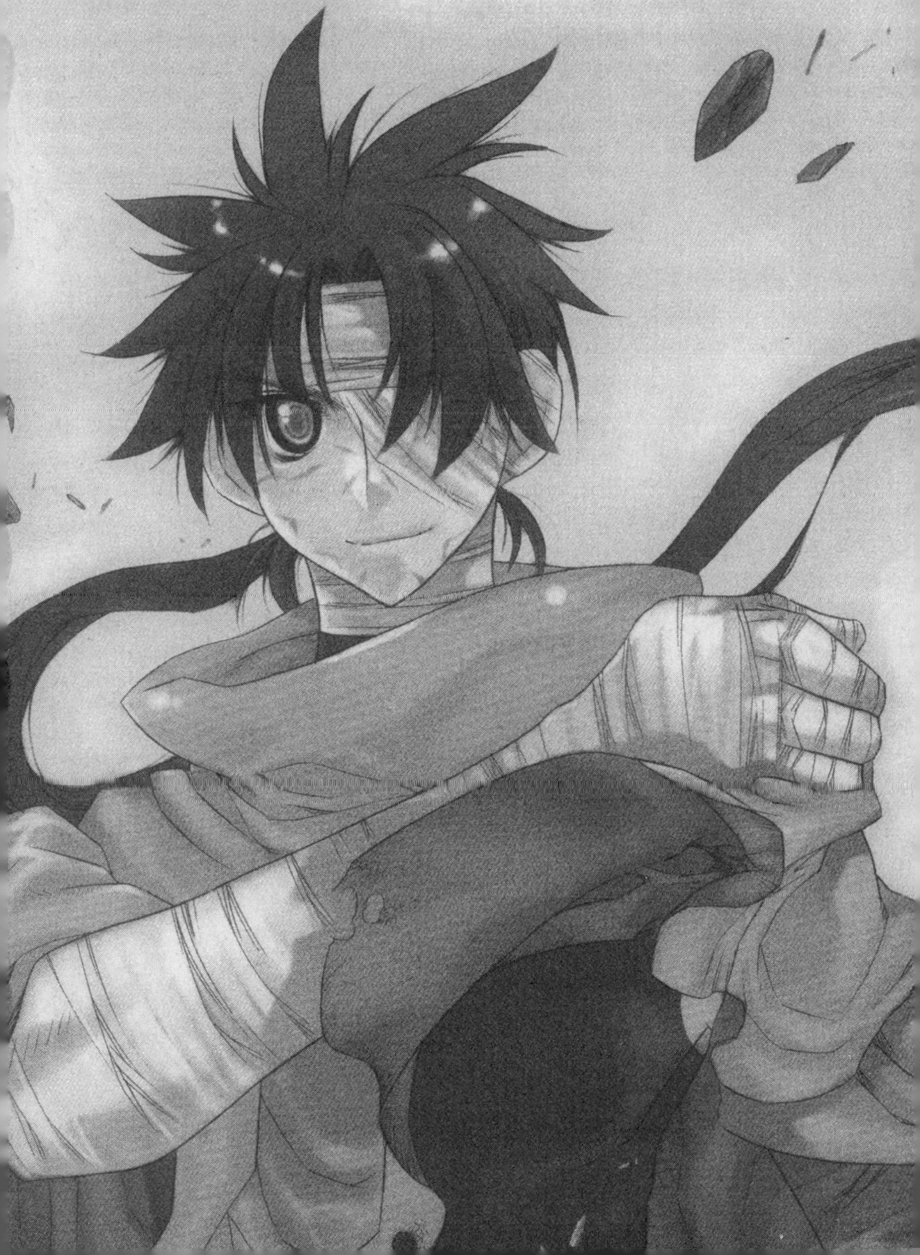

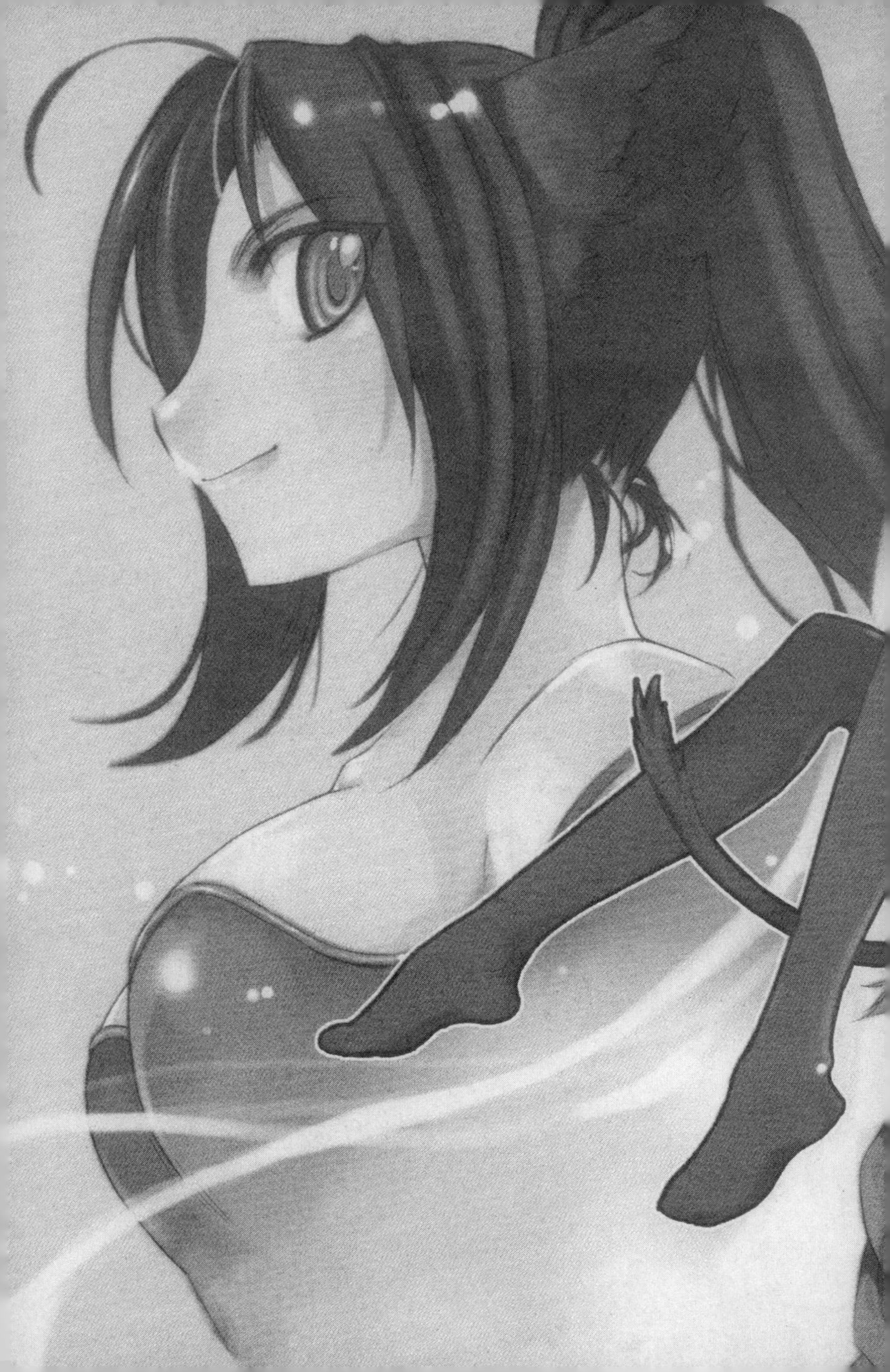

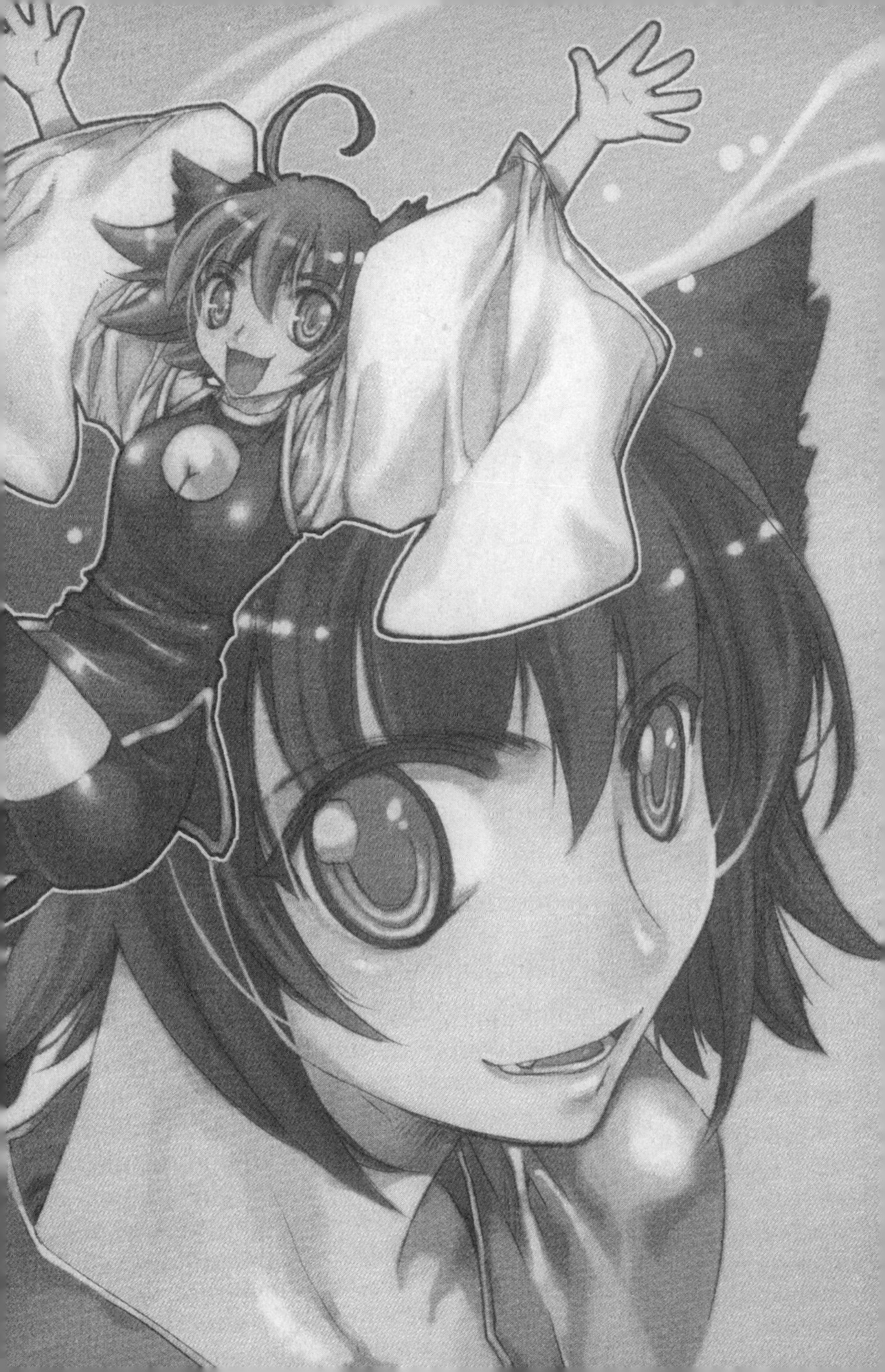

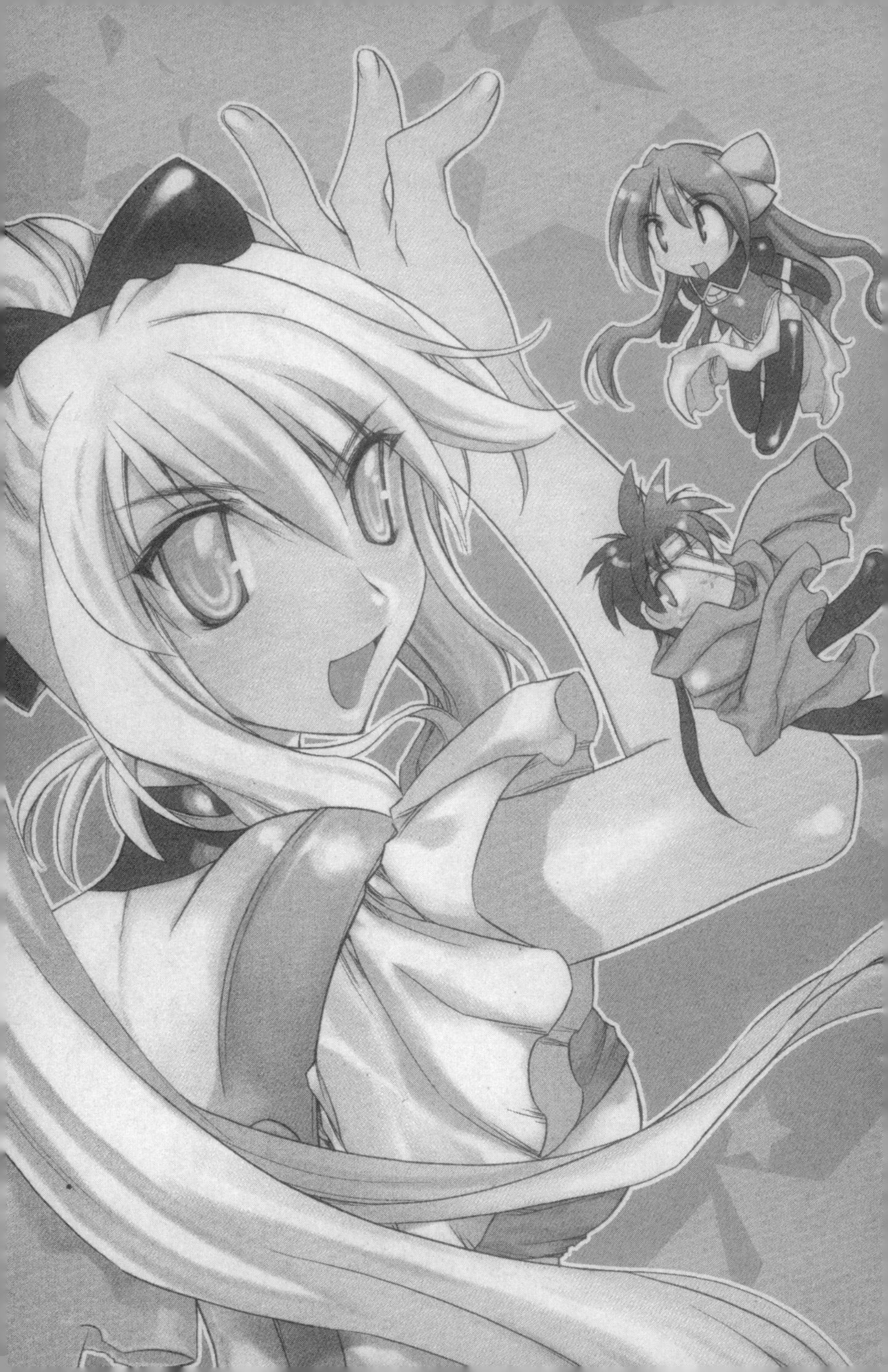

CHRONICLES OF THE CURSED SWORD

Volume 12

Story by
YEO BEOP-RYONG
Art by
PARK HUI-JIN

HAMBURG // LONDON // LOS ANGELES // TOKYO

Chronicles of the Cursed Sword Vol. 12
written by Yeo Beop-Ryong
illustrated by Park Hui-Jin

Translation - Yongju Ryu
English Adaptation - Matt Varosky
Copy Editor - Suzanne Waldman
Retouch and Lettering - Pete Sattler
Production Artist - Gloria Wu
Cover Design - Kyle Plummer

Editor - Aaron Suhr
Digital Imaging Manager - Chris Buford
Pre-Press Manager - Antonio DePietro
Production Managers - Jennifer Miller and Mutsumi Miyazaki
Art Director - Matt Alford
Managing Editor - Jill Freshney
VP of Production - Ron Klamert
Editor-in-Chief - Mike Kiley
President and C.O.O. - John Parker
Publisher and C.E.O. - Stuart Levy

A  Manga

TOKYOPOP Inc.
5900 Wilshire Blvd. Suite 2000
Los Angeles, CA 90036

E-mail: info@TOKYOPOP.com
Come visit us online at www.TOKYOPOP.com

ISBN: 1-59532-389-9

First TOKYOPOP printing: June 2005
10 9 8 7 6 5 4 3 2 1
Printed in the USA

Chronicles

CHRONICLES OF THE CURSED SWORD

the cast of characters

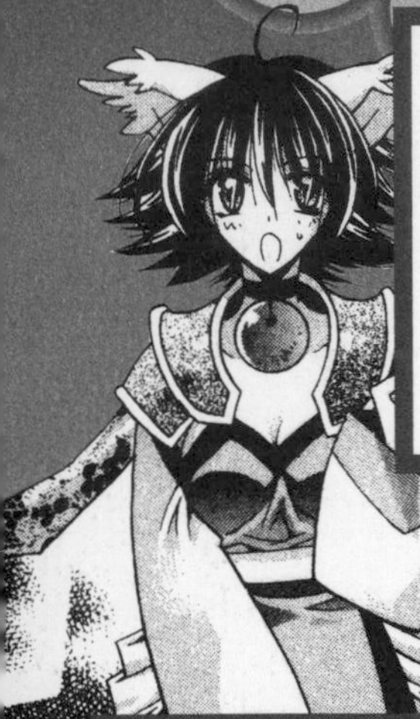

MINGLING

A lesser demon with feline qualities, Mingling is now the loyal follower of Shyao Lin. She lives in fear of Rey, who still doesn't trust her.

THE PASA SWORD

A living sword that hungers for demon blood. It grants its user incredible power, but at a great cost - it can take over the user's body and, in time, his soul.

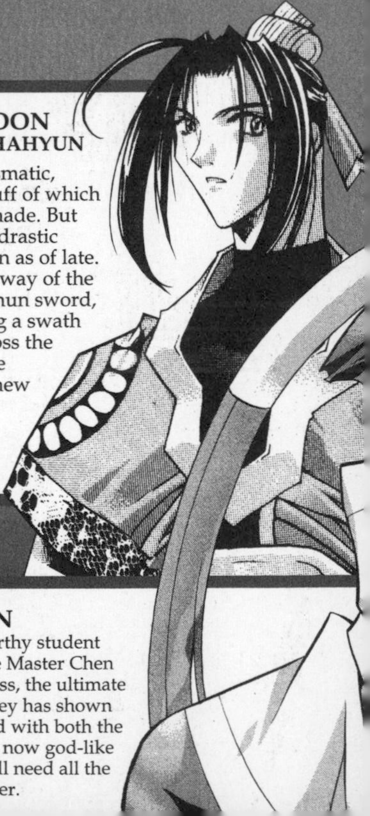

JARYOON
KING OF HAHYUN

Noble and charismatic, Jaryoon is the stuff of which great kings are made. But there has been a drastic change in Jaryoon as of late. Now under the sway of the spirit of the PaChun sword, Jaryoon is cutting a swath of humanity across the countryside as he searches for his new prey: Rey.

SHYAO LIN

A sorceress, previously Rey's traveling companion and greatest ally. Shyao has recently discovered that she is, in fact, one of the Eight Sages of the Azure Pavilion, sent to gather information in the Human Realm. Much to her dismay, she has been told that she must now kill Rey Yan.

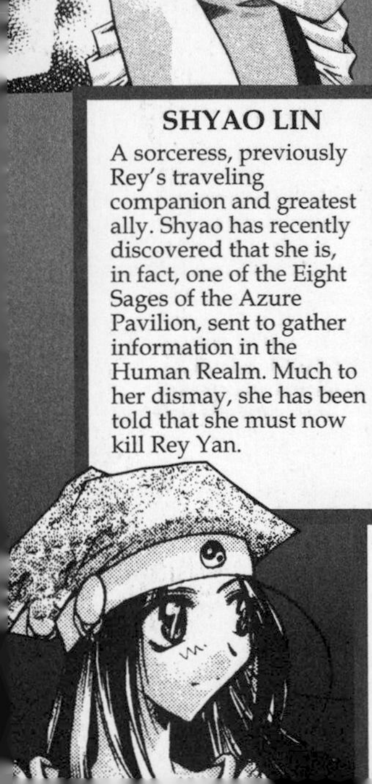

REY YAN

Rey has proven to be a worthy student of the wise and diminutive Master Chen Kaihu. At the Mujin Fortress, the ultimate warrior testing grounds, Rey has shown his martial arts mettle. And with both the possessed Jaryoon and the now god-like Shyao after his blood—he'll need all the survival skills he can muster.

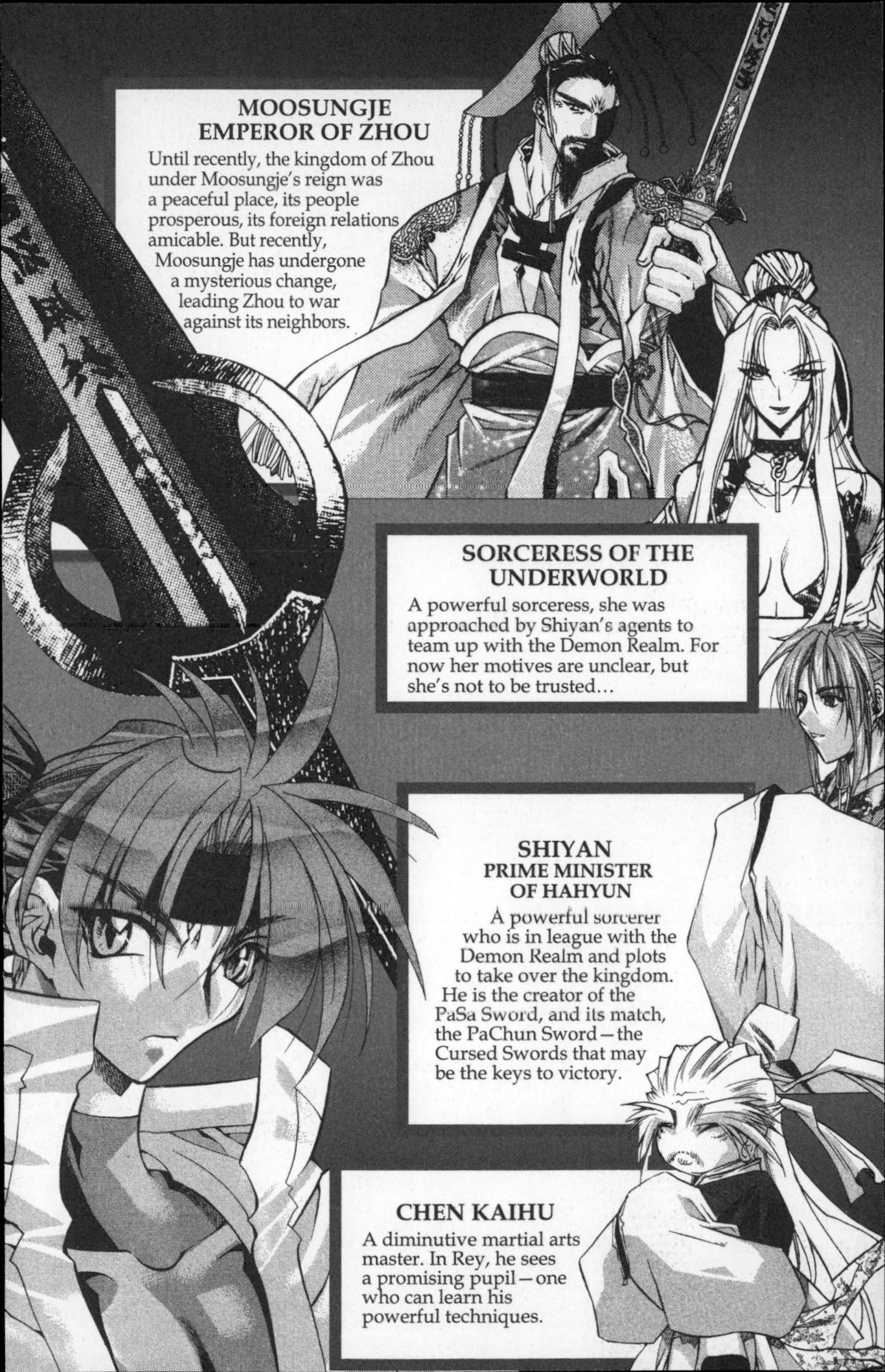
MOOSUNGJE
EMPEROR OF ZHOU
Until recently, the kingdom of Zhou under Moosungje's reign was a peaceful place, its people prosperous, its foreign relations amicable. But recently, Moosungje has undergone a mysterious change, leading Zhou to war against its neighbors.
SORCERESS OF THE UNDERWORLD
A powerful sorceress, she was approached by Shiyan's agents to team up with the Demon Realm. For now her motives are unclear, but she's not to be trusted...
SHIYAN
PRIME MINISTER OF HAHYUN
A powerful sorcerer who is in league with the Demon Realm and plots to take over the kingdom. He is the creator of the PaSa Sword, and its match, the PaChun Sword—the Cursed Swords that may be the keys to victory.
CHEN KAIHU
A diminutive martial arts master. In Rey, he sees a promising pupil—one who can learn his powerful techniques.

Thus Far In...

CHRONICLES OF THE
CURSED SWORD

In an era of warring states, warlords become kings, dynasties crumble, and heroes can rise from the most unlikely places. Rey yan was an orphan with no home no skills and no purpose. But when he comes upon the PaSa sword, a cursed blade made from the bones of the Demon Emperor, he suddenly finds himself with the power to be a great hero...

In preparation for the demon invasion on Human realm, the Demon Emperor is out to eliminate all potential threats...including Lady Hyacia. After being betrayed by her once-loyal subjects, Lady Hyacia is barely able to escape, however her body has only days to live if it is not reunited with her captive soul! Rey and his rag-tag team are in a race against time to save Lady Hyacia's life.

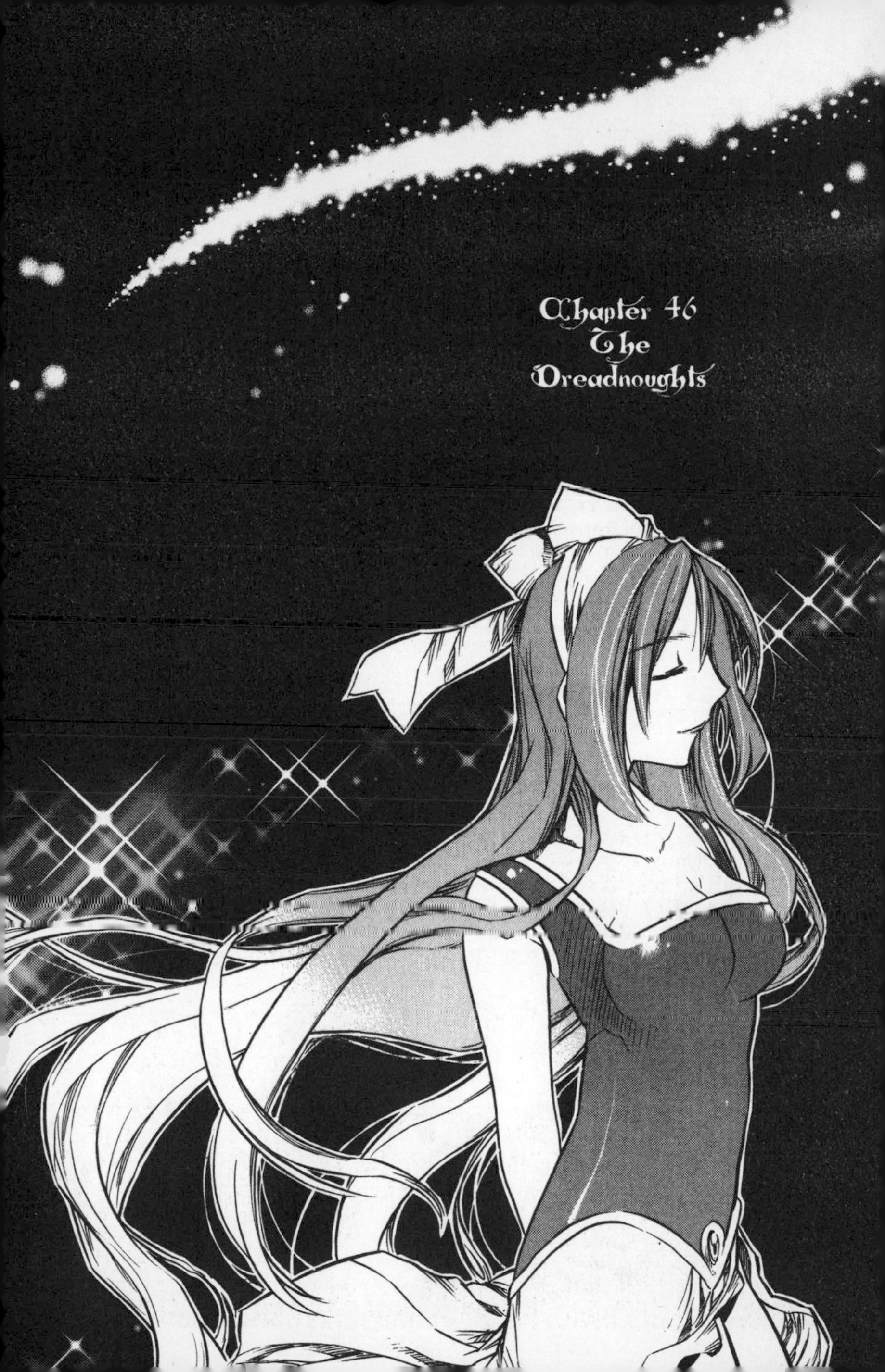
Chapter 46
The
Dreadnoughts

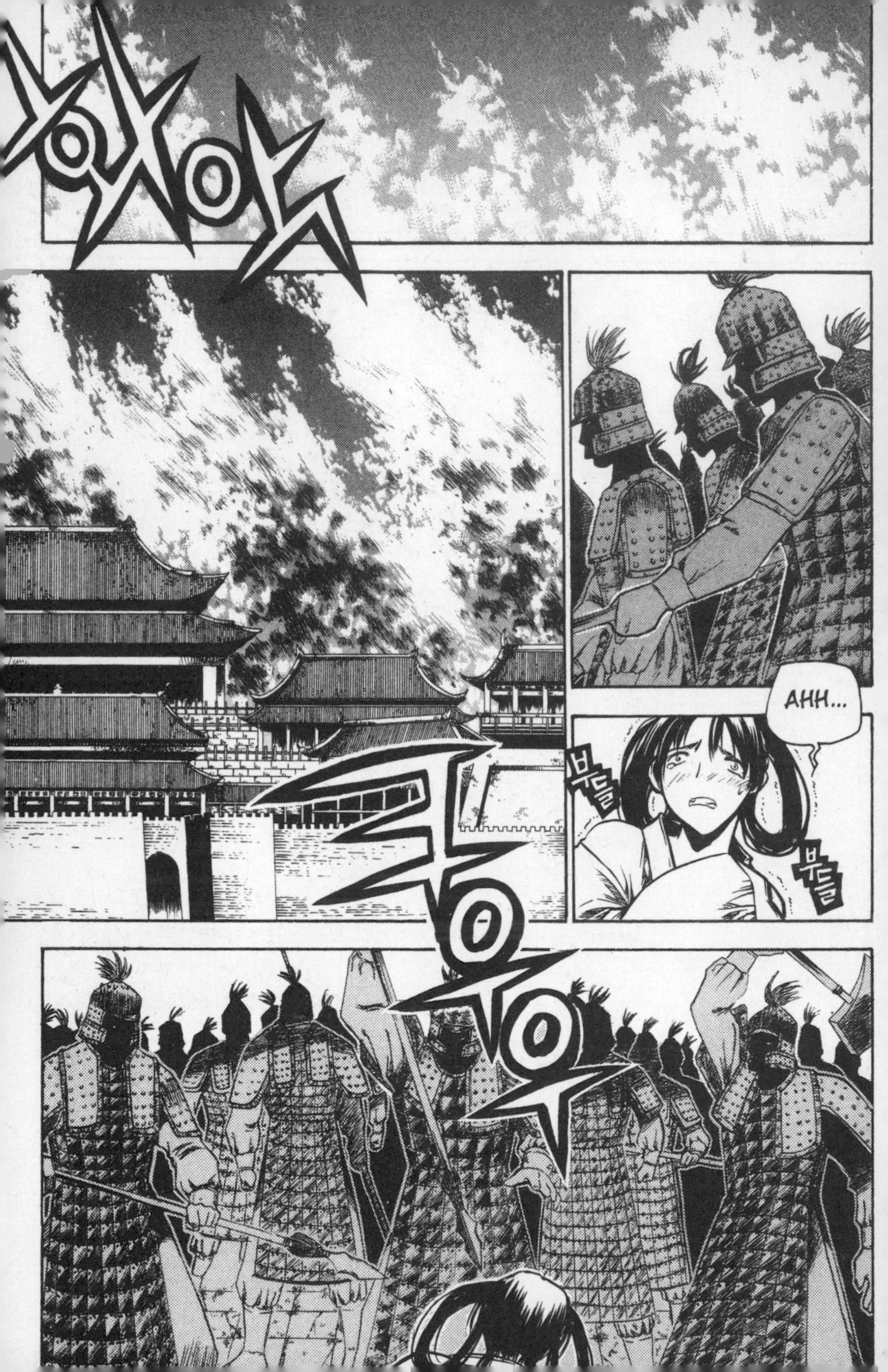
AHH...
부들
부들

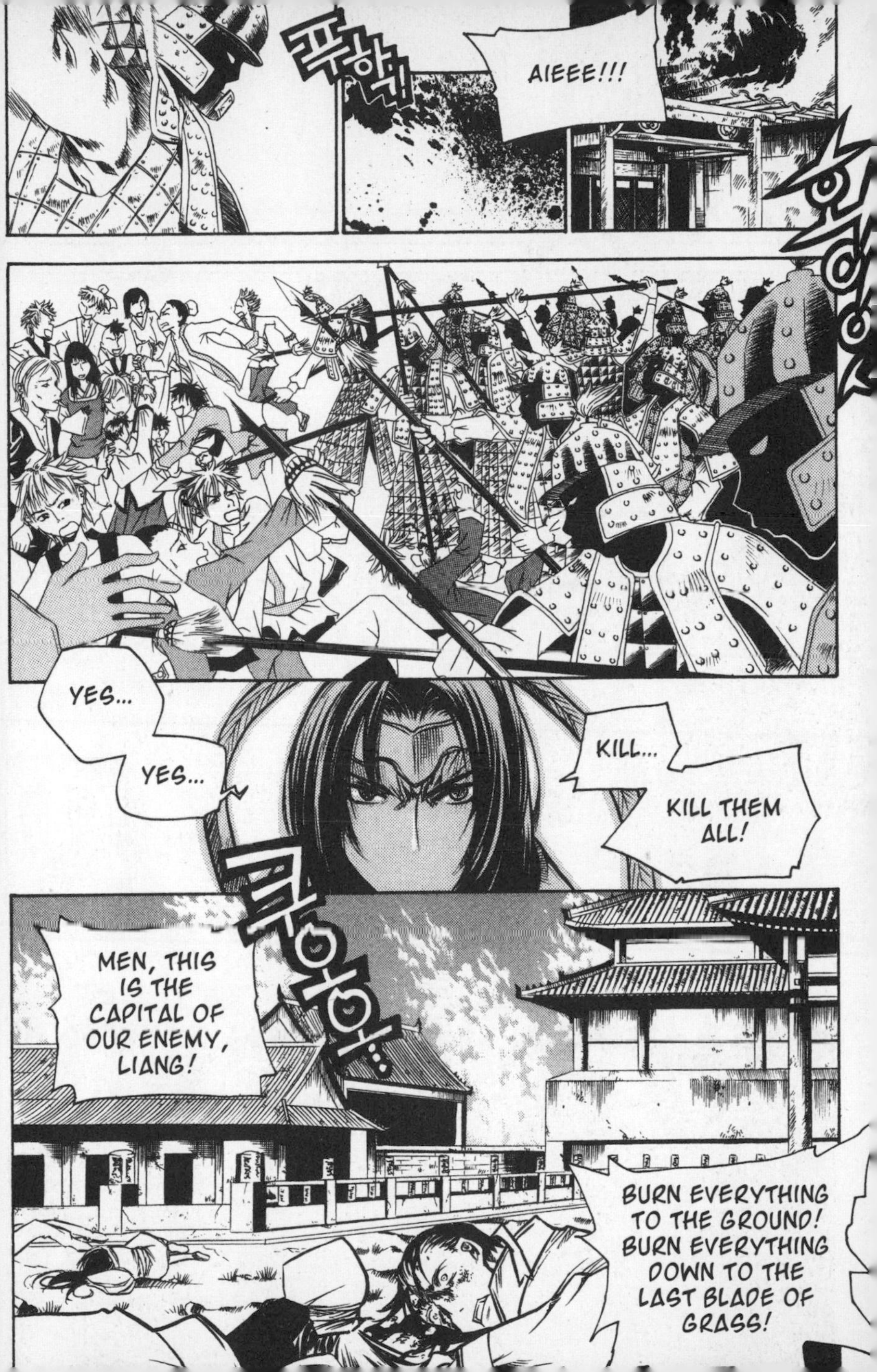
푸학!
AIEEE!!!
와아아
YES...
YES...
KILL...
KILL THEM ALL!
타아아...
MEN, THIS IS THE CAPITAL OF OUR ENEMY, LIANG!
BURN EVERYTHING TO THE GROUND! BURN EVERYTHING DOWN TO THE LAST BLADE OF GRASS!

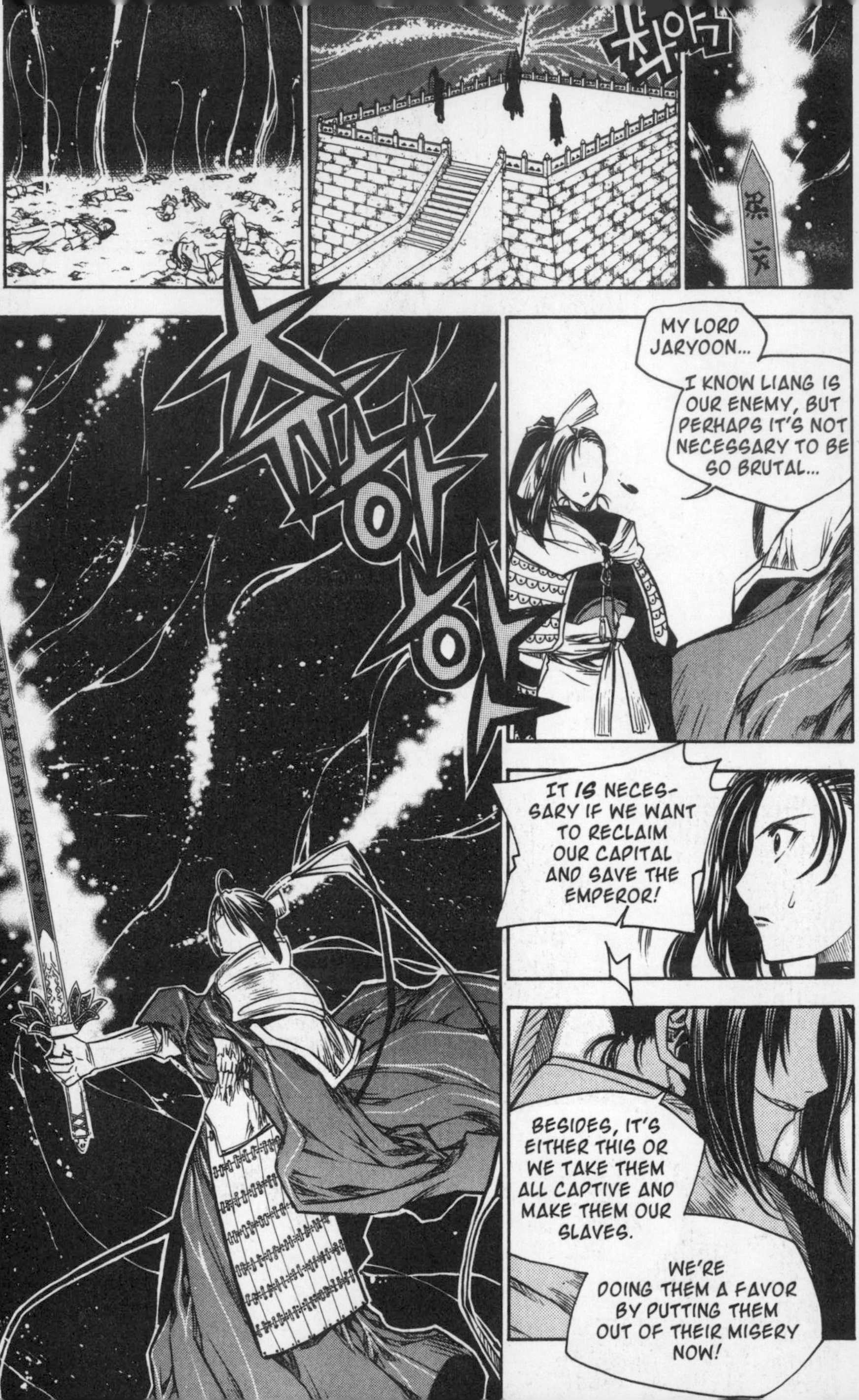
MY LORD JARYOON...
I KNOW LIANG IS OUR ENEMY, BUT PERHAPS IT'S NOT NECESSARY TO BE SO BRUTAL...
IT IS NECES-SARY IF WE WANT TO RECLAIM OUR CAPITAL AND SAVE THE EMPEROR!
BESIDES, IT'S EITHER THIS OR WE TAKE THEM ALL CAPTIVE AND MAKE THEM OUR SLAVES.
WE'RE DOING THEM A FAVOR BY PUTTING THEM OUT OF THEIR MISERY NOW!

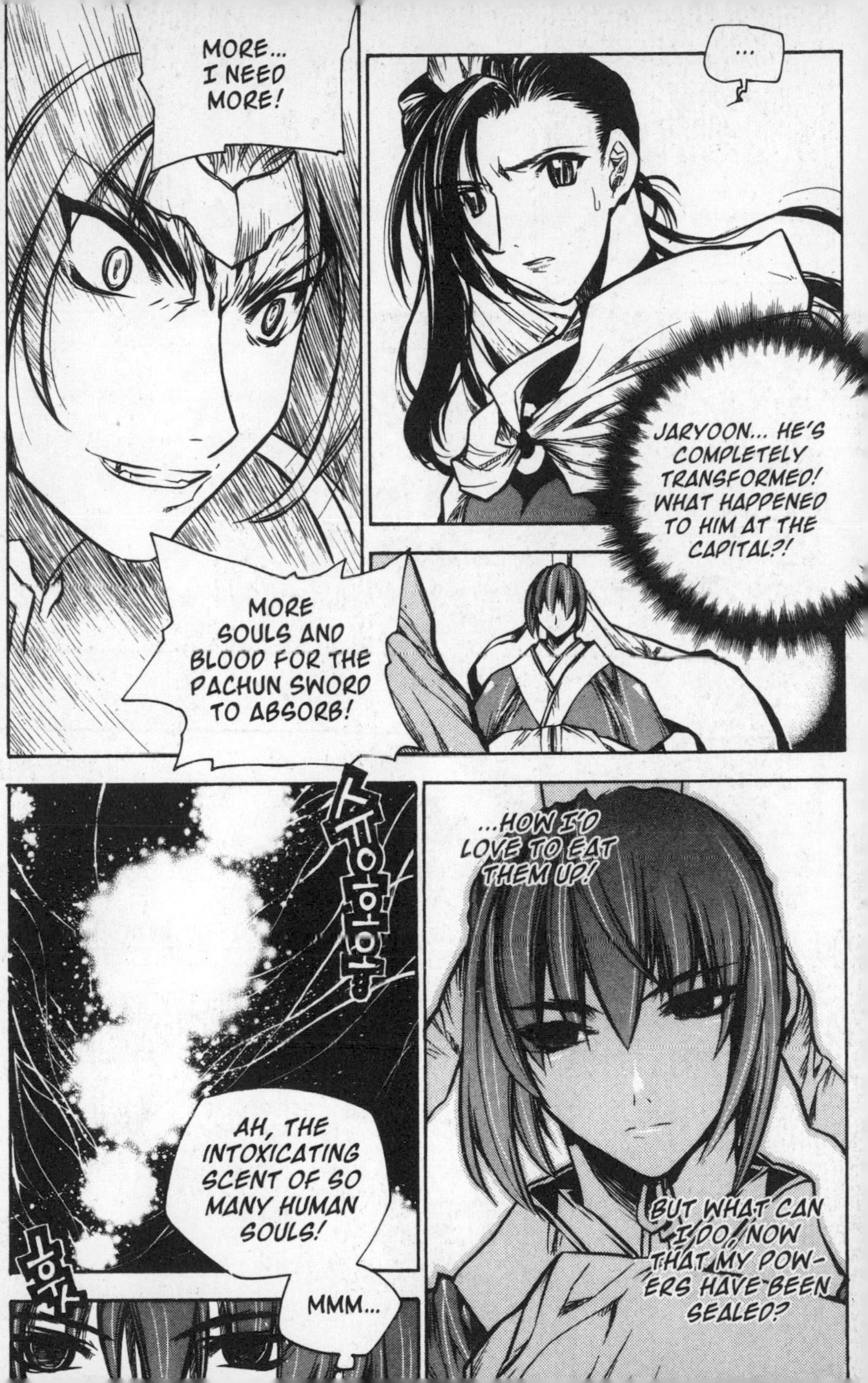
MORE... I NEED MORE!
MORE SOULS AND BLOOD FOR THE PACHUN SWORD TO ABSORB!
...
JARYOON... HE'S COMPLETELY TRANSFORMED! WHAT HAPPENED TO HIM AT THE CAPITAL?!
AH, THE INTOXICATING SCENT OF SO MANY HUMAN SOULS!
MMM...
...HOW I'D LOVE TO EAT THEM UP!
BUT WHAT CAN I DO, NOW THAT MY POWERS HAVE BEEN SEALED?

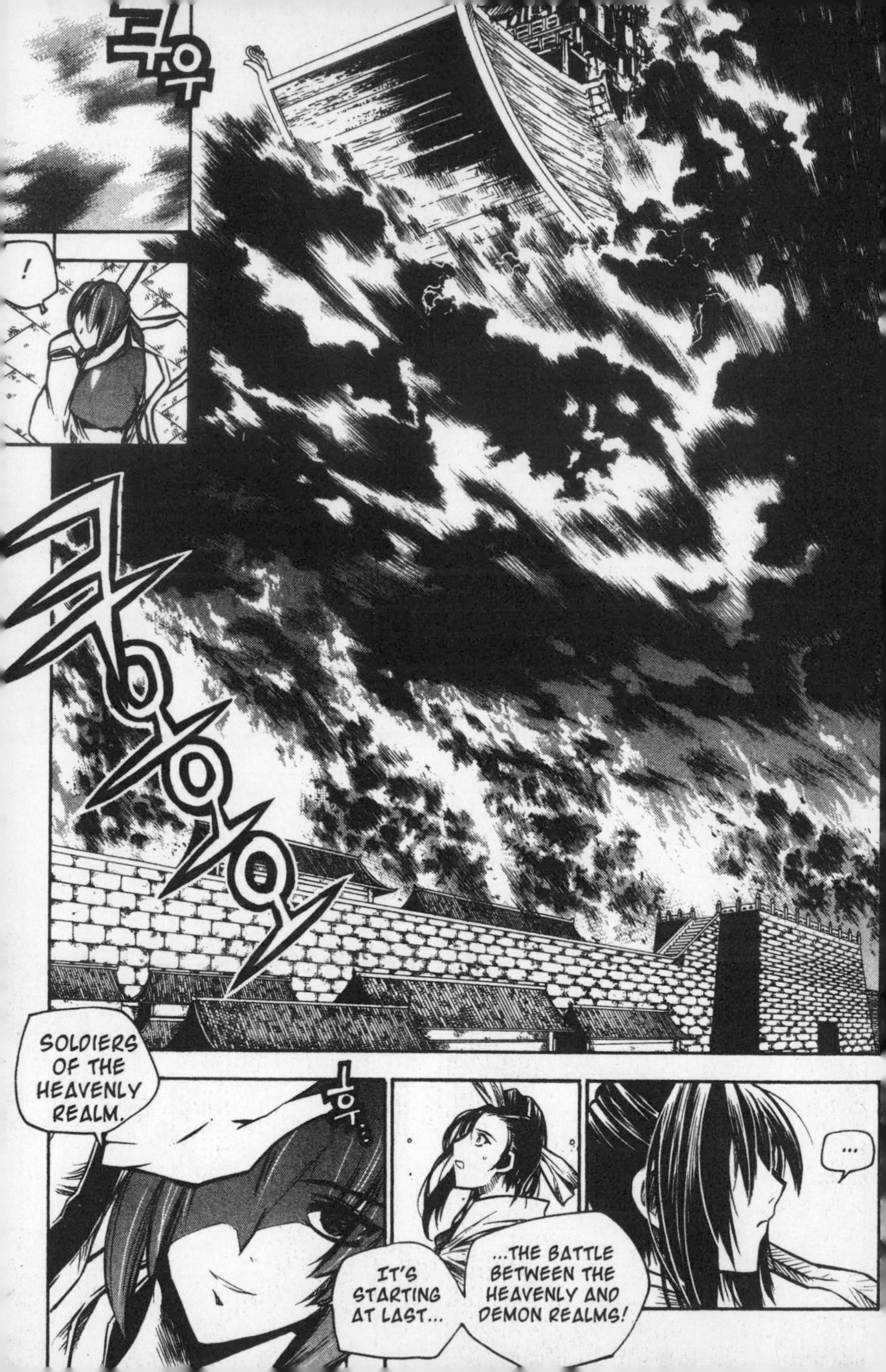
!
SOLDIERS OF THE HEAVENLY REALM.
IT'S STARTING AT LAST...
...THE BATTLE BETWEEN THE HEAVENLY AND DEMON REALMS!
...

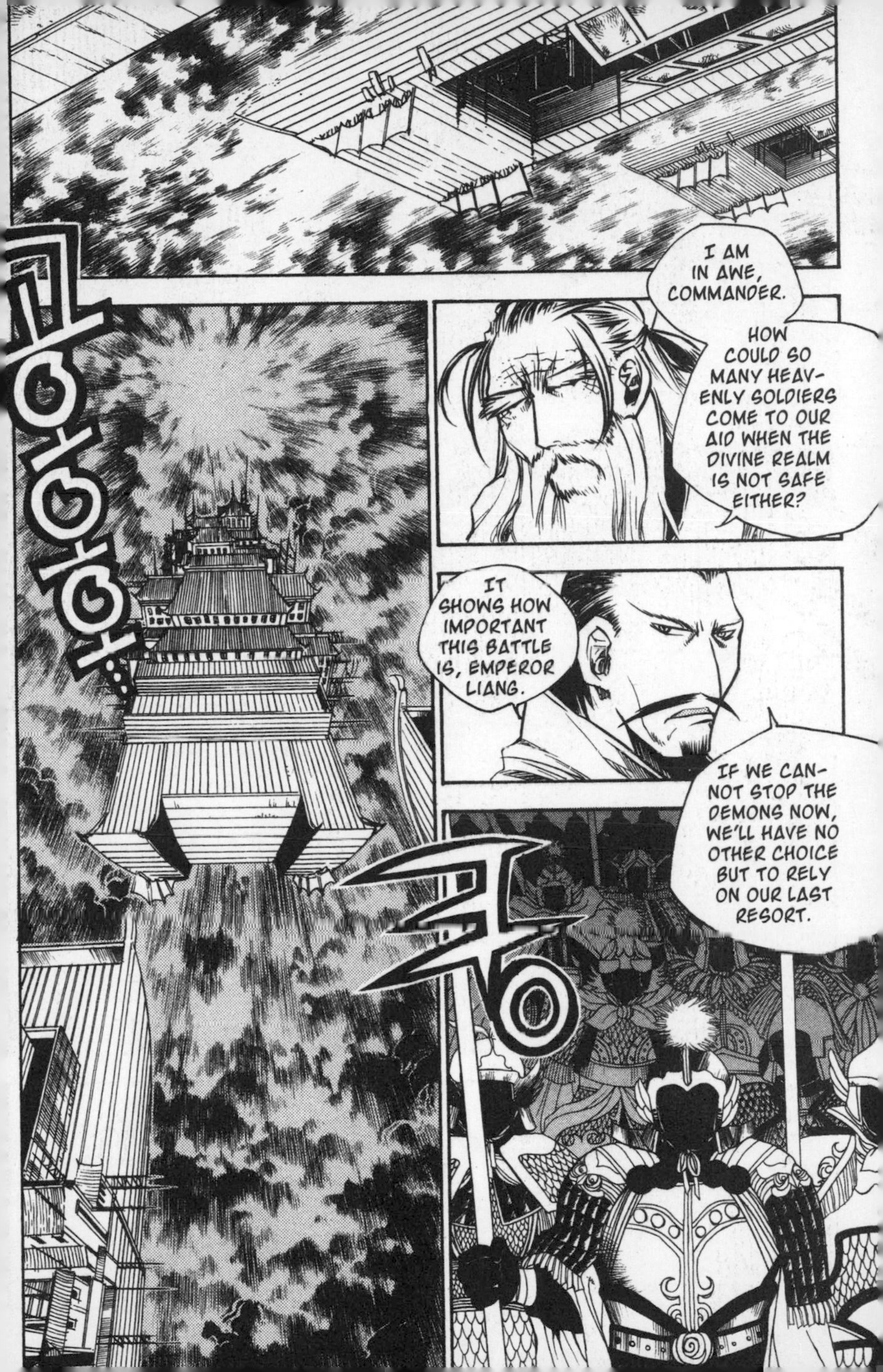
I AM IN AWE, COMMANDER.
HOW COULD SO MANY HEAVENLY SOLDIERS COME TO OUR AID WHEN THE DIVINE REALM IS NOT SAFE EITHER?
IT SHOWS HOW IMPORTANT THIS BATTLE IS, EMPEROR LIANG.
IF WE CANNOT STOP THE DEMONS NOW, WE'LL HAVE NO OTHER CHOICE BUT TO RELY ON OUR LAST RESORT.

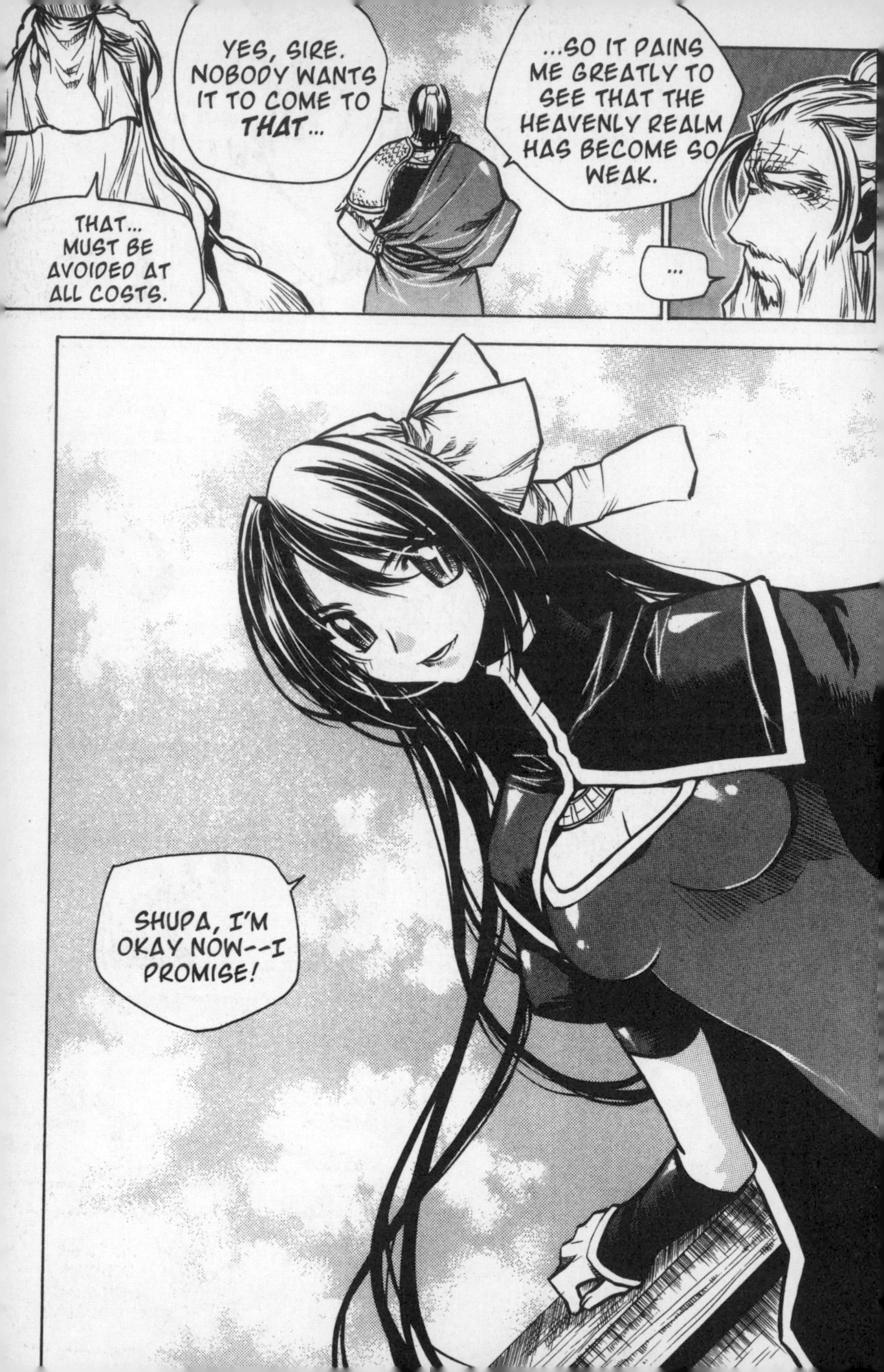
YES, SIRE. NOBODY WANTS IT TO COME TO THAT...
THAT... MUST BE AVOIDED AT ALL COSTS.
...SO IT PAINS ME GREATLY TO SEE THAT THE HEAVENLY REALM HAS BECOME SO WEAK.
...
SHUPA, I'M OKAY NOW--I PROMISE!

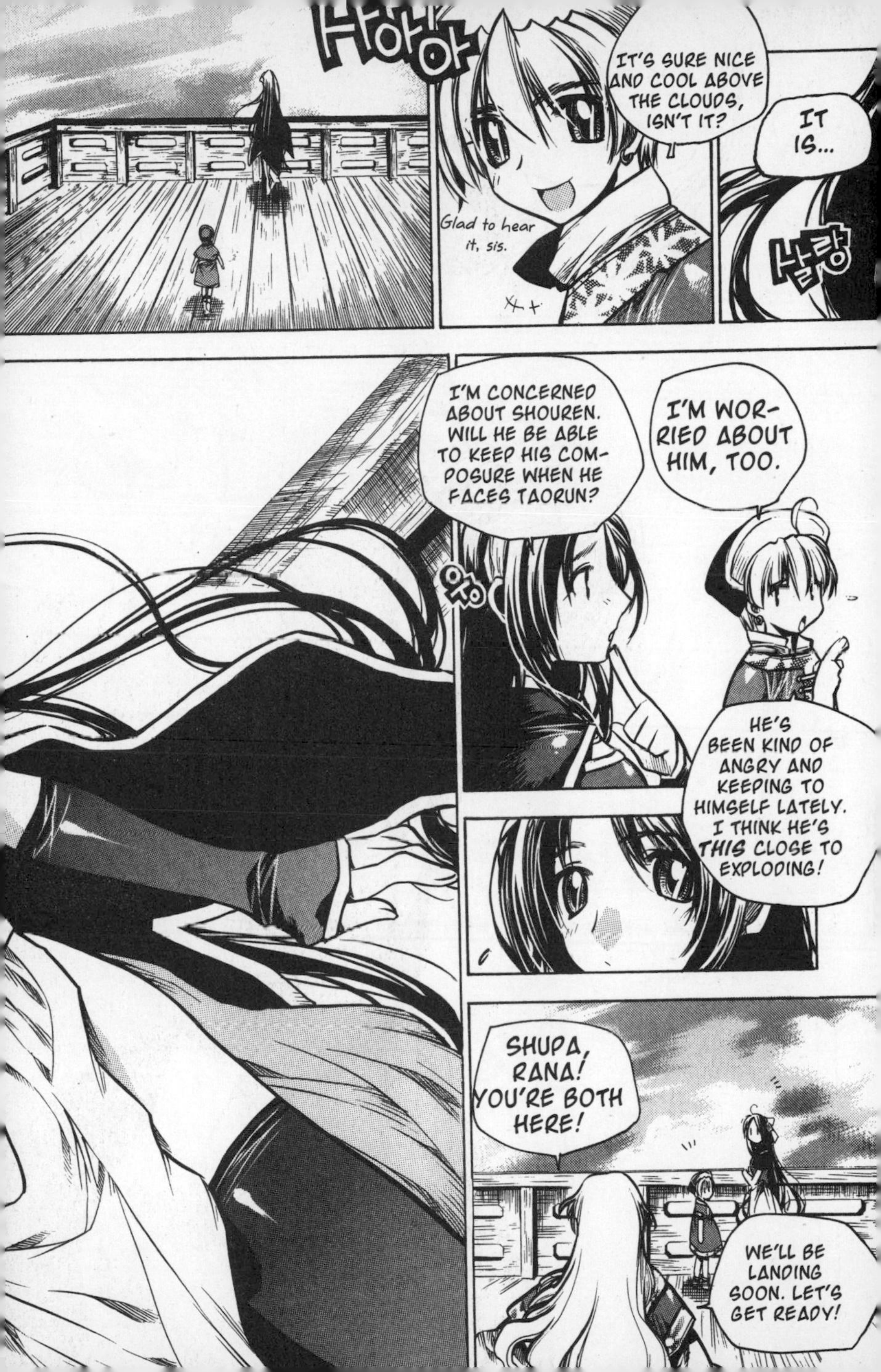
IT'S SURE NICE AND COOL ABOVE THE CLOUDS, ISN'T IT?
Glad to hear it, sis.
IT IS...
I'M CONCERNED ABOUT SHOUREN. WILL HE BE ABLE TO KEEP HIS COMPOSURE WHEN HE FACES TAORUN?
I'M WORRIED ABOUT HIM, TOO.
HE'S BEEN KIND OF ANGRY AND KEEPING TO HIMSELF LATELY. I THINK HE'S THIS CLOSE TO EXPLODING!
SHUPA, RANA! YOU'RE BOTH HERE!
WE'LL BE LANDING SOON. LET'S GET READY!

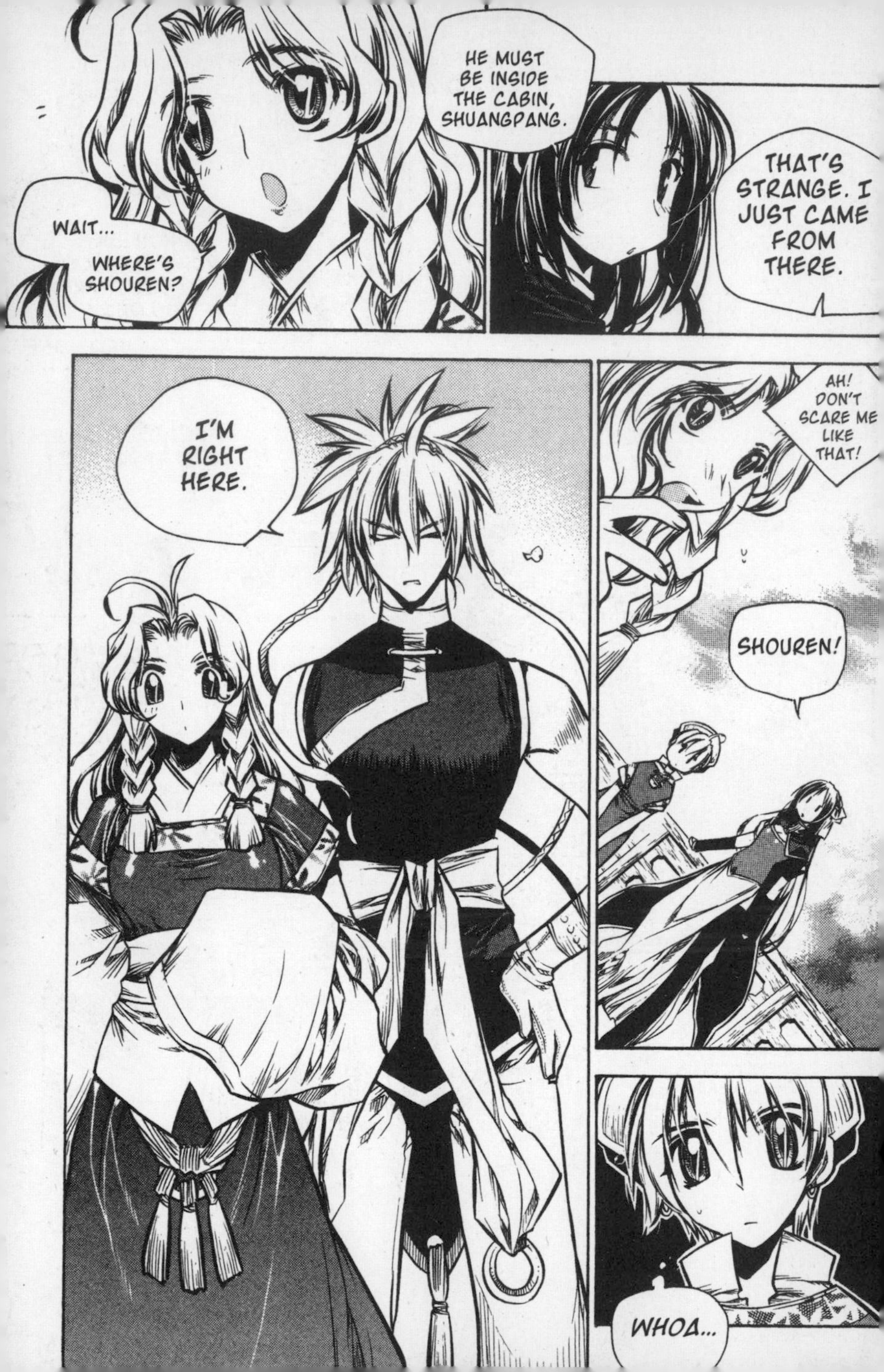
WAIT... WHERE'S SHOUREN?
HE MUST BE INSIDE THE CABIN, SHUANGPANG.
THAT'S STRANGE. I JUST CAME FROM THERE.
I'M RIGHT HERE.
AH! DON'T SCARE ME LIKE THAT!
SHOUREN!
WHOA...

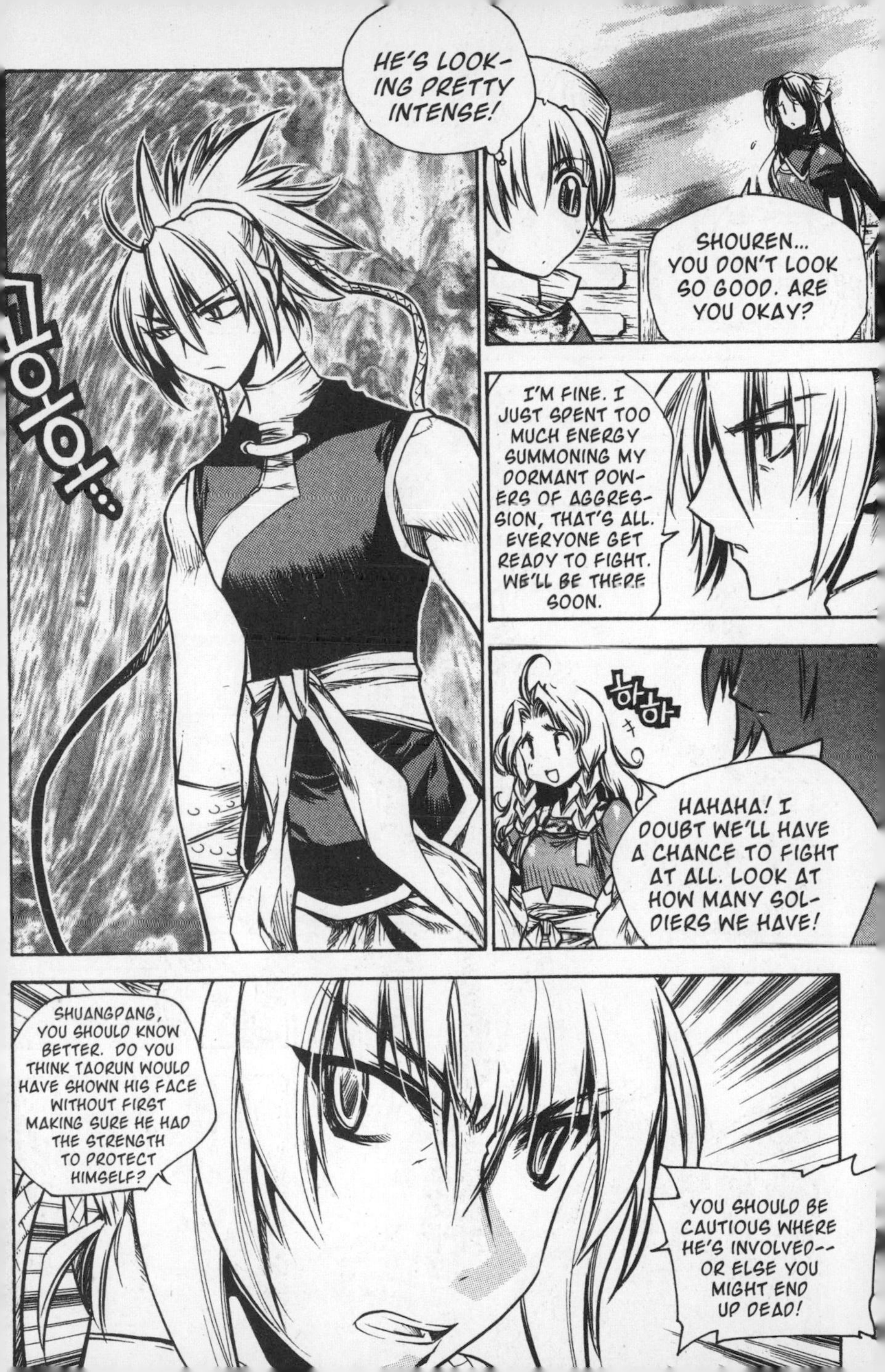
HE'S LOOKING PRETTY INTENSE!
SHOUREN... YOU DON'T LOOK SO GOOD. ARE YOU OKAY?
I'M FINE. I JUST SPENT TOO MUCH ENERGY SUMMONING MY DORMANT POWERS OF AGGRESSION, THAT'S ALL. EVERYONE GET READY TO FIGHT. WE'LL BE THERE SOON.
하하
HAHAHA! I DOUBT WE'LL HAVE A CHANCE TO FIGHT AT ALL. LOOK AT HOW MANY SOLDIERS WE HAVE!
SHUANGPANG, YOU SHOULD KNOW BETTER. DO YOU THINK TAORUN WOULD HAVE SHOWN HIS FACE WITHOUT FIRST MAKING SURE HE HAD THE STRENGTH TO PROTECT HIMSELF?
YOU SHOULD BE CAUTIOUS WHERE HE'S INVOLVED--OR ELSE YOU MIGHT END UP DEAD!

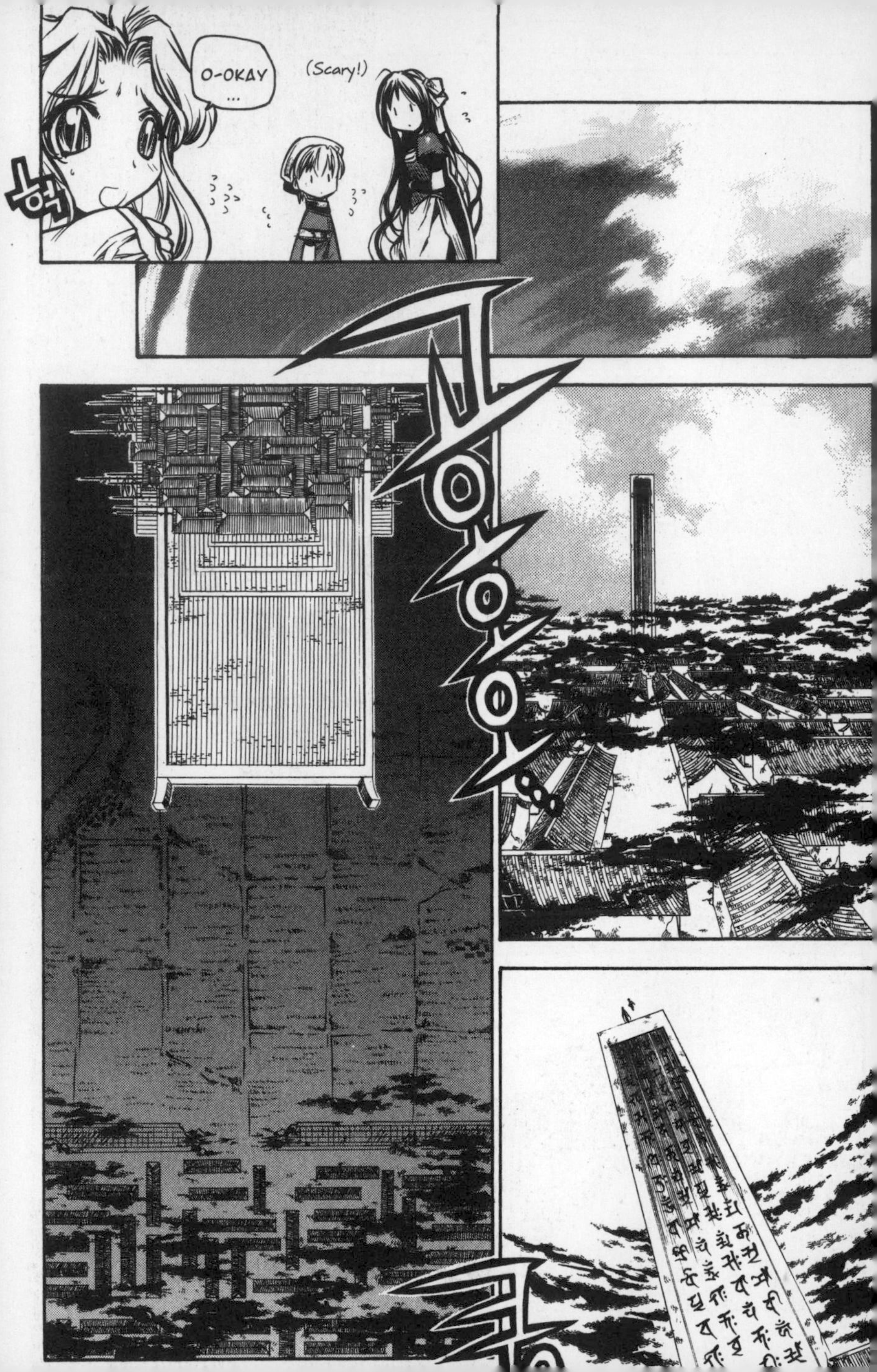
O-OKAY ...
(Scary!)

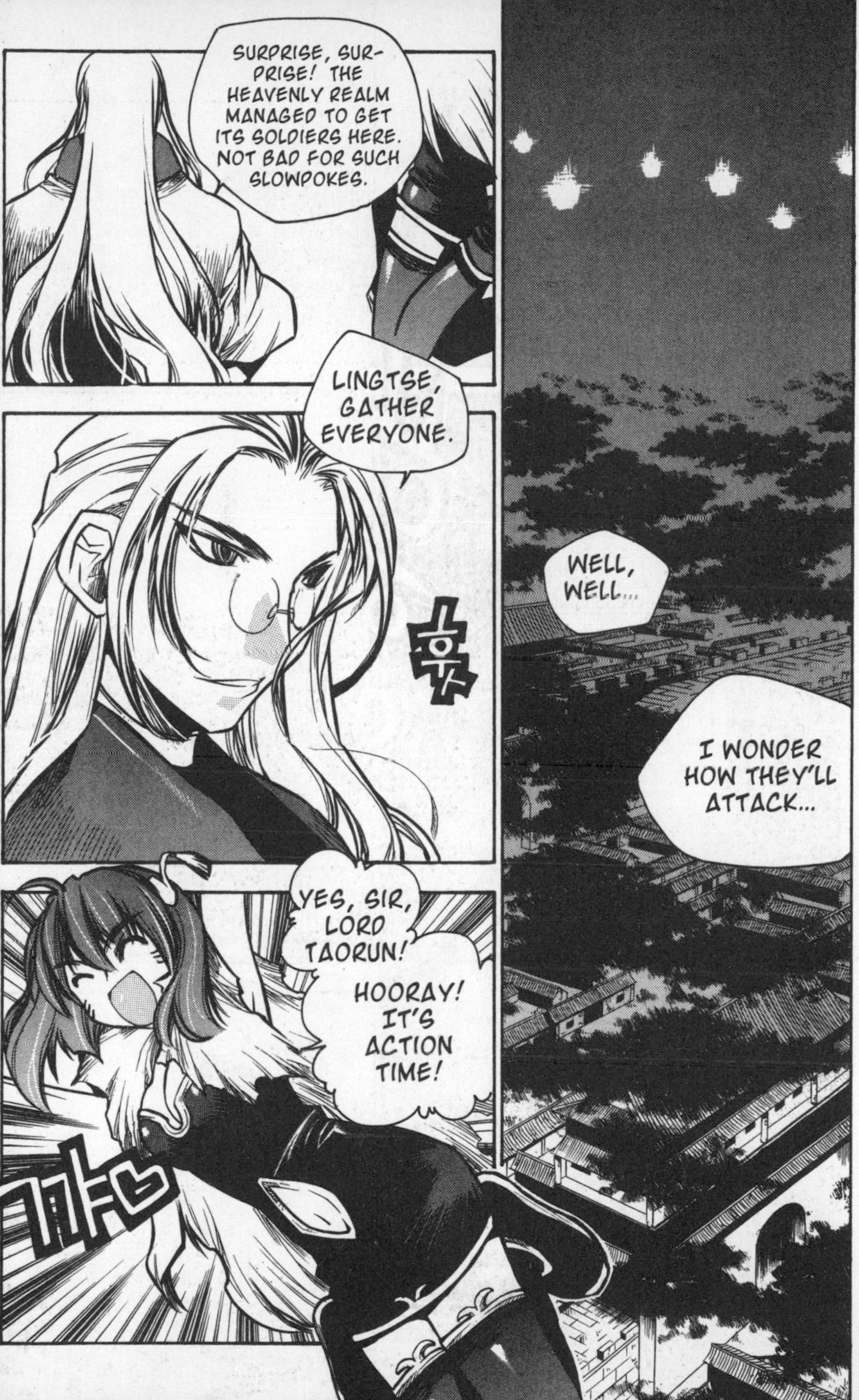
SURPRISE, SURPRISE! THE HEAVENLY REALM MANAGED TO GET ITS SOLDIERS HERE. NOT BAD FOR SUCH SLOWPOKES.
LINGTSE, GATHER EVERYONE.
YES, SIR, LORD TAORUN!
HOORAY! IT'S ACTION TIME!
WELL, WELL...
I WONDER HOW THEY'LL ATTACK...

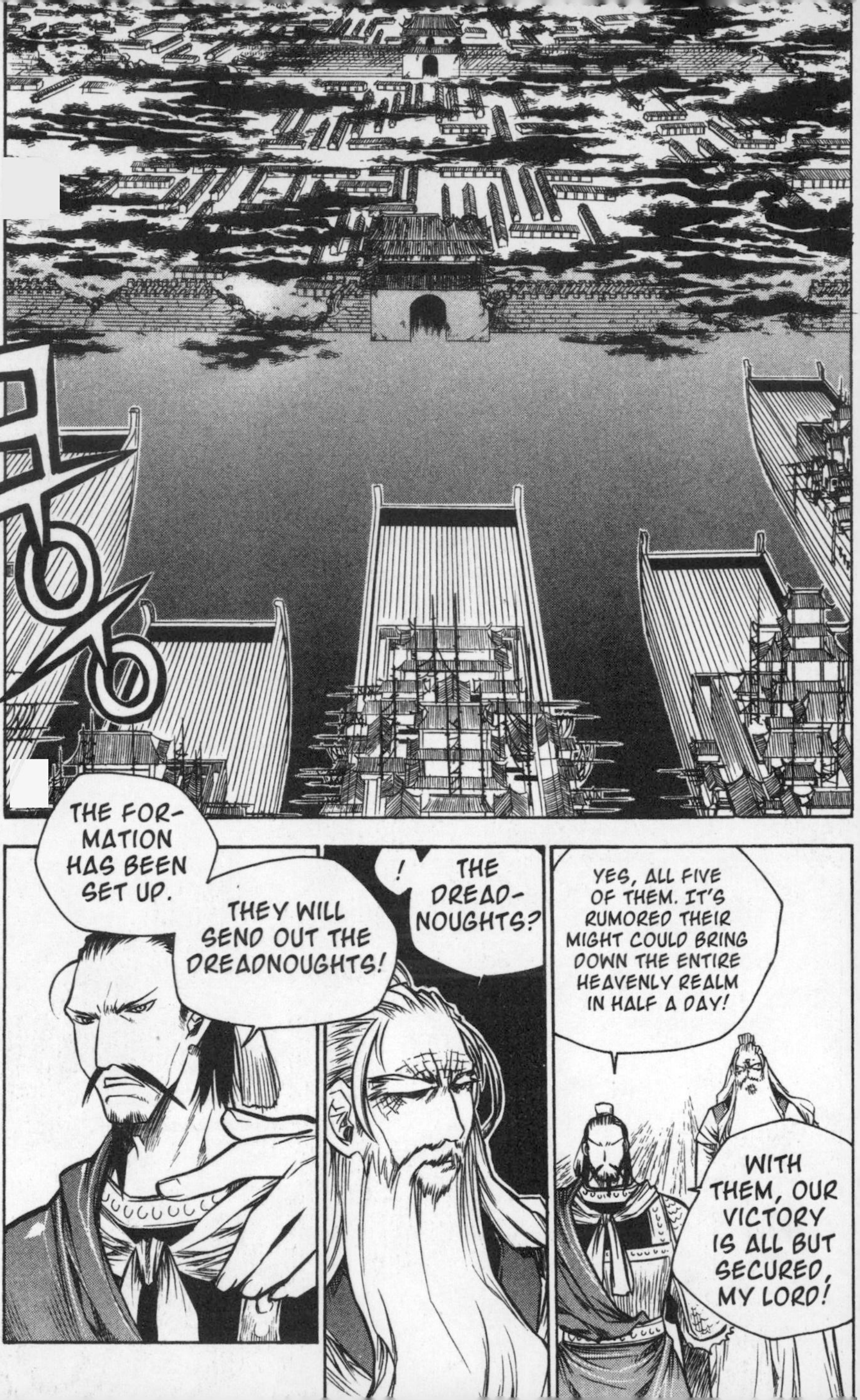
THE FOR-MATION HAS BEEN SET UP.
THEY WILL SEND OUT THE DREADNOUGHTS!
!
THE DREAD-NOUGHTS?
YES, ALL FIVE OF THEM. IT'S RUMORED THEIR MIGHT COULD BRING DOWN THE ENTIRE HEAVENLY REALM IN HALF A DAY!
WITH THEM, OUR VICTORY IS ALL BUT SECURED, MY LORD!

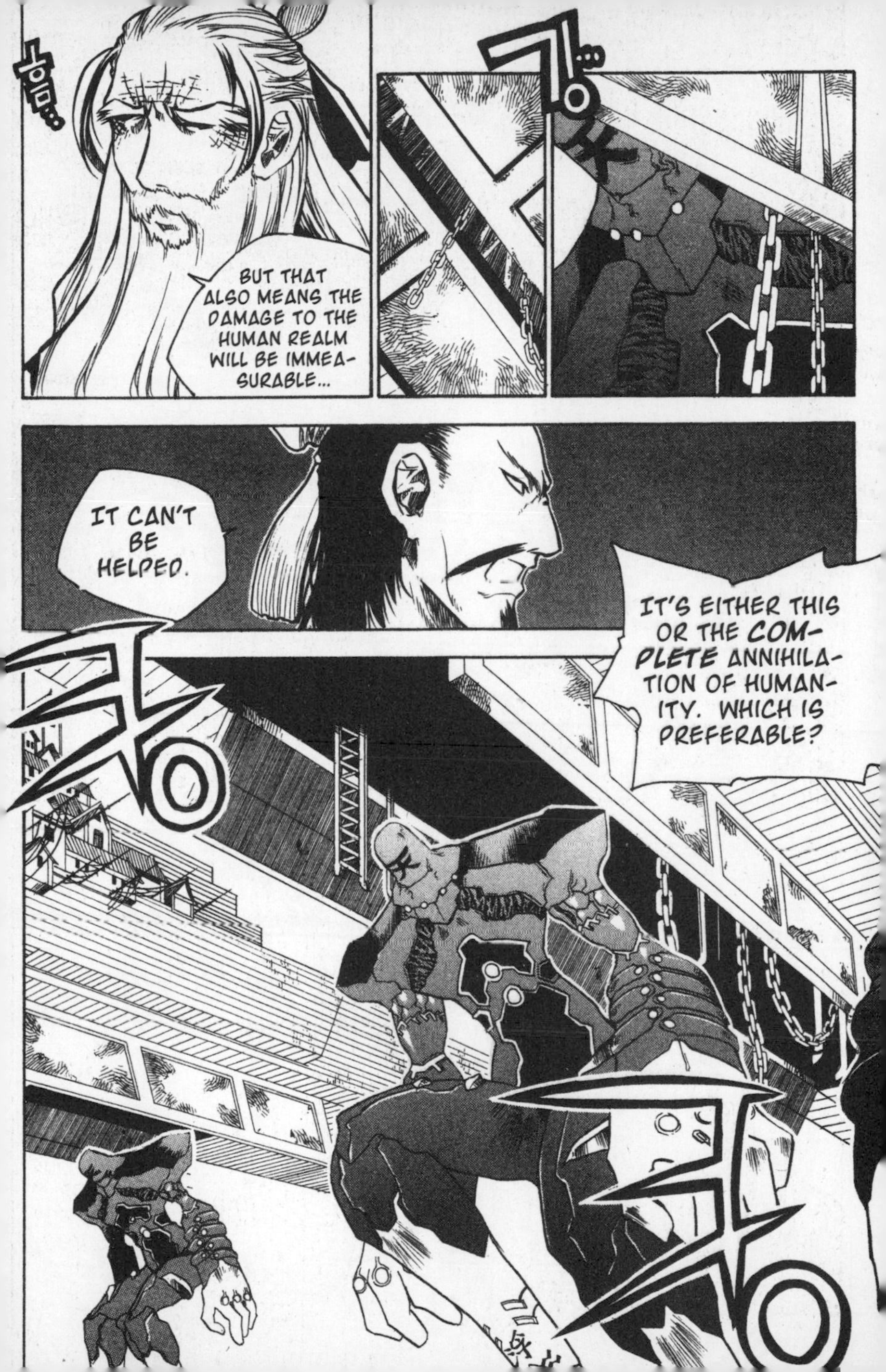
BUT THAT ALSO MEANS THE DAMAGE TO THE HUMAN REALM WILL BE IMMEA-SURABLE...
IT CAN'T BE HELPED.
IT'S EITHER THIS OR THE **COM-PLETE** ANNIHILA-TION OF HUMAN-ITY. WHICH IS PREFERABLE?

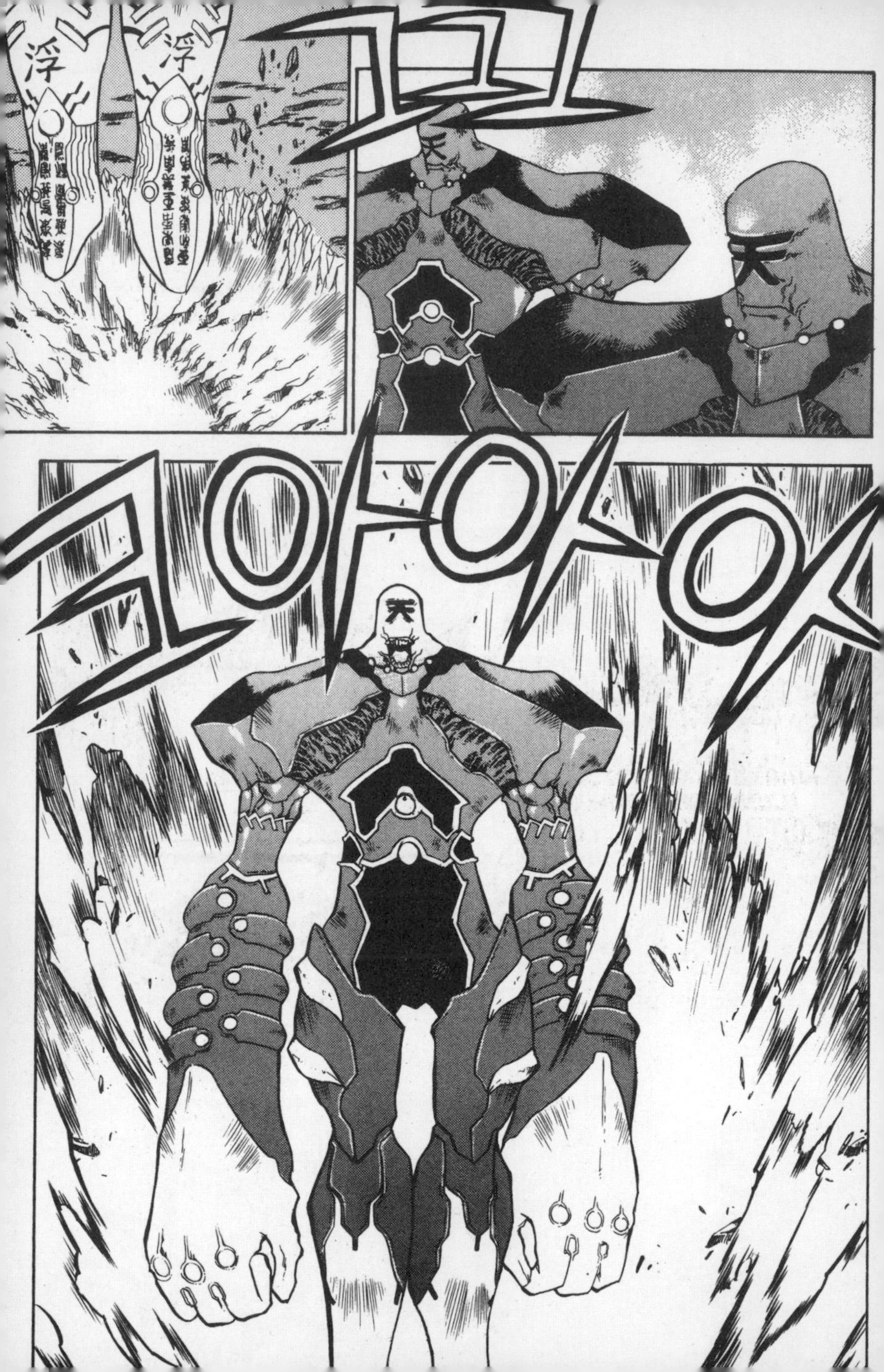

浮
浮

Chapter 47
Sorcerer Kumwa, the Golden Toad

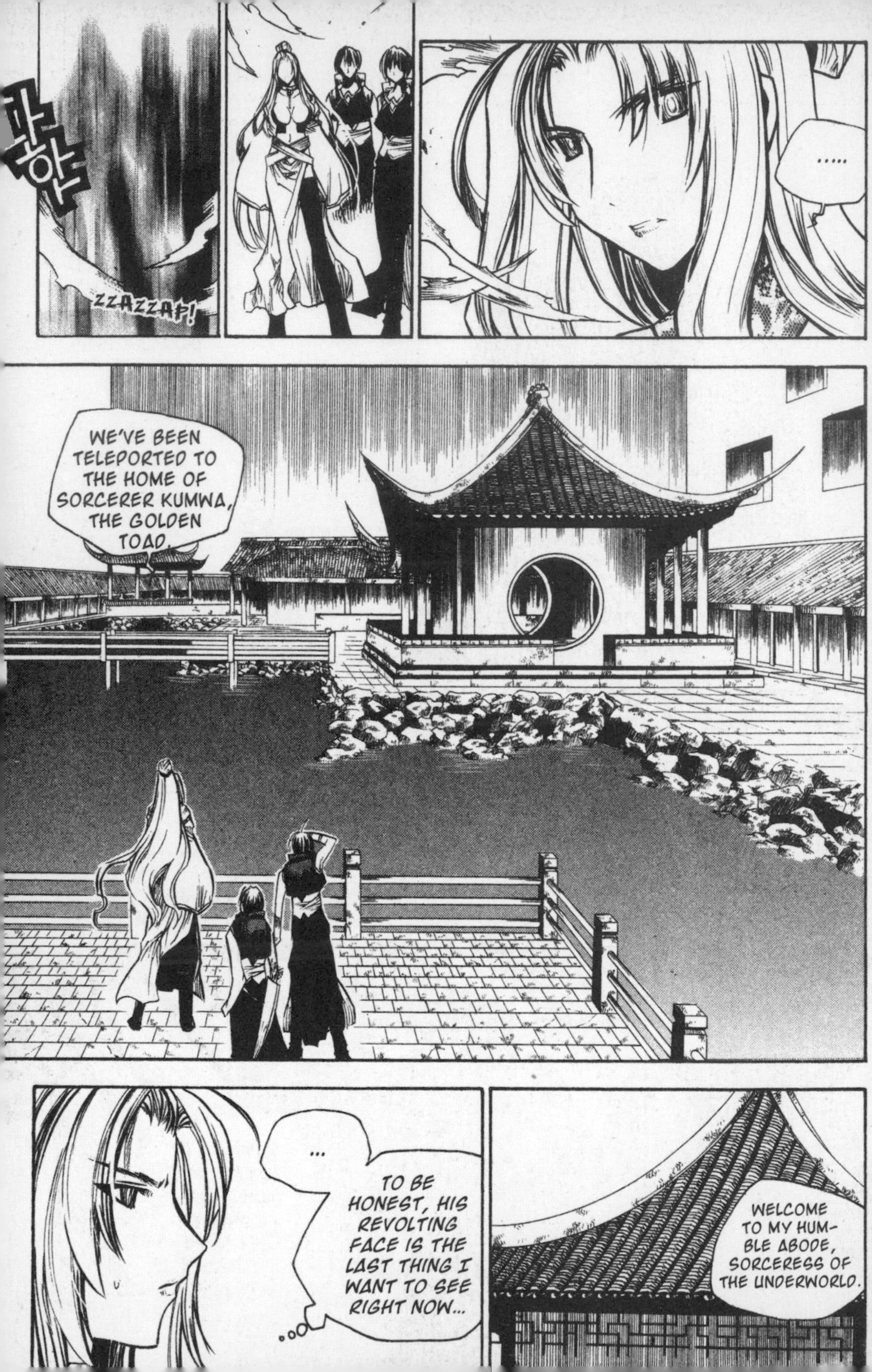
ZZAZZAP!
.....
WE'VE BEEN TELEPORTED TO THE HOME OF SORCERER KUMWA, THE GOLDEN TOAD.
...
TO BE HONEST, HIS REVOLTING FACE IS THE LAST THING I WANT TO SEE RIGHT NOW...
WELCOME TO MY HUM-BLE ABODE, SORCERESS OF THE UNDERWORLD.

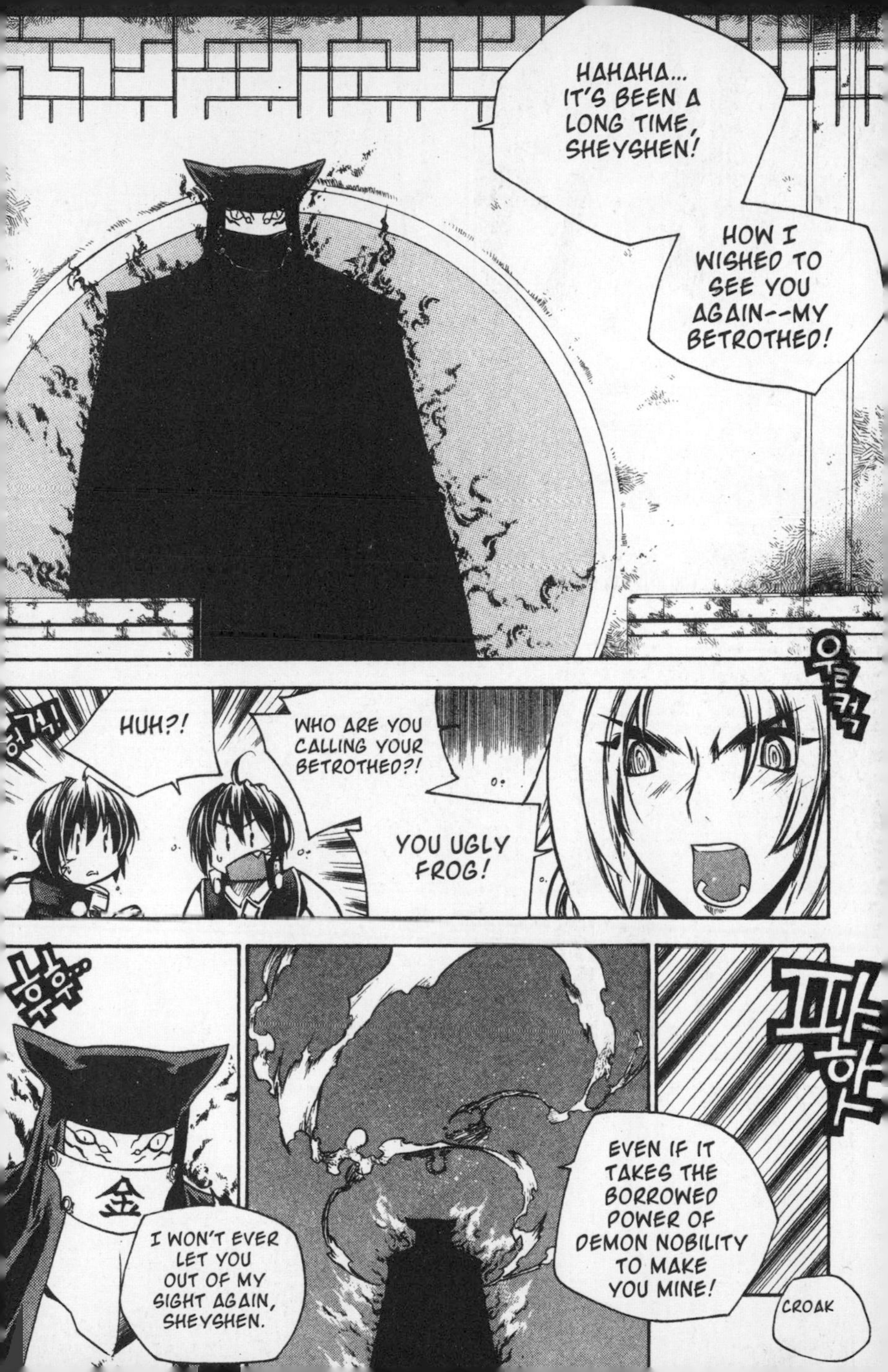
HAHAHA... IT'S BEEN A LONG TIME, SHEYSHEN!
HOW I WISHED TO SEE YOU AGAIN--MY BETROTHED!
HUH?!
WHO ARE YOU CALLING YOUR BETROTHED?!
YOU UGLY FROG!
I WON'T EVER LET YOU OUT OF MY SIGHT AGAIN, SHEYSHEN.
EVEN IF IT TAKES THE BORROWED POWER OF DEMON NOBILITY TO MAKE YOU MINE!
CROAK

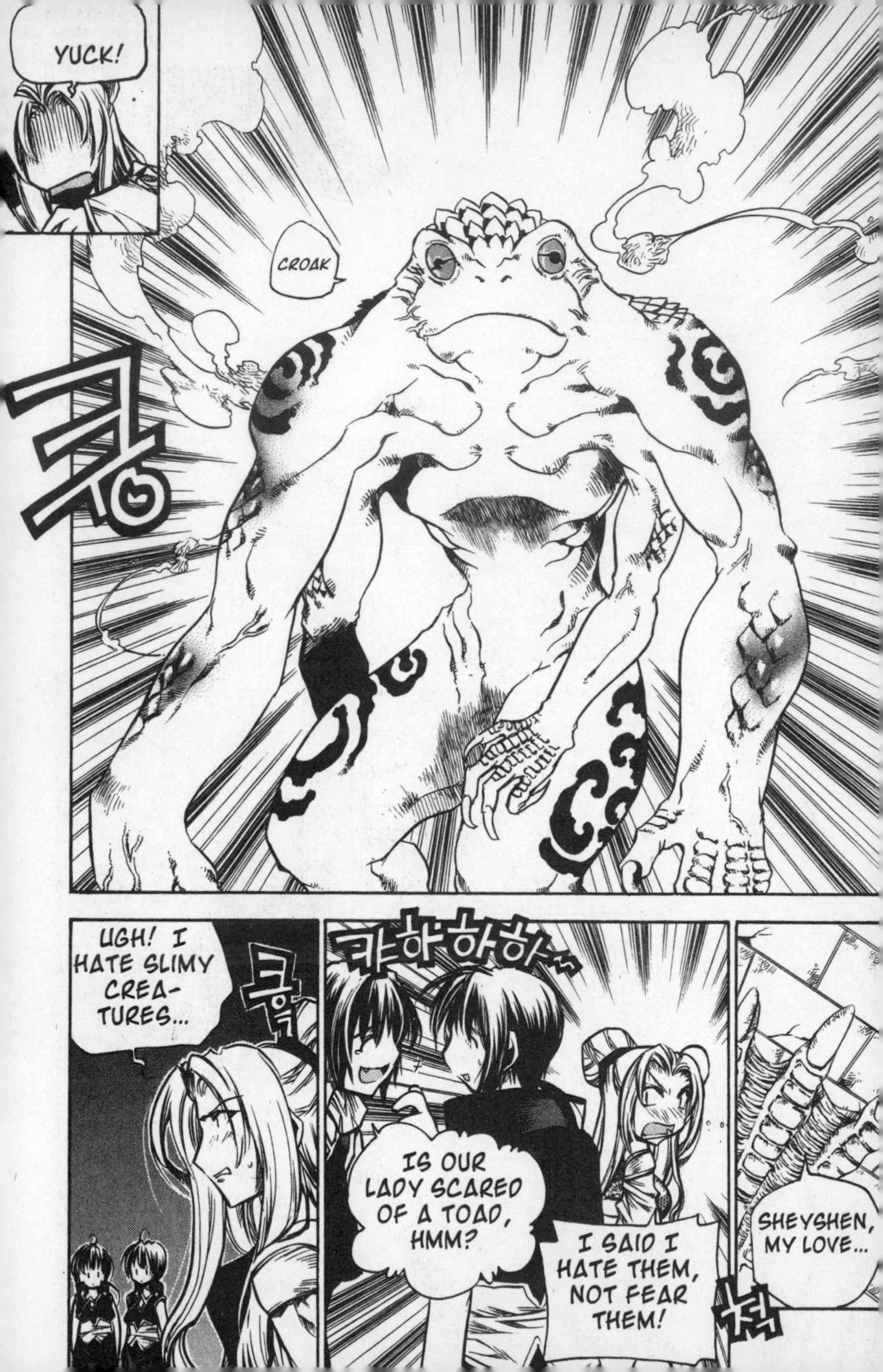
YUCK!
CROAK
쿵
UGH! I HATE SLIMY CREA-TURES...
캬하하하~
IS OUR LADY SCARED OF A TOAD, HMM?
I SAID I HATE THEM, NOT FEAR THEM!
SHEYSHEN, MY LOVE...

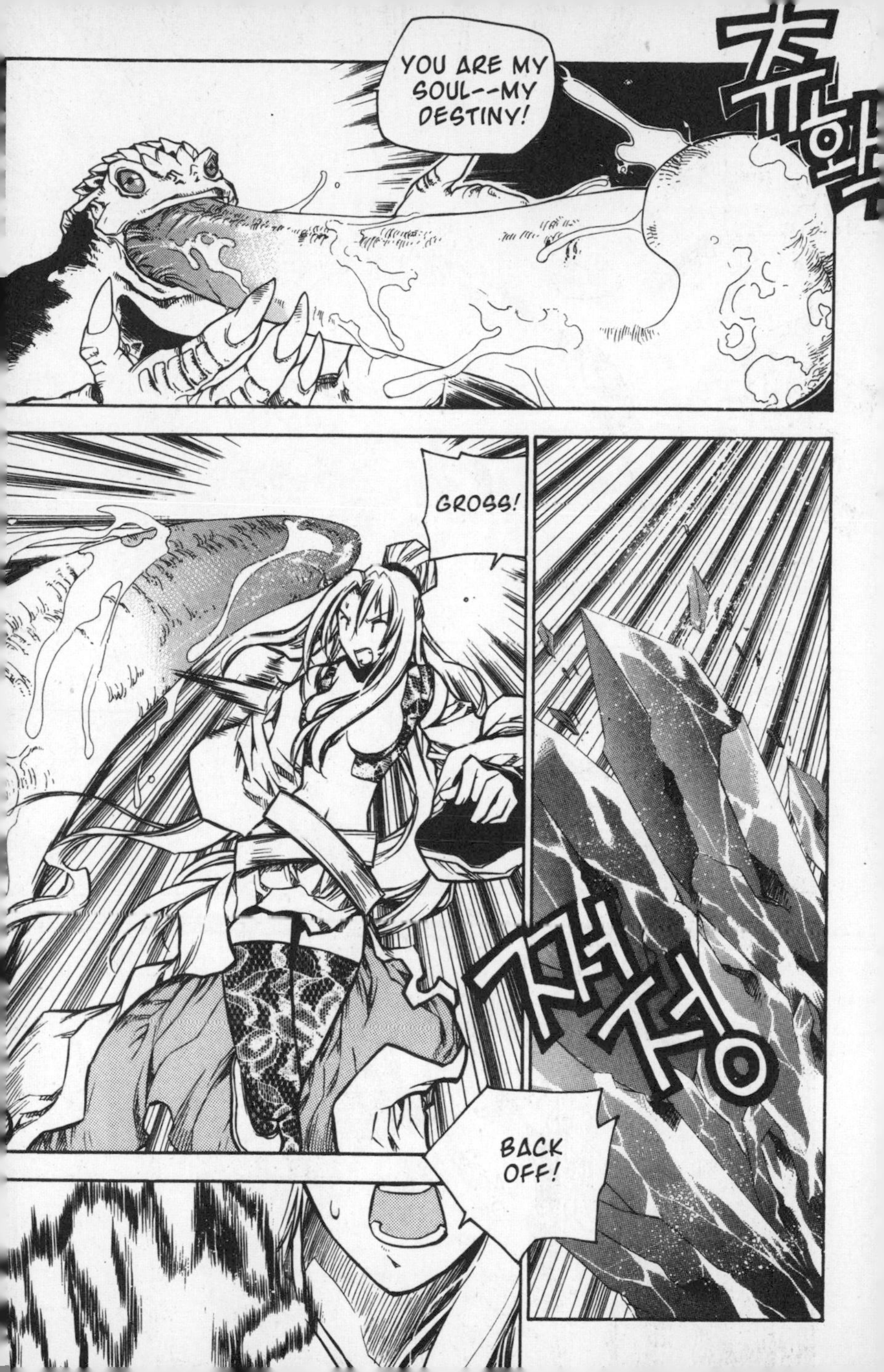
YOU ARE MY SOUL--MY DESTINY!
GROSS!
BACK OFF!

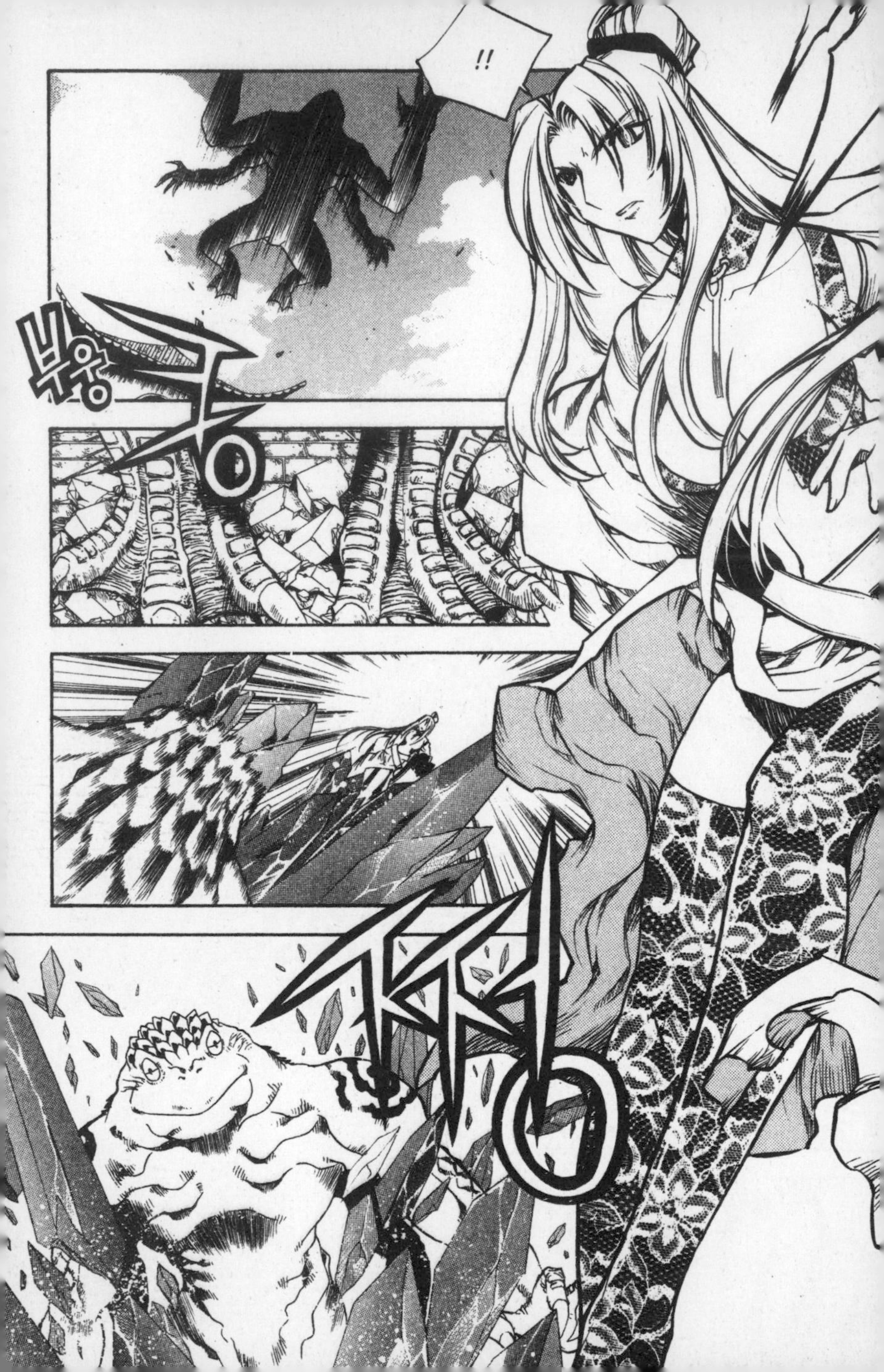
!!
부웅
쿵
쩡

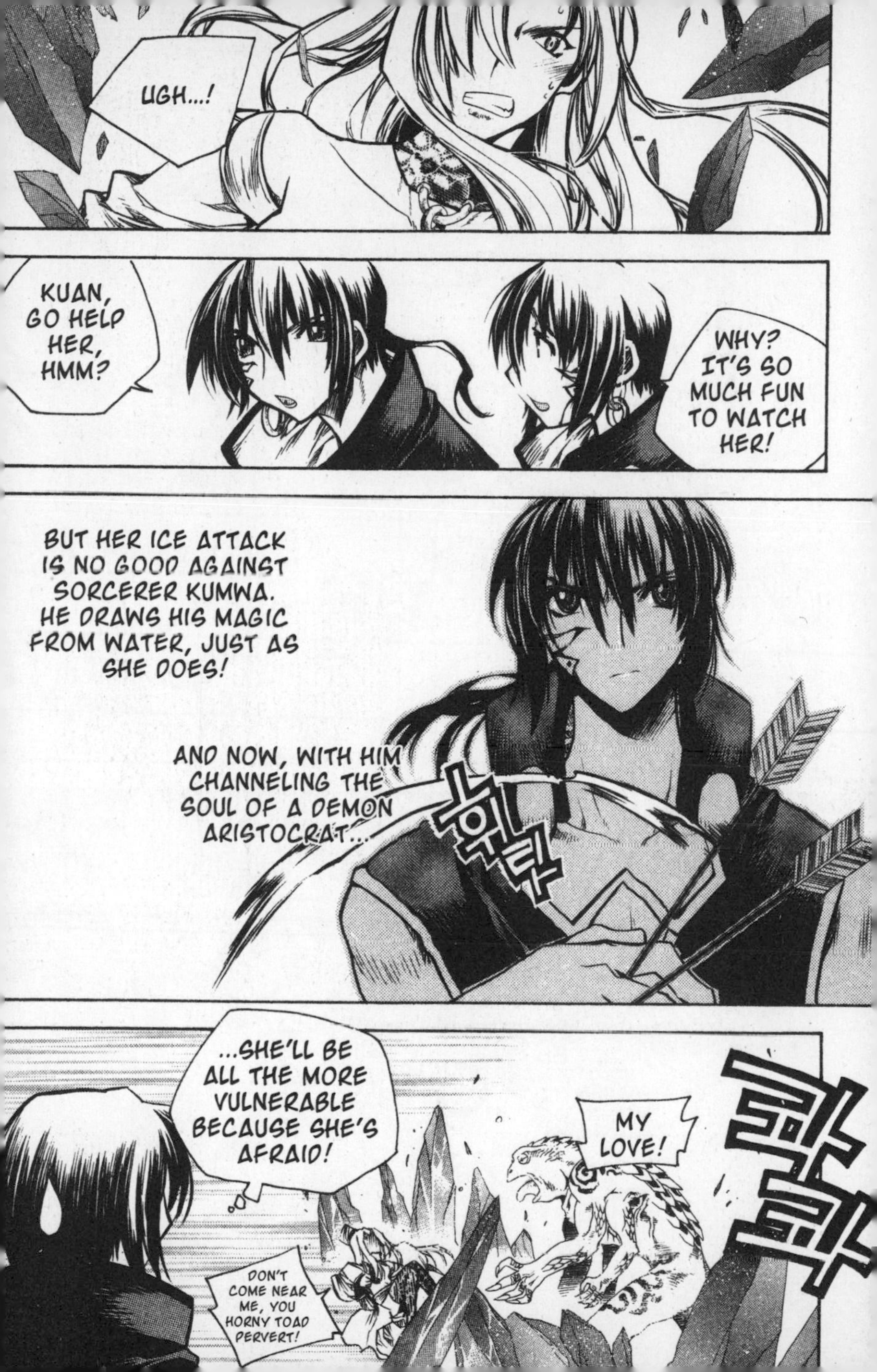
UGH...!
KUAN, GO HELP HER, HMM?
WHY? IT'S SO MUCH FUN TO WATCH HER!
BUT HER ICE ATTACK IS NO GOOD AGAINST SORCERER KUMWA. HE DRAWS HIS MAGIC FROM WATER, JUST AS SHE DOES!
AND NOW, WITH HIM CHANNELING THE SOUL OF A DEMON ARISTOCRAT...
...SHE'LL BE ALL THE MORE VULNERABLE BECAUSE SHE'S AFRAID!
MY LOVE!
DON'T COME NEAR ME, YOU HORNY TOAD PERVERT!

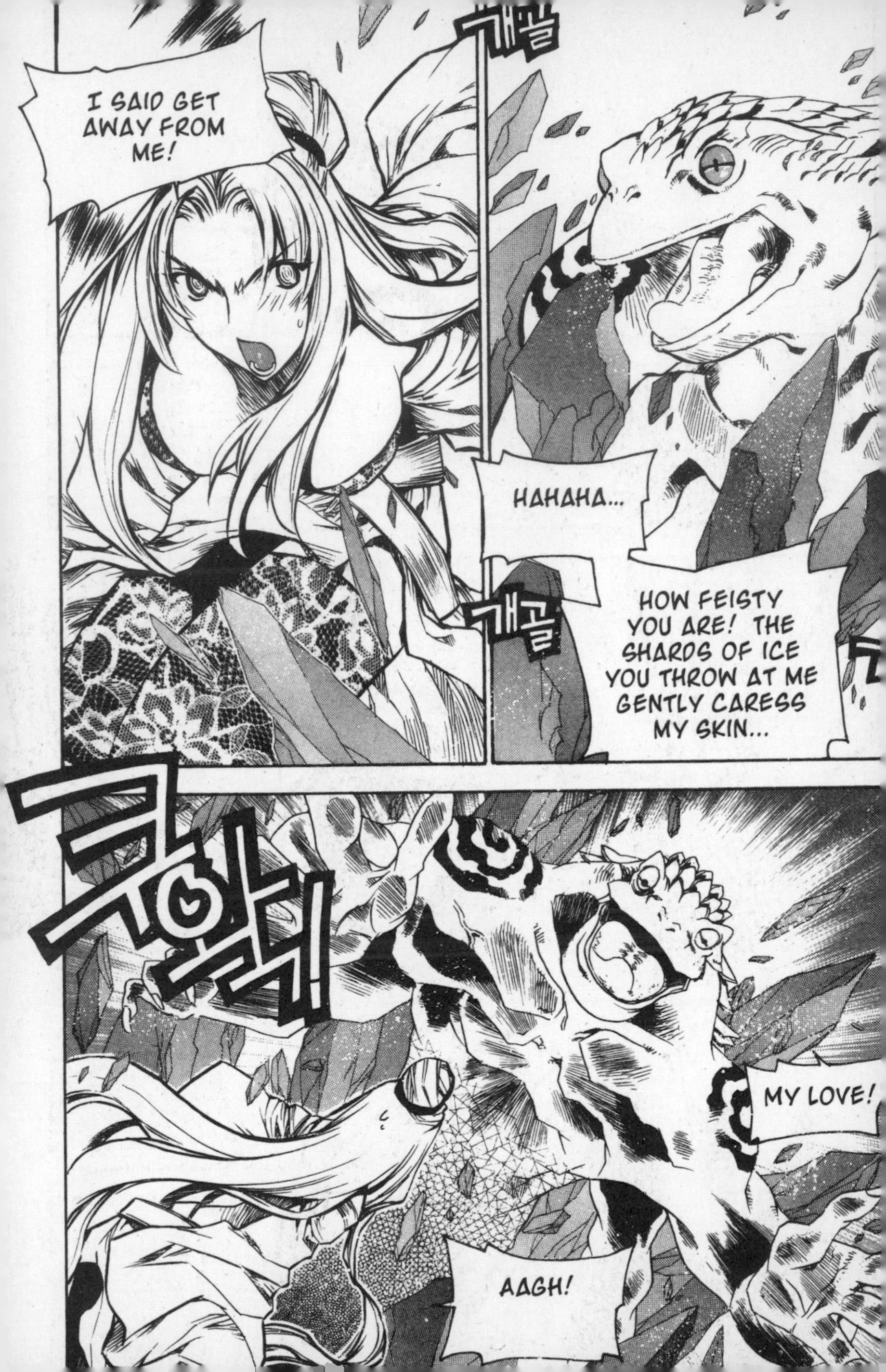
I SAID GET AWAY FROM ME!
개골
HAHAHA...
개골
HOW FEISTY YOU ARE! THE SHARDS OF ICE YOU THROW AT ME GENTLY CARESS MY SKIN...
MY LOVE!
AAGH!

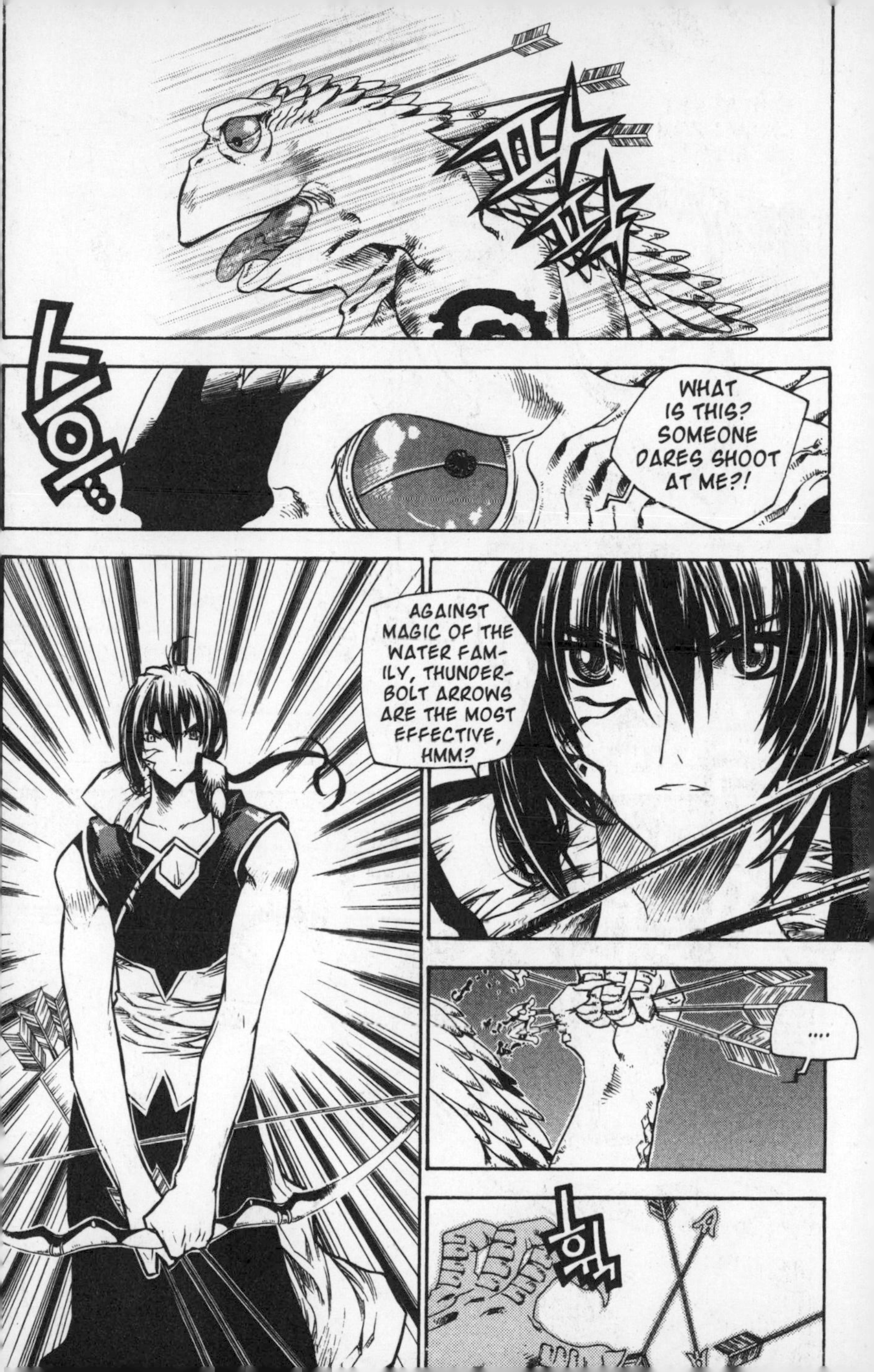
WHAT IS THIS? SOMEONE DARES SHOOT AT ME?!
AGAINST MAGIC OF THE WATER FAMILY, THUNDERBOLT ARROWS ARE THE MOST EFFECTIVE, HMM?
....

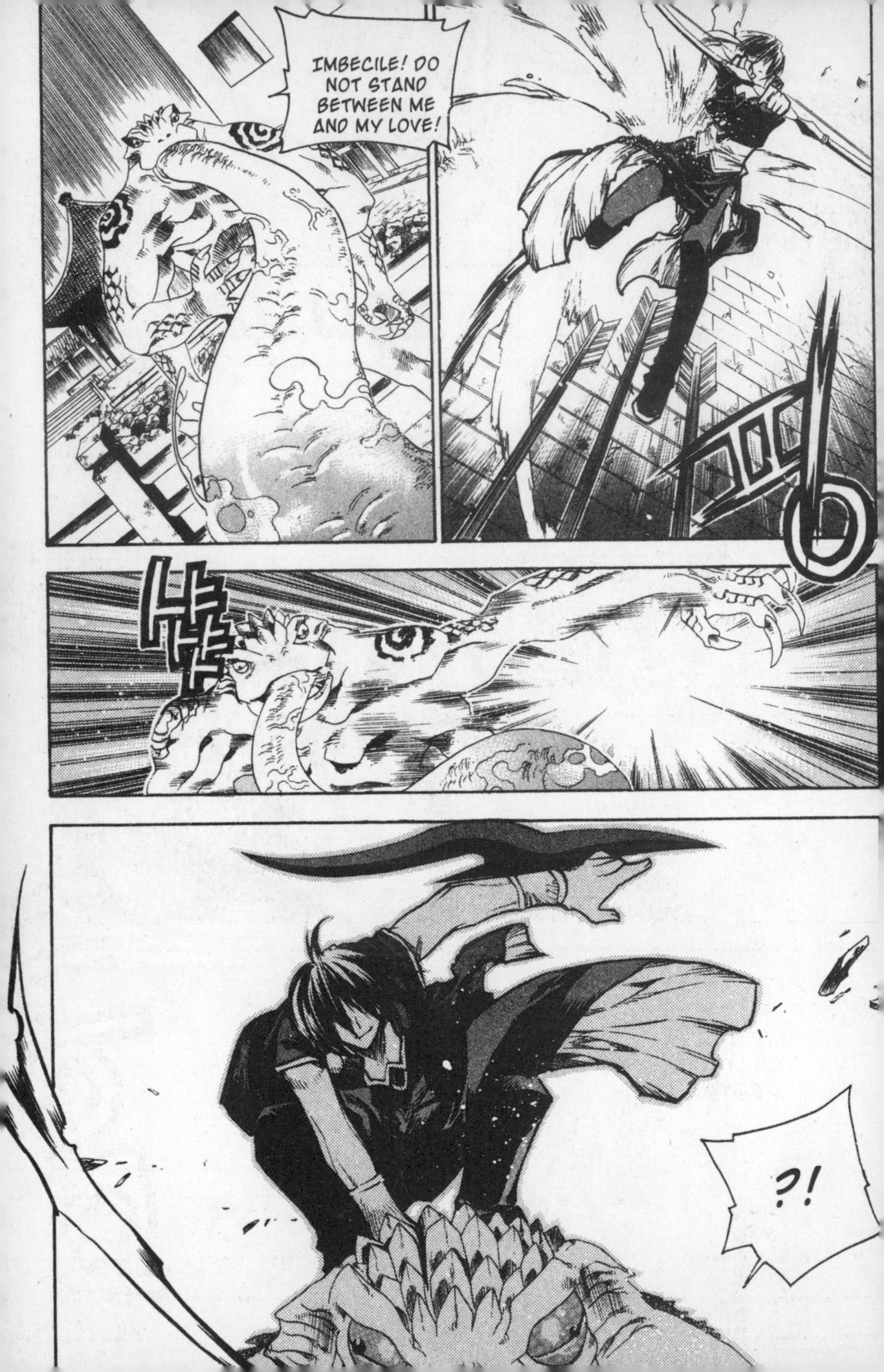
IMBECILE! DO NOT STAND BETWEEN ME AND MY LOVE!
?!

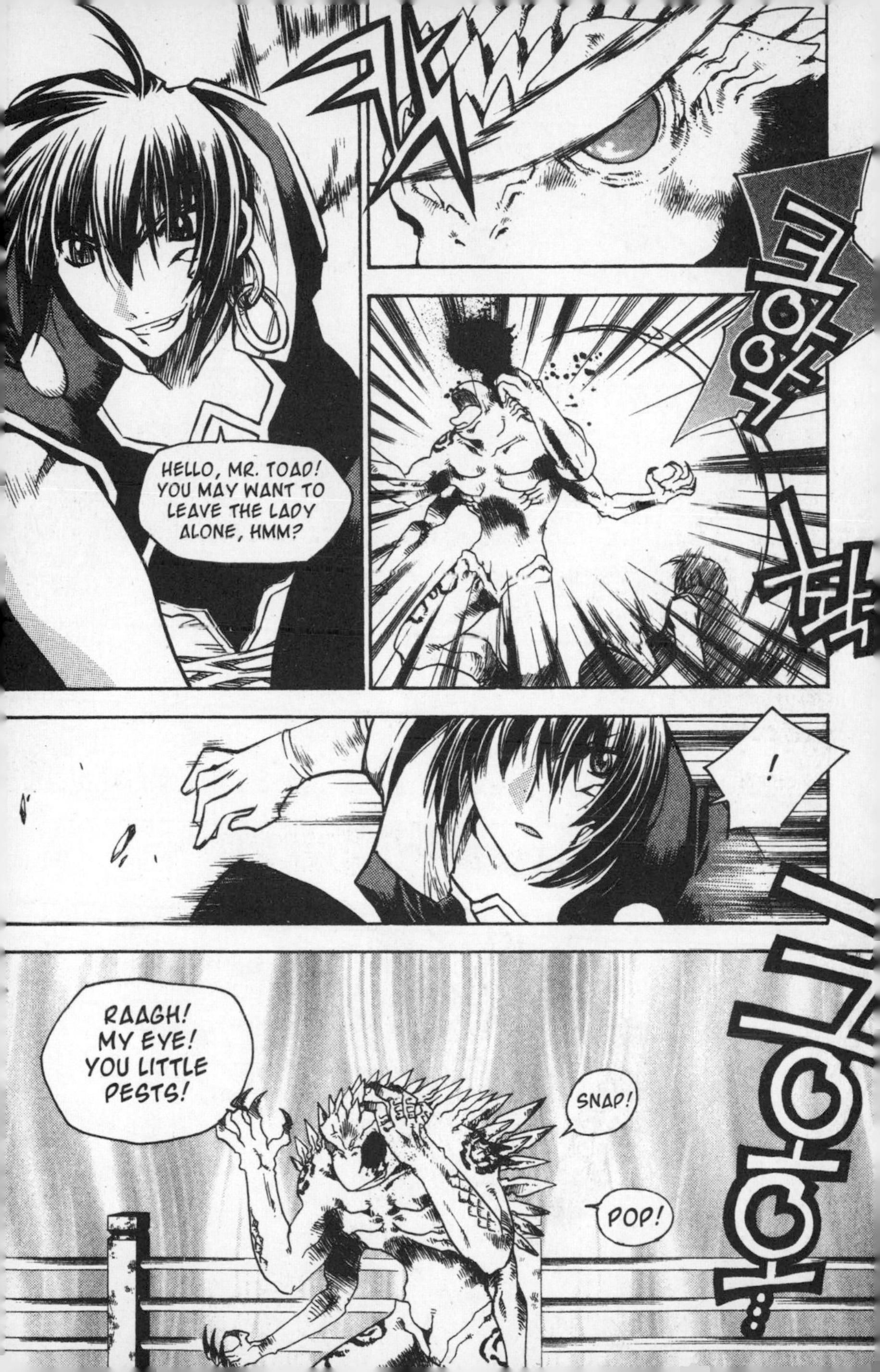
HELLO, MR. TOAD! YOU MAY WANT TO LEAVE THE LADY ALONE, HMM?
!
RAAGH! MY EYE! YOU LITTLE PESTS!
SNAP!
POP!

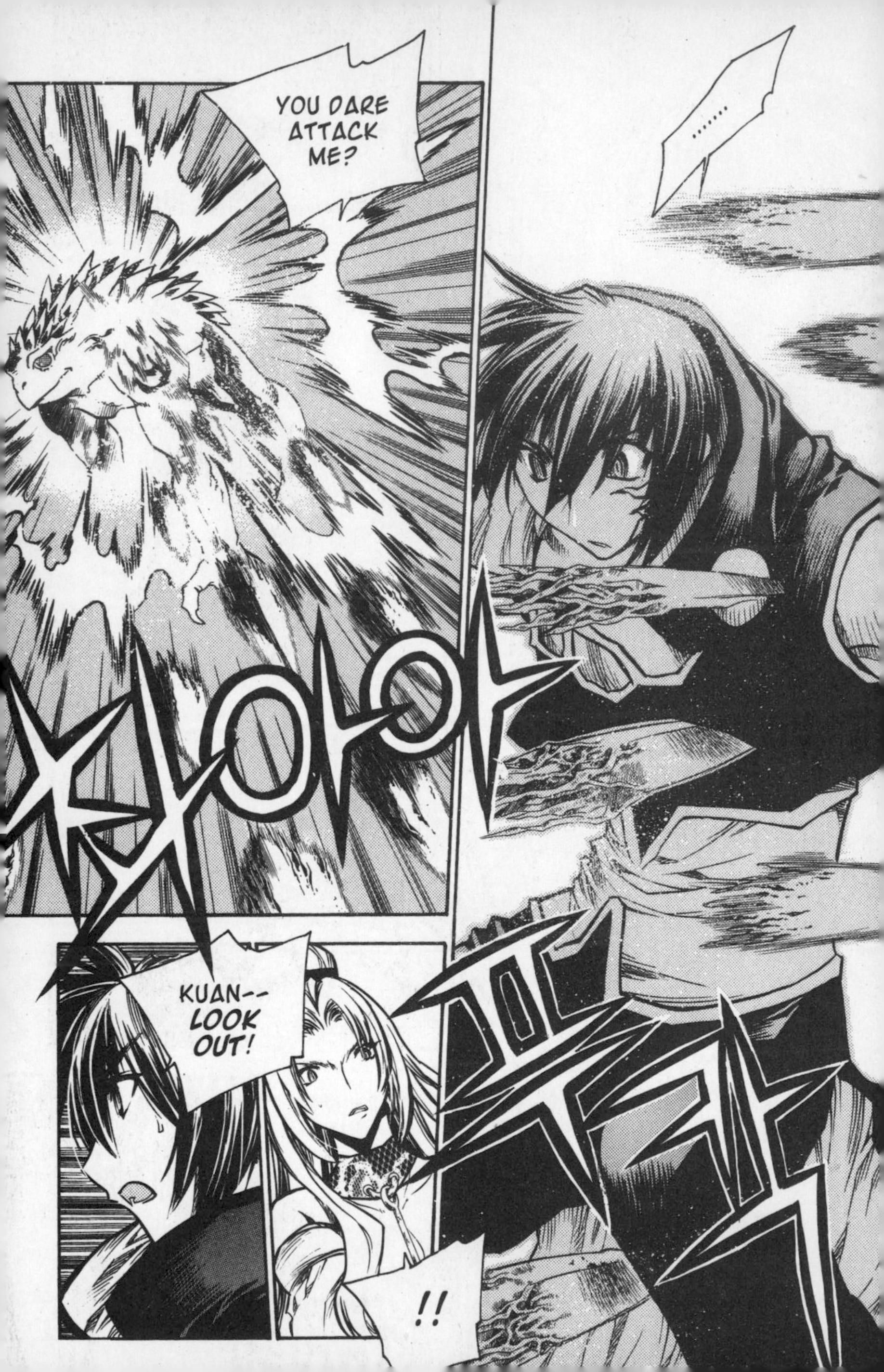
YOU DARE ATTACK ME?
KUAN-- LOOK OUT!
!!
......

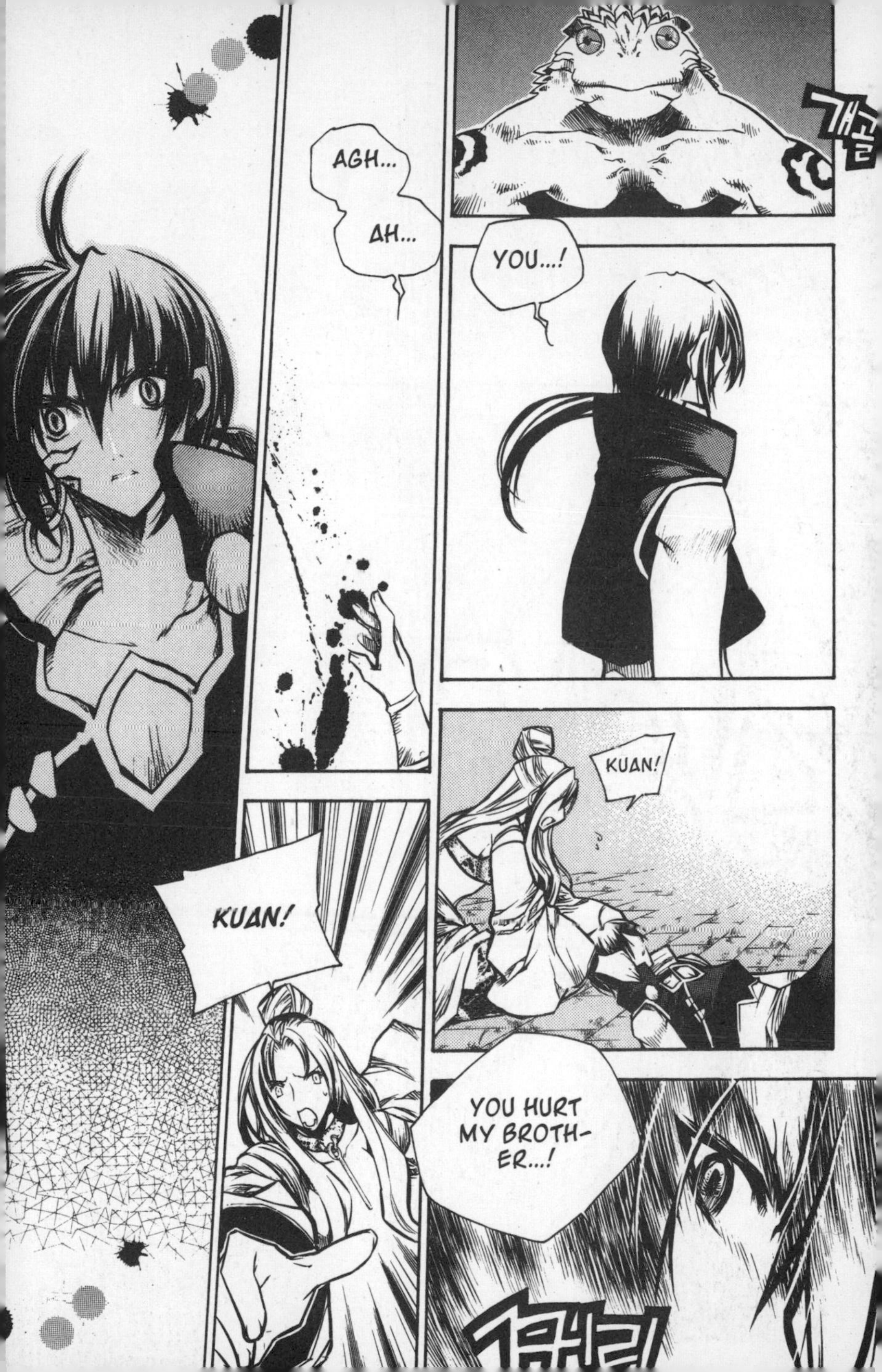
AGH...
AH...
KUAN!
YOU...!
KUAN!
YOU HURT MY BROTHER-ER...!

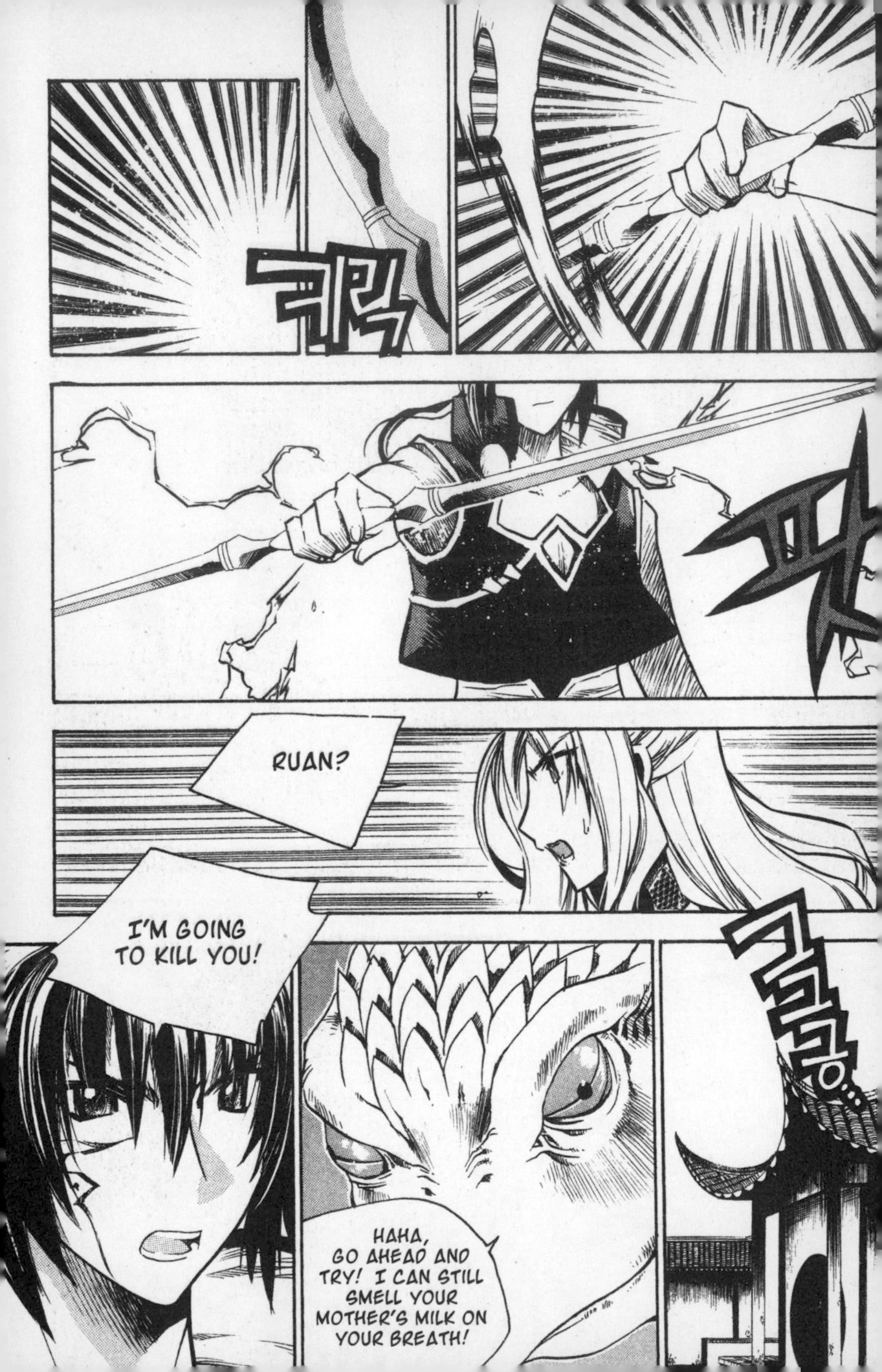
RUAN?
I'M GOING TO KILL YOU!
HAHA, GO AHEAD AND TRY! I CAN STILL SMELL YOUR MOTHER'S MILK ON YOUR BREATH!

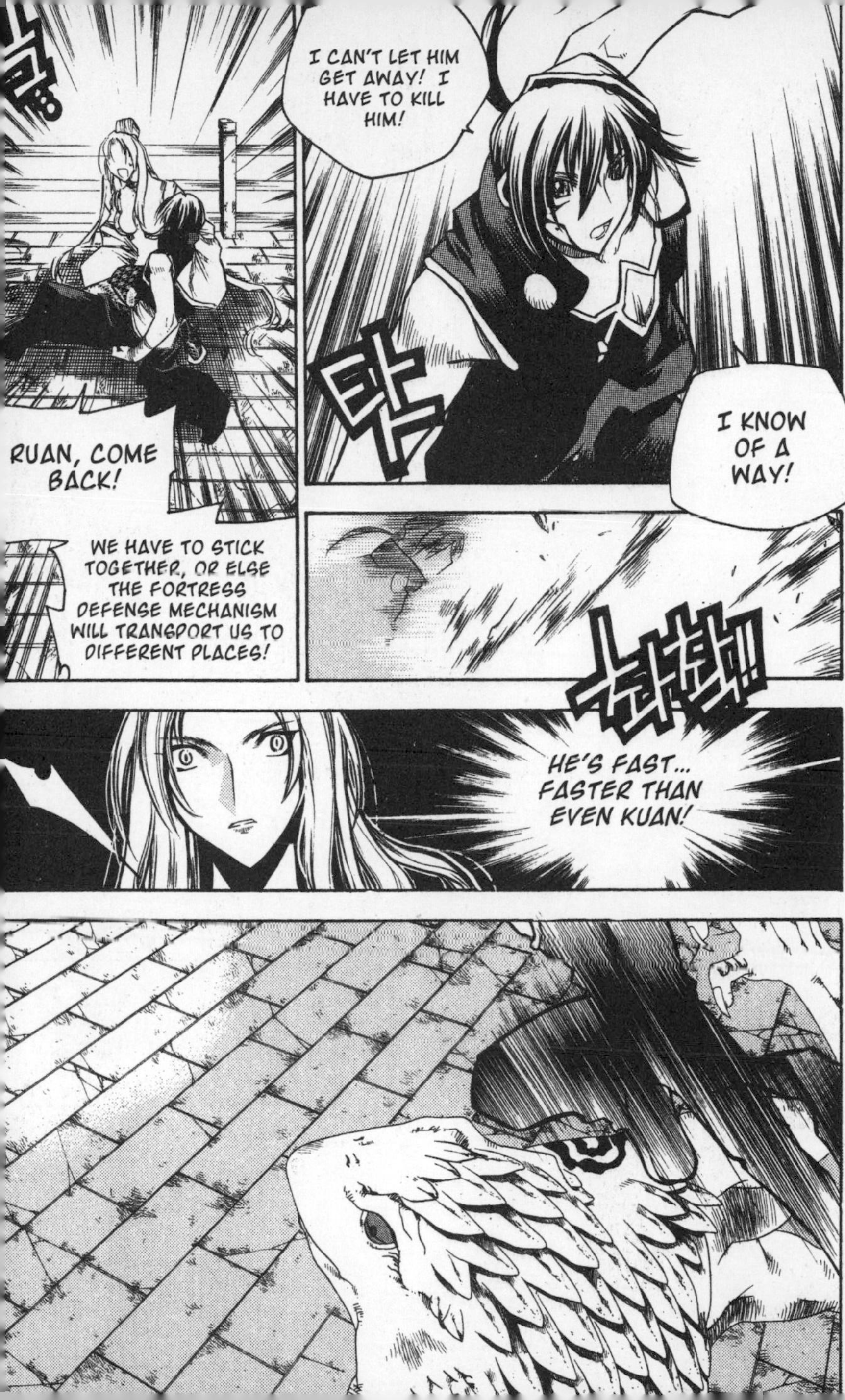
RUAN, COME BACK!
WE HAVE TO STICK TOGETHER, OR ELSE THE FORTRESS DEFENSE MECHANISM WILL TRANSPORT US TO DIFFERENT PLACES!
I CAN'T LET HIM GET AWAY! I HAVE TO KILL HIM!
I KNOW OF A WAY!
HE'S FAST... FASTER THAN EVEN KUAN!

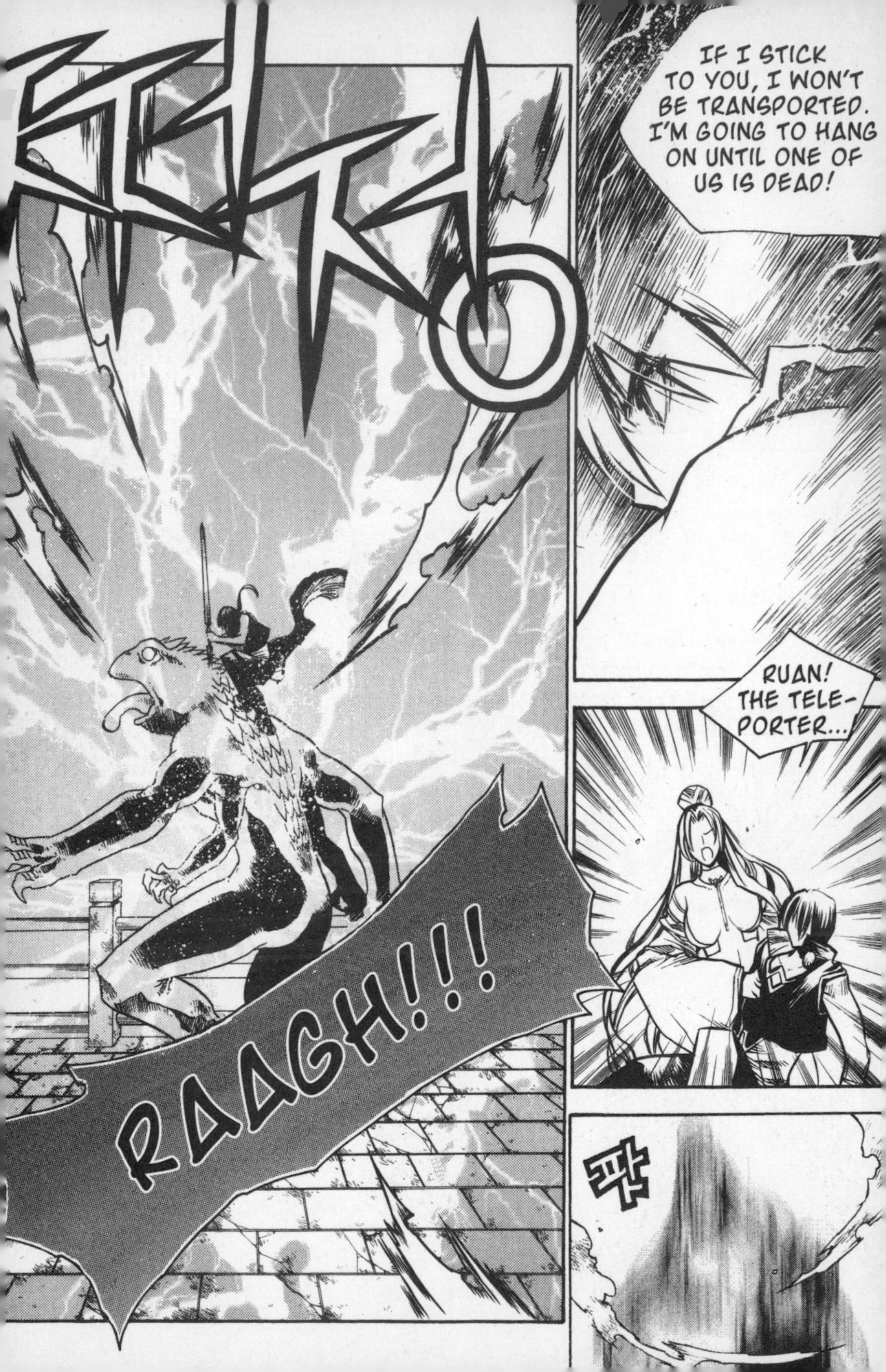
RAAGH!!!
IF I STICK TO YOU, I WON'T BE TRANSPORTED. I'M GOING TO HANG ON UNTIL ONE OF US IS DEAD!
RUAN! THE TELE-PORTER...
팍

Chapter 48
Undead or Alive

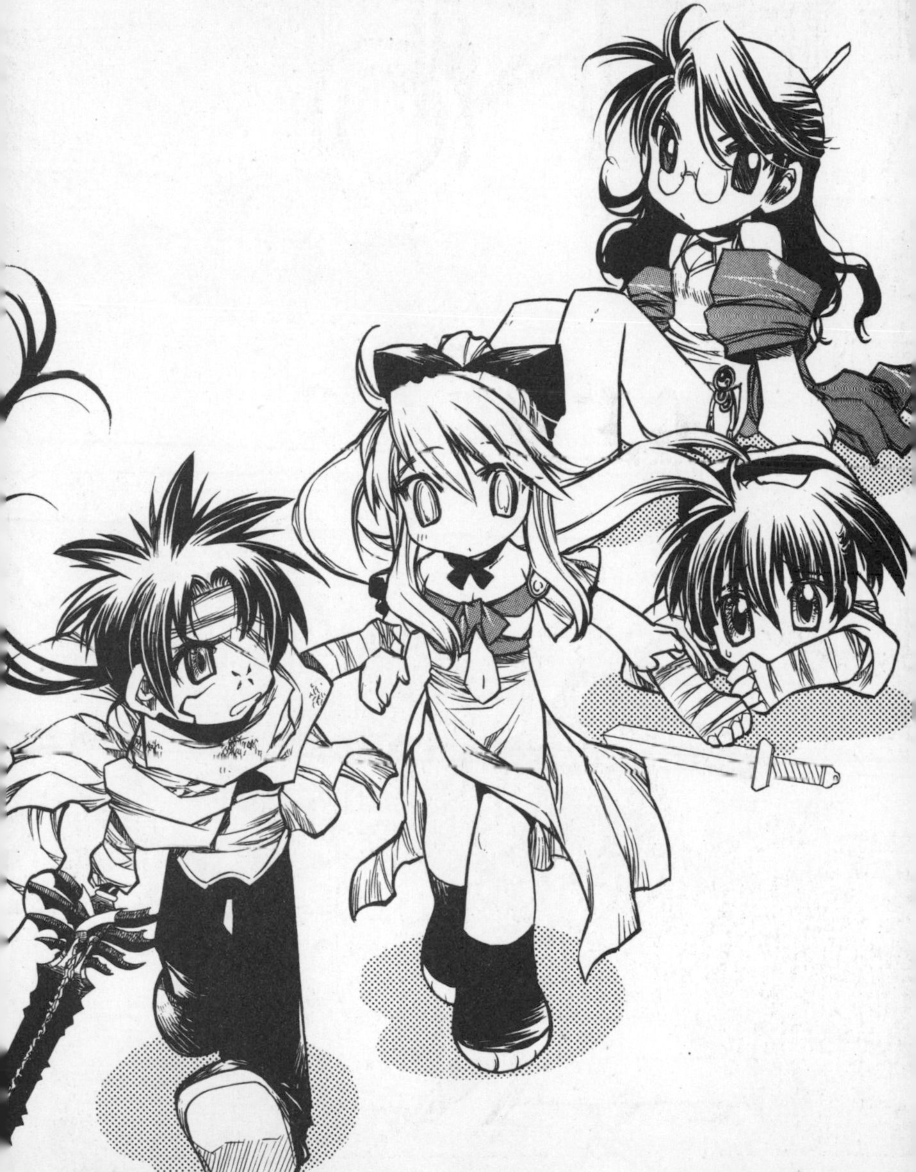

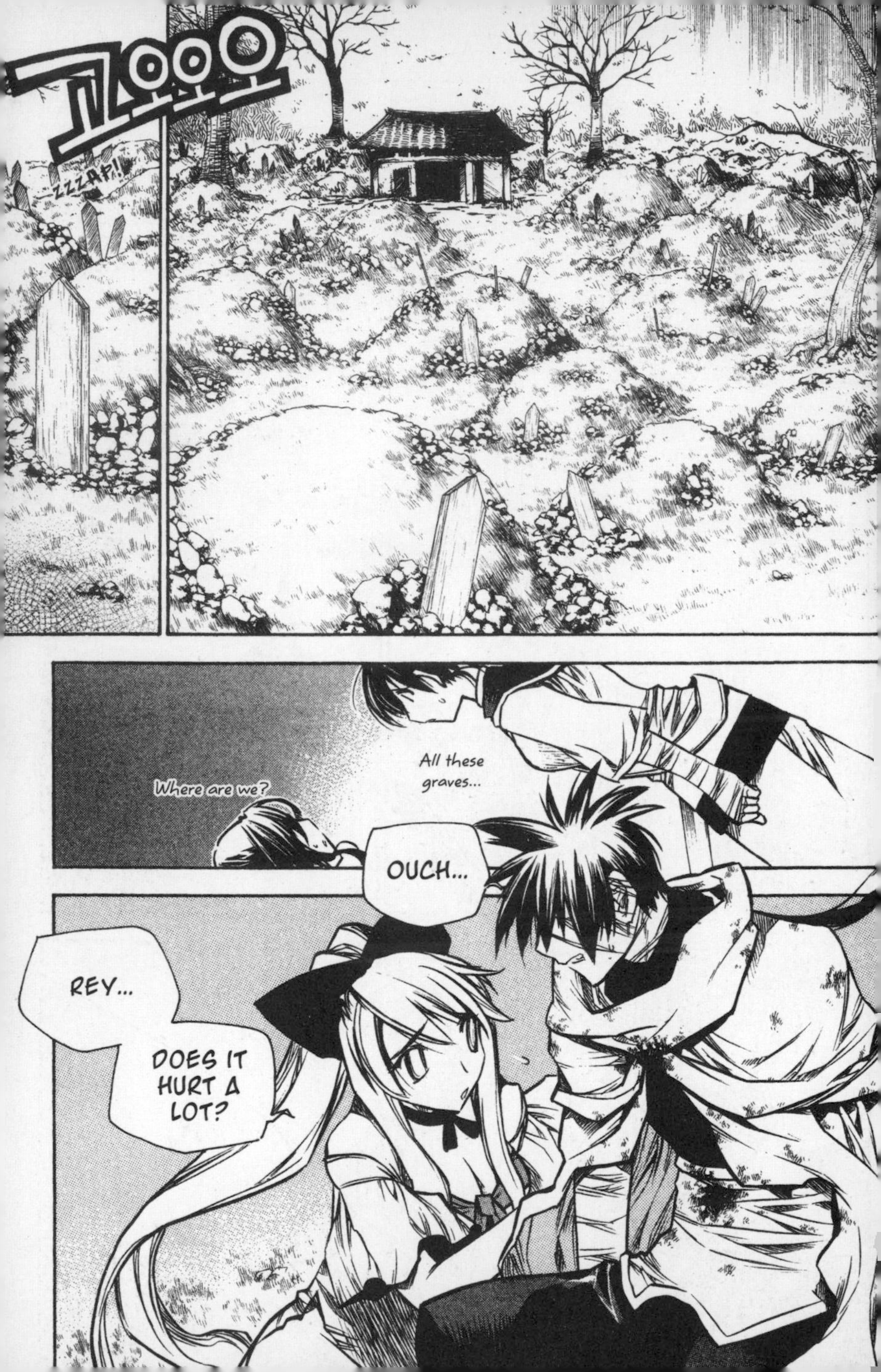
ZZZAP!!
Where are we?
All these graves...
OUCH...
REY...
DOES IT HURT A LOT?

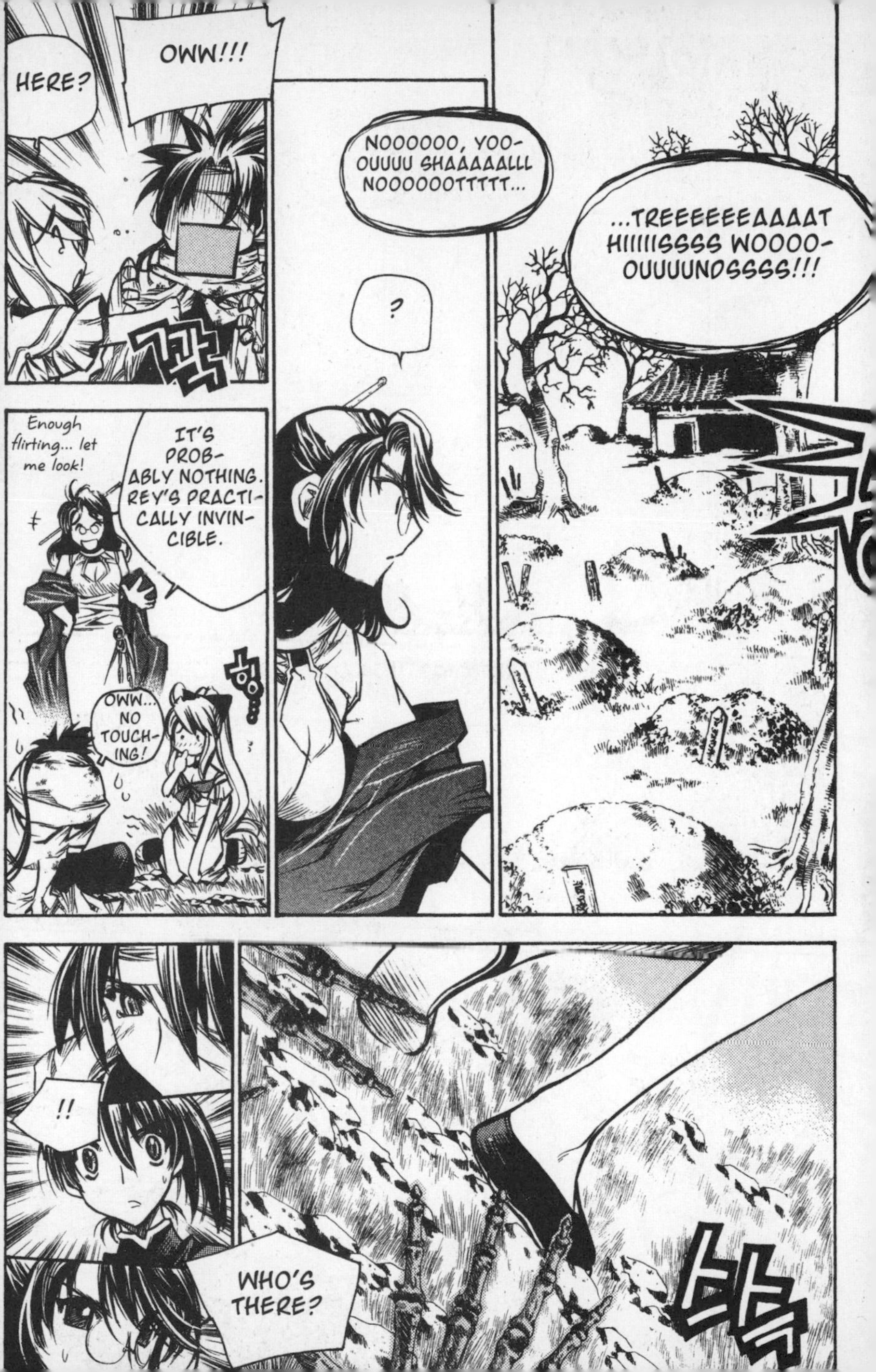
HERE?
OWW!!!
Enough flirting... let me look!
IT'S PROB-ABLY NOTHING. REY'S PRACTI-CALLY INVIN-CIBLE.
OWW... NO TOUCH-ING!
NOOOOOO, YOO-OUUUU SHAAAAALLL NOOOOOOTTTTT...
?
...TREEEEEEAAAAT HIIIIISSSS WOOOO-OUUUUNDSSSS!!!
!!
WHO'S THERE?

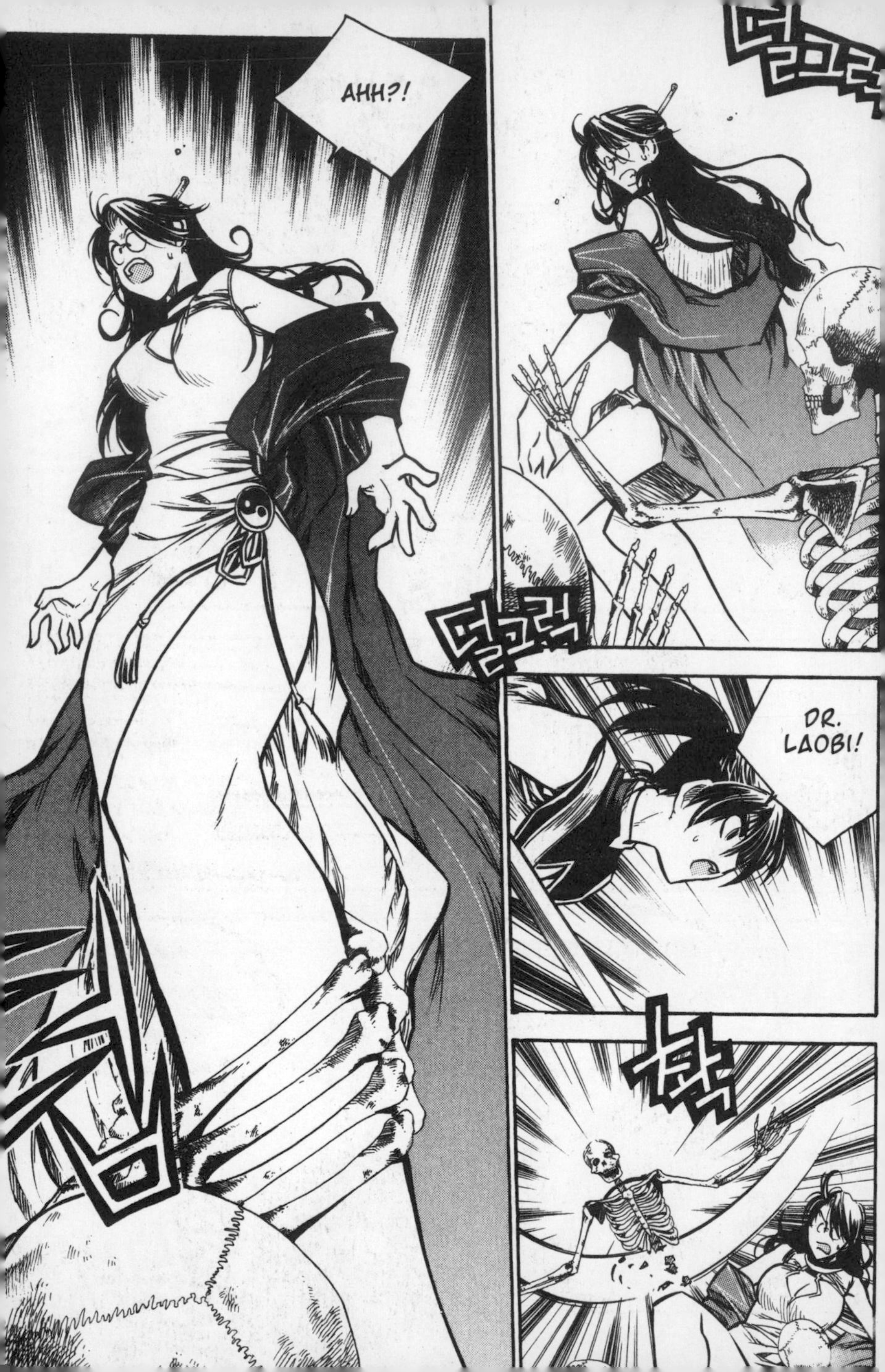
AHH?!
덜그럭
덜그럭
DR. LAOBI!
확

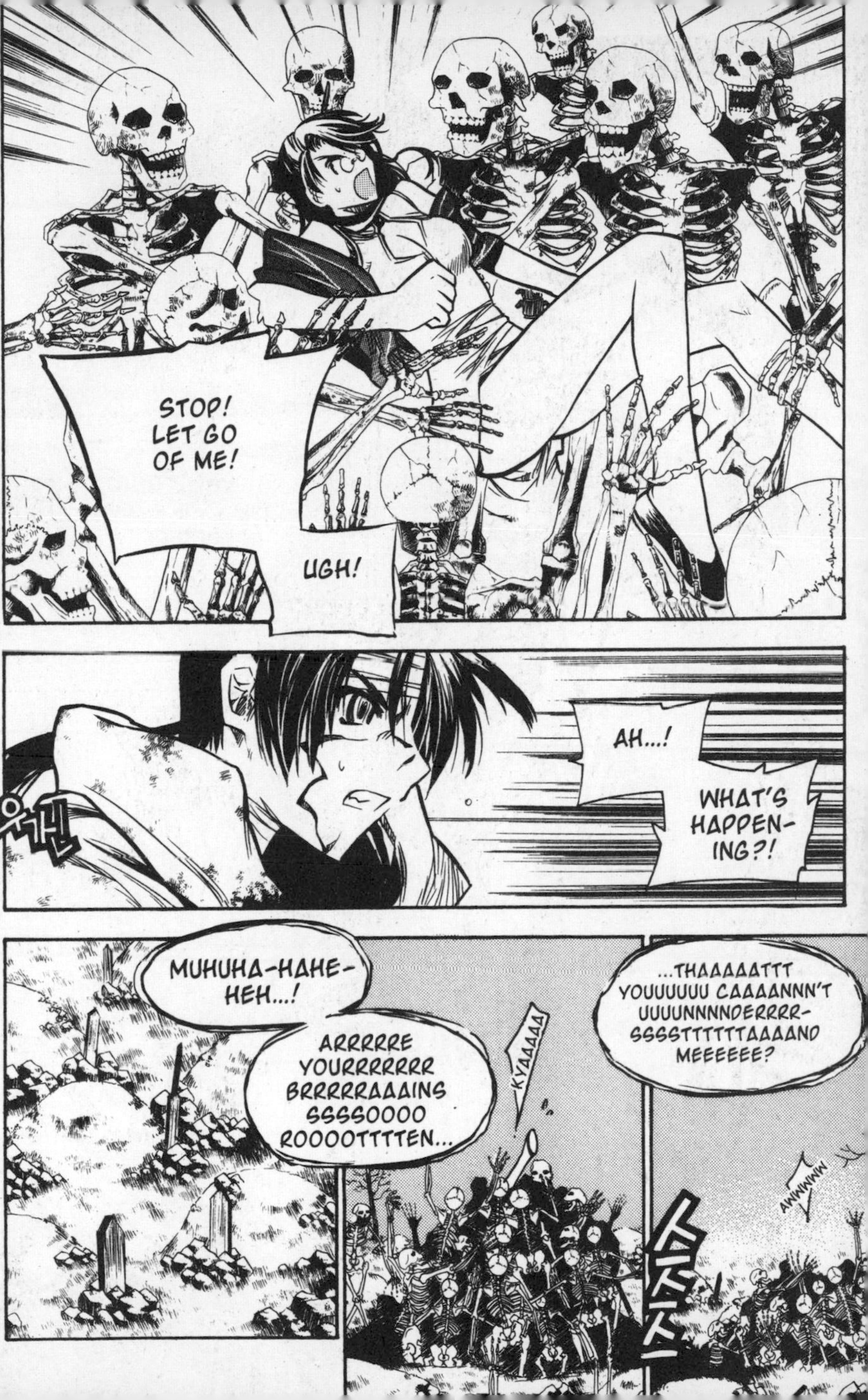
STOP! LET GO OF ME!
UGH!
AH...!
WHAT'S HAPPEN-ING?!
MUHUHA-HAHE-HEH...!
ARRRRRE YOURRRRRRR BRRRRRAAAINS SSSSOOOO ROOOOTTTTEN...
KYAAAAA
...THAAAAATTT YOUUUUUU CAAAANNN'T UUUUNNNNDERRRR-SSSSTTTTTTAAAAND MEEEEEE?
AWWWWW

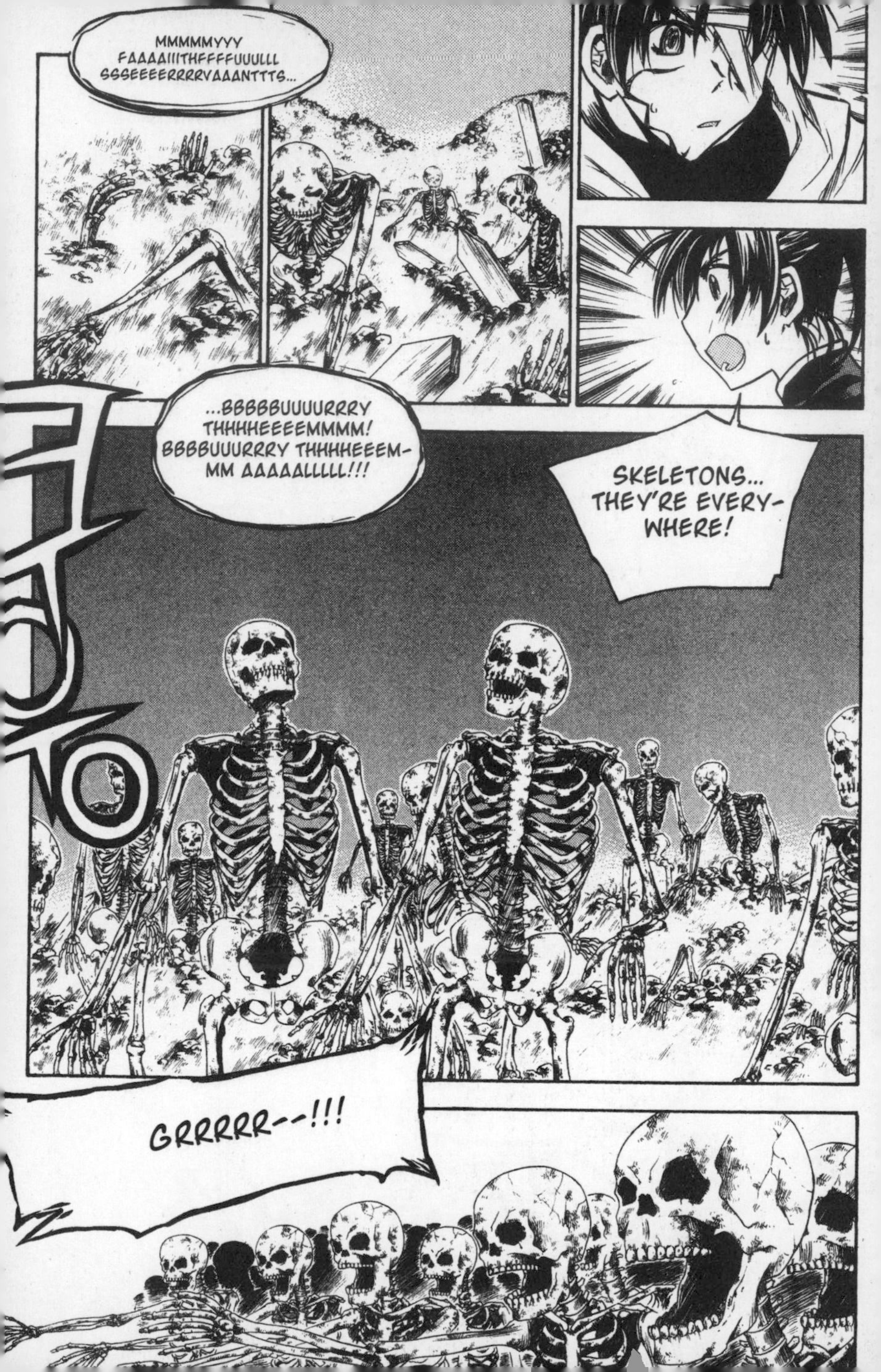
MMMMMYYY FAAAAIIIITHFFFFUUULLL SSSEEEEERRRRVAAANTTTS...
...BBBBBUUUURRRY THHHHEEEEMMMM! BBBBUUURRRY THHHHEEEM-MM AAAAALLLLL!!!
SKELETONS... THEY'RE EVERY-WHERE!
GRRRRR--!!!

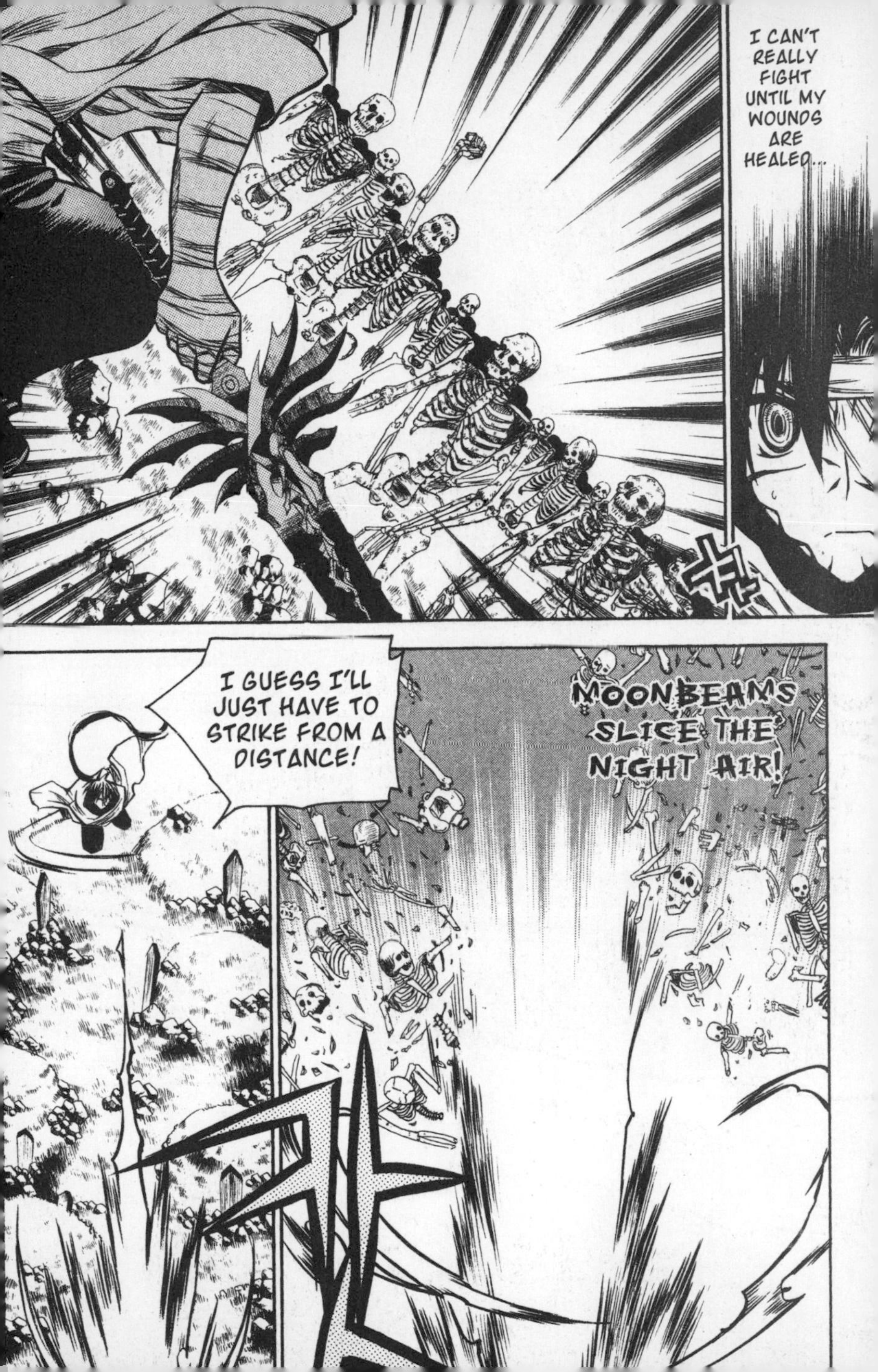
I CAN'T REALLY FIGHT UNTIL MY WOUNDS ARE HEALED...
I GUESS I'LL JUST HAVE TO STRIKE FROM A DISTANCE!
MOONBEAMS SLICE THE NIGHT AIR!

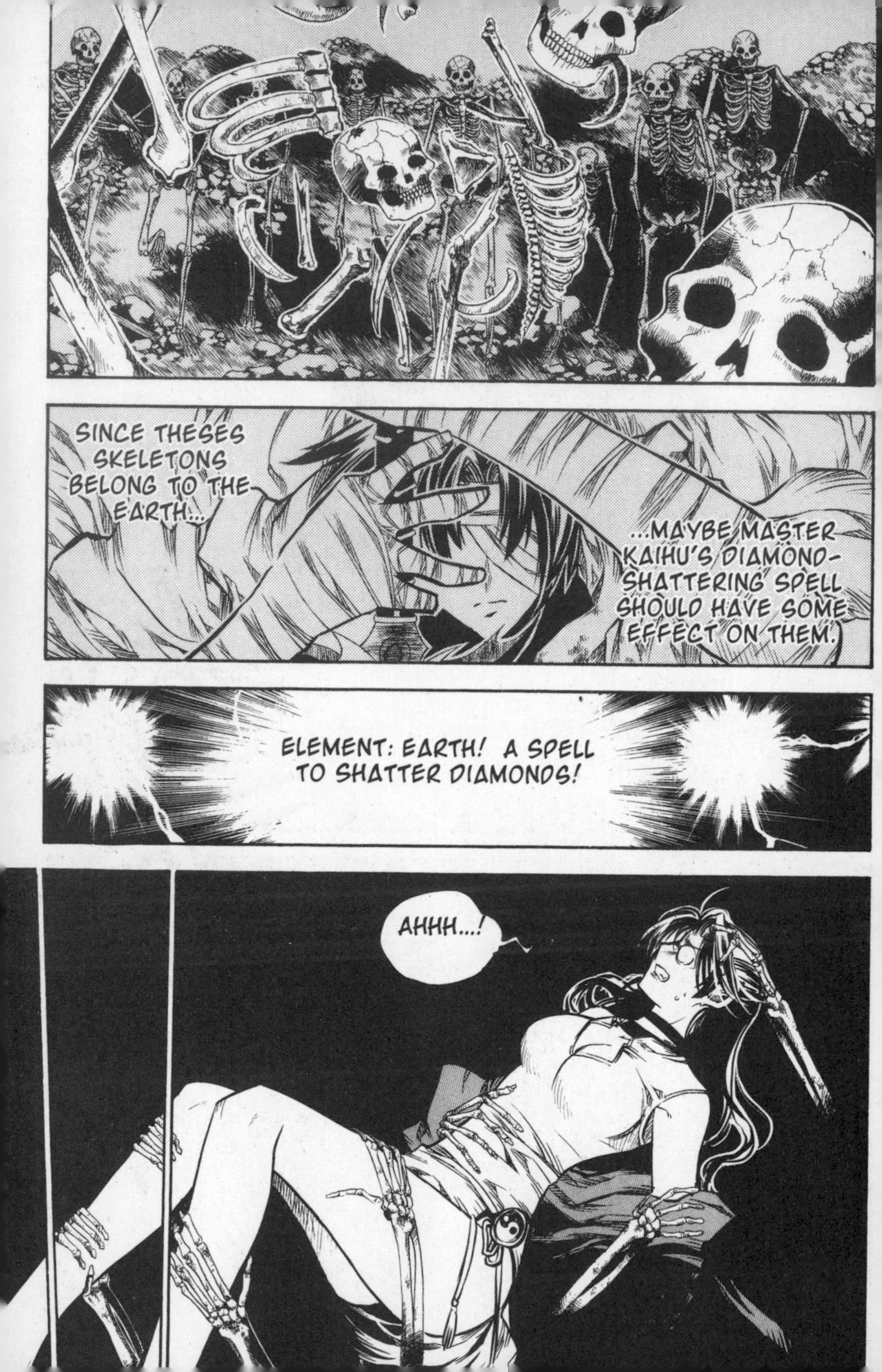
SINCE THESES SKELETONS BELONG TO THE EARTH...
...MAYBE MASTER KAIHU'S DIAMOND-SHATTERING SPELL SHOULD HAVE SOME EFFECT ON THEM.
ELEMENT: EARTH! A SPELL TO SHATTER DIAMONDS!
AHHH...!

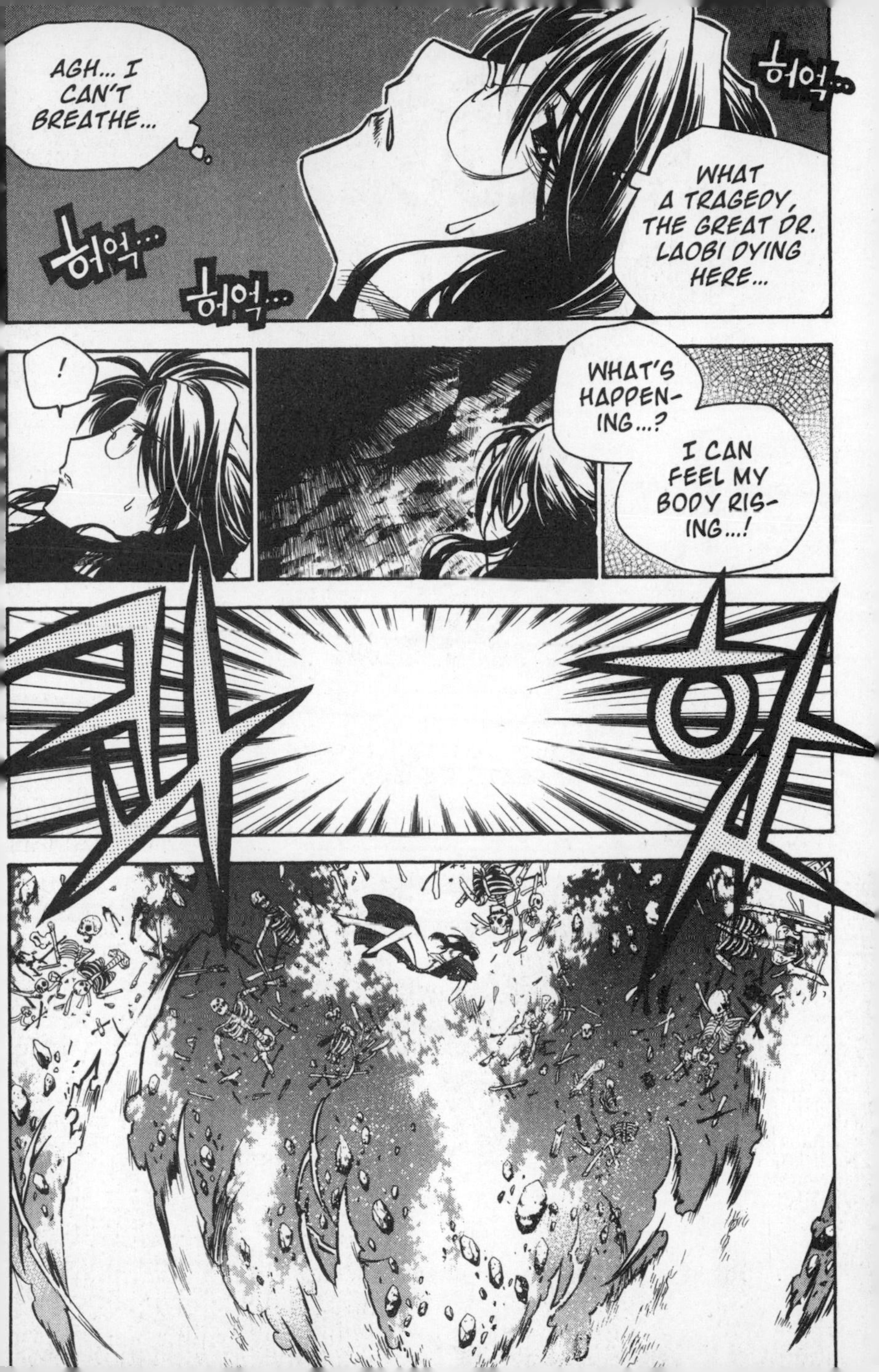
AGH... I CAN'T BREATHE...
허억...
WHAT A TRAGEDY, THE GREAT DR. LAOBI DYING HERE...
허억...
허억...
!
WHAT'S HAPPEN-ING...?
I CAN FEEL MY BODY RIS-ING...!
콰
앙

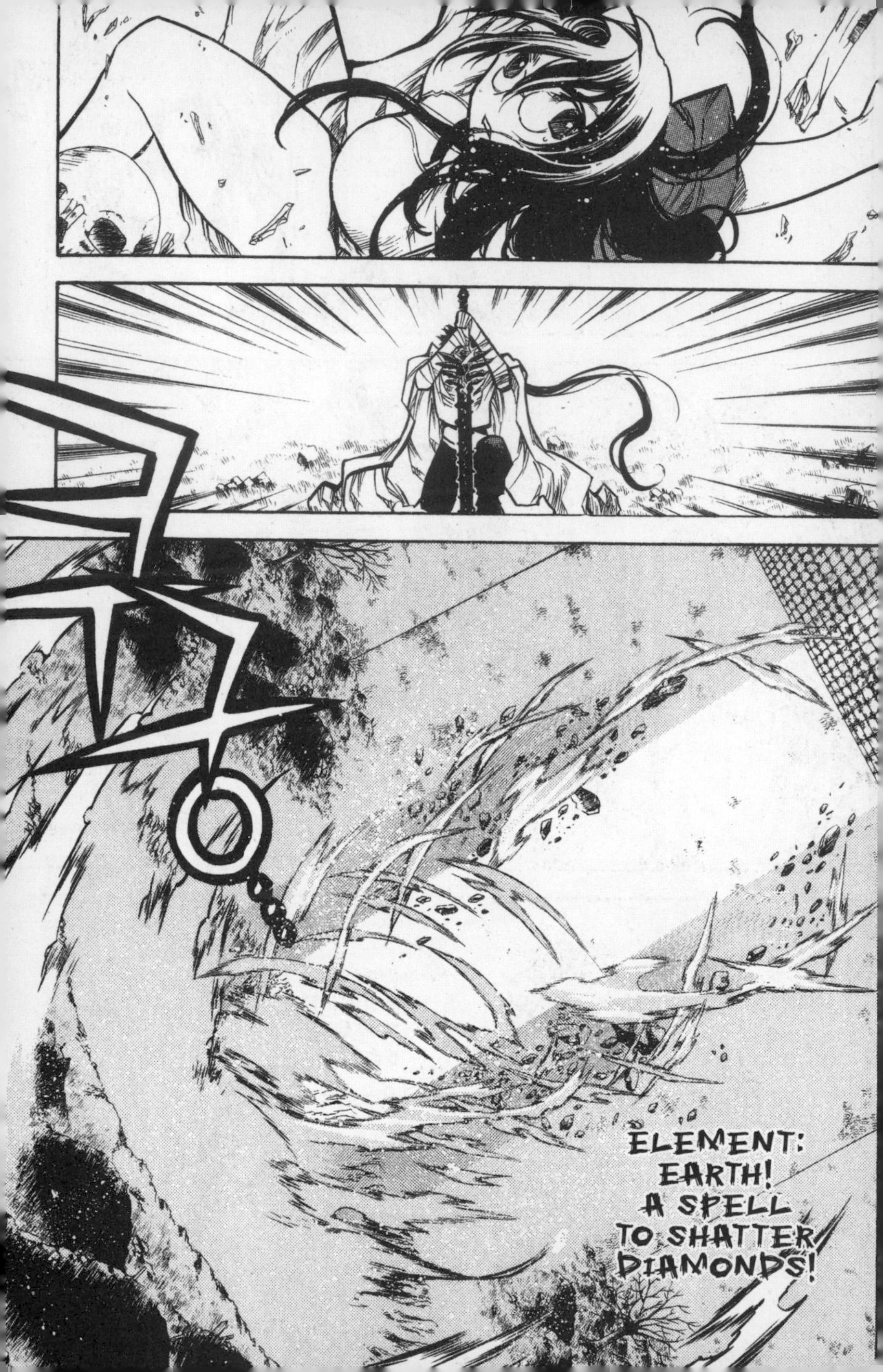
ELEMENT: EARTH! A SPELL TO SHATTER DIAMONDS!

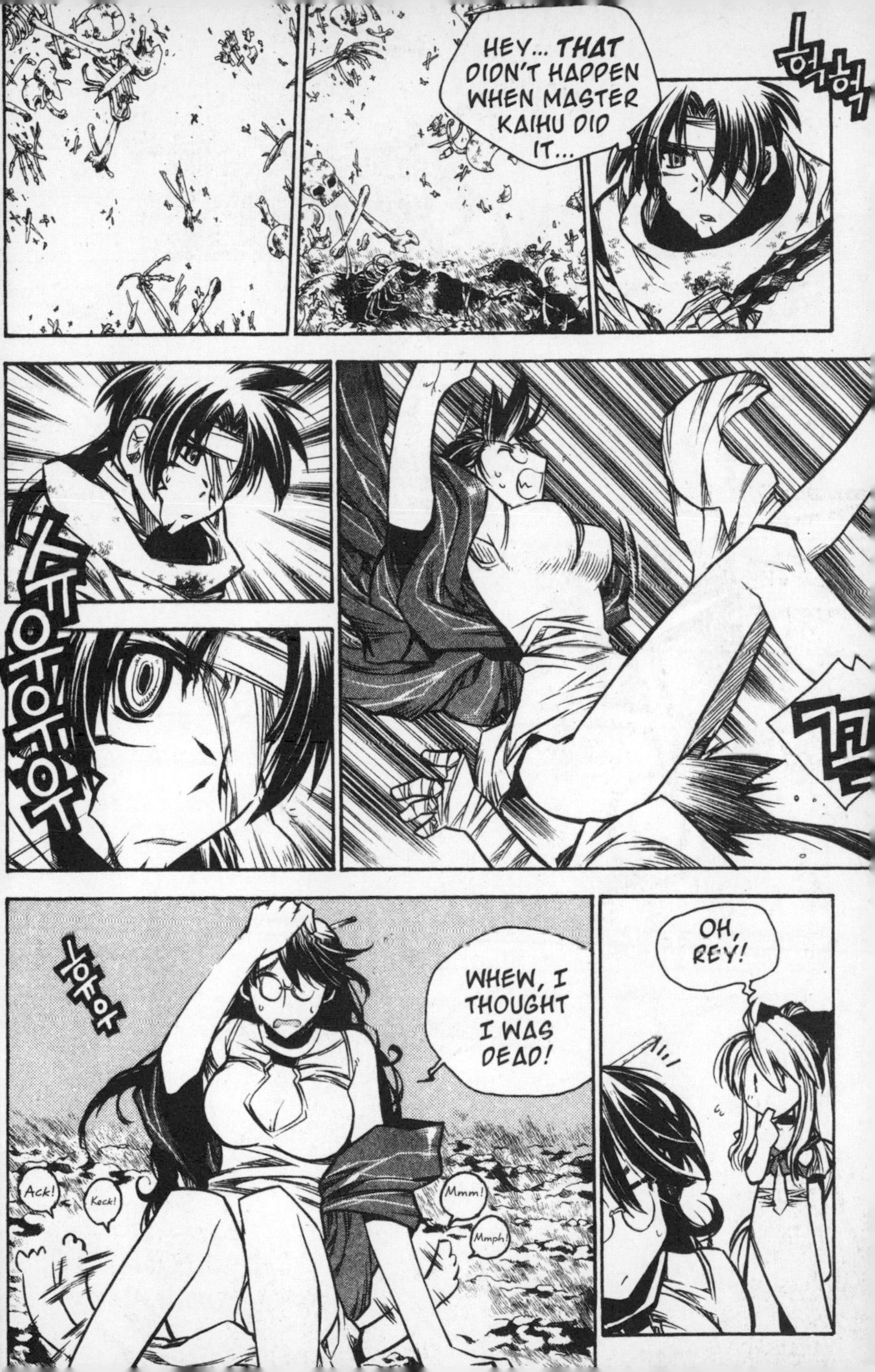
HEY... THAT DIDN'T HAPPEN WHEN MASTER KAIHU DID IT...
헉헉
WHEW, I THOUGHT I WAS DEAD!
Ack!
Keck!
Mmm!
Mmph!
OH, REY!

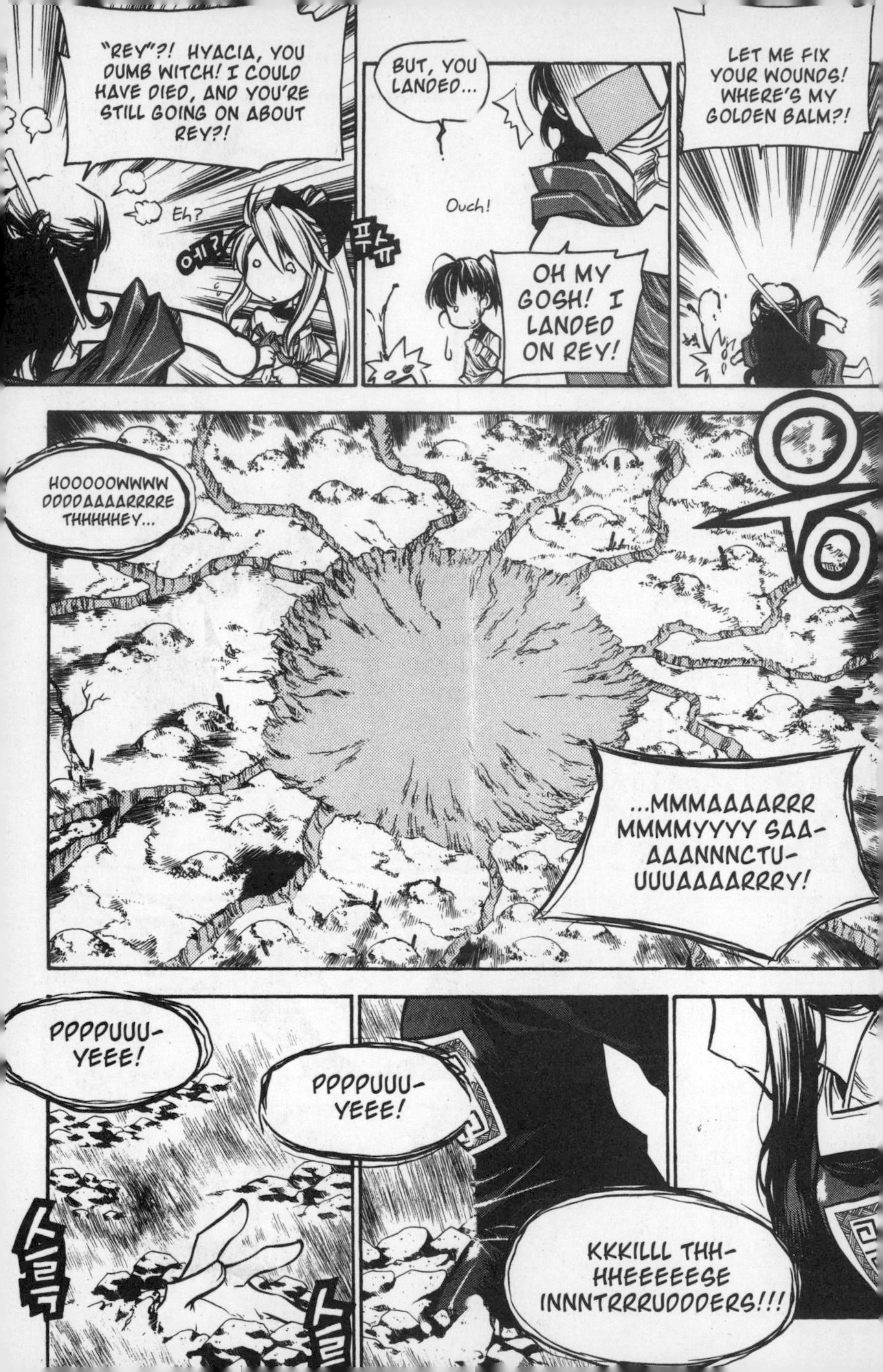
"REY"?! HYACIA, YOU DUMB WITCH! I COULD HAVE DIED, AND YOU'RE STILL GOING ON ABOUT REY?!
Eh?
BUT, YOU LANDED...
Ouch!
OH MY GOSH! I LANDED ON REY!
LET ME FIX YOUR WOUNDS! WHERE'S MY GOLDEN BALM?!
HOOOOOWWWW DDDDAAAARRRRE THHHHHEY...
...MMMAAAAARRR MMMMYYYY SAA-AAANNNCTU-UUUAAAARRRY!
PPPPUUU-YEEE!
PPPPUUU-YEEE!
KKKILLL THH-HHEEEEESE INNNTRRRUDDDERS!!!

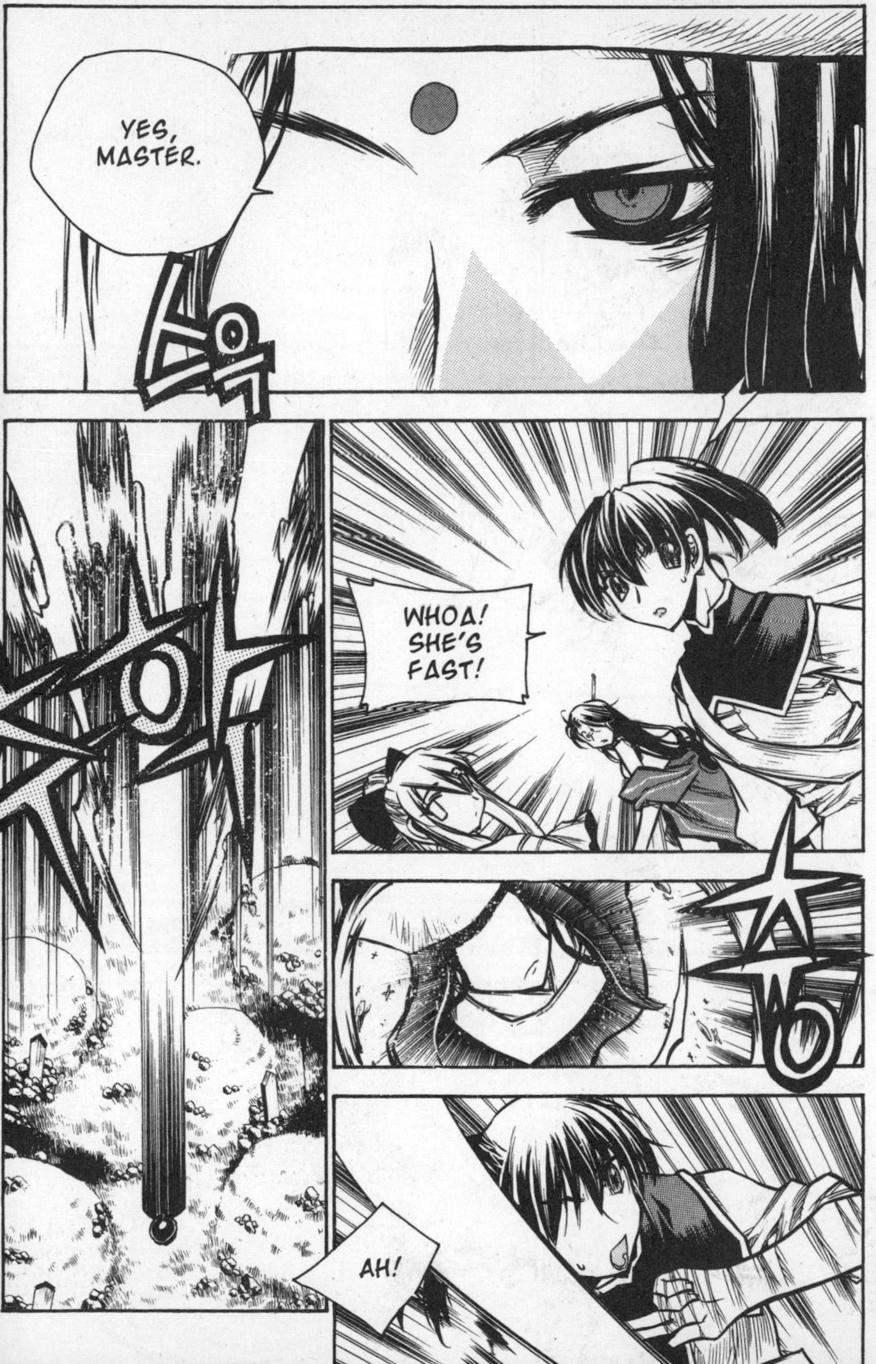
YES, MASTER.
WHOA! SHE'S FAST!
AH!

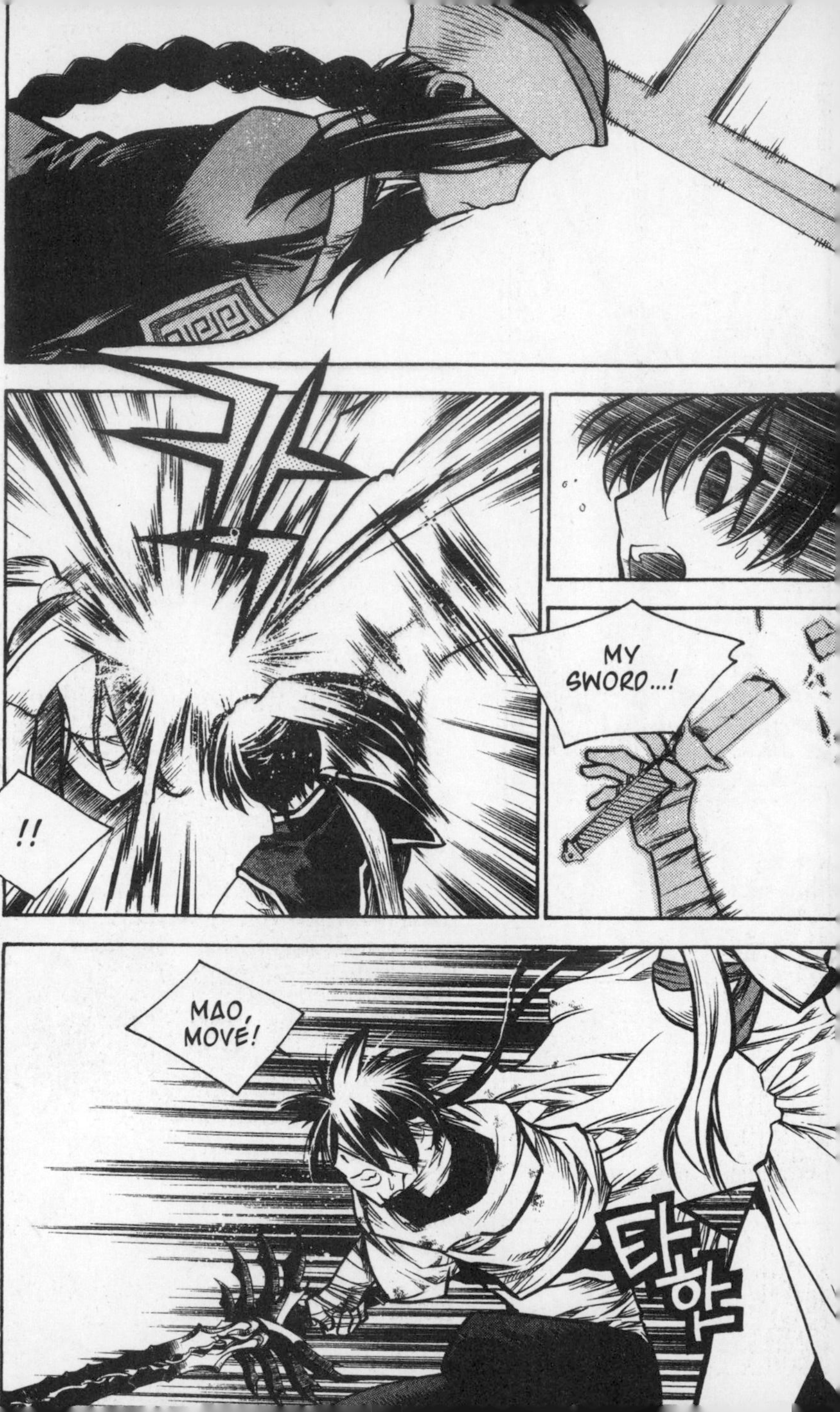
MY SWORD...!
!!
MAO, MOVE!
타앙

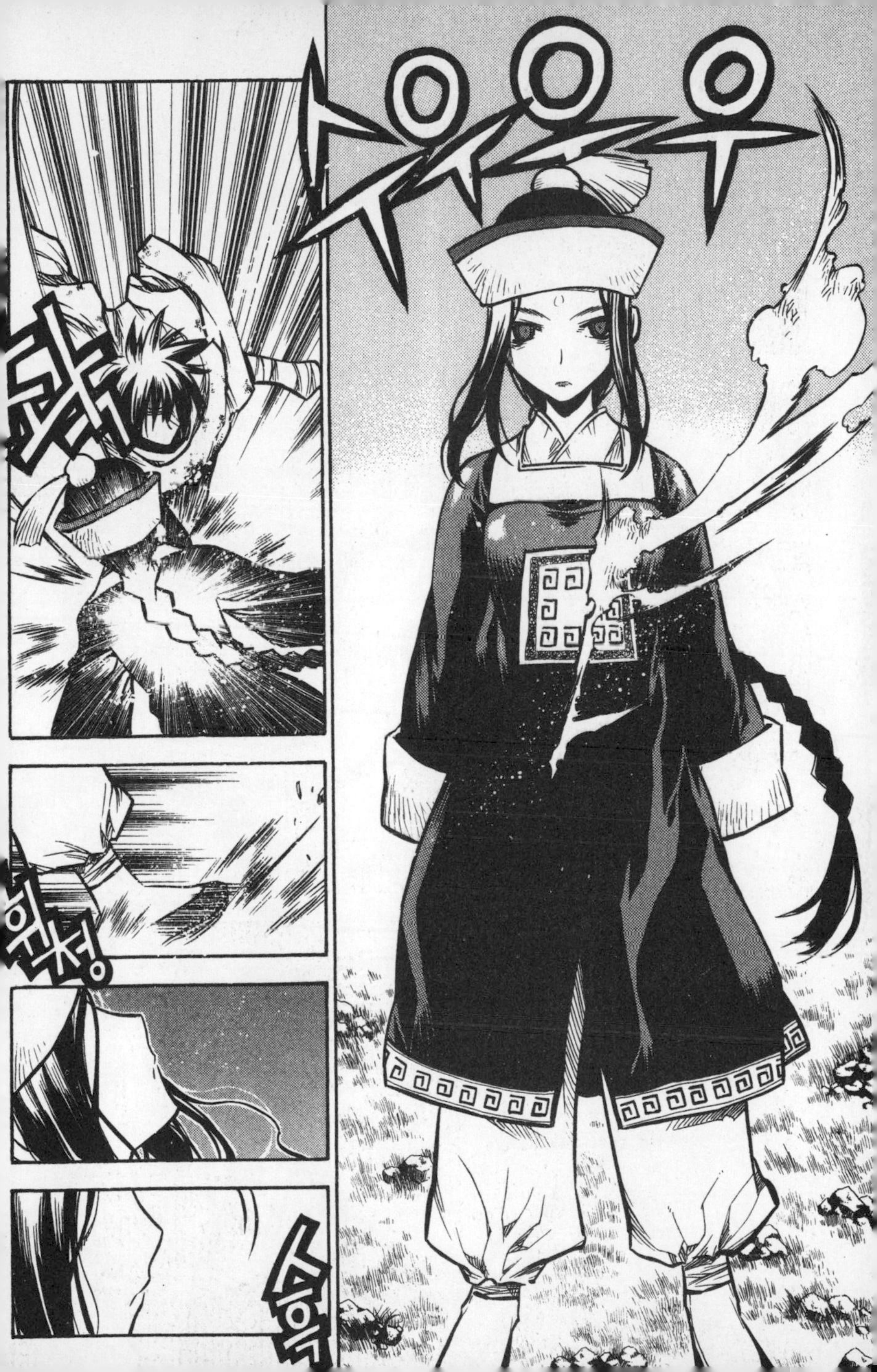
휘청!

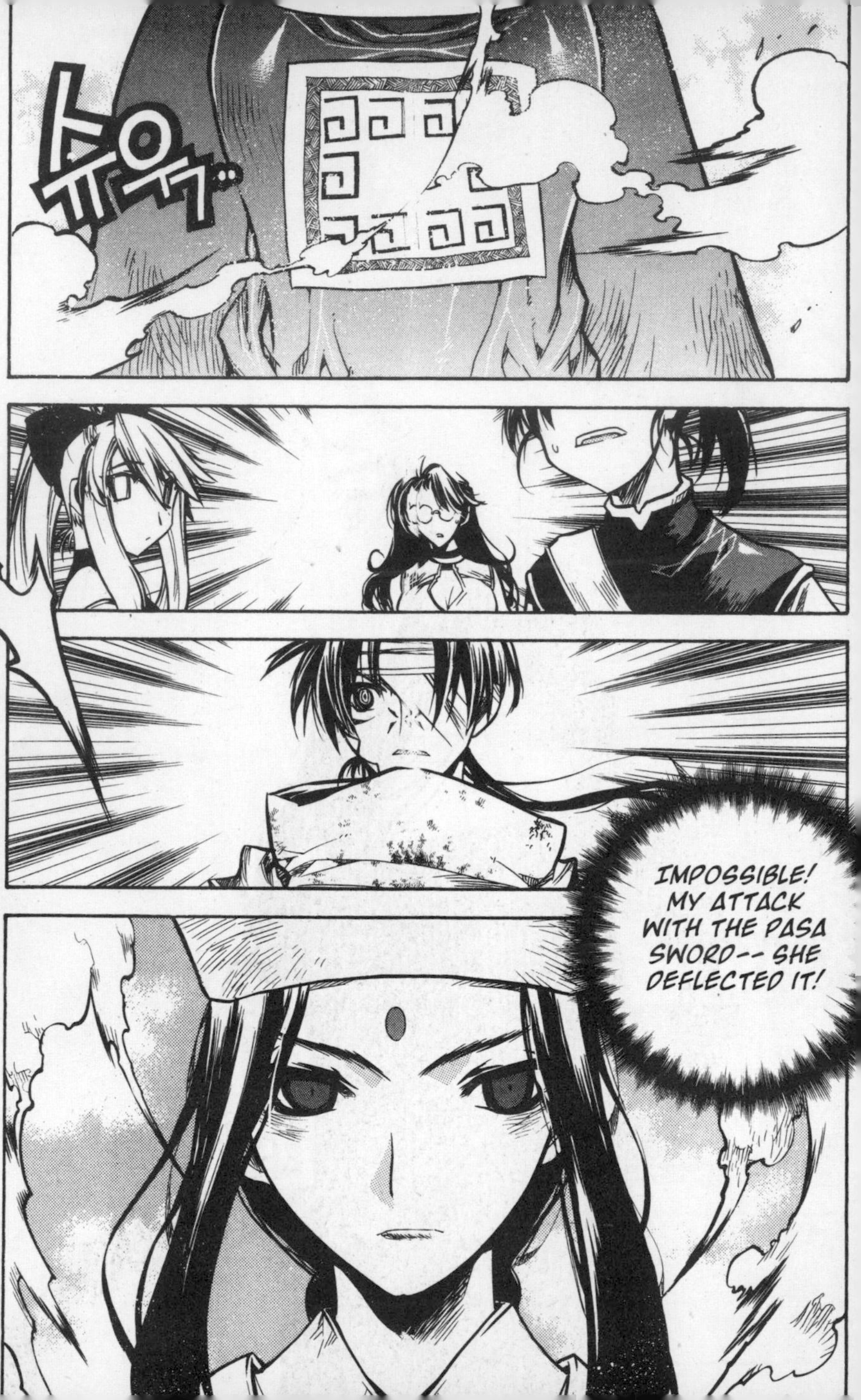
IMPOSSIBLE! MY ATTACK WITH THE PASA SWORD-- SHE DEFLECTED IT!

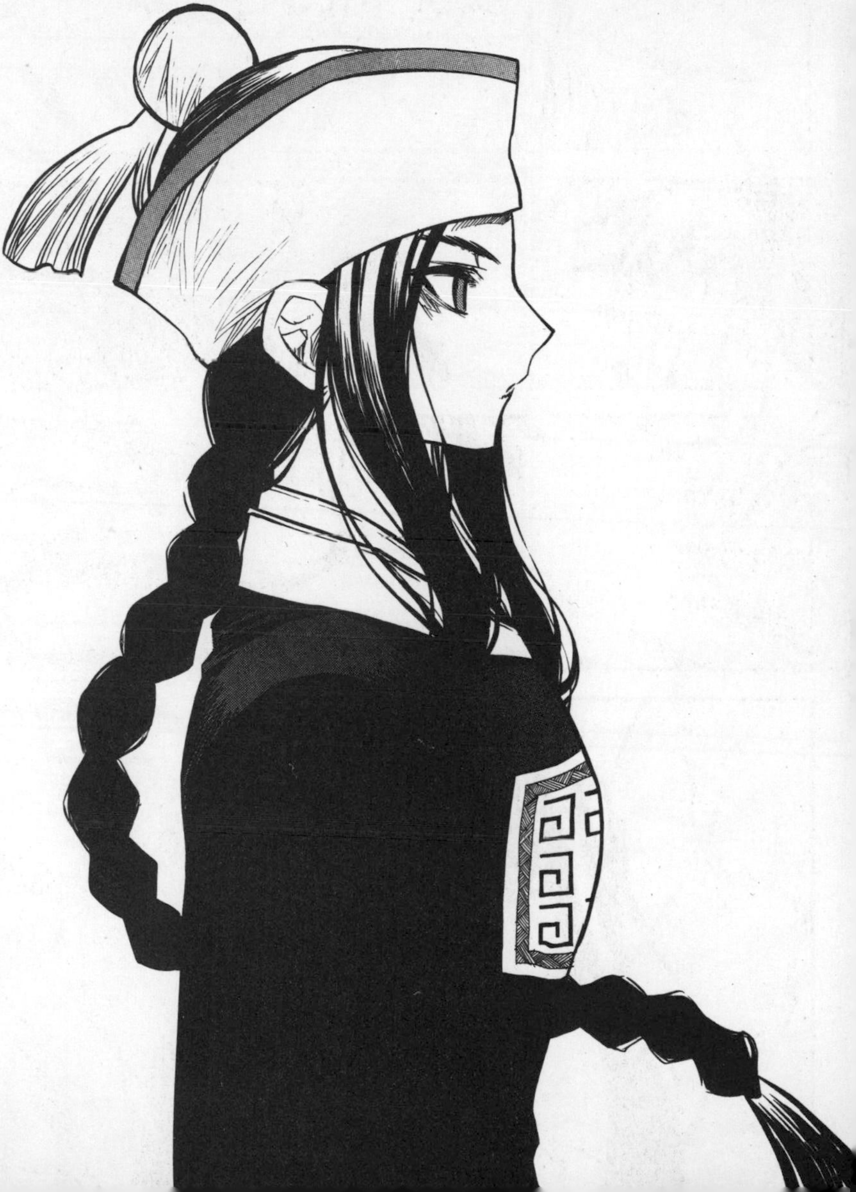

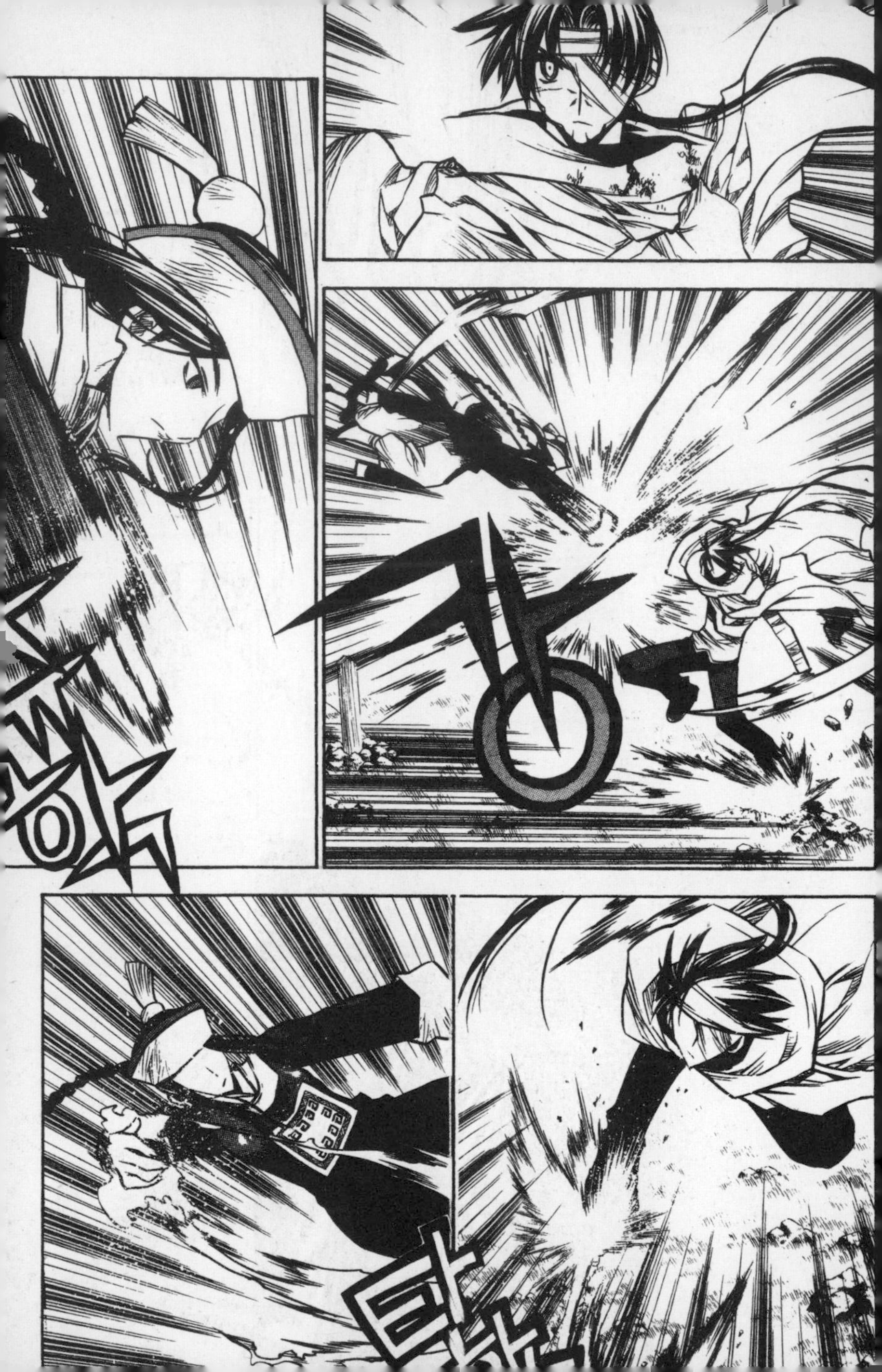

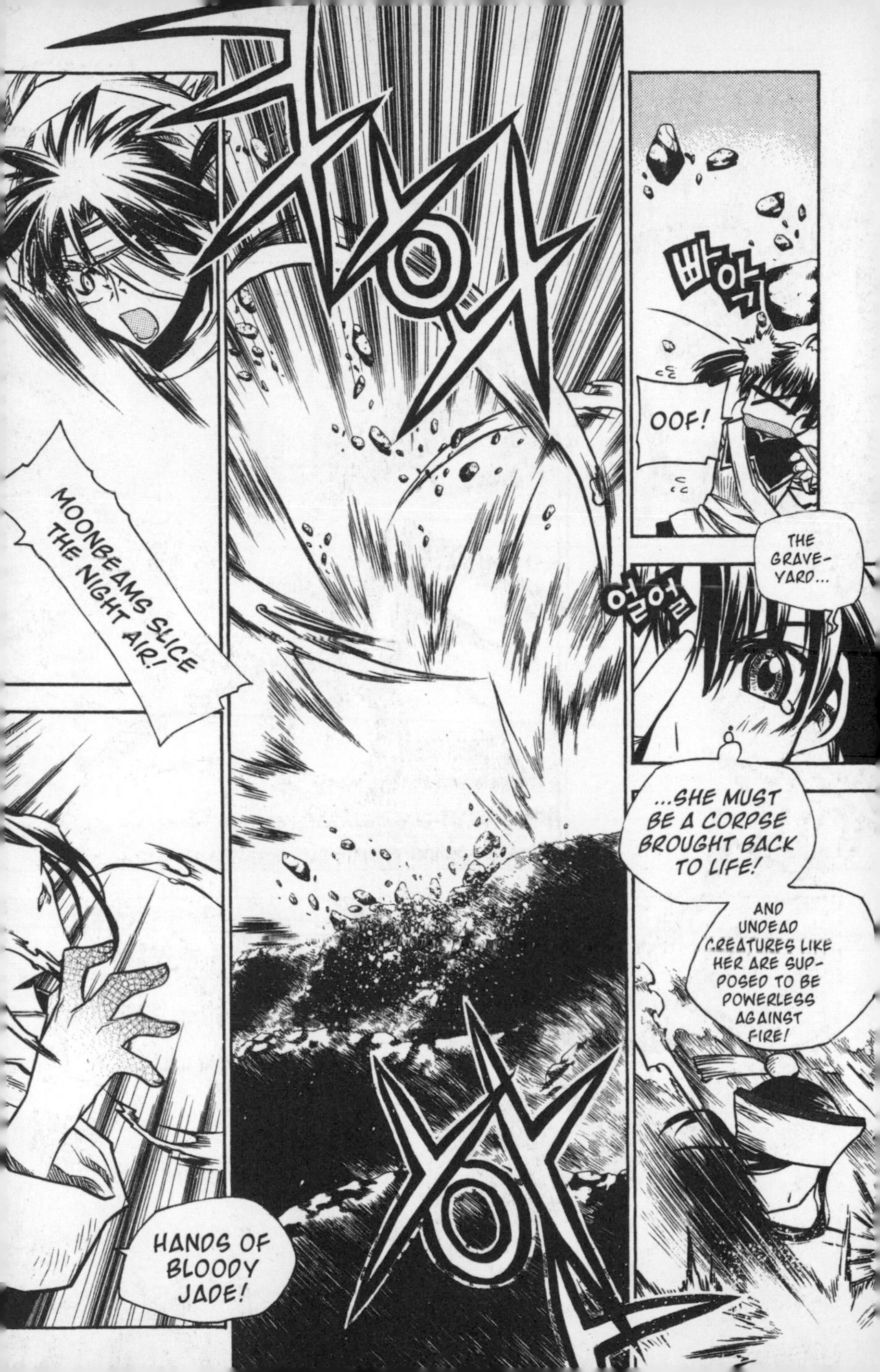
MOONBEAMS SLICE THE NIGHT AIR!
HANDS OF BLOODY JADE!
빠악
OOF!
얼얼
THE GRAVE-YARD...
...SHE MUST BE A CORPSE BROUGHT BACK TO LIFE!
AND UNDEAD CREATURES LIKE HER ARE SUP-POSED TO BE POWERLESS AGAINST FIRE!

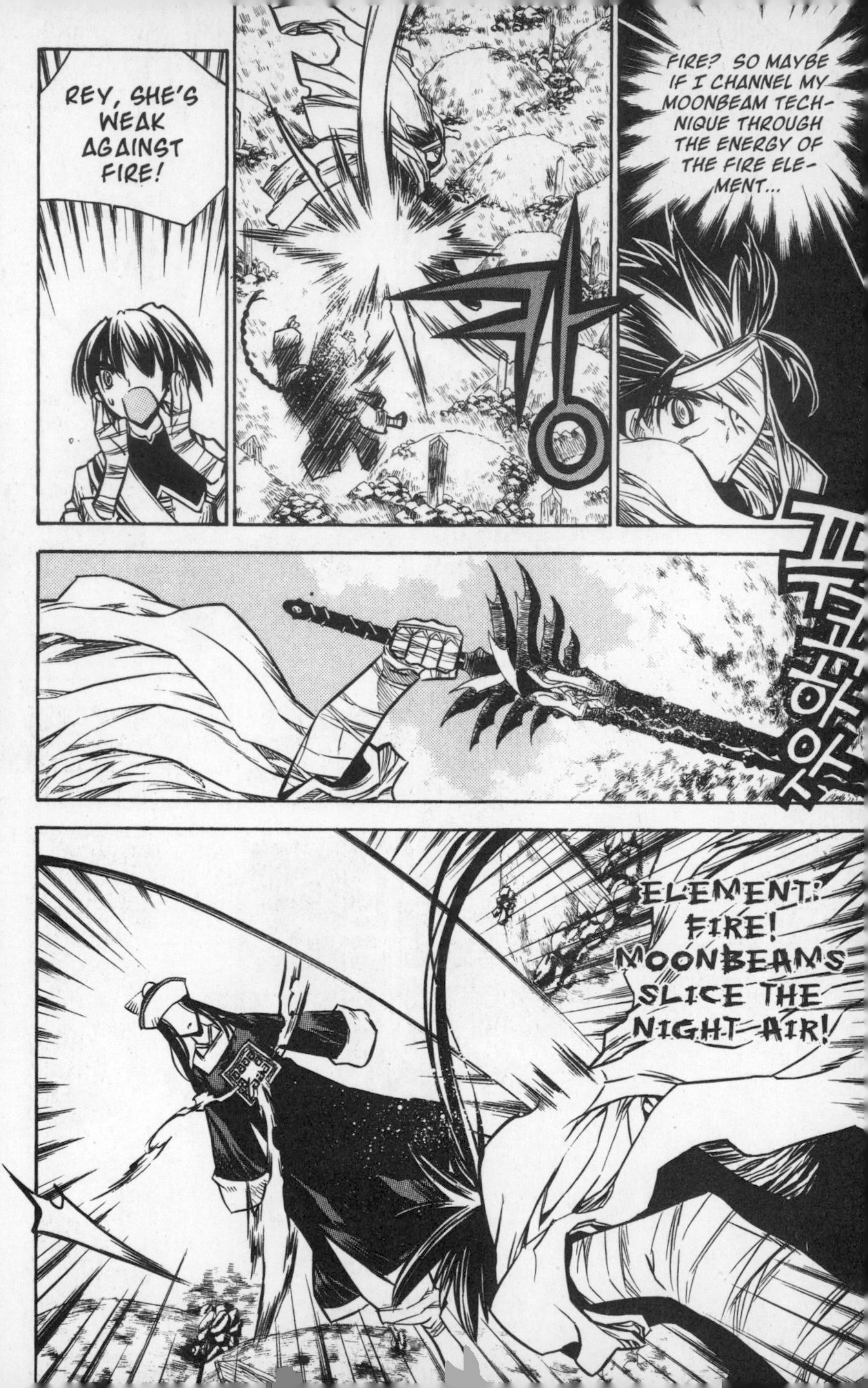
REY, SHE'S WEAK AGAINST FIRE!
FIRE? SO MAYBE IF I CHANNEL MY MOONBEAM TECH-NIQUE THROUGH THE ENERGY OF THE FIRE ELE-MENT...
ELEMENT: FIRE! MOONBEAMS SLICE THE NIGHT AIR!

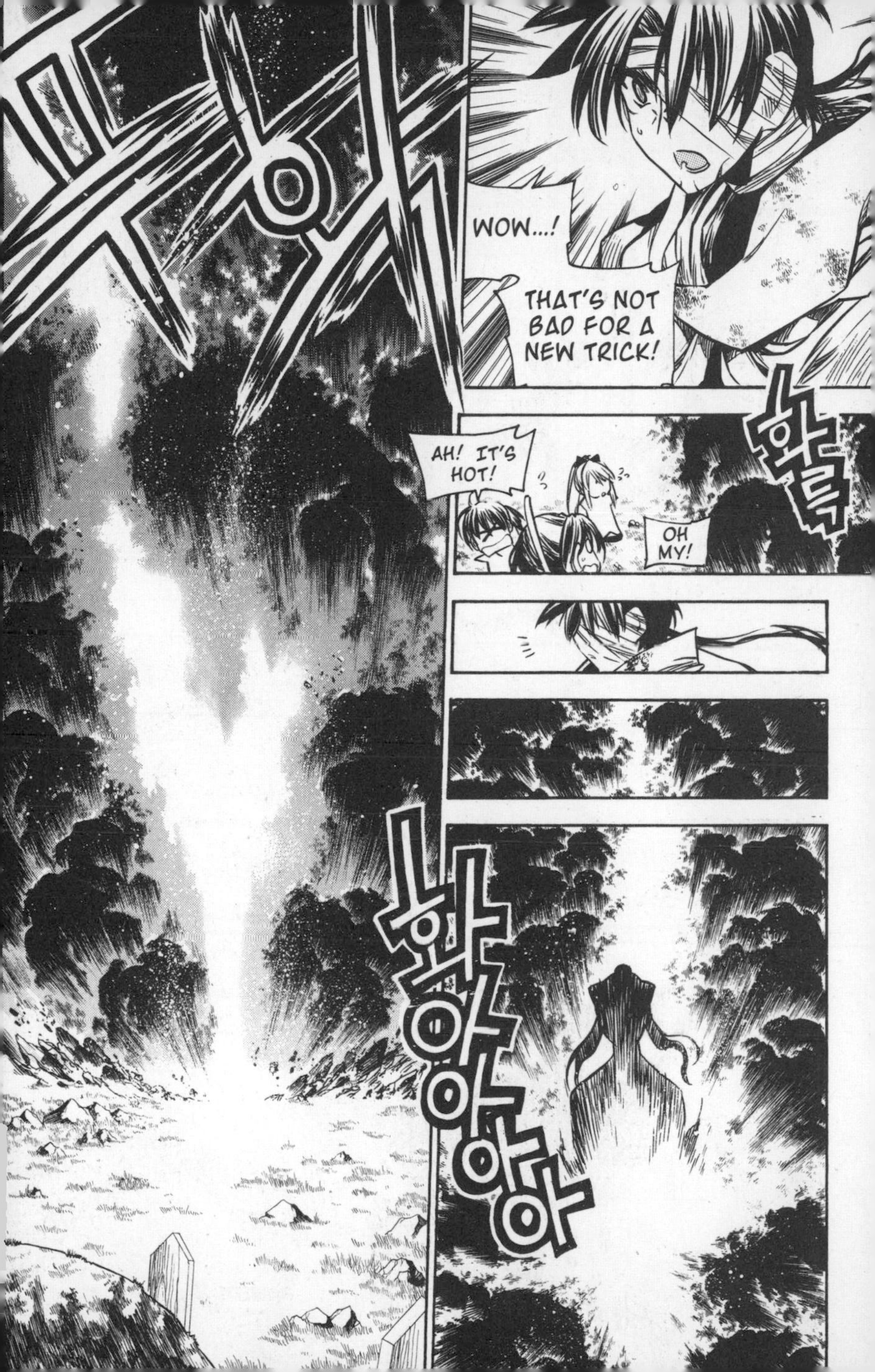
WOW...!
THAT'S NOT BAD FOR A NEW TRICK!
화륵
AH! IT'S HOT!
OH MY!
화아아아아

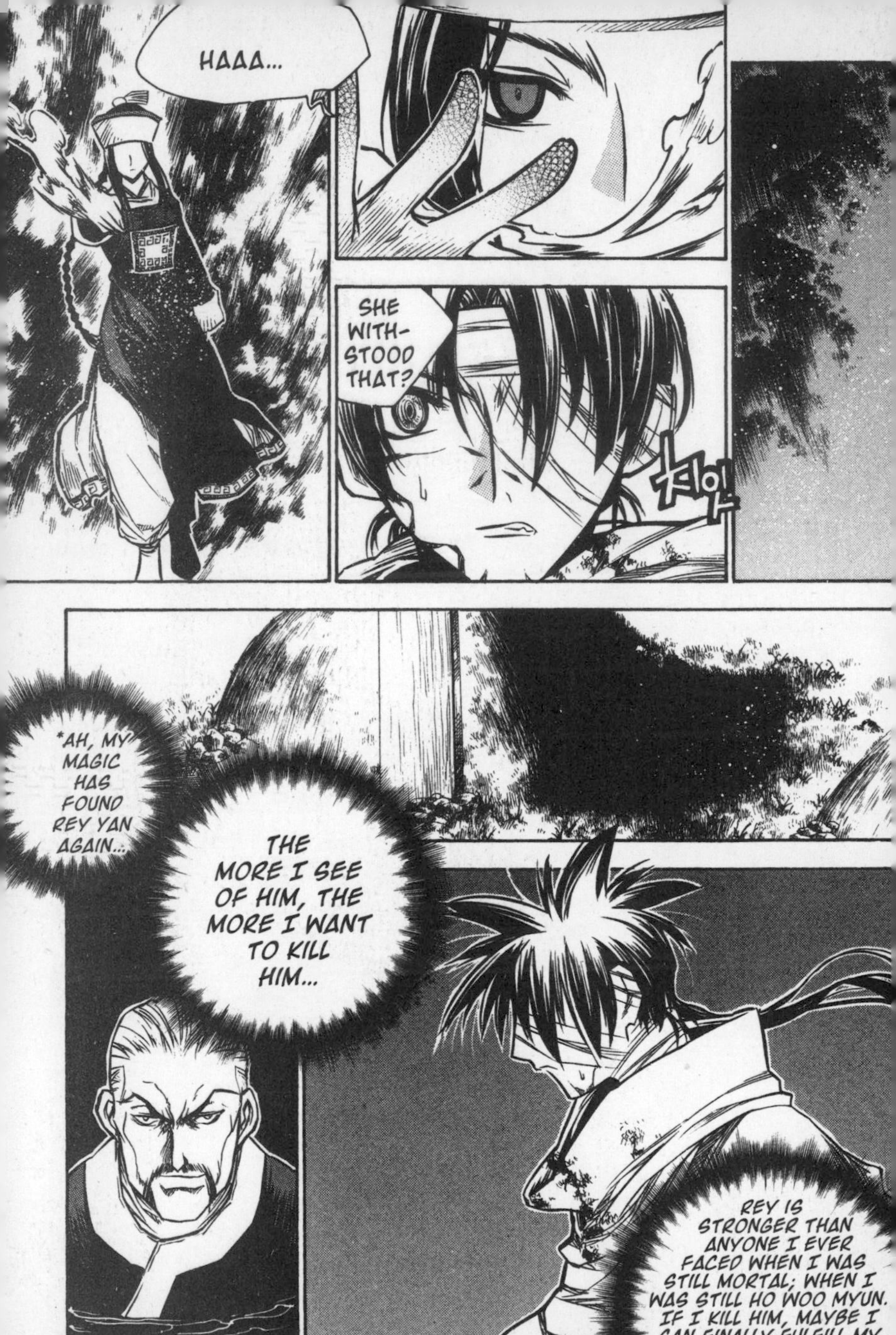
HAAA...
SHE WITH-STOOD THAT?
*AH, MY MAGIC HAS FOUND REY YAN AGAIN...
THE MORE I SEE OF HIM, THE MORE I WANT TO KILL HIM...
REY IS STRONGER THAN ANYONE I EVER FACED WHEN I WAS STILL MORTAL; WHEN I WAS STILL HO WOO MYUN. IF I KILL HIM, MAYBE I CAN FINALLY FULFILL MY LONG-TIME WISH!

*Editor's Note: This is Hwansa, the Sorcerer of Illusions, from whom Rey and the others barely escaped in the last volume.

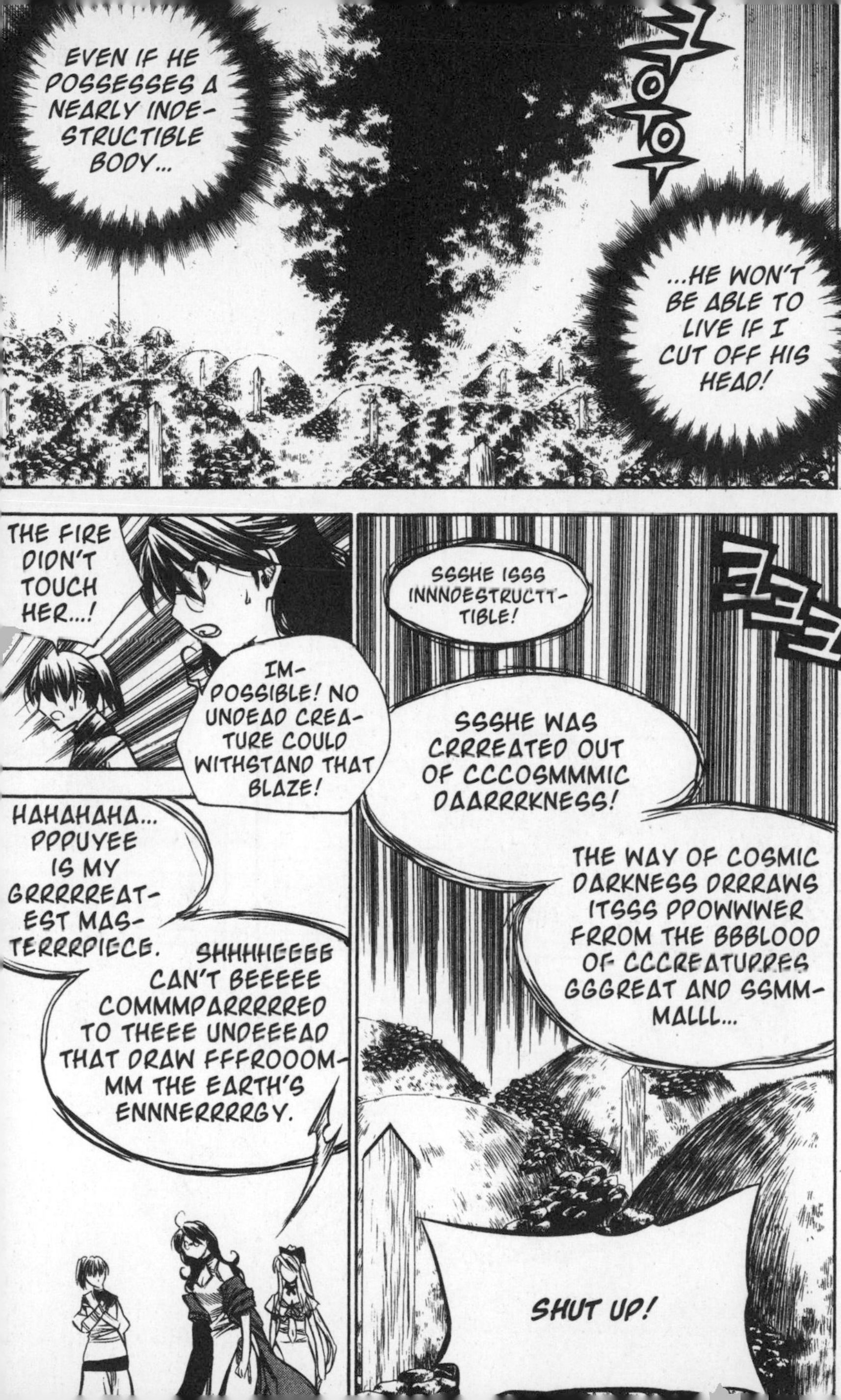
EVEN IF HE POSSESSES A NEARLY INDE-STRUCTIBLE BODY...
...HE WON'T BE ABLE TO LIVE IF I CUT OFF HIS HEAD!
THE FIRE DIDN'T TOUCH HER...!
IM-POSSIBLE! NO UNDEAD CREA-TURE COULD WITHSTAND THAT BLAZE!
HAHAHAHA... PPPUYEE IS MY GRRRRREAT-EST MAS-TERRRPIECE.
SHHHHEEEE CAN'T BEEEEE COMMMPARRRRRED TO THEEE UNDEEEAD THAT DRAW FFFROOOM-MM THE EARTH'S ENNNERRRRGY.
SSSHE ISSS INNNDESTRUCTT-TIBLE!
SSSHE WAS CRRREATED OUT OF CCCOSMMMIC DAARRRKNESS!
THE WAY OF COSMIC DARKNESS DRRRAWS ITSSS PPOWWWER FRROM THE BBBLOOD OF CCCREATURRES GGGREAT AND SSMM-MALLL...
SHUT UP!

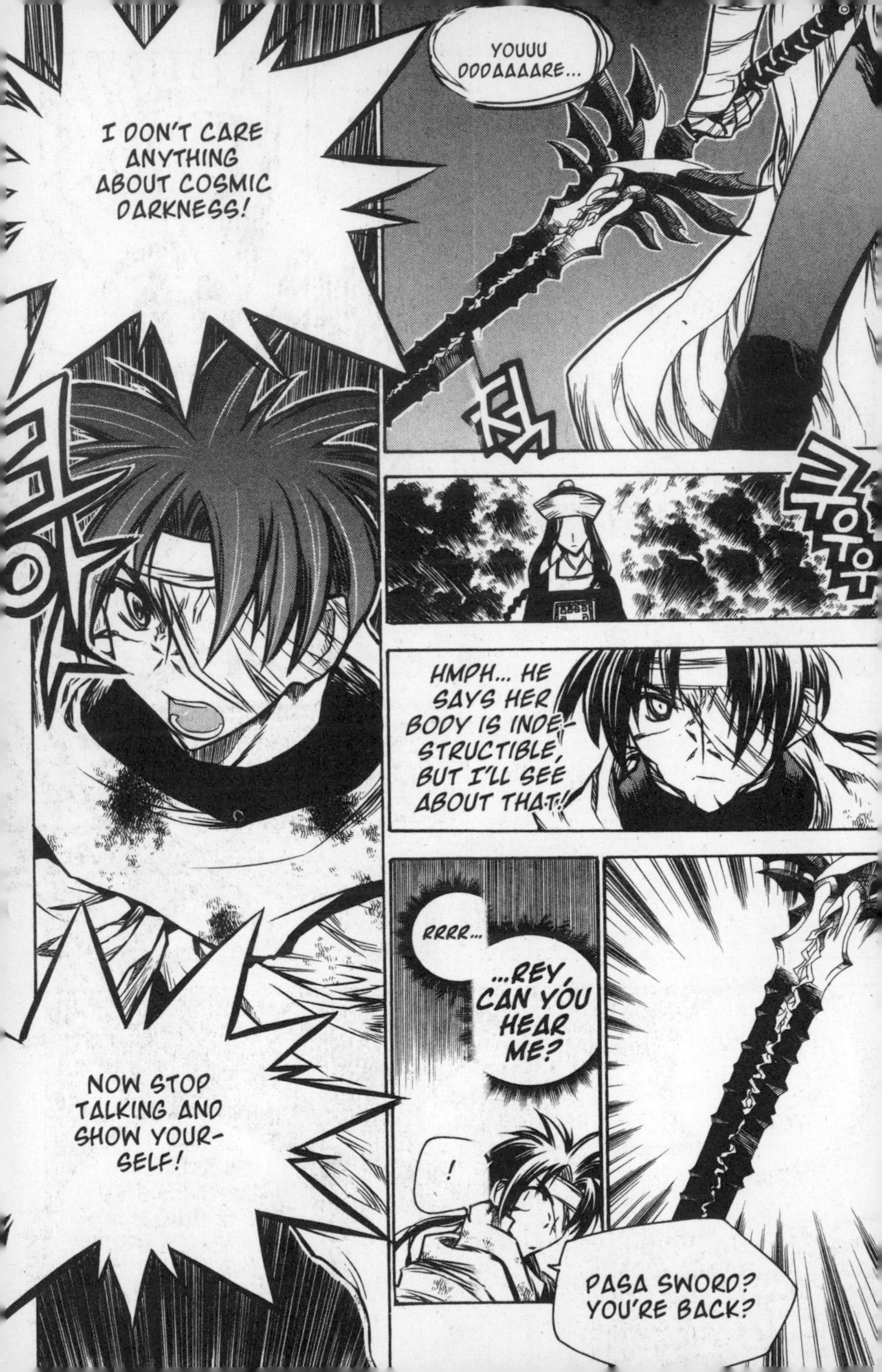
I DON'T CARE ANYTHING ABOUT COSMIC DARKNESS!
NOW STOP TALKING AND SHOW YOUR-SELF!
YOUUU OOOAAAARE...
HMPH... HE SAYS HER BODY IS INDE-STRUCTIBLE, BUT I'LL SEE ABOUT THAT!
RRRR...
...REY, CAN YOU HEAR ME?
!
PASA SWORD? YOU'RE BACK?

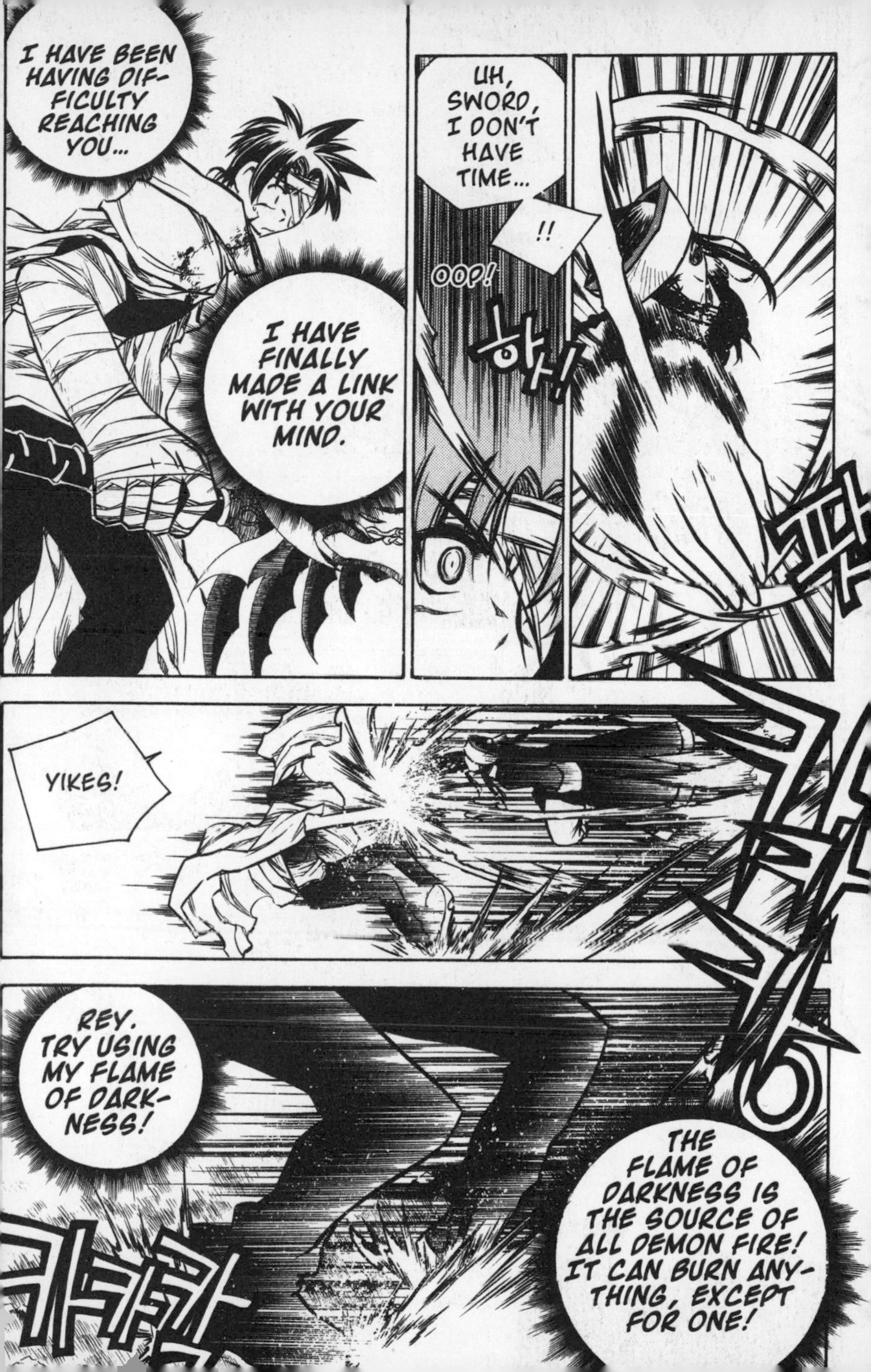
I HAVE BEEN HAVING DIF-FICULTY REACHING YOU...
I HAVE FINALLY MADE A LINK WITH YOUR MIND.
UH, SWORD, I DON'T HAVE TIME...
!!
OOP!
YIKES!
REY. TRY USING MY FLAME OF DARK-NESS!
THE FLAME OF DARKNESS IS THE SOURCE OF ALL DEMON FIRE! IT CAN BURN ANY-THING, EXCEPT FOR ONE!

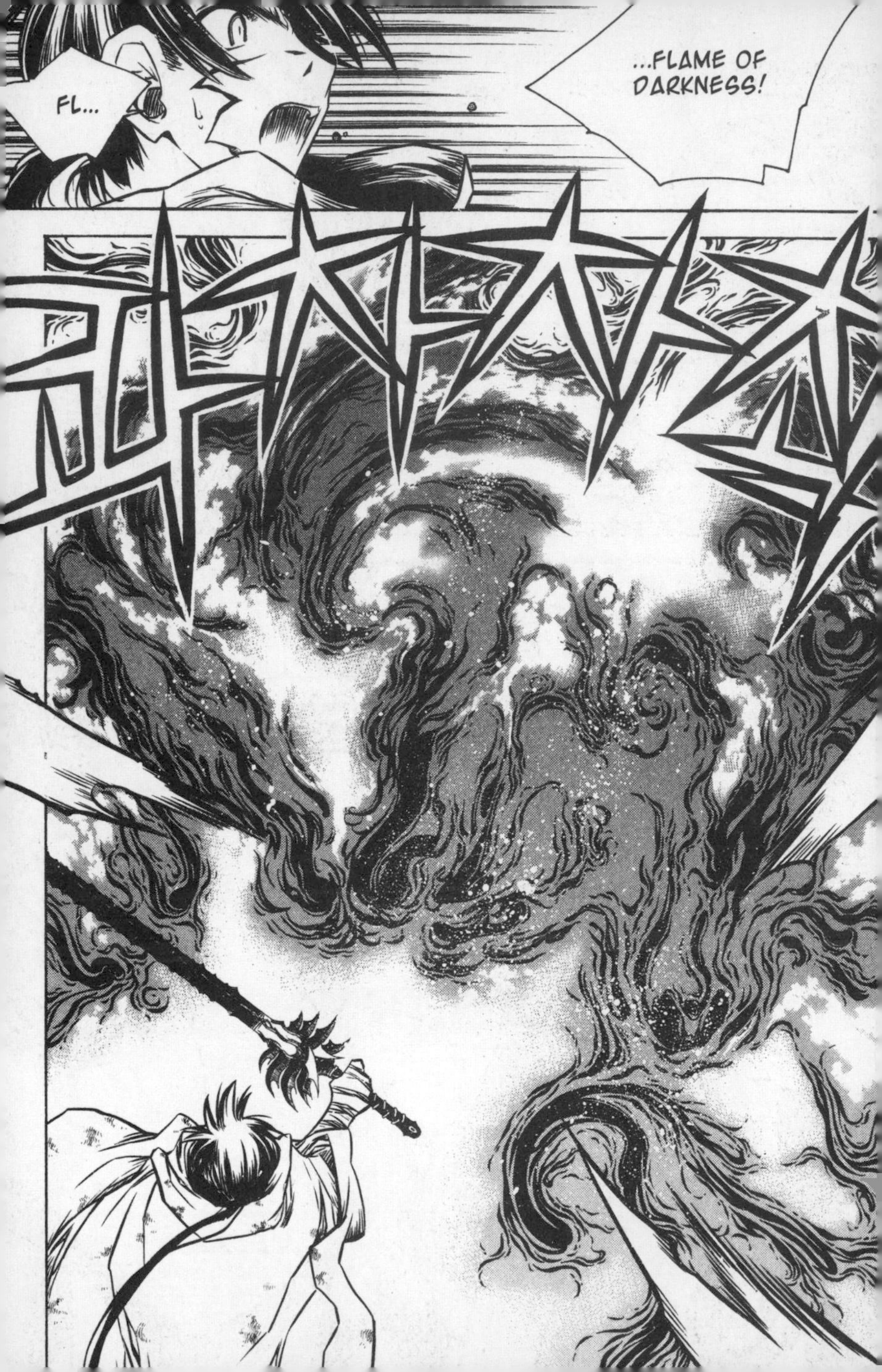
FL...
...FLAME OF DARKNESS!

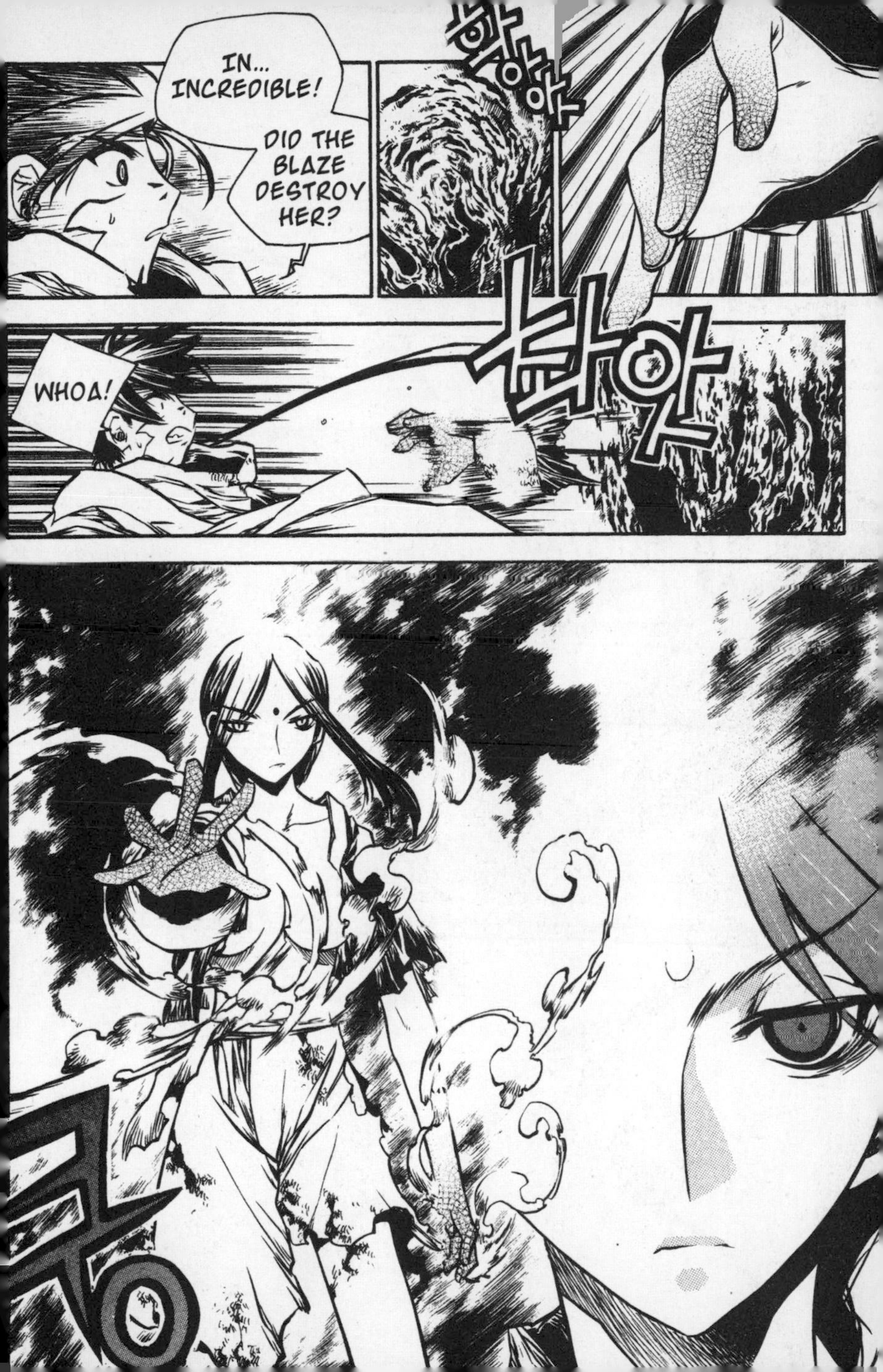
IN... INCREDIBLE!
DID THE BLAZE DESTROY HER?
WHOA!

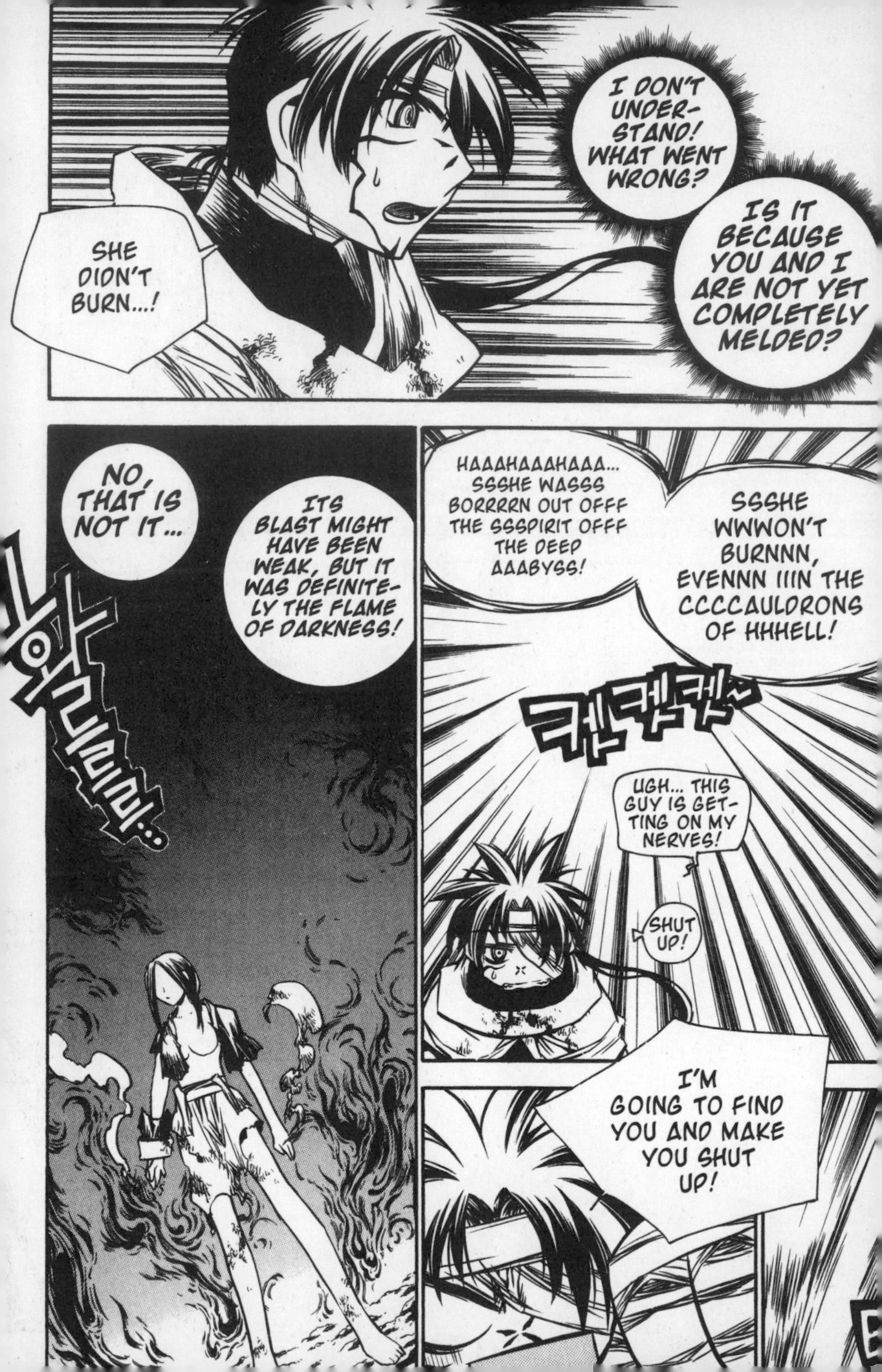
SHE DIDN'T BURN...!
I DON'T UNDER-STAND! WHAT WENT WRONG?
IS IT BECAUSE YOU AND I ARE NOT YET COMPLETELY MELDED?
NO, THAT IS NOT IT...
ITS BLAST MIGHT HAVE BEEN WEAK, BUT IT WAS DEFINITE-LY THE FLAME OF DARKNESS!
HAAAHAAAHAAA... SSSHE WASSS BORRRRN OUT OFFF THE SSSPIRIT OFFF THE DEEP AAABYSS!
SSSHE WWWON'T BURNNN, EVENNN IIIN THE CCCCAULDRONS OF HHHELL!
켁켁켁~
UGH... THIS GUY IS GET-TING ON MY NERVES!
SHUT UP!
I'M GOING TO FIND YOU AND MAKE YOU SHUT UP!

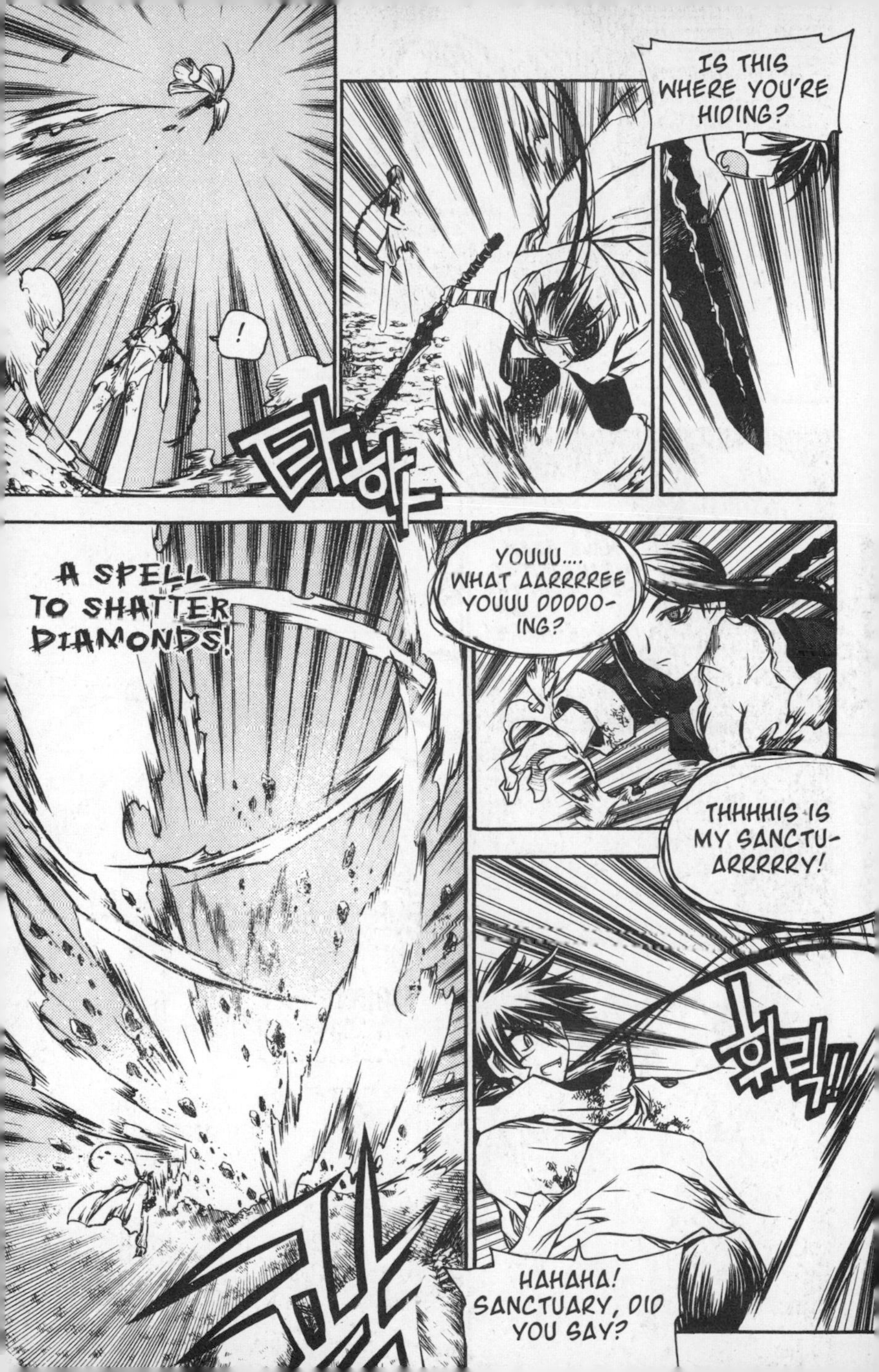
!
IS THIS WHERE YOU'RE HIDING?
A SPELL TO SHATTER DIAMONDS!
YOUUU.... WHAT AARRRREE YOUUU DDDDO-ING?
THHHHIS IS MY SANCTU-ARRRRRY!
휘릭!!
HAHAHA! SANCTUARY, DID YOU SAY?

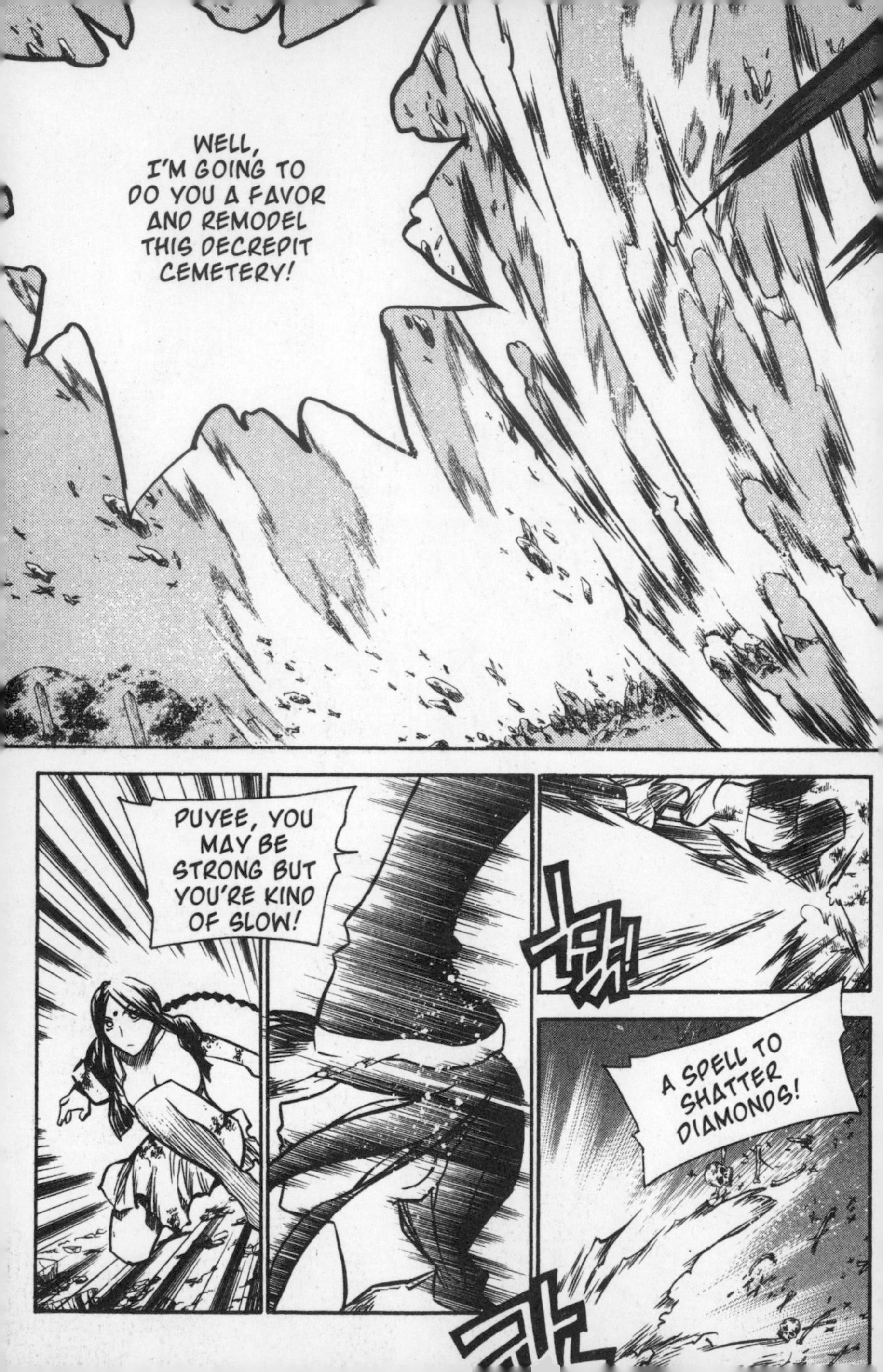
WELL, I'M GOING TO DO YOU A FAVOR AND REMODEL THIS DECREPIT CEMETERY!
PUYEE, YOU MAY BE STRONG BUT YOU'RE KIND OF SLOW!
A SPELL TO SHATTER DIAMONDS!

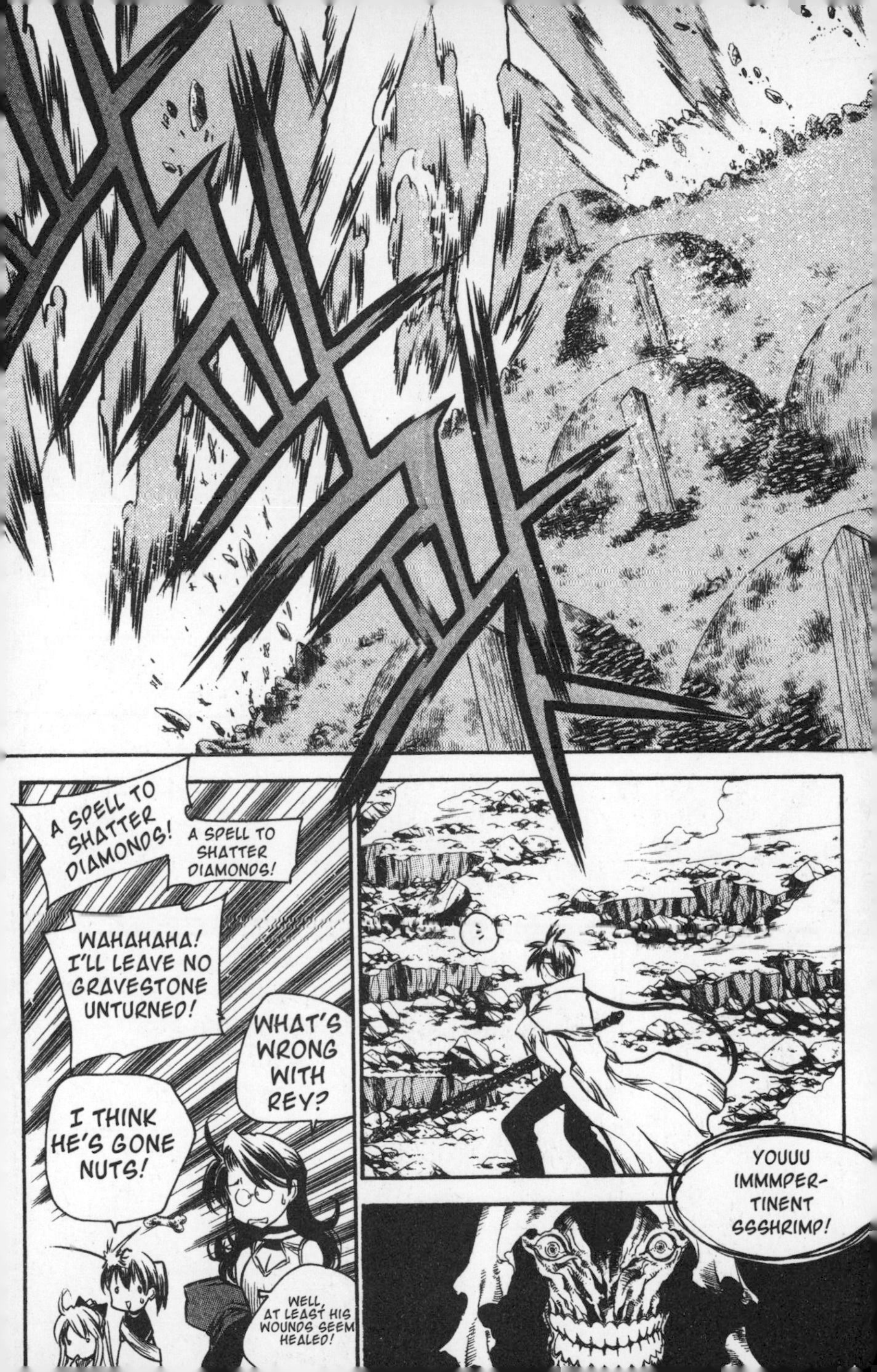
A SPELL TO SHATTER DIAMONDS!
A SPELL TO SHATTER DIAMONDS!
WAHAHAHA! I'LL LEAVE NO GRAVESTONE UNTURNED!
WHAT'S WRONG WITH REY?
I THINK HE'S GONE NUTS!
WELL, AT LEAST HIS WOUNDS SEEM HEALED!
YOUUU IMMMPER-TINENT SSSHRIMP!

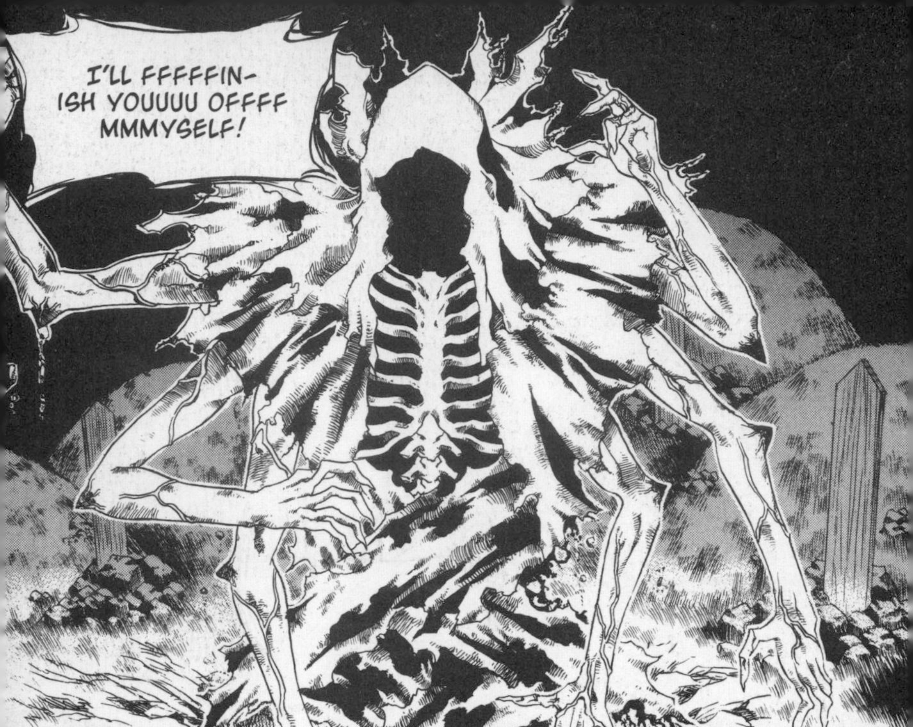
I'LL FFFFFIN-ISH YOUUUU OFFFF MMMYSELF!

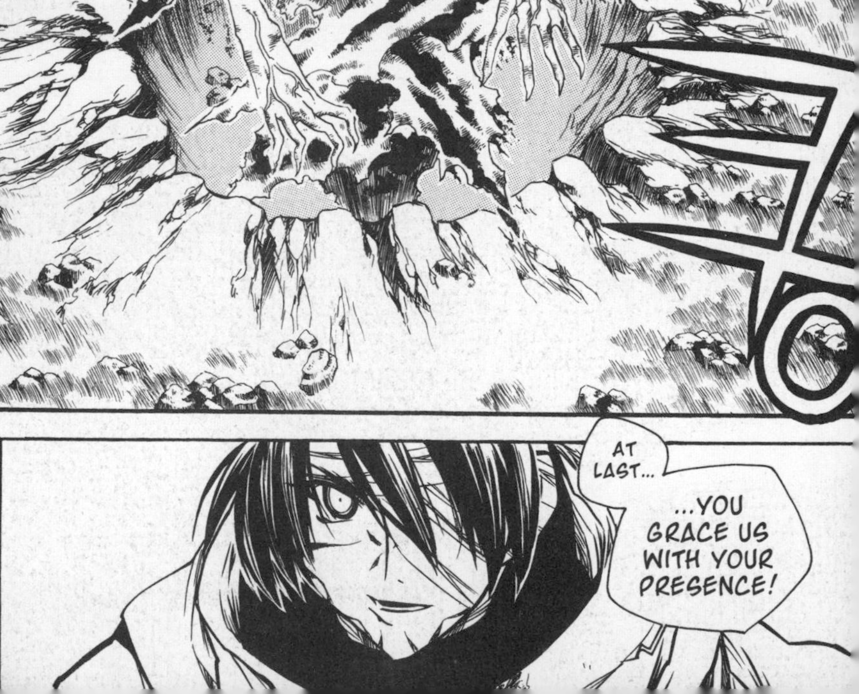
AT LAST...
...YOU GRACE US WITH YOUR PRESENCE!

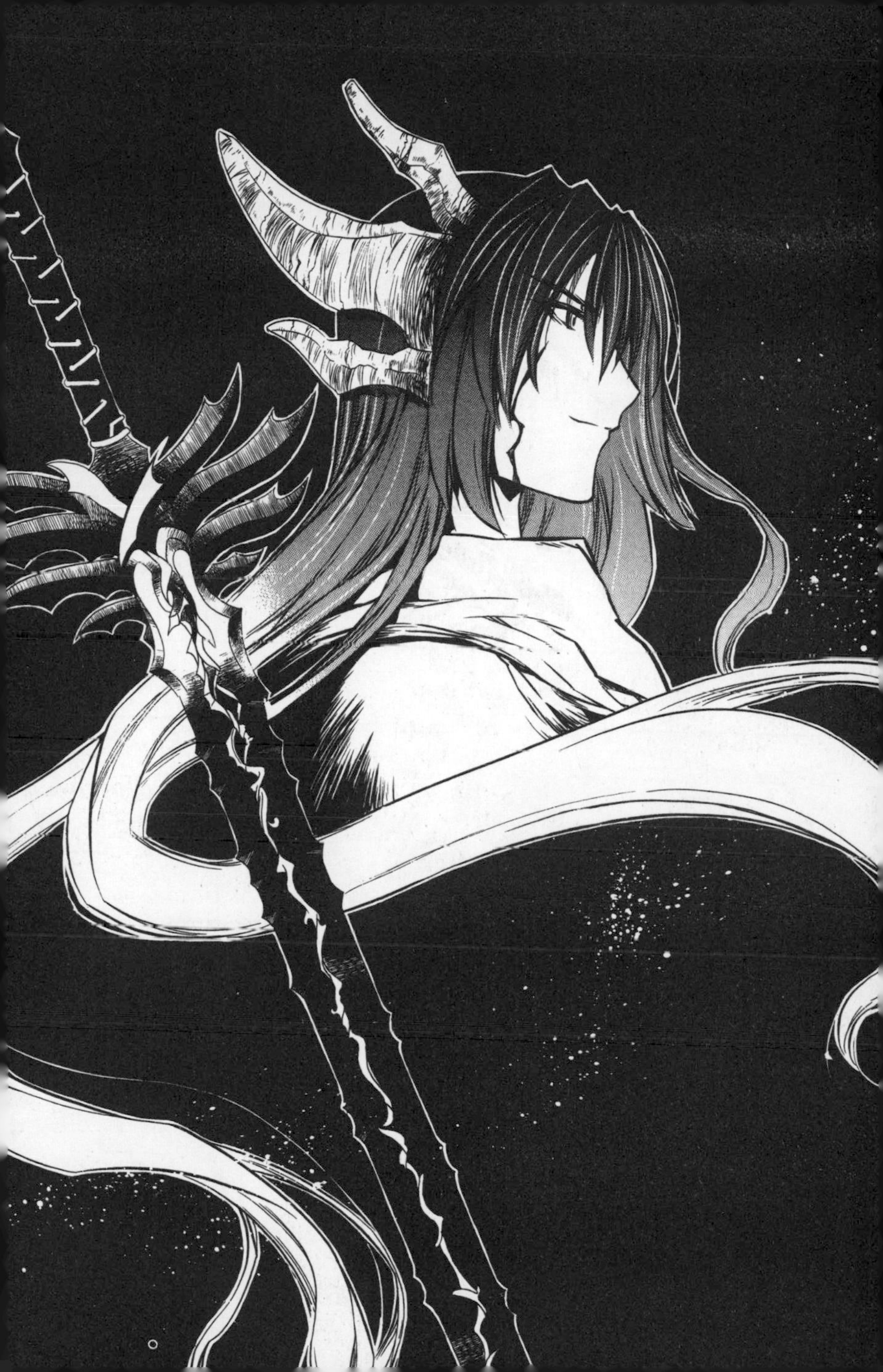

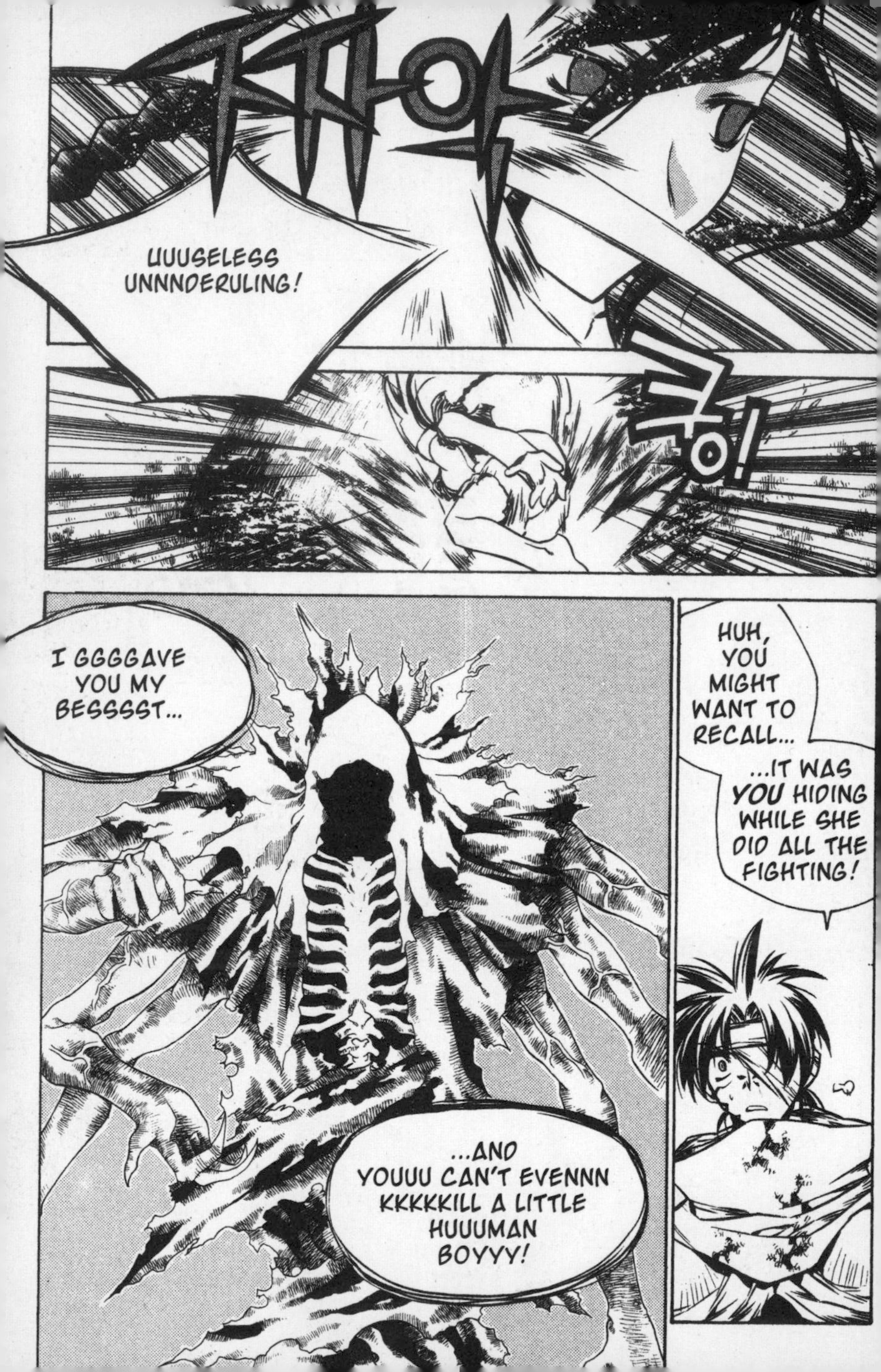
UUUSELESS UNNNDERULING!
I GGGGAVE YOU MY BESSSST...
...AND YOUUU CAN'T EVENNN KKKKKILL A LITTLE HUUUMAN BOYYY!
HUH, YOU MIGHT WANT TO RECALL...
...IT WAS *YOU* HIDING WHILE SHE DID ALL THE FIGHTING!

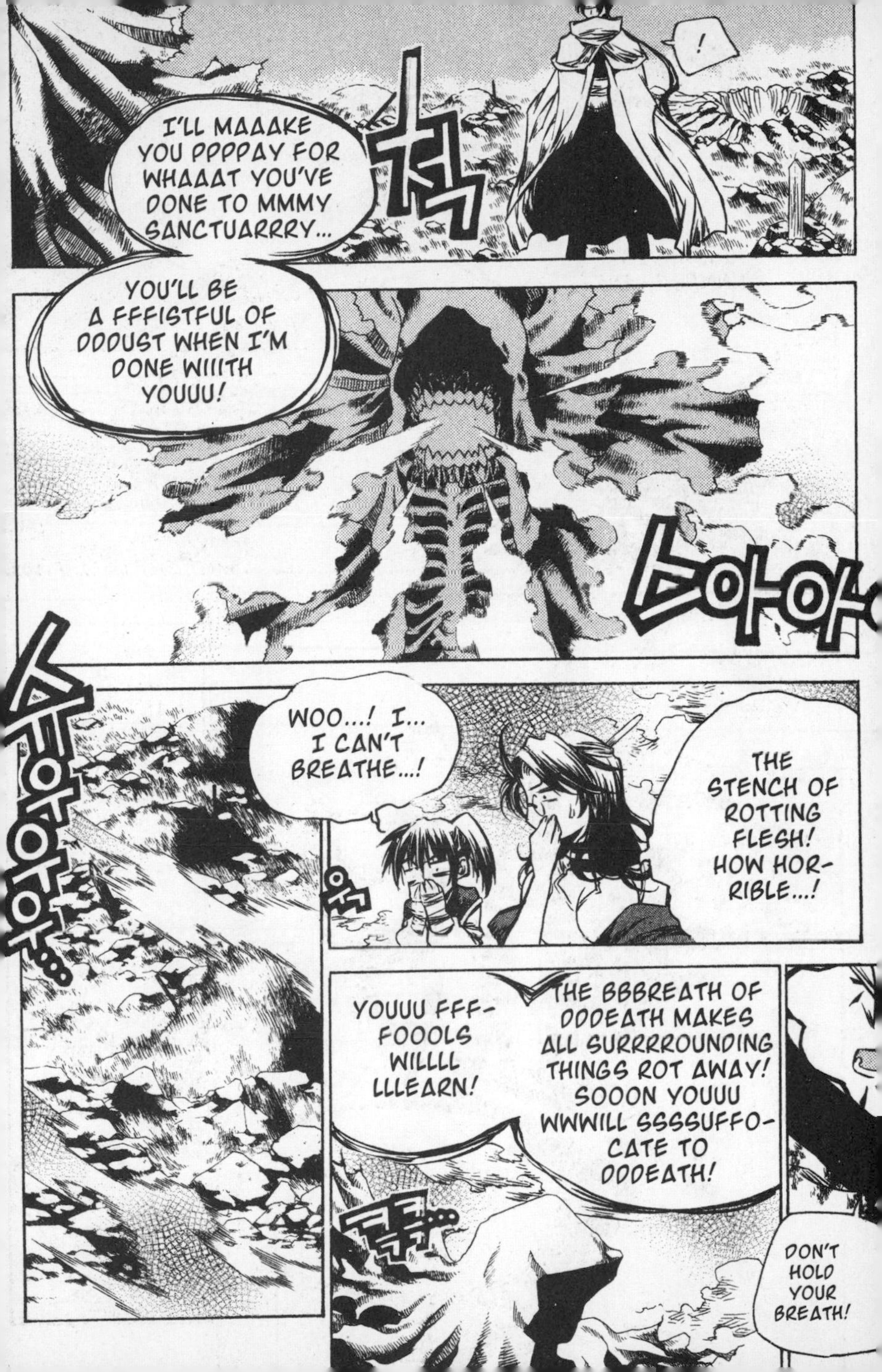
I'LL MAAAKE YOU PPPPAY FOR WHAAAT YOU'VE DONE TO MMMY SANCTUARRRY...
!
YOU'LL BE A FFFISTFUL OF DDDUST WHEN I'M DONE WIIITH YOUUU!
WOO...! I... I CAN'T BREATHE...!
THE STENCH OF ROTTING FLESH! HOW HOR-RIBLE...!
YOUUU FFF-FOOOLS WILLLL LLLEARN!
THE BBBREATH OF DDDEATH MAKES ALL SURRRROUNDING THINGS ROT AWAY! SOOON YOUUU WWWILL SSSSUFFO-CATE TO DDDEATH!
DON'T HOLD YOUR BREATH!

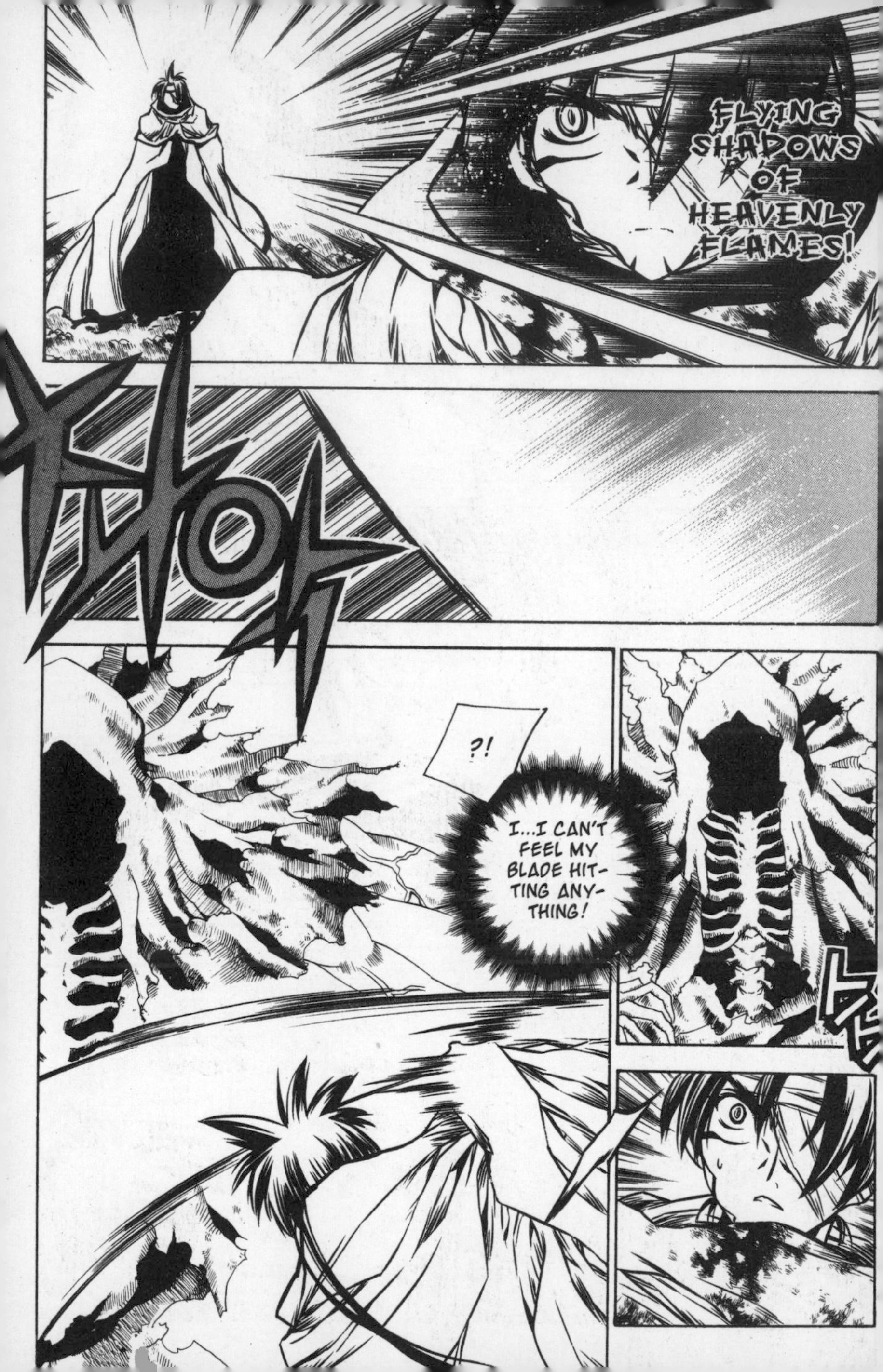
FLYING SHADOWS OF HEAVENLY FLAMES!
?!
I...I CAN'T FEEL MY BLADE HIT-TING ANY-THING!

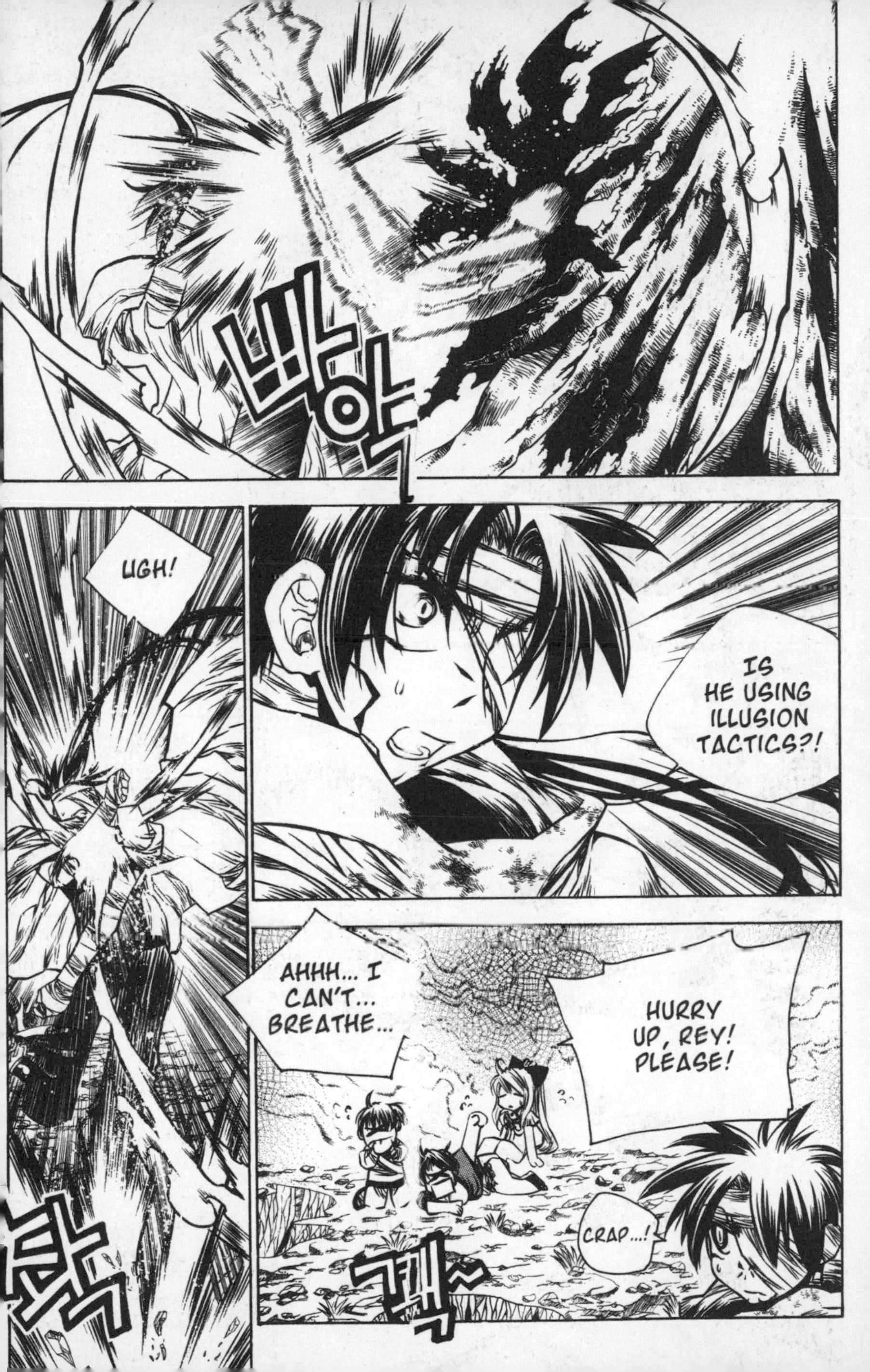

UGH!
IS HE USING ILLUSION TACTICS?!
AHHH... I CAN'T... BREATHE...
HURRY UP, REY! PLEASE!
CRAP...!

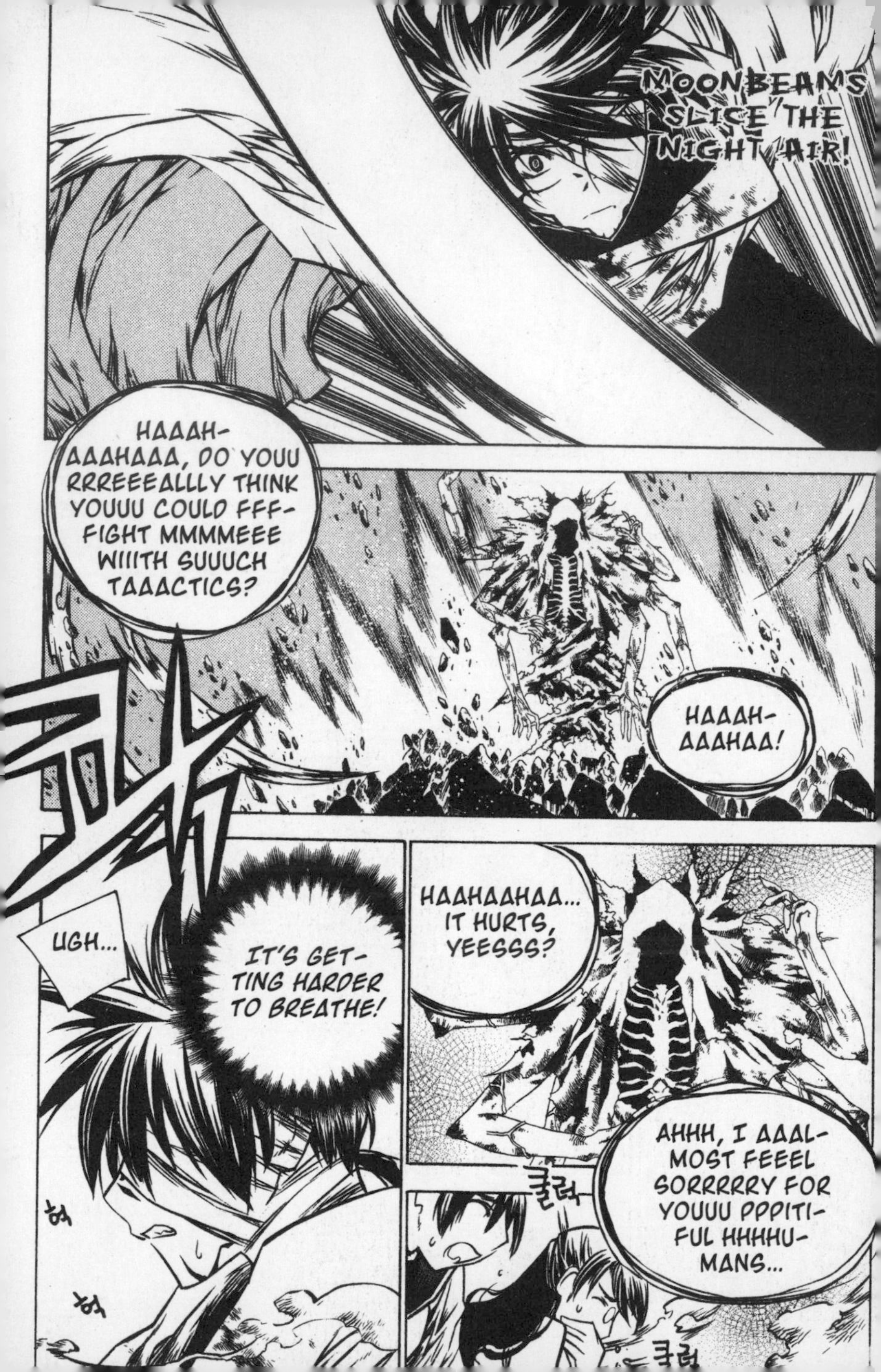
MOONBEAMS SLICE THE NIGHT AIR!
HAAAH-AAAHAAA, DO YOUU RRREEEALLLY THINK YOUUU COULD FFF-FIGHT MMMMEEE WIIITH SUUUCH TAAACTICS?
HAAAH-AAAHAA!
UGH...
IT'S GET-TING HARDER TO BREATHE!
헉
헉
HAAHAAHAA... IT HURTS, YEESSS?
AHHH, I AAAL-MOST FEEEL SORRRRRY FOR YOUUU PPPITI-FUL HHHHU-MANS...
쿨럭
쿨럭

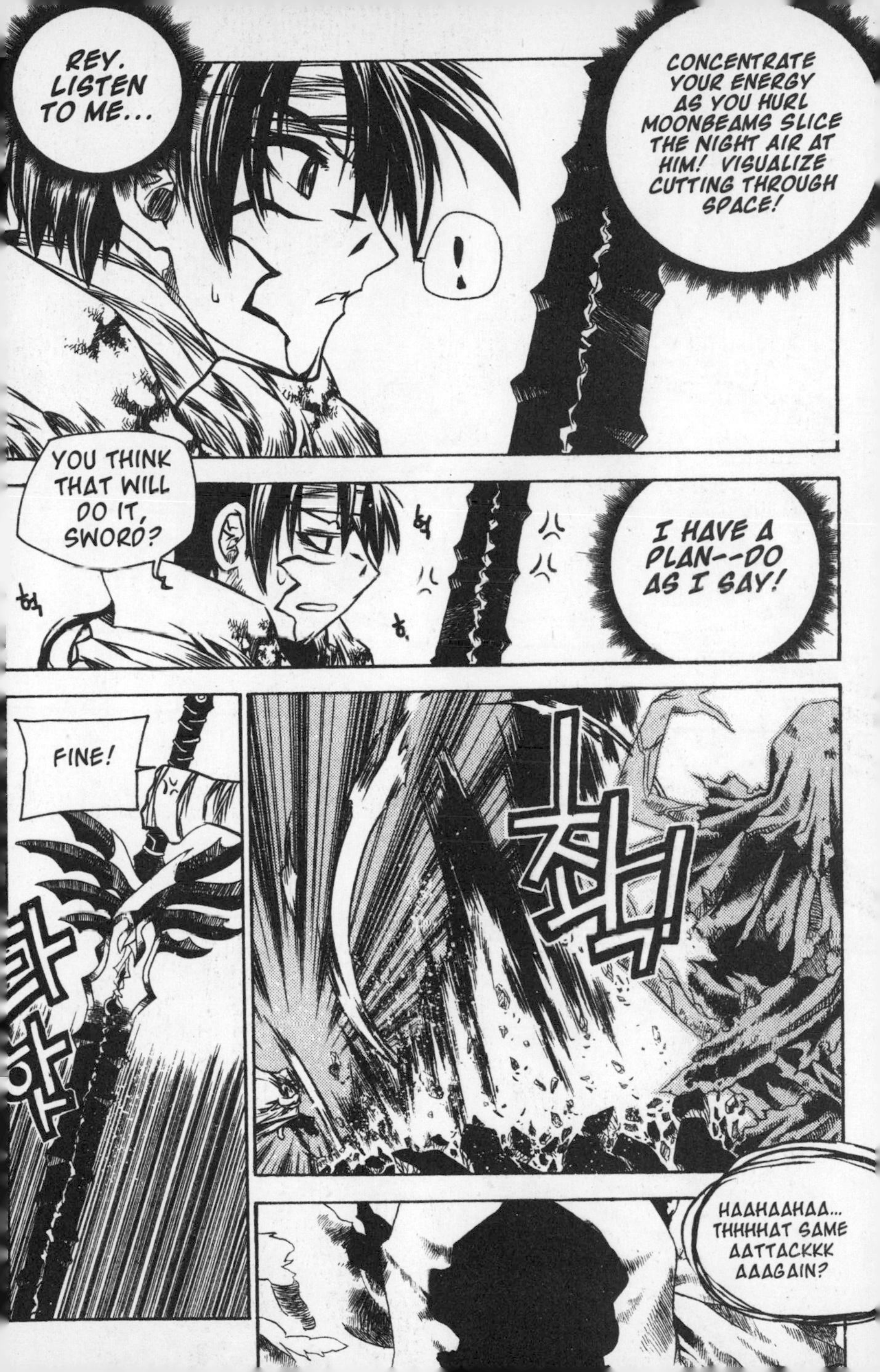
REY. LISTEN TO ME...
!
CONCENTRATE YOUR ENERGY AS YOU HURL MOONBEAMS SLICE THE NIGHT AIR AT HIM! VISUALIZE CUTTING THROUGH SPACE!
YOU THINK THAT WILL DO IT, SWORD?
I HAVE A PLAN--DO AS I SAY!
FINE!
HAAHAAHAA... THHHHAT SAME AATTACKKK AAAGAIN?

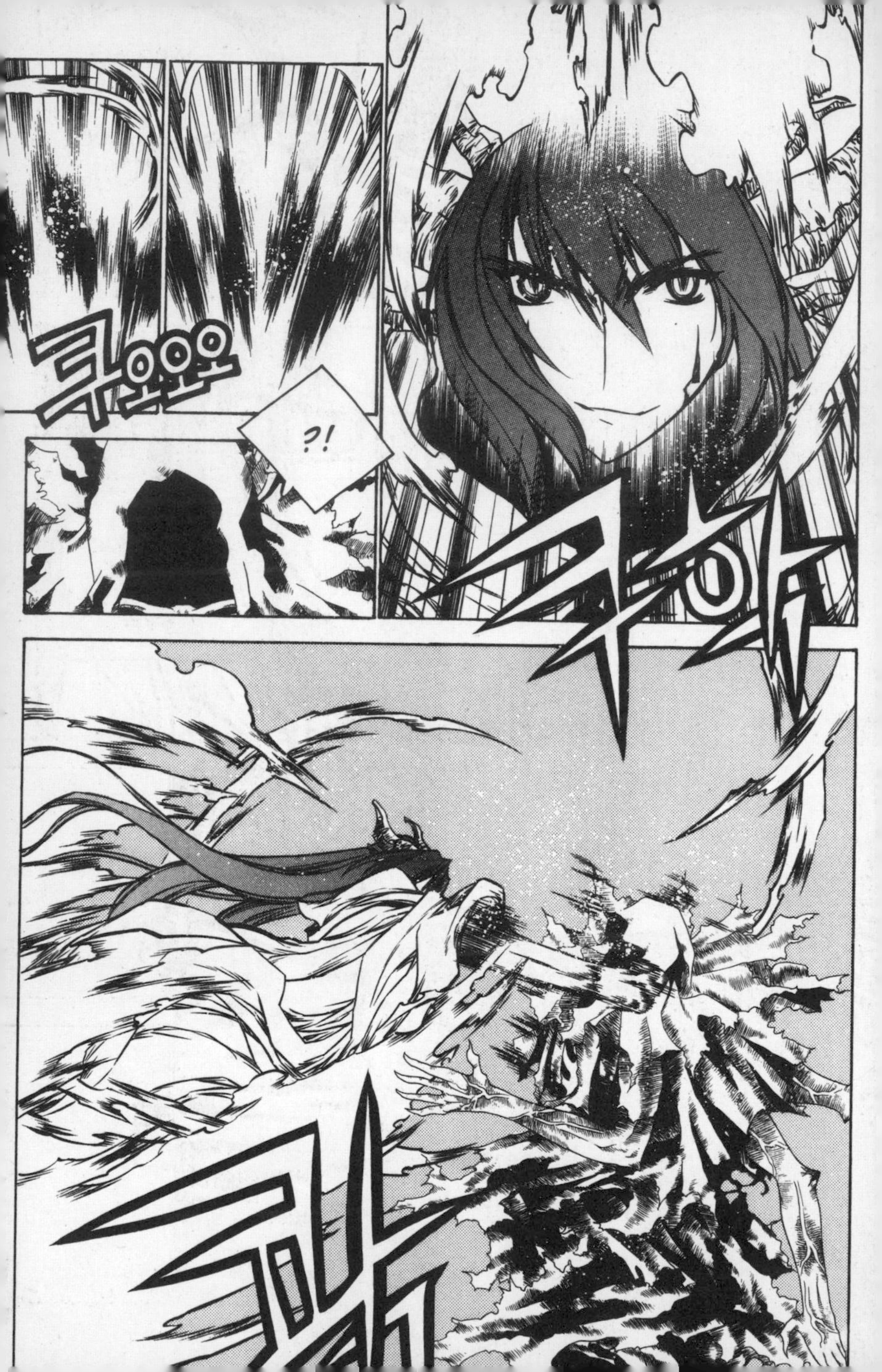
쿠오오오
?!
콰아

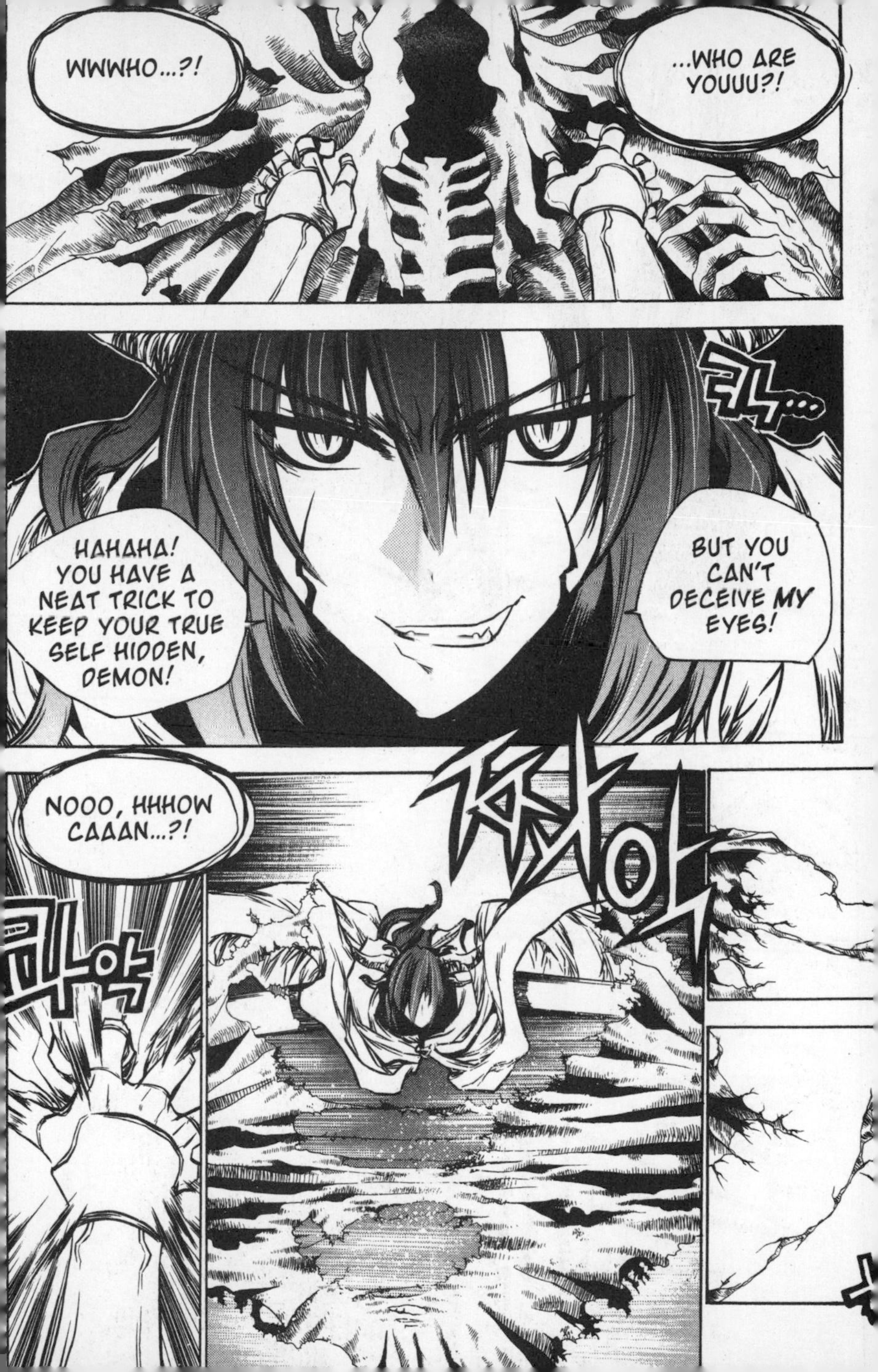
WWWHO...?!
...WHO ARE YOUUU?!
HAHAHA! YOU HAVE A NEAT TRICK TO KEEP YOUR TRUE SELF HIDDEN, DEMON!
BUT YOU CAN'T DECEIVE MY EYES!
NOOO, HHHOW CAAAN...?!

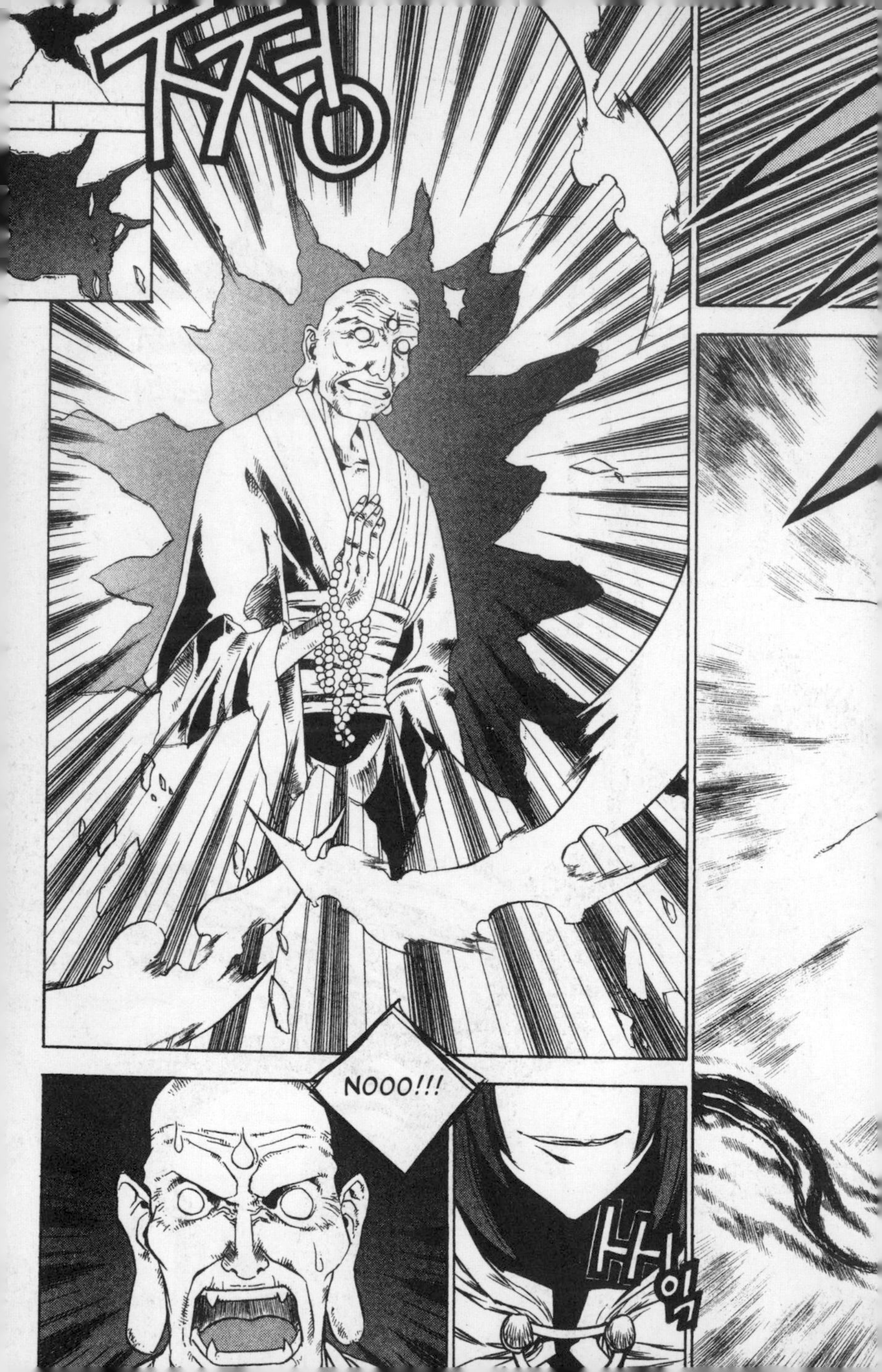
NOOO!!!

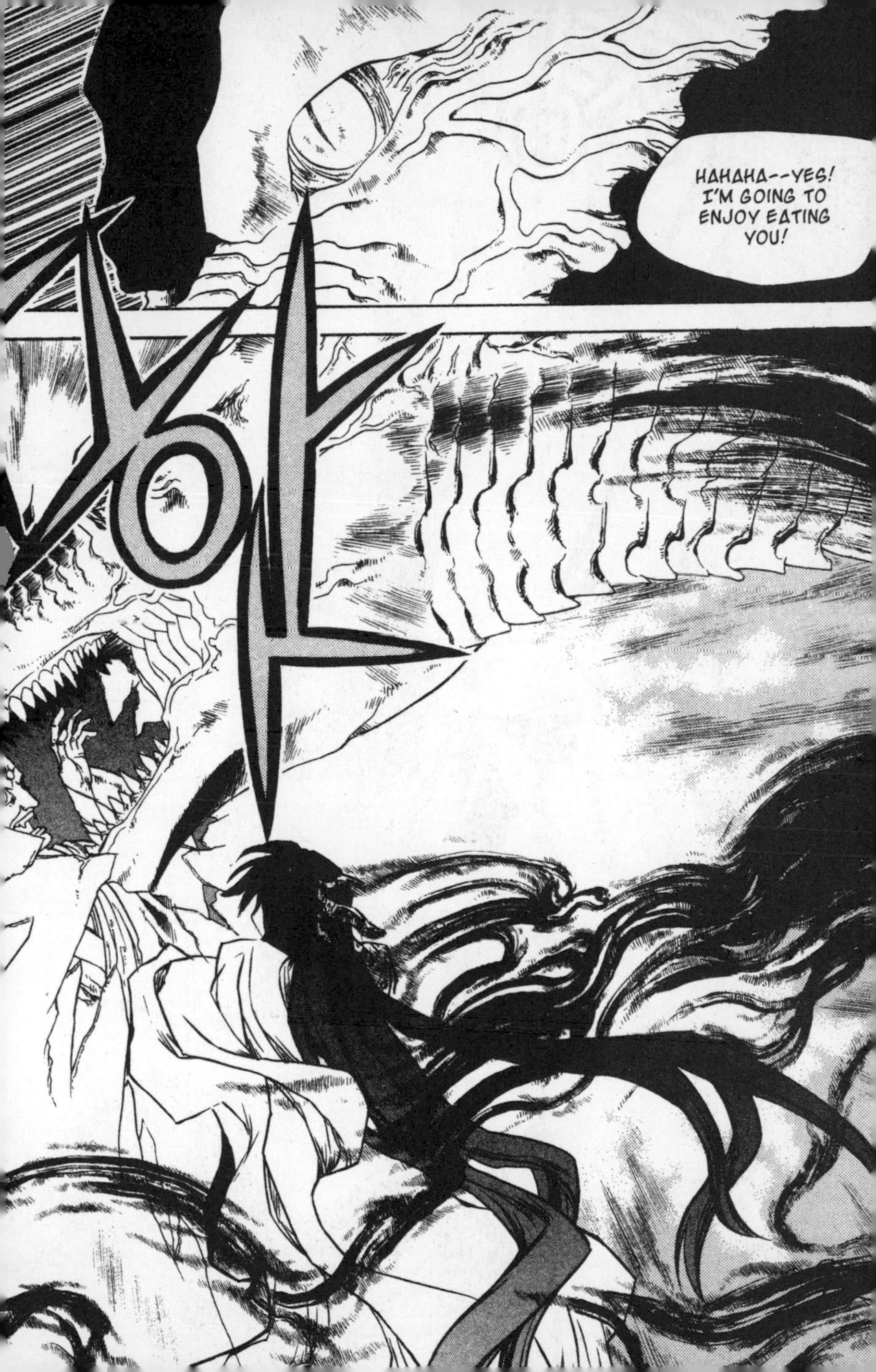
HAHAHA--YES! I'M GOING TO ENJOY EATING YOU!

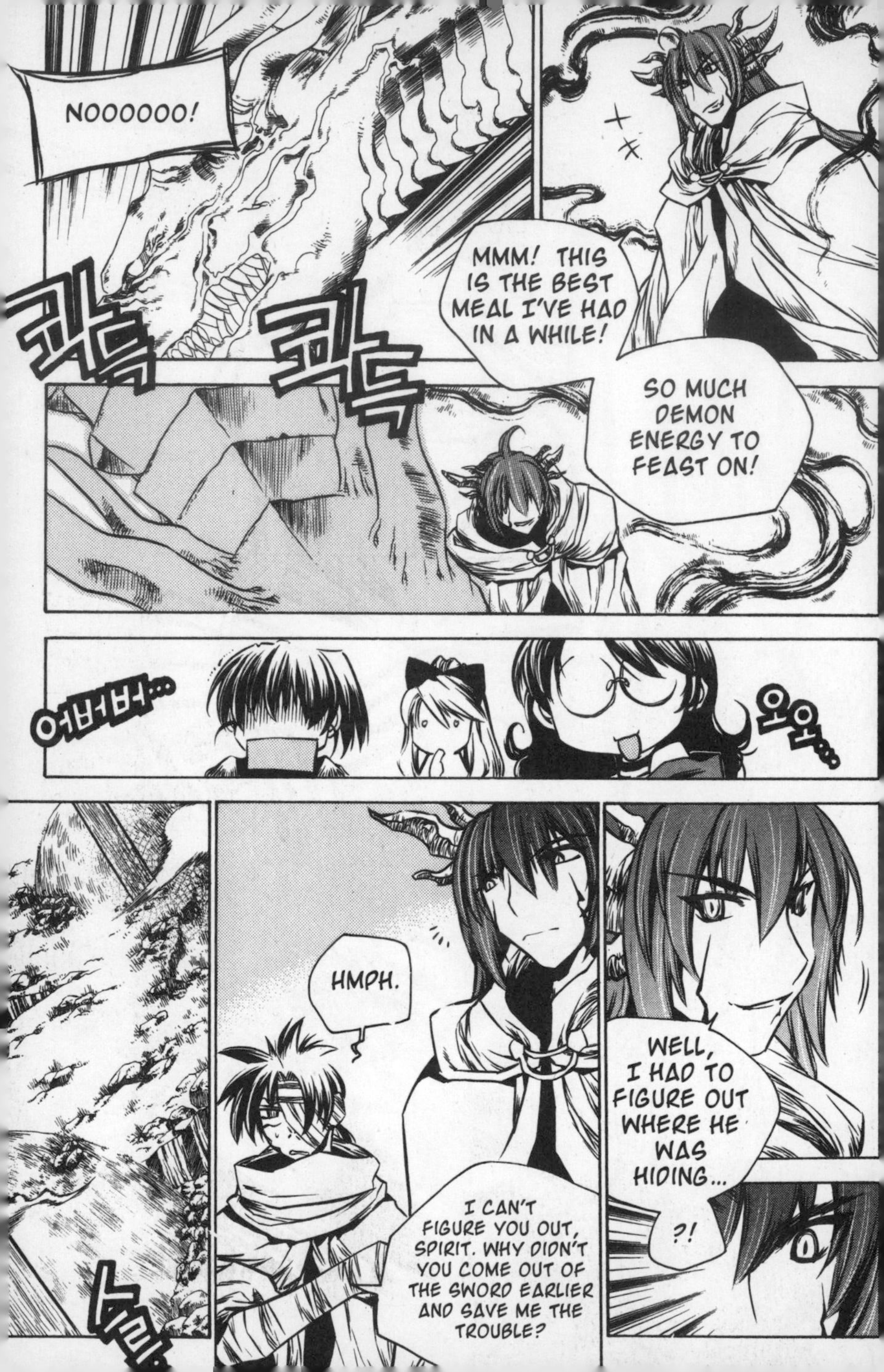
NOOOOOO!
콰득
콰득
MMM! THIS IS THE BEST MEAL I'VE HAD IN A WHILE!
SO MUCH DEMON ENERGY TO FEAST ON!
어버버...
오오...
HMPH.
WELL, I HAD TO FIGURE OUT WHERE HE WAS HIDING...
I CAN'T FIGURE YOU OUT, SPIRIT. WHY DIDN'T YOU COME OUT OF THE SWORD EARLIER AND SAVE ME THE TROUBLE?
?!

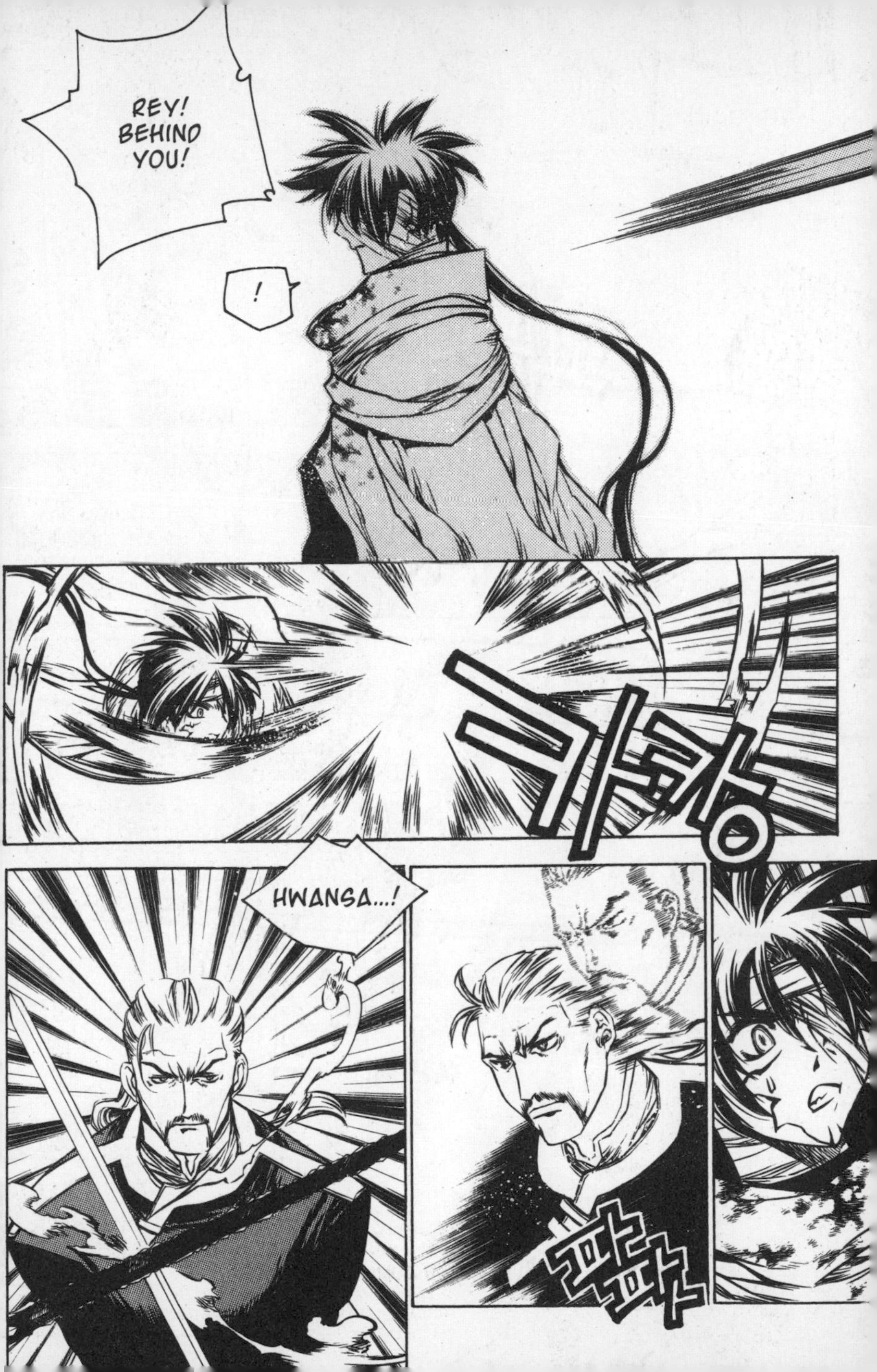
REY! BEHIND YOU!
!
HWANSA...!

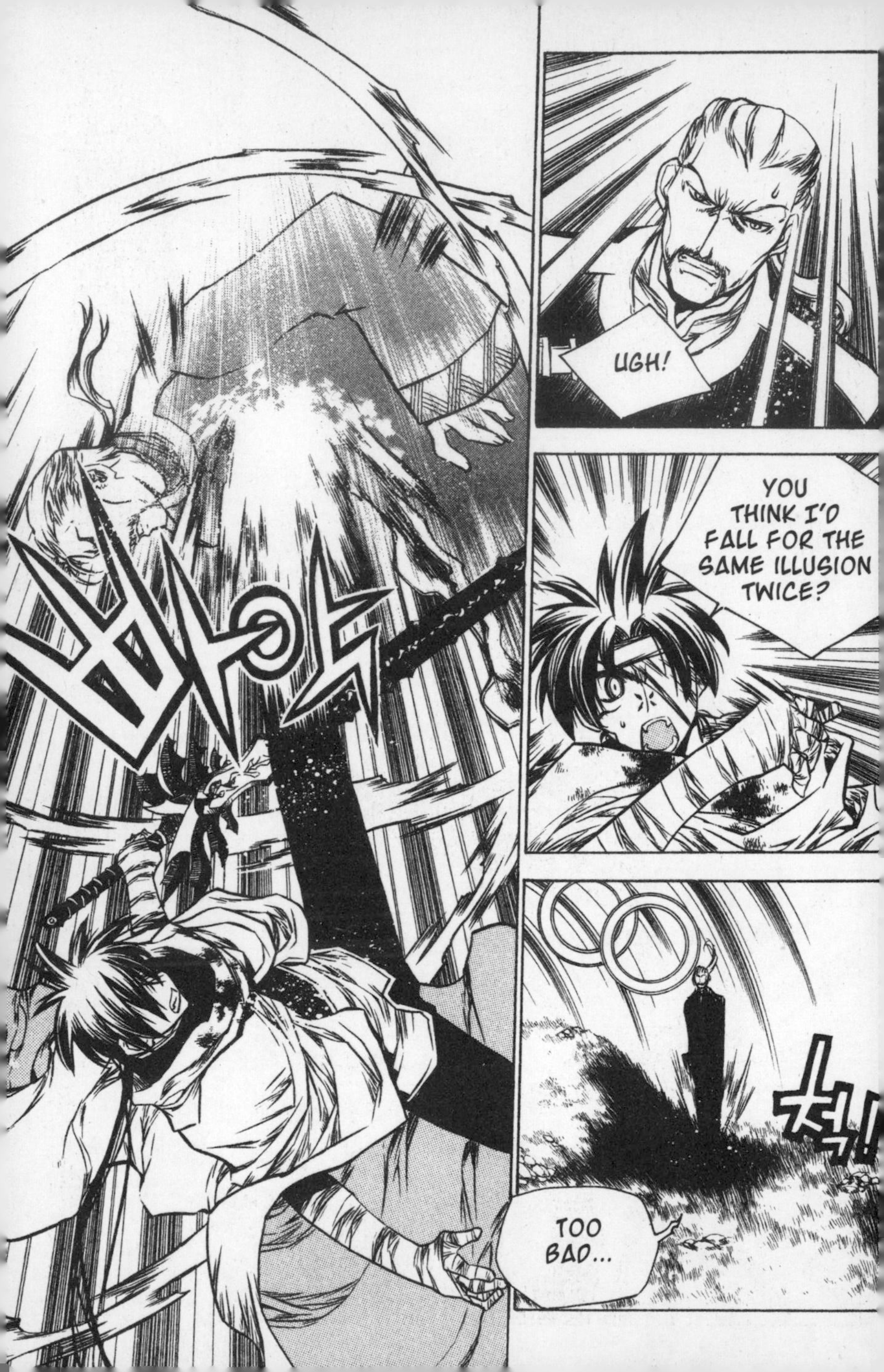
UGH!
YOU THINK I'D FALL FOR THE SAME ILLUSION TWICE?
TOO BAD...

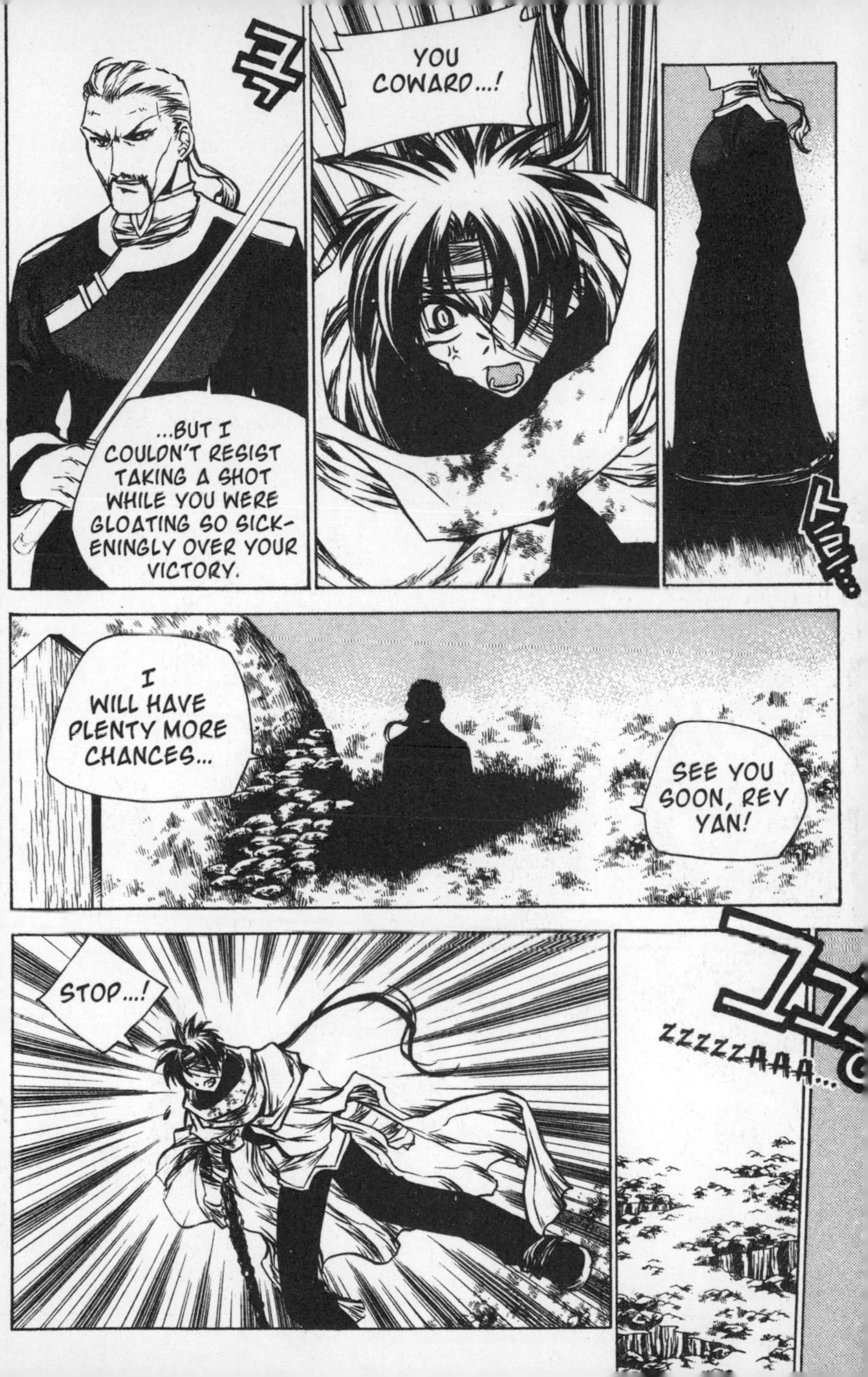
...BUT I COULDN'T RESIST TAKING A SHOT WHILE YOU WERE GLOATING SO SICK-ENINGLY OVER YOUR VICTORY.
YOU COWARD...!
I WILL HAVE PLENTY MORE CHANCES...
SEE YOU SOON, REY YAN!
STOP...!
ZZZZZZAAA...

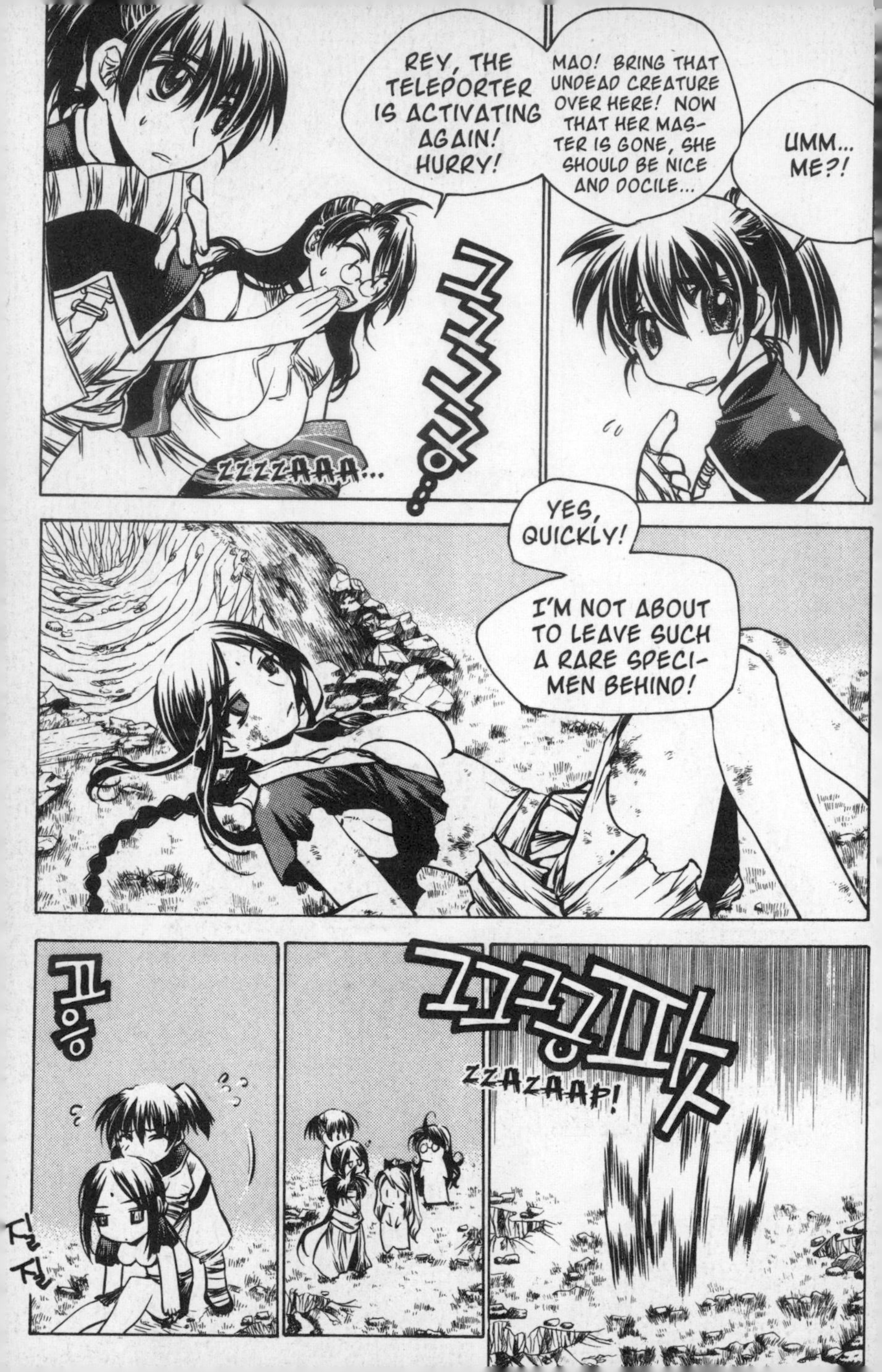
REY, THE TELEPORTER IS ACTIVATING AGAIN! HURRY!
ZZZZAAA...
MAO! BRING THAT UNDEAD CREATURE OVER HERE! NOW THAT HER MASTER IS GONE, SHE SHOULD BE NICE AND DOCILE...
UMM... ME?!
YES, QUICKLY!
I'M NOT ABOUT TO LEAVE SUCH A RARE SPECIMEN BEHIND!
ZZAZAAAP!

Chapter 49
Hyulgum, Sorcerer of the Sword

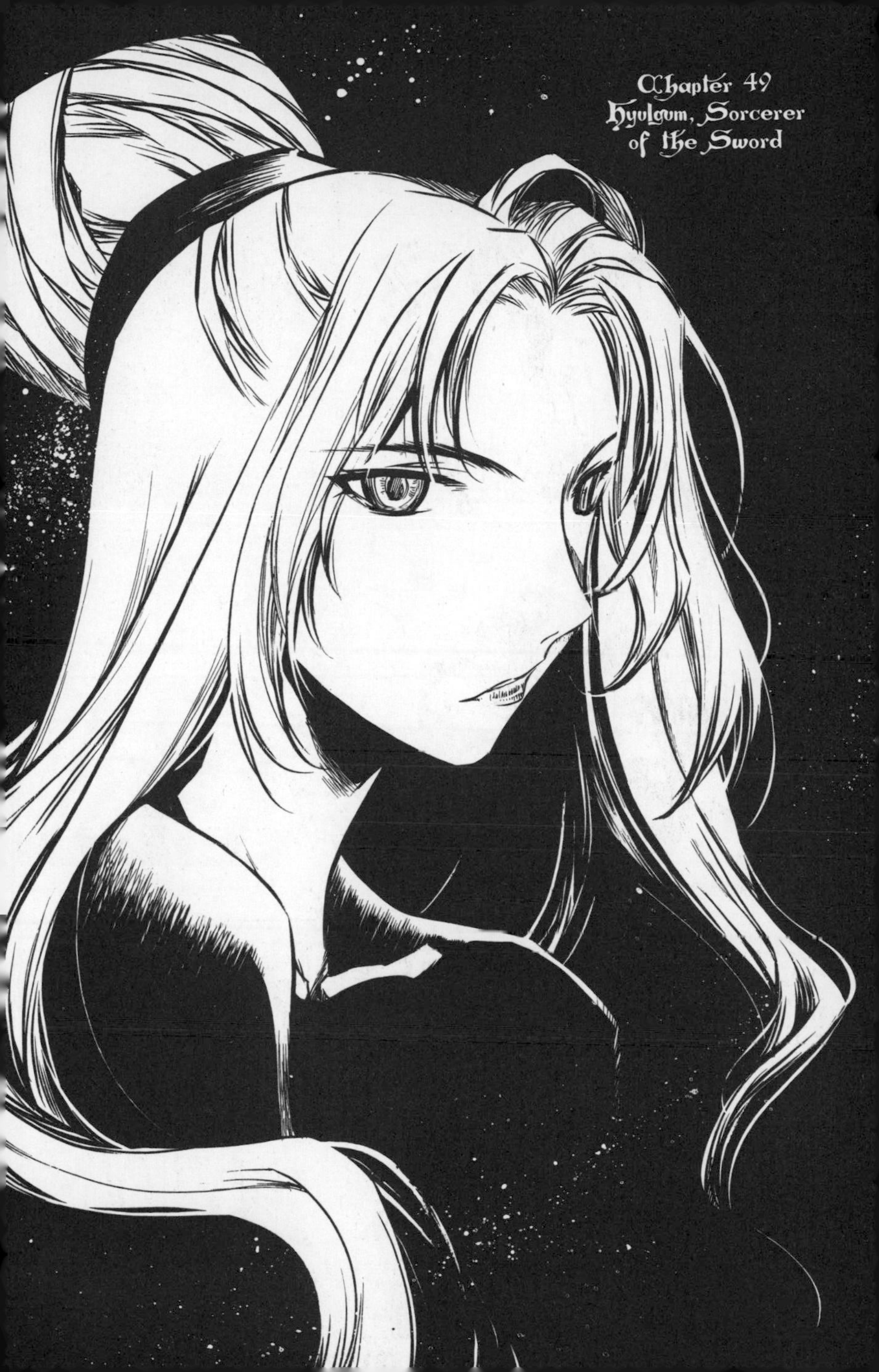

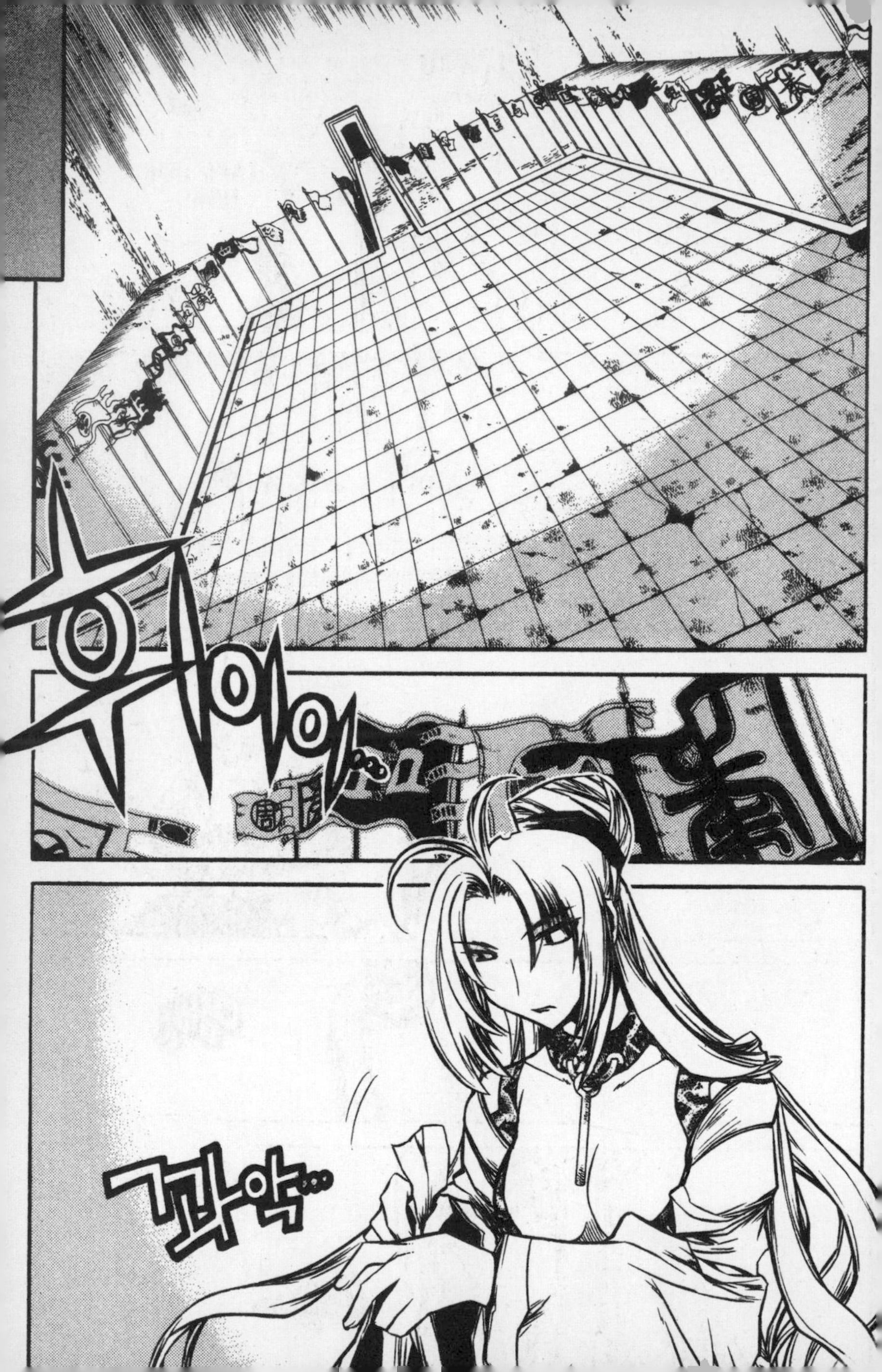
아아아아...ㅁ
꽈악...

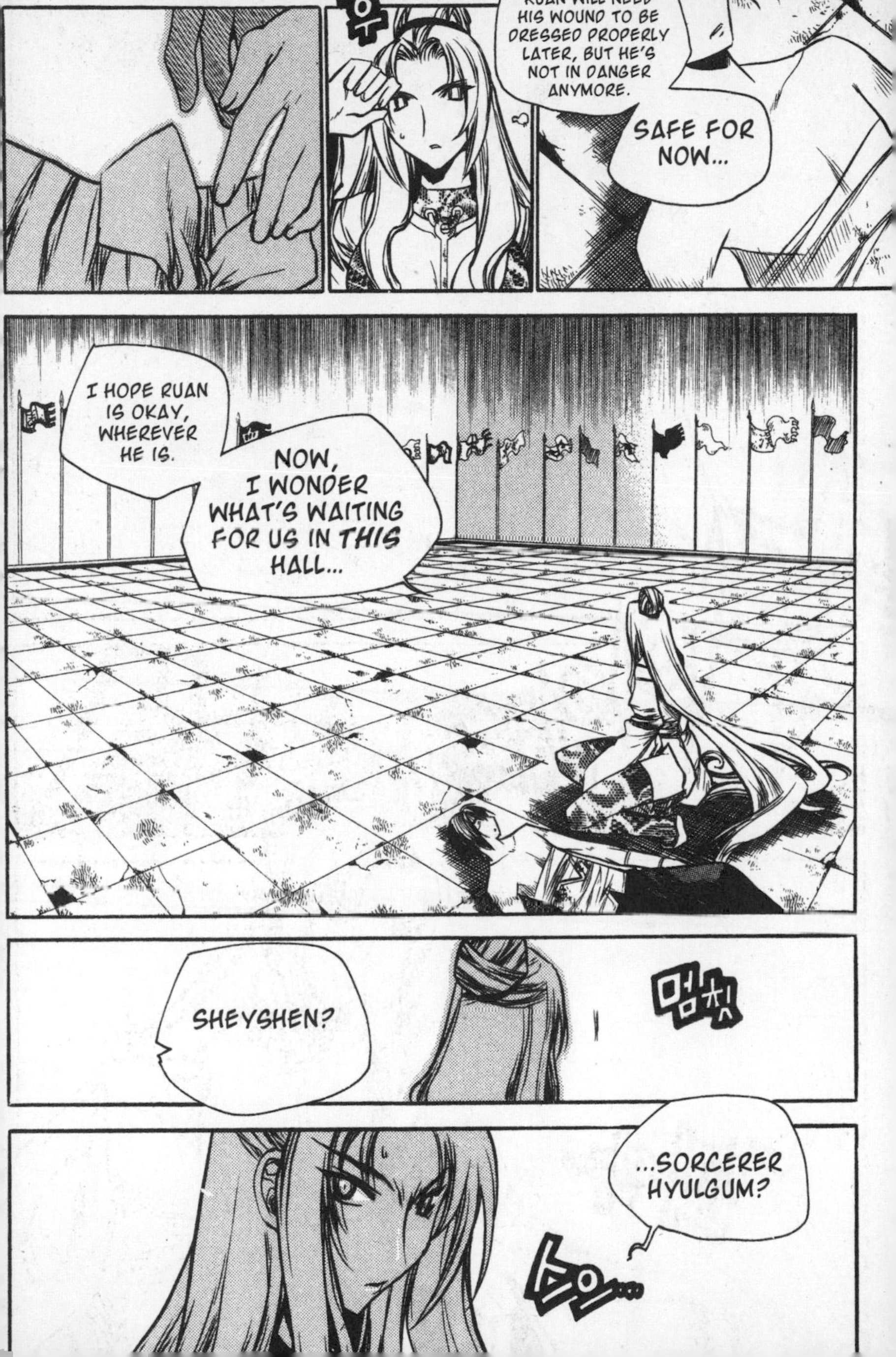
KUAN WILL NEED HIS WOUND TO BE DRESSED PROPERLY LATER, BUT HE'S NOT IN DANGER ANYMORE.
SAFE FOR NOW...
I HOPE RUAN IS OKAY, WHEREVER HE IS.
NOW, I WONDER WHAT'S WAITING FOR US IN THIS HALL...
SHEYSHEN?
멈칫
...SORCERER HYULGUM?

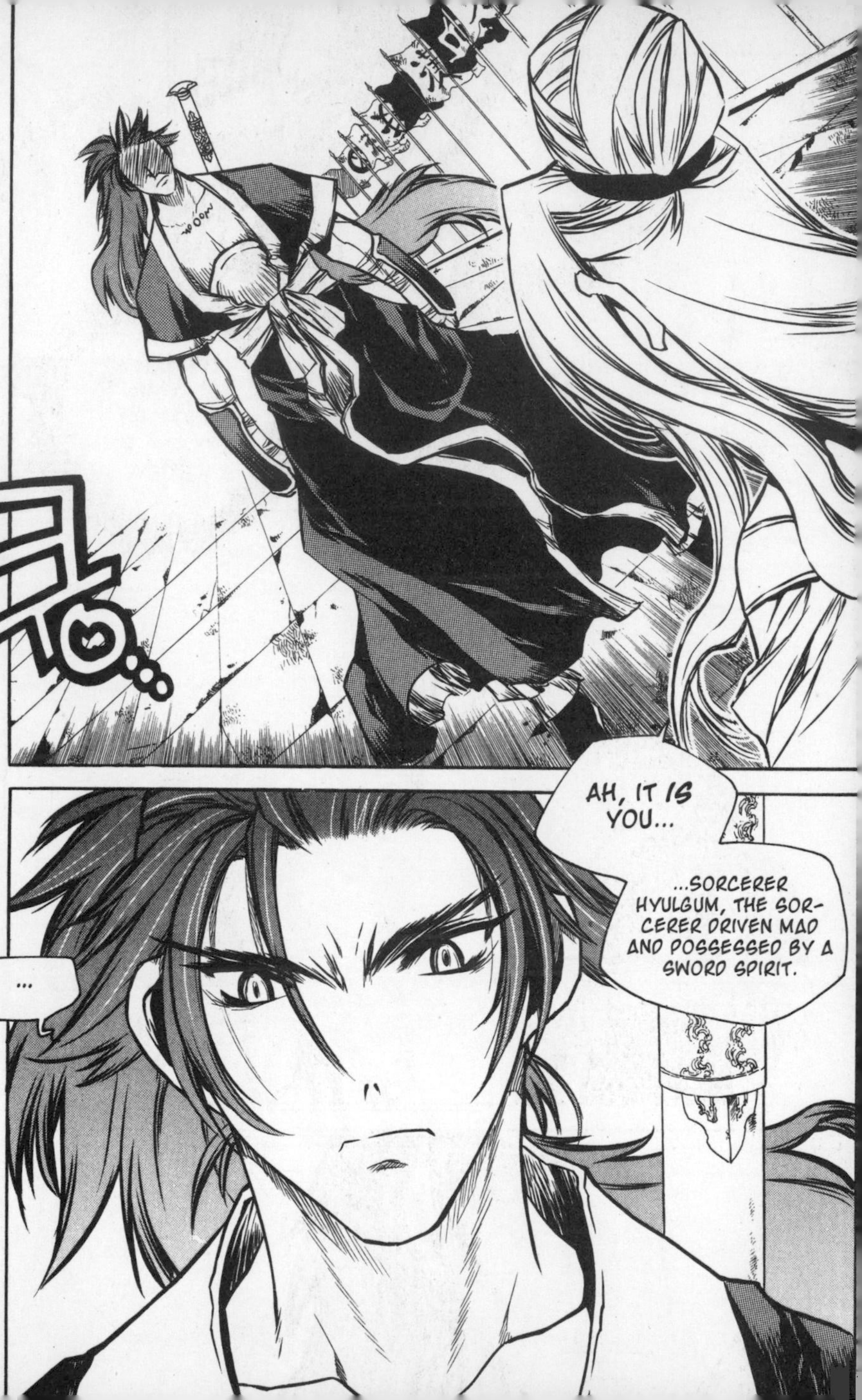
AH, IT IS YOU...
...SORCERER HYULGUM, THE SOR-CERER DRIVEN MAD AND POSSESSED BY A SWORD SPIRIT.
...

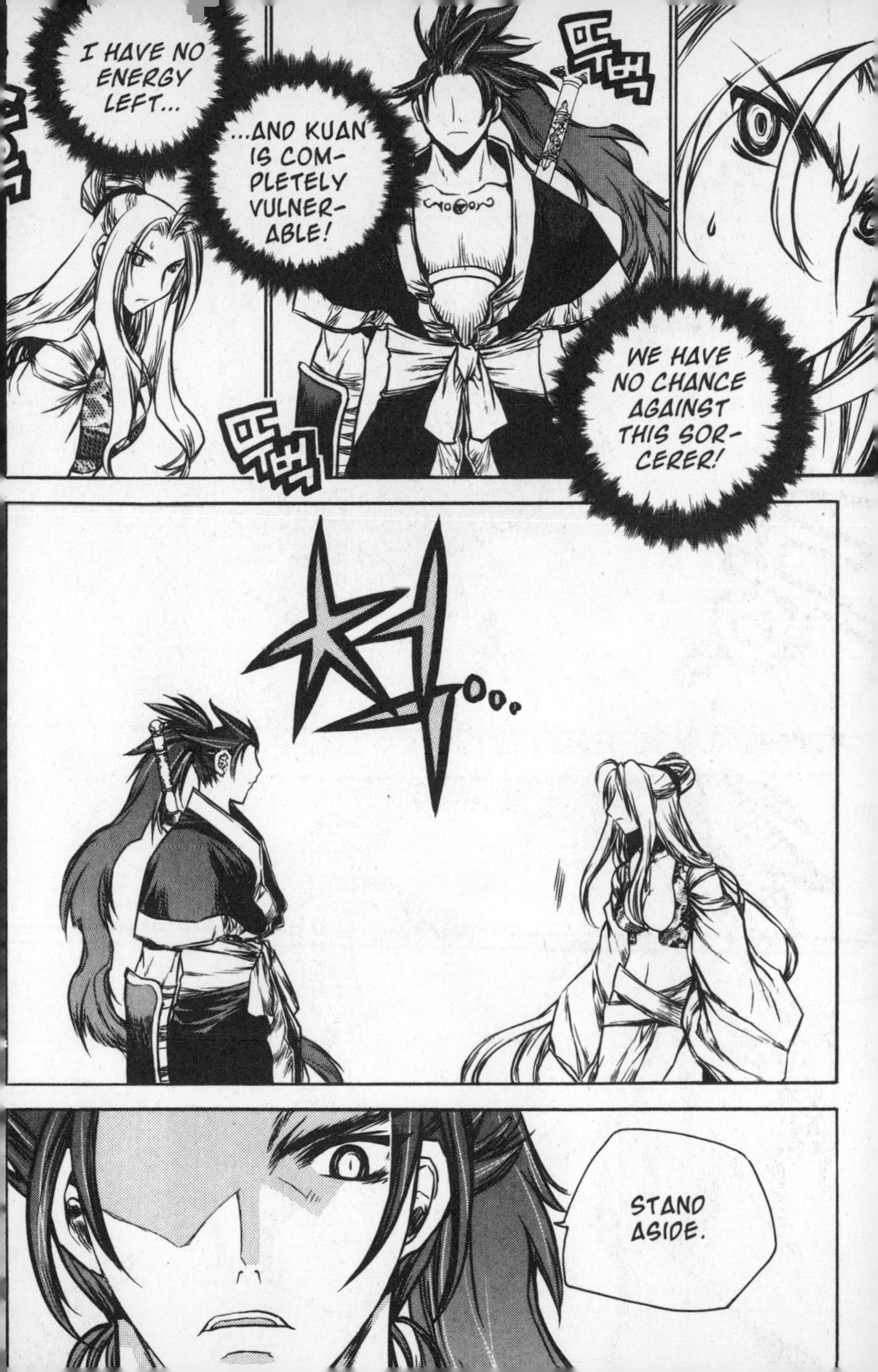
I HAVE NO ENERGY LEFT...
...AND KUAN IS COMPLETELY VULNERABLE!
WE HAVE NO CHANCE AGAINST THIS SORCERER!
STAND ASIDE.

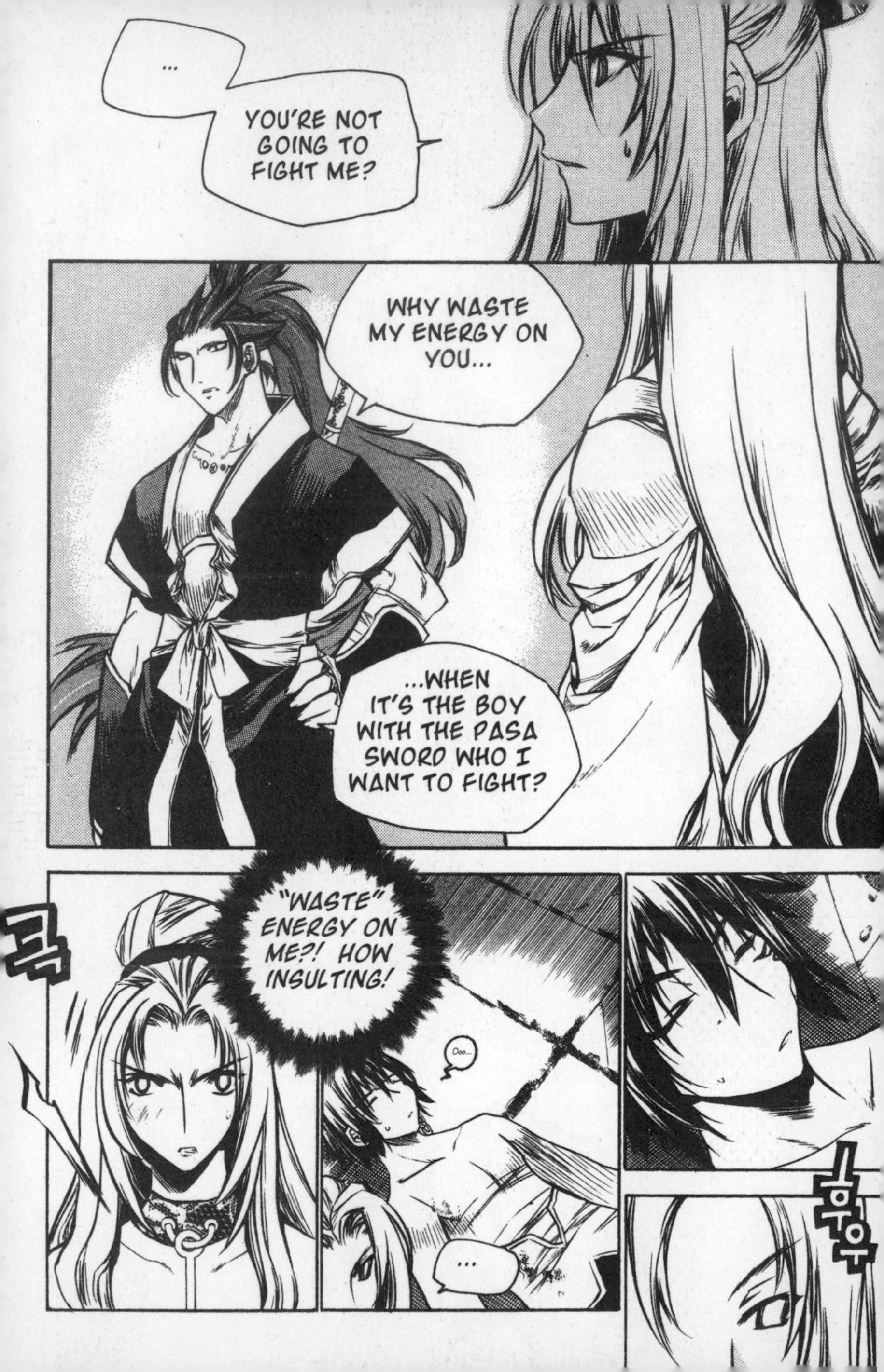
...
YOU'RE NOT GOING TO FIGHT ME?
WHY WASTE MY ENERGY ON YOU...
...WHEN IT'S THE BOY WITH THE PASA SWORD WHO I WANT TO FIGHT?
"WASTE" ENERGY ON ME?! HOW INSULTING!
Ooo...
...

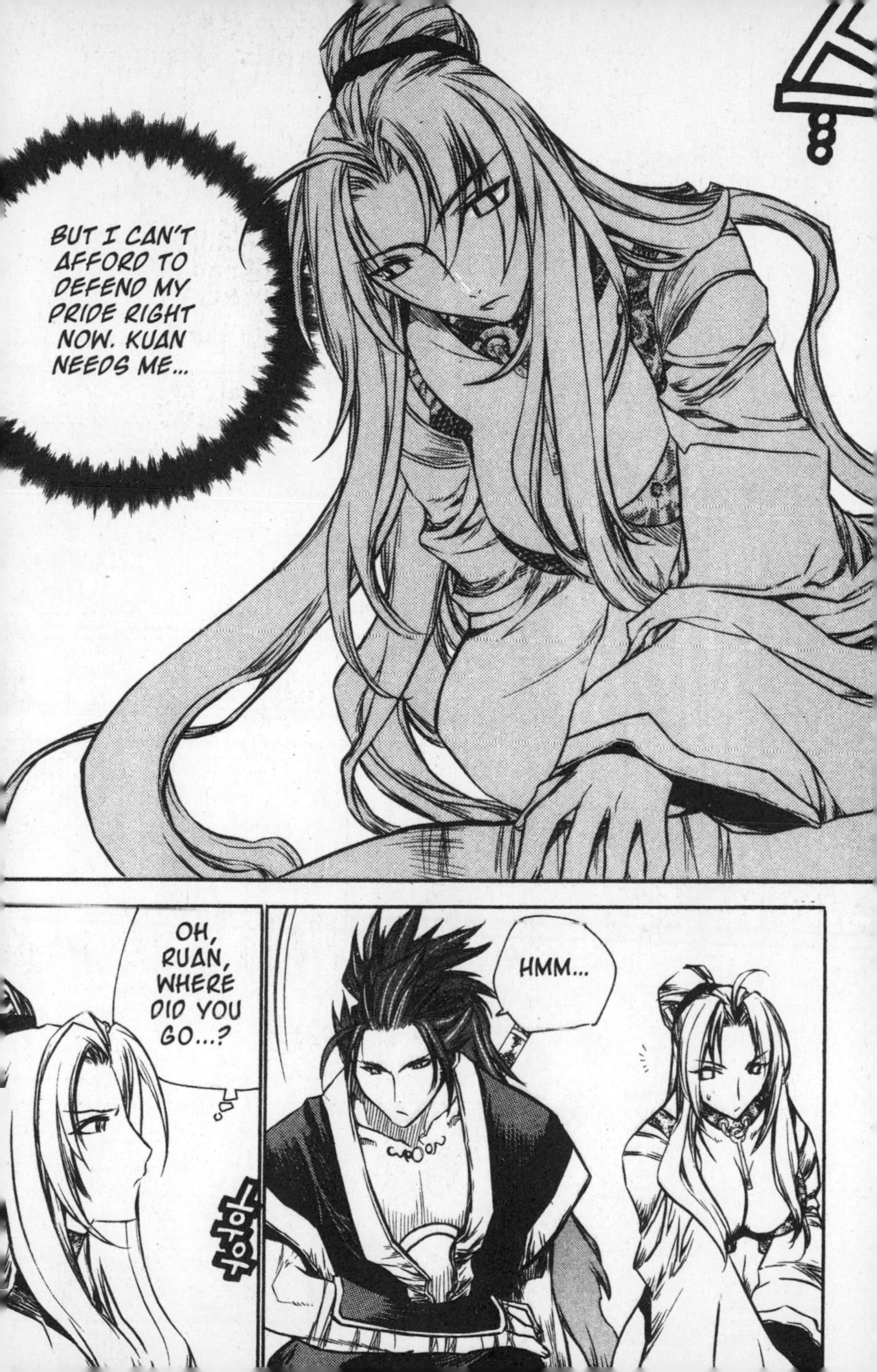
BUT I CAN'T AFFORD TO DEFEND MY PRIDE RIGHT NOW. KUAN NEEDS ME...
OH, RUAN, WHERE DID YOU GO...?
HMM...

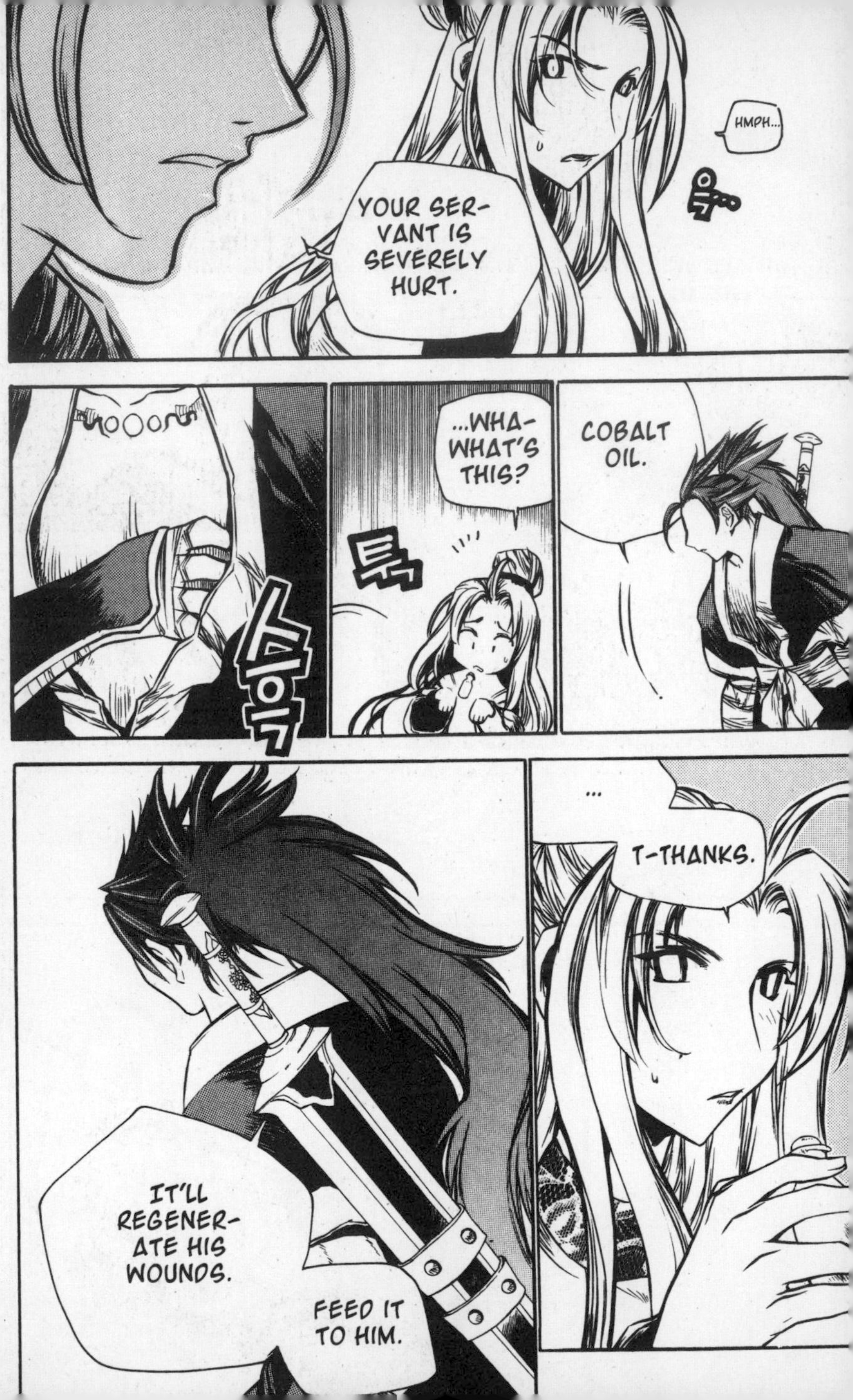
YOUR SER-VANT IS SEVERELY HURT.
HMPH...
...WHA-WHAT'S THIS?
툭
COBALT OIL.
IT'LL REGENER-ATE HIS WOUNDS.
FEED IT TO HIM.
...
T-THANKS.

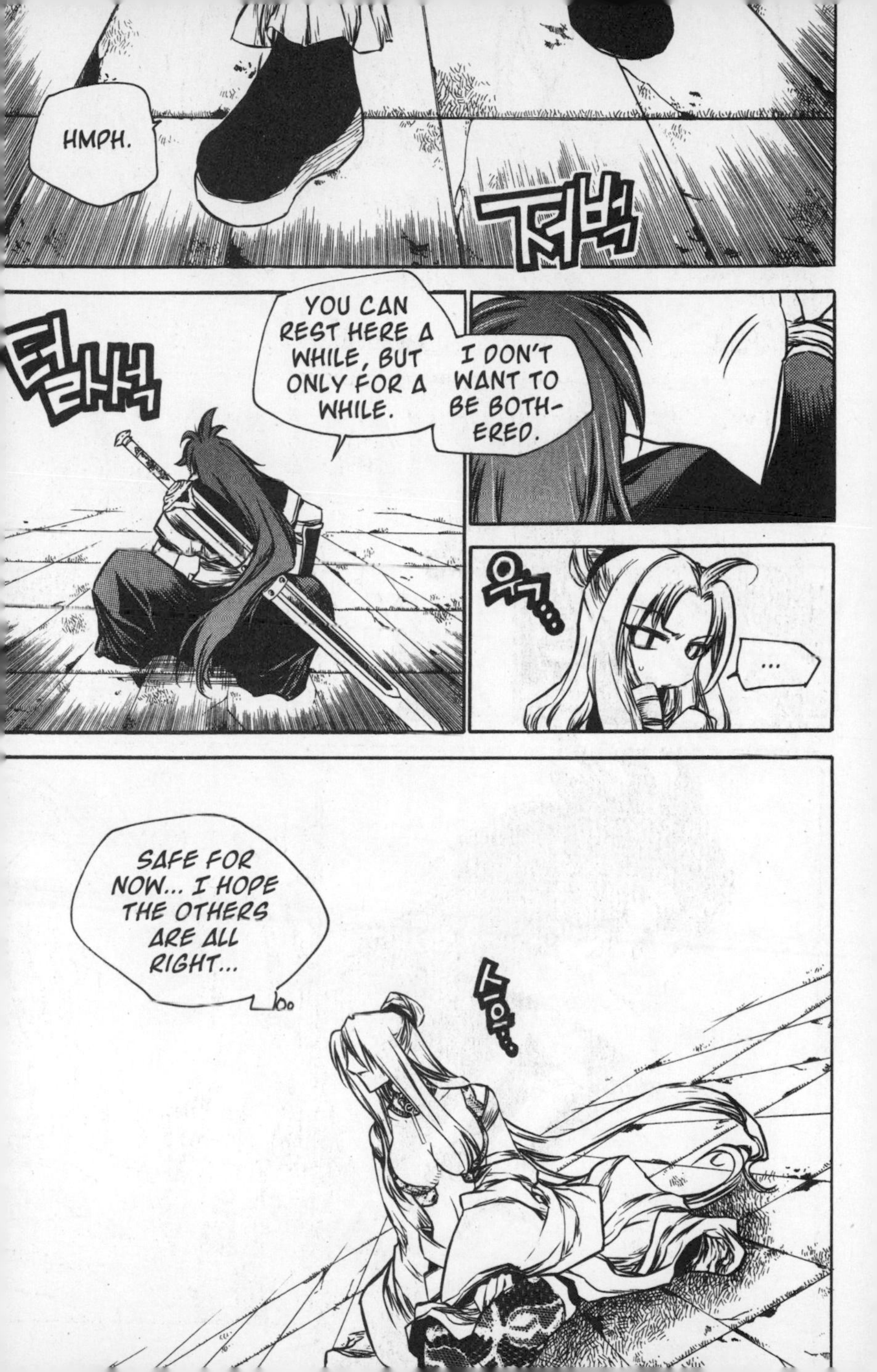
HMPH.
YOU CAN REST HERE A WHILE, BUT ONLY FOR A WHILE.
I DON'T WANT TO BE BOTH-ERED.
...
SAFE FOR NOW... I HOPE THE OTHERS ARE ALL RIGHT...

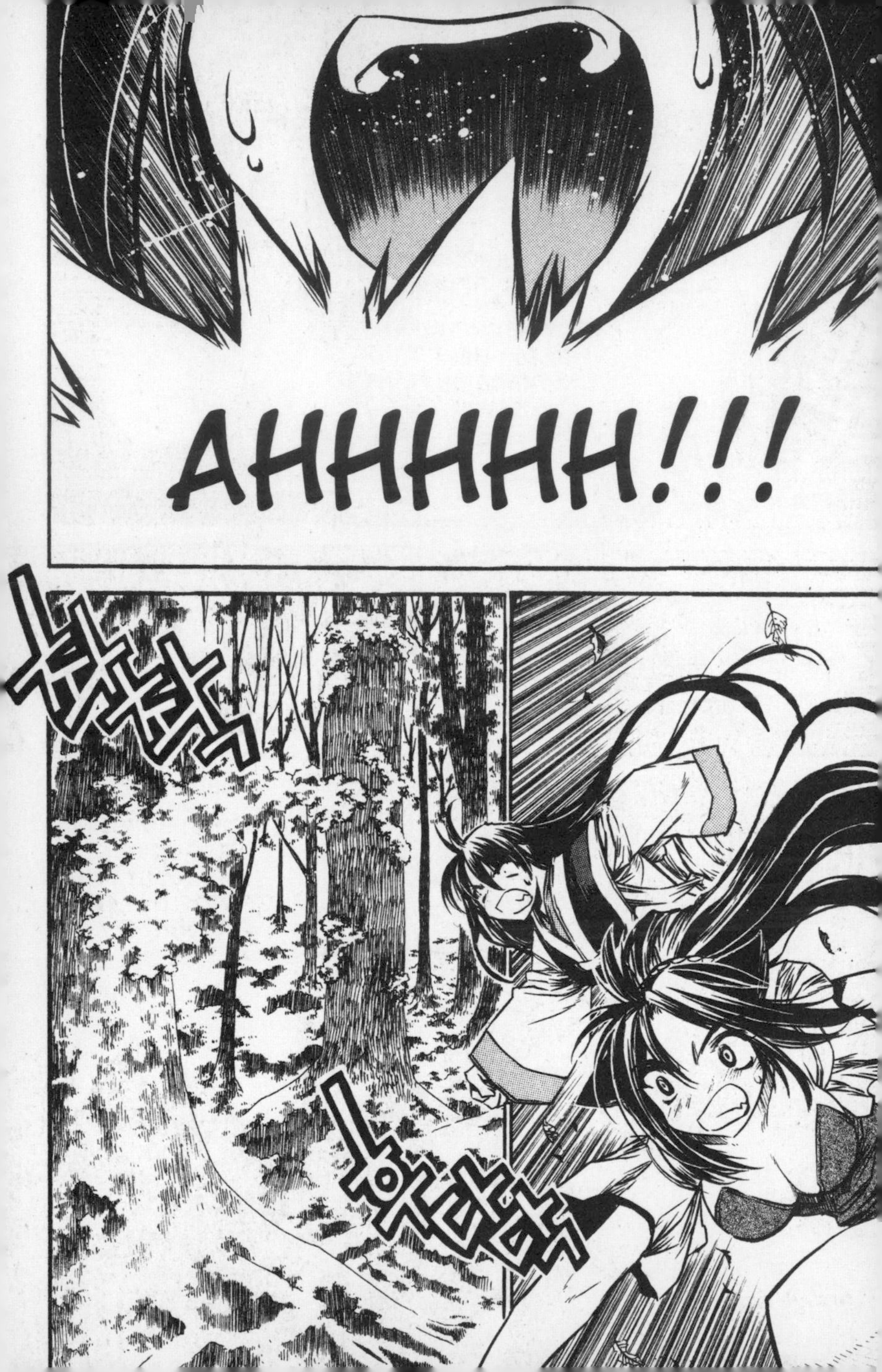
AHHHHH!!!

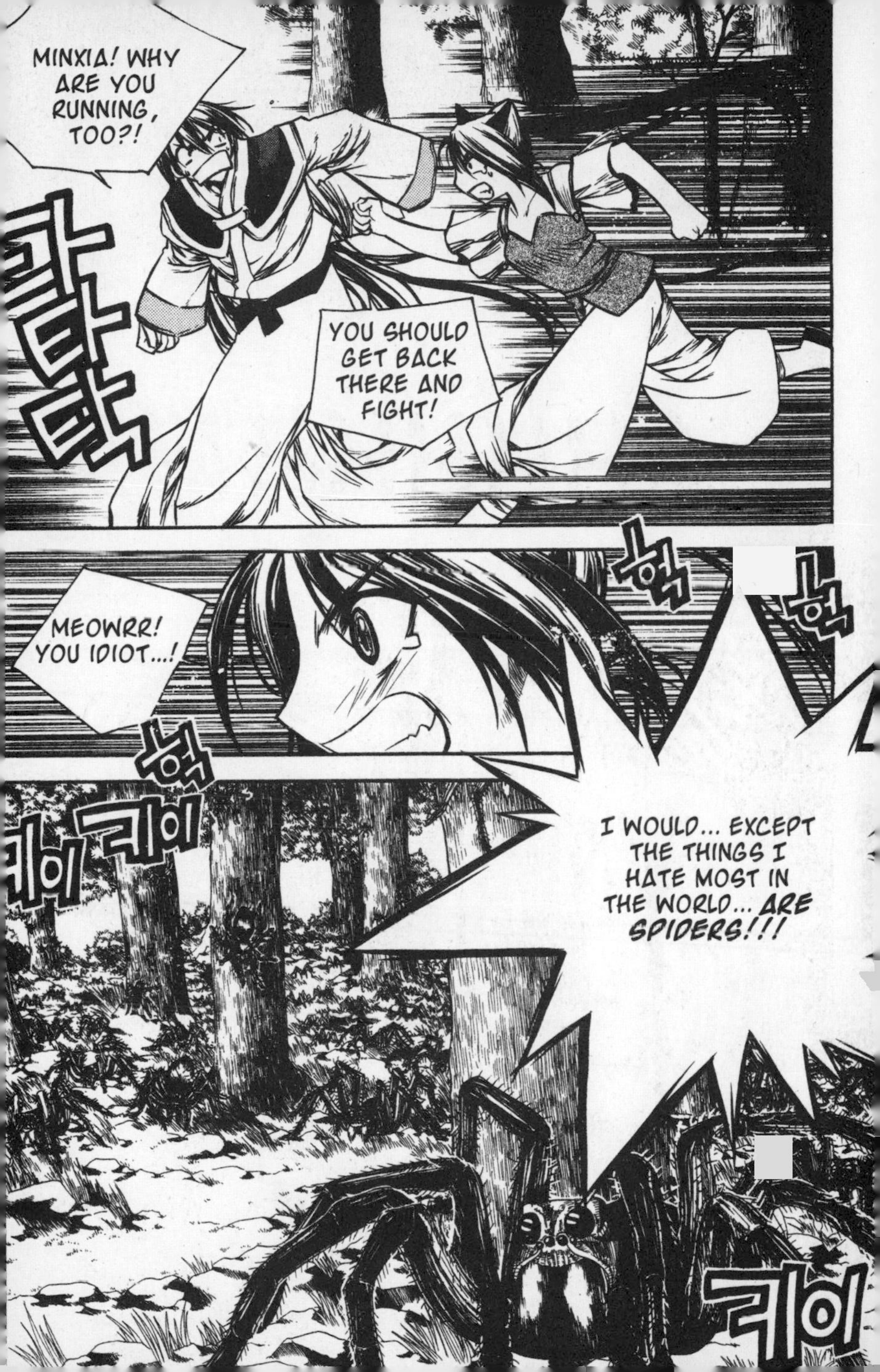
MINXIA! WHY ARE YOU RUNNING, TOO?!
YOU SHOULD GET BACK THERE AND FIGHT!
MEOWRR! YOU IDIOT...!
헉
헉
헉
I WOULD... EXCEPT THE THINGS I HATE MOST IN THE WORLD... ***ARE SPIDERS!!!***
키이
키이

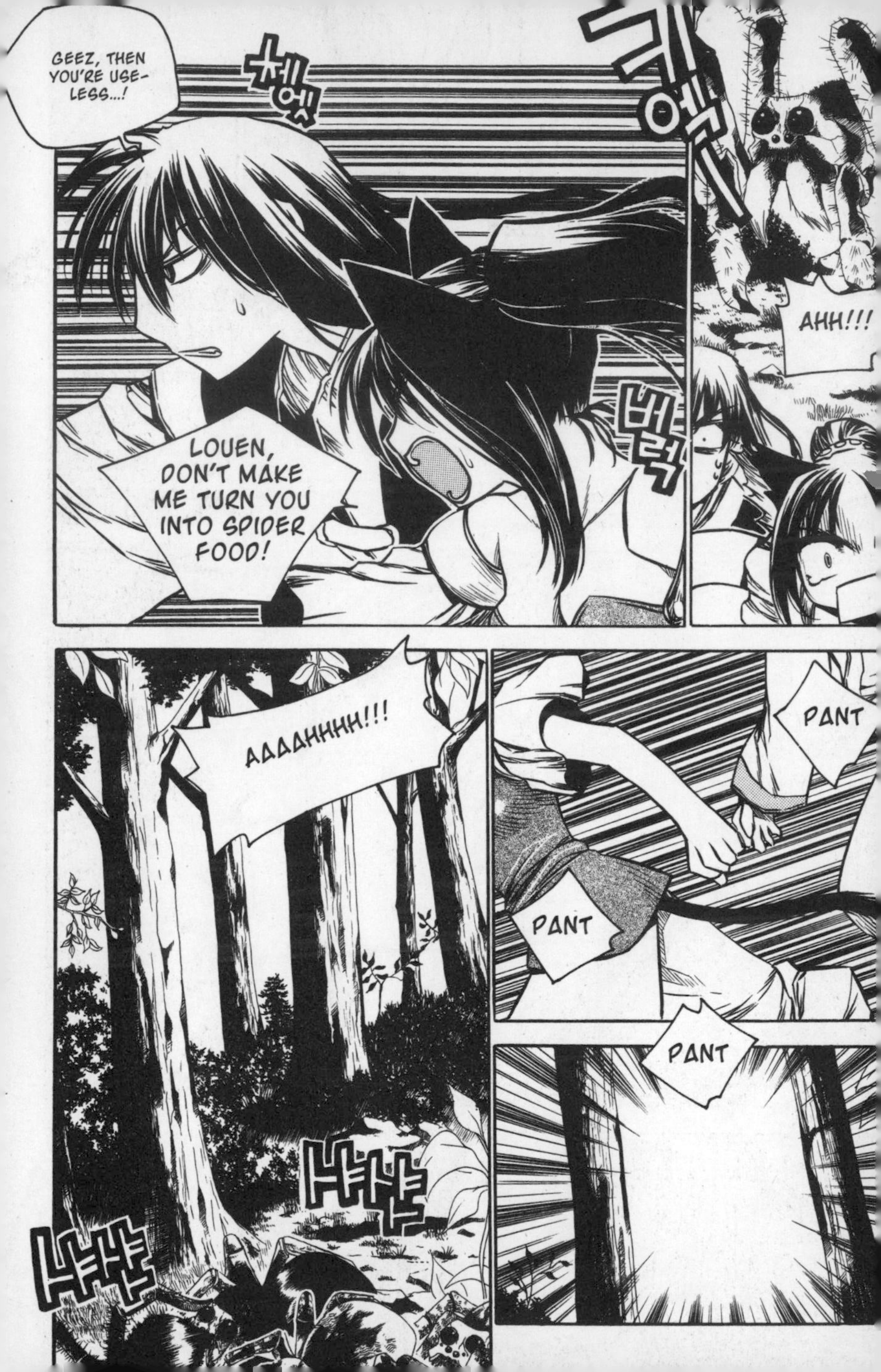
GEEZ, THEN YOU'RE USE-LESS...!
LOUEN, DON'T MAKE ME TURN YOU INTO SPIDER FOOD!
AHH!!!
AAAAHHHH!!!
PANT
PANT
PANT

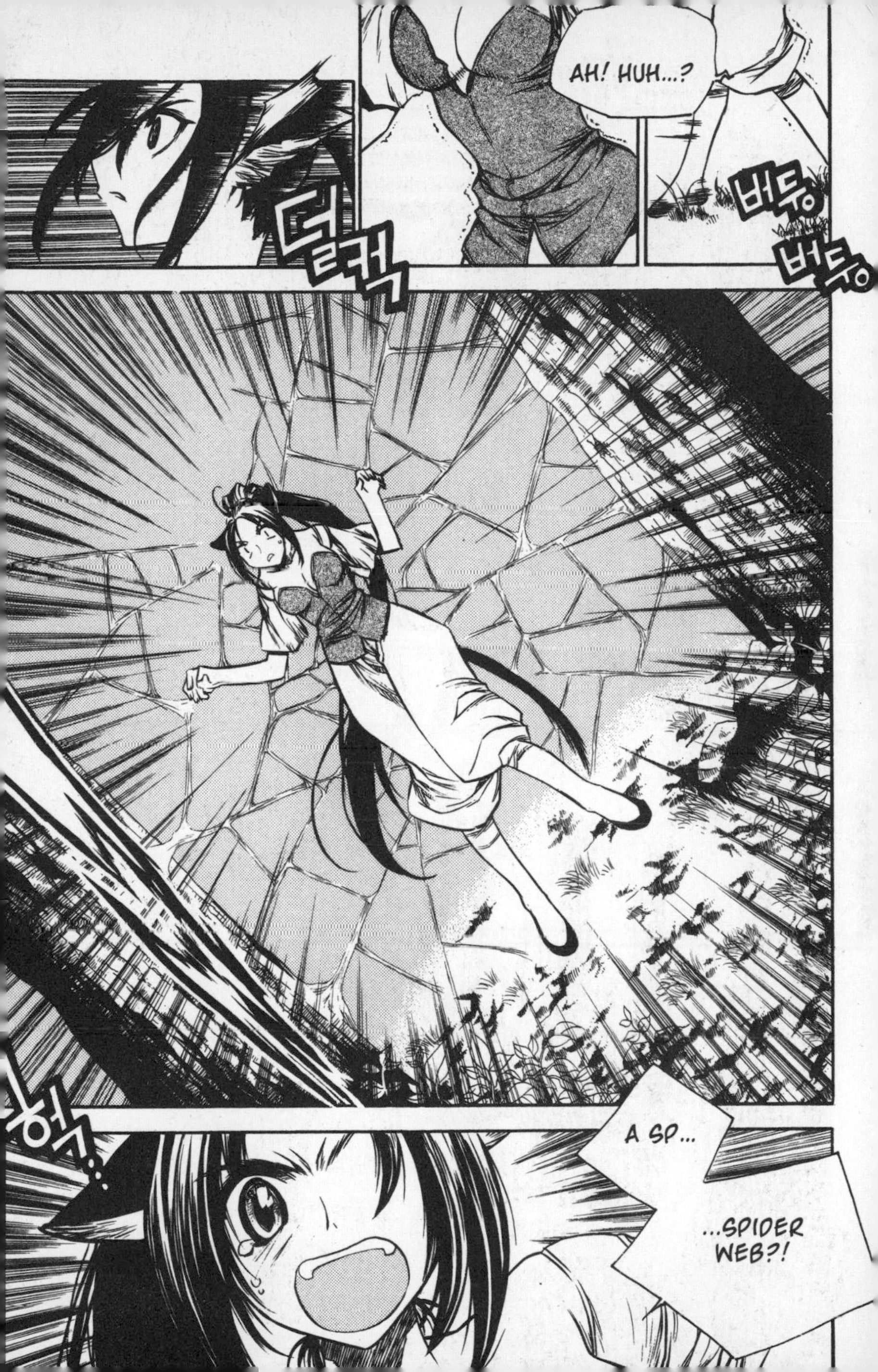
덜컥
AH! HUH...?
버둥
버둥
A SP...
...SPIDER WEB?!

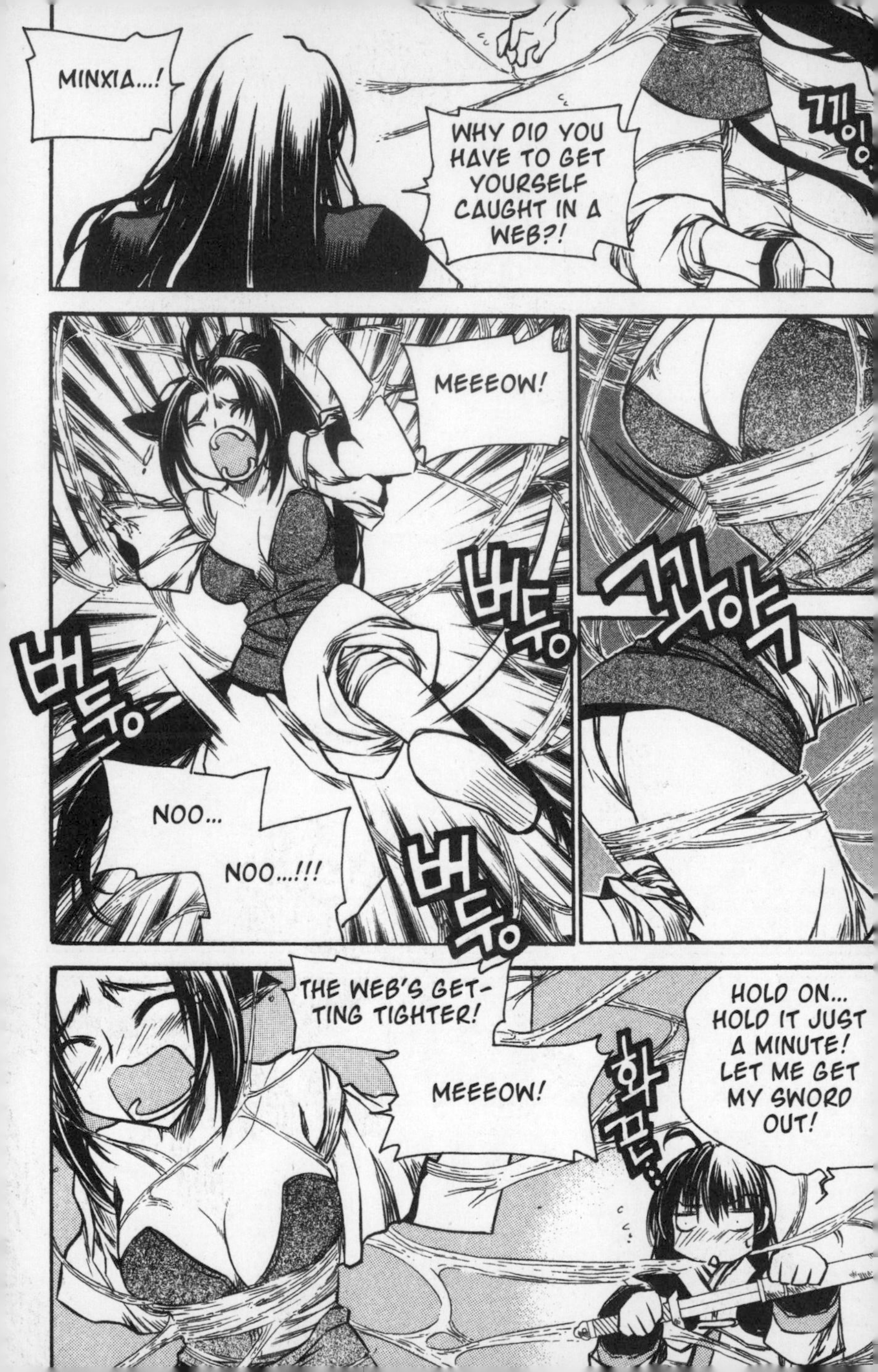
MINXIA...!
WHY DID YOU HAVE TO GET YOURSELF CAUGHT IN A WEB?!
끼이이...
MEEEOW!
버둥
버둥
버둥
NOO...
NOO...!!!
끼야악
THE WEB'S GET-TING TIGHTER!
MEEEOW!
화끈
HOLD ON... HOLD IT JUST A MINUTE! LET ME GET MY SWORD OUT!

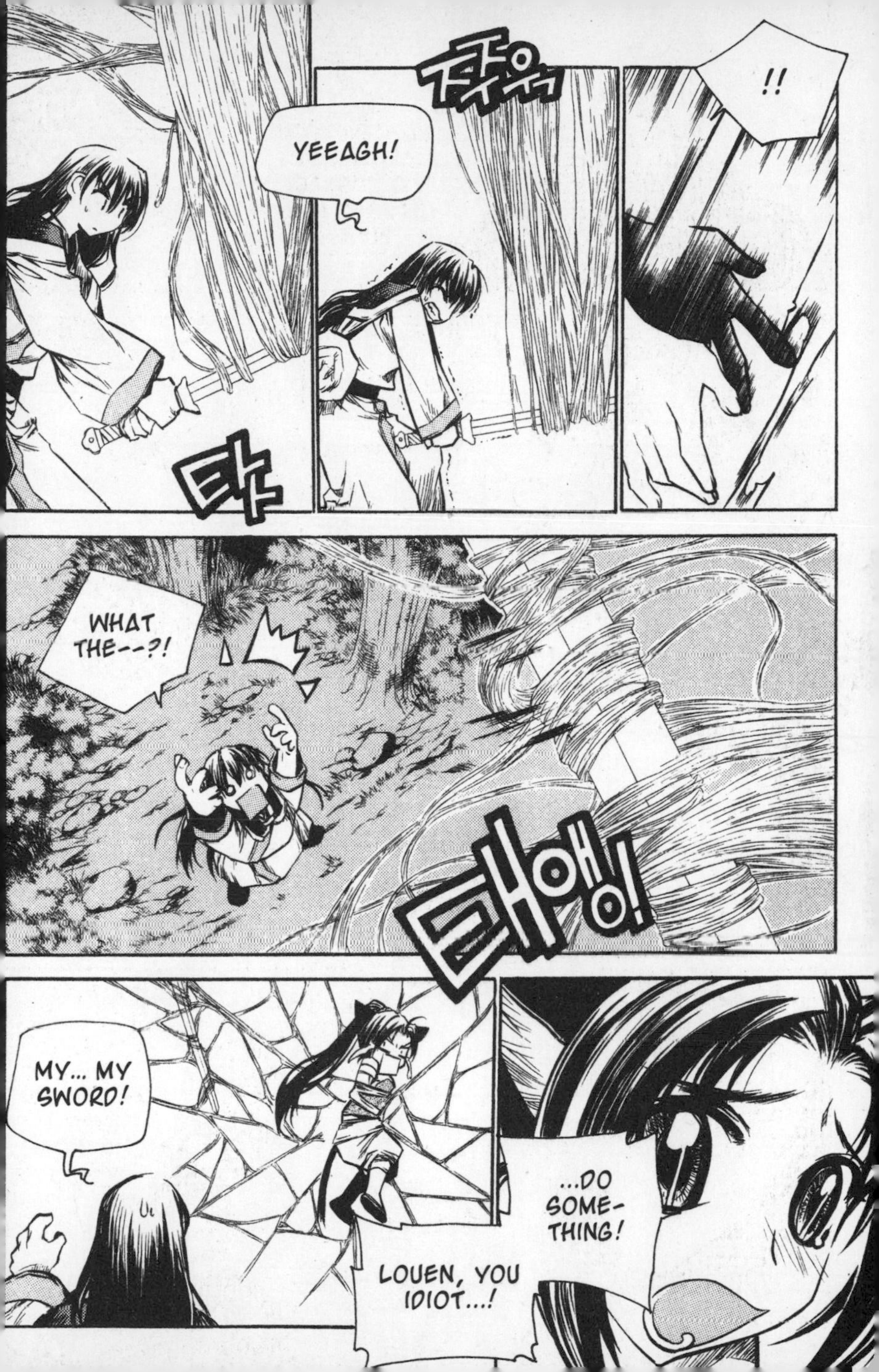
YEEAGH!
!!
WHAT THE--?!
MY... MY SWORD!
LOUEN, YOU IDIOT...!
...DO SOMETHING!

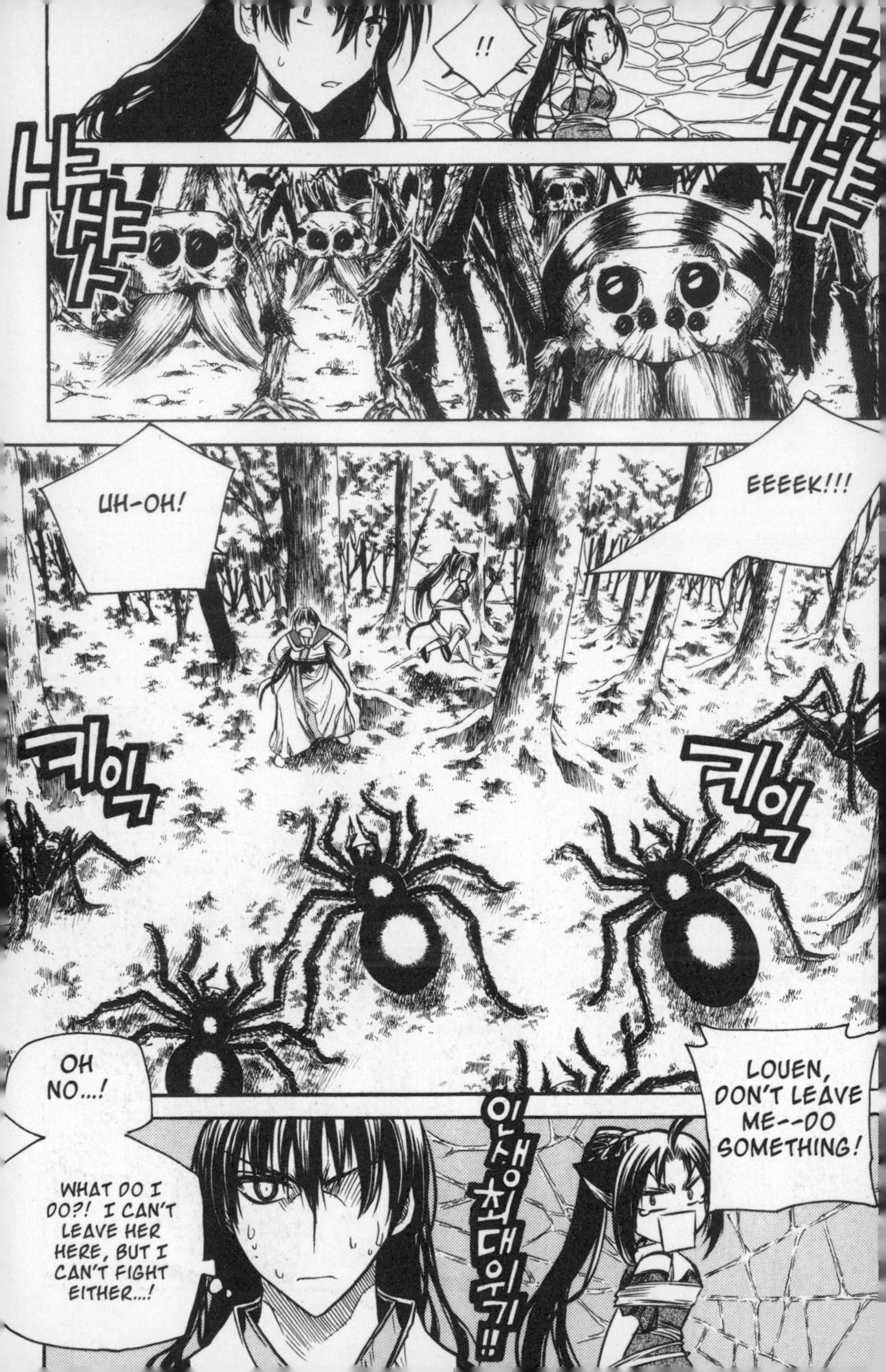
!!
UH-OH!
EEEEK!!!
OH NO...!
WHAT DO I DO?! I CAN'T LEAVE HER HERE, BUT I CAN'T FIGHT EITHER...!
인생최대위기!!
LOUEN, DON'T LEAVE ME--DO SOMETHING!

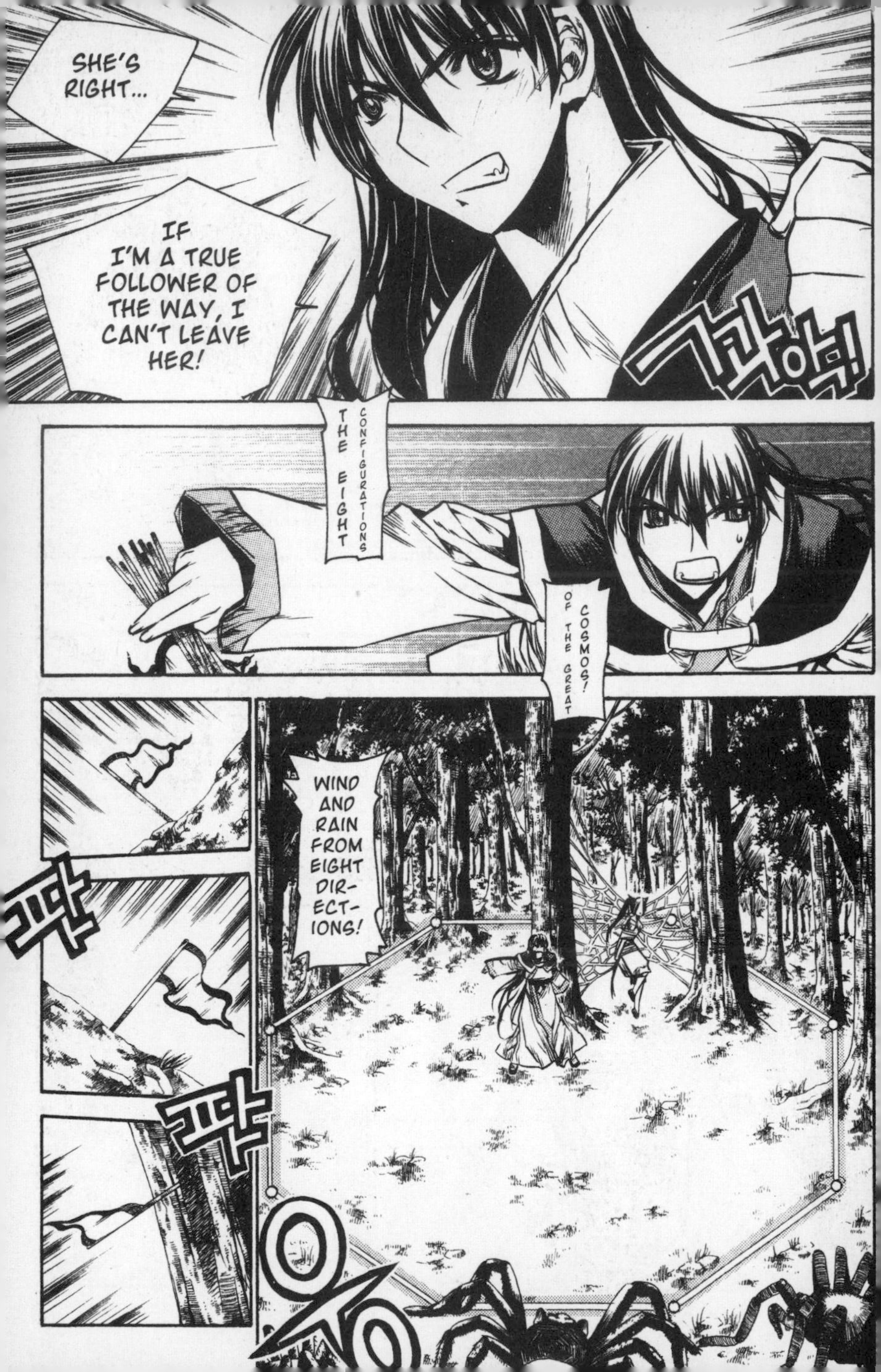
SHE'S RIGHT...
IF I'M A TRUE FOLLOWER OF THE WAY, I CAN'T LEAVE HER!
THE EIGHT CONFIGURATIONS
OF THE GREAT COSMOS!
WIND AND RAIN FROM EIGHT DIR-ECT-IONS!

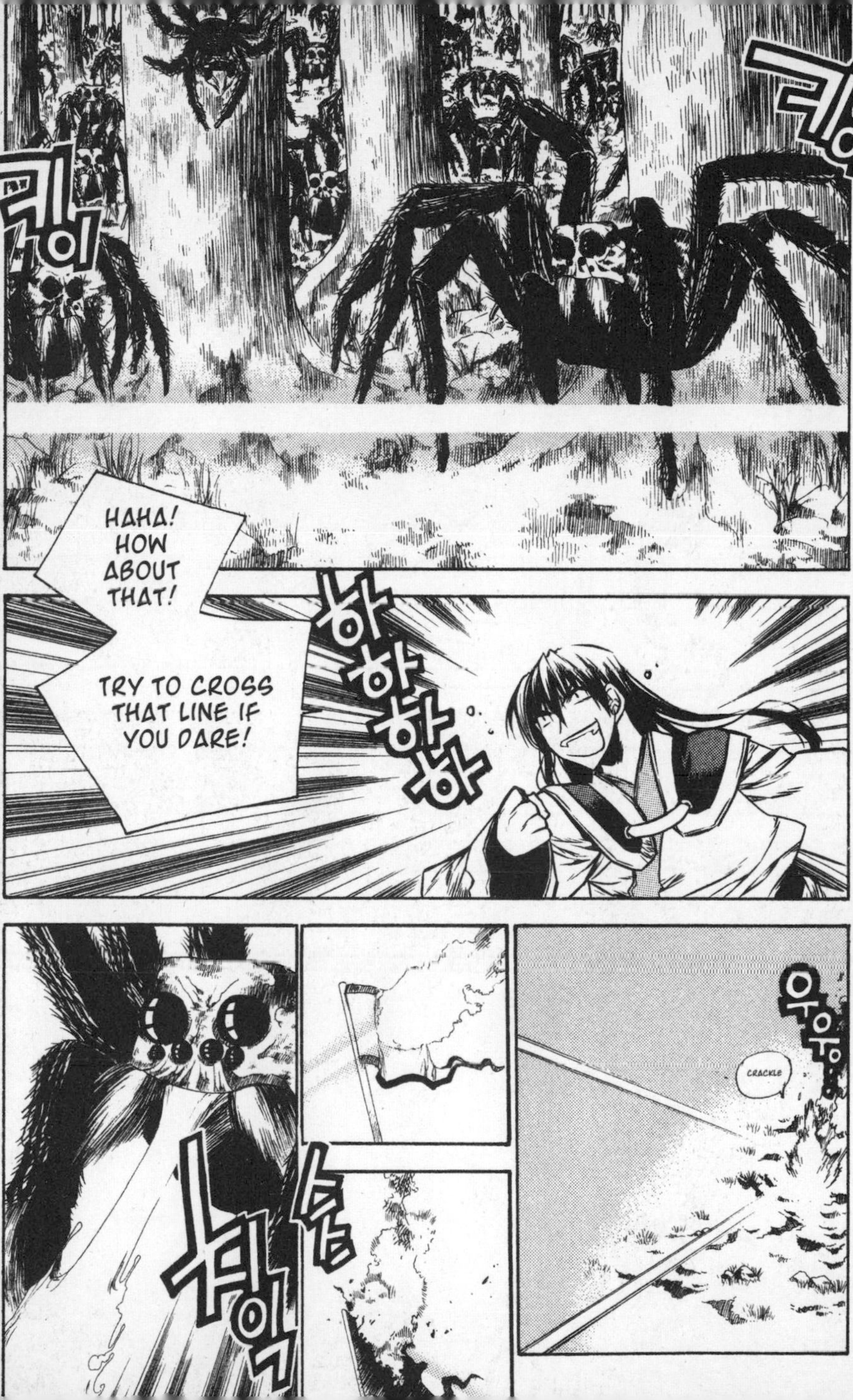
HAHA! HOW ABOUT THAT!
TRY TO CROSS THAT LINE IF YOU DARE!
하하하하
CRACKLE

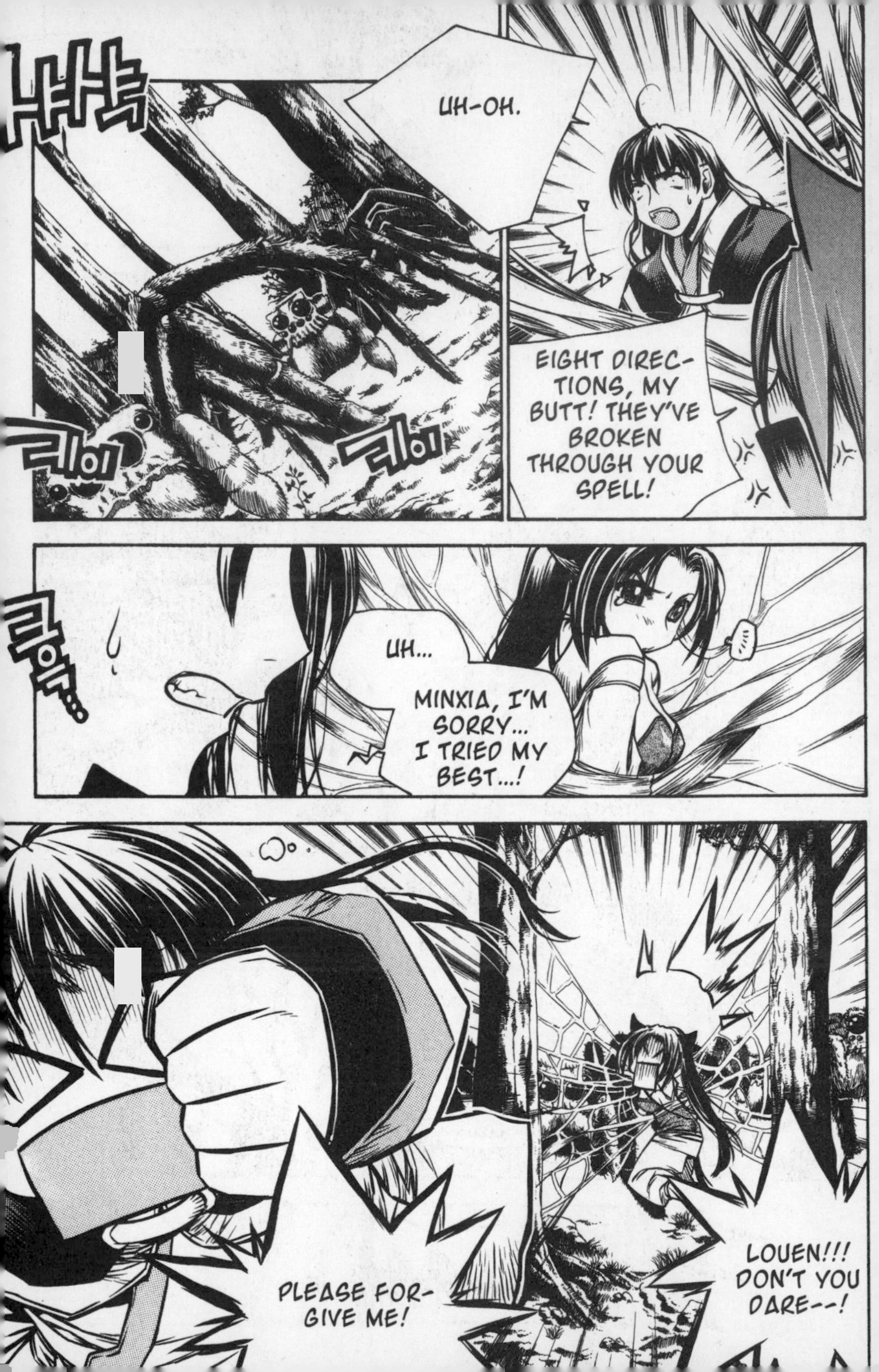
UH-OH.
EIGHT DIREC-TIONS, MY BUTT! THEY'VE BROKEN THROUGH YOUR SPELL!
UH...
MINXIA, I'M SORRY... I TRIED MY BEST...!
PLEASE FOR-GIVE ME!
LOUEN!!! DON'T YOU DARE--!

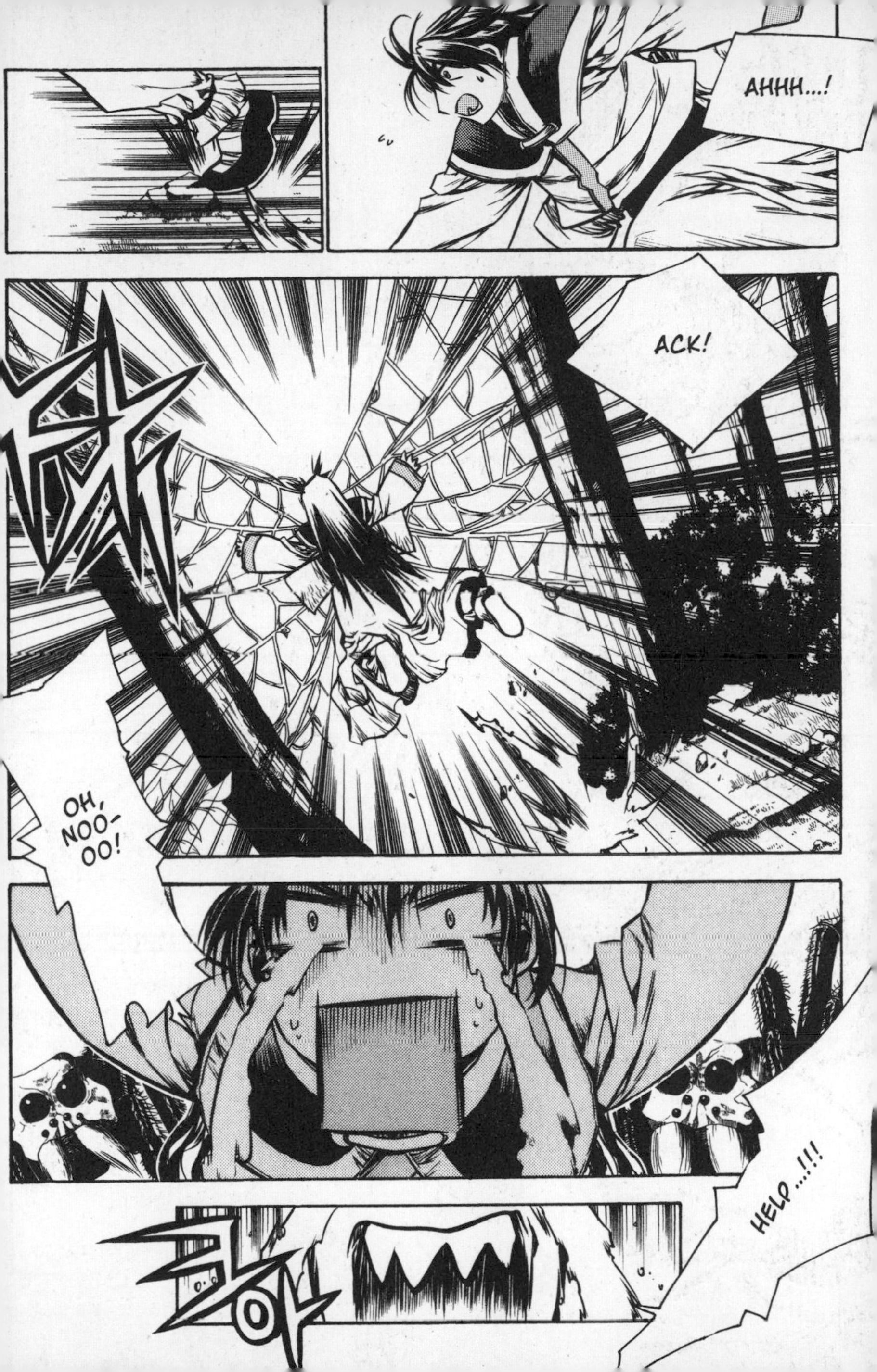
AHHH...!
ACK!
OH, NOO-OO!
HELP...!!!!

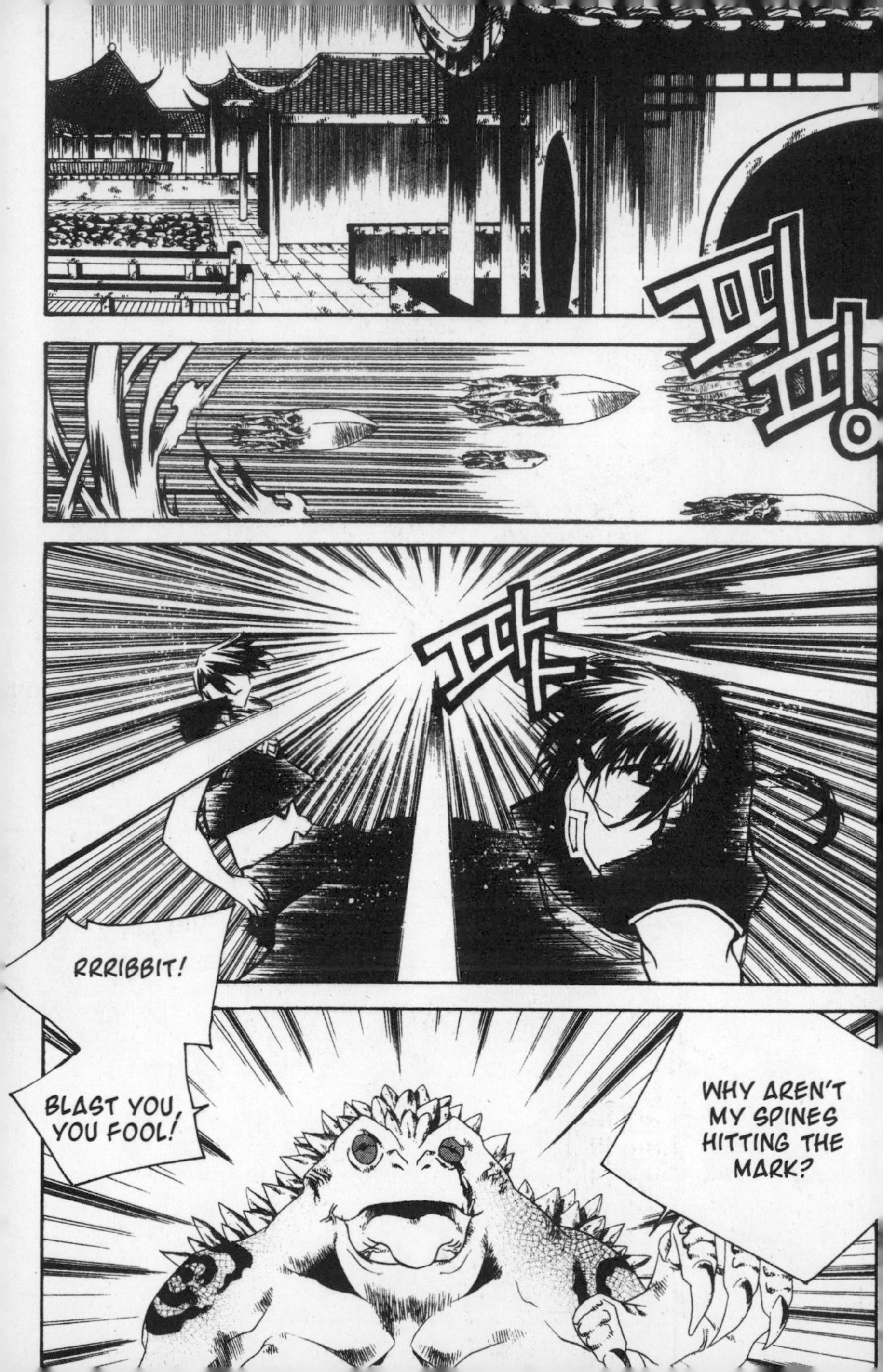
RRRIBBIT!
BLAST YOU, YOU FOOL!
WHY AREN'T MY SPINES HITTING THE MARK?

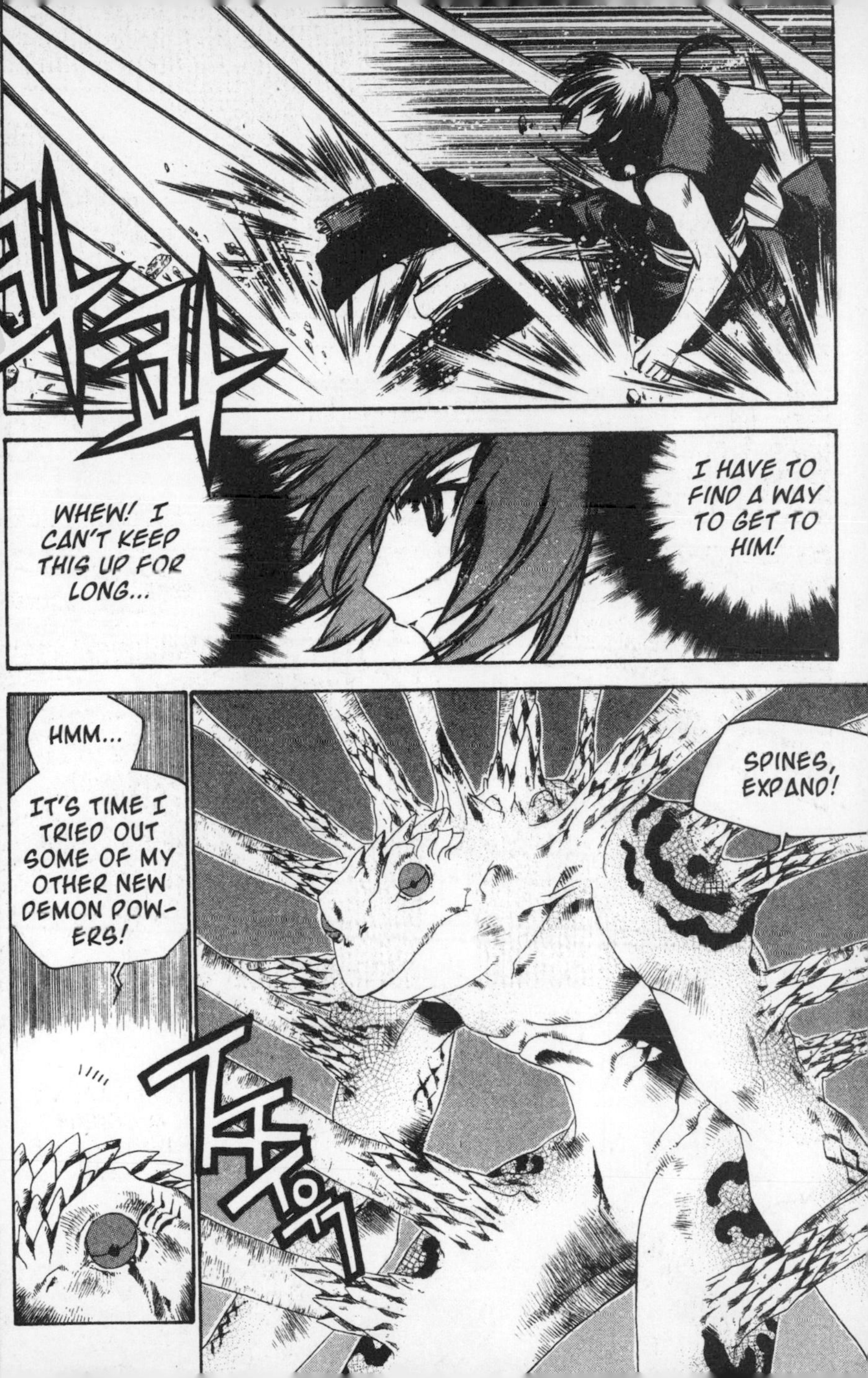
WHEW! I CAN'T KEEP THIS UP FOR LONG...
I HAVE TO FIND A WAY TO GET TO HIM!
HMM...
IT'S TIME I TRIED OUT SOME OF MY OTHER NEW DEMON POWERS!
SPINES, EXPAND!

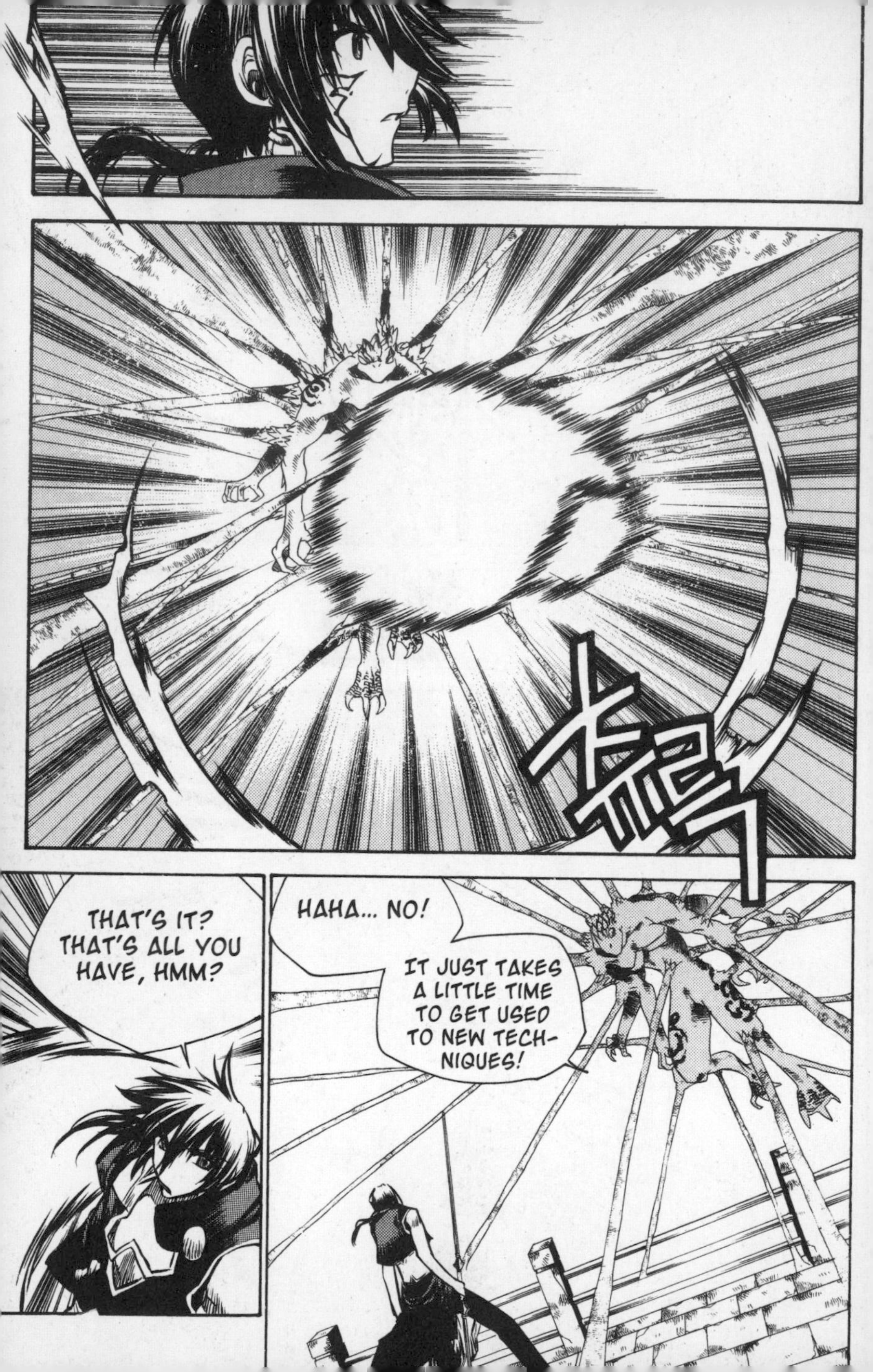
THAT'S IT? THAT'S ALL YOU HAVE, HMM?
HAHA... NO!
IT JUST TAKES A LITTLE TIME TO GET USED TO NEW TECH-NIQUES!

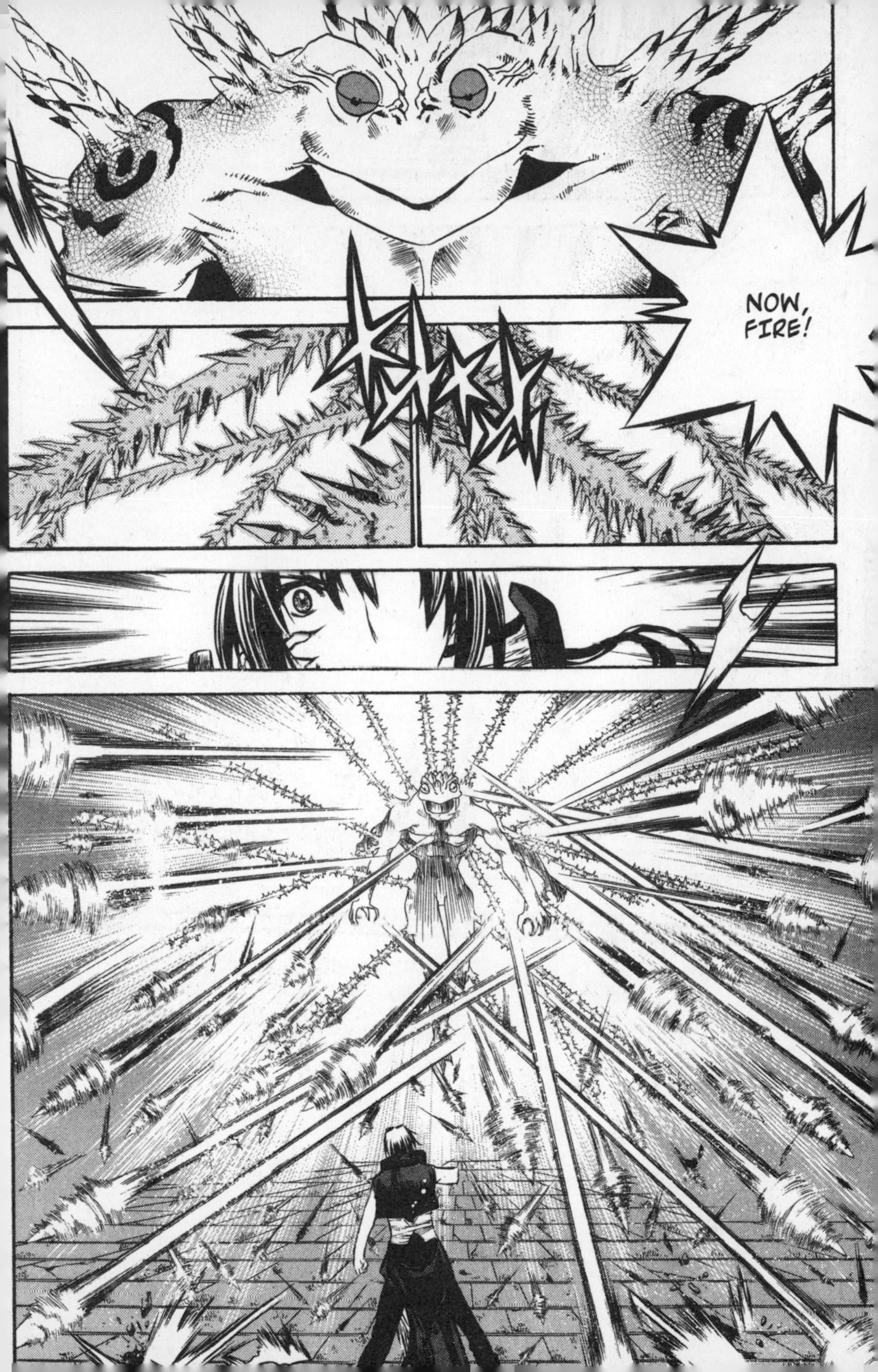
NOW, FIRE!

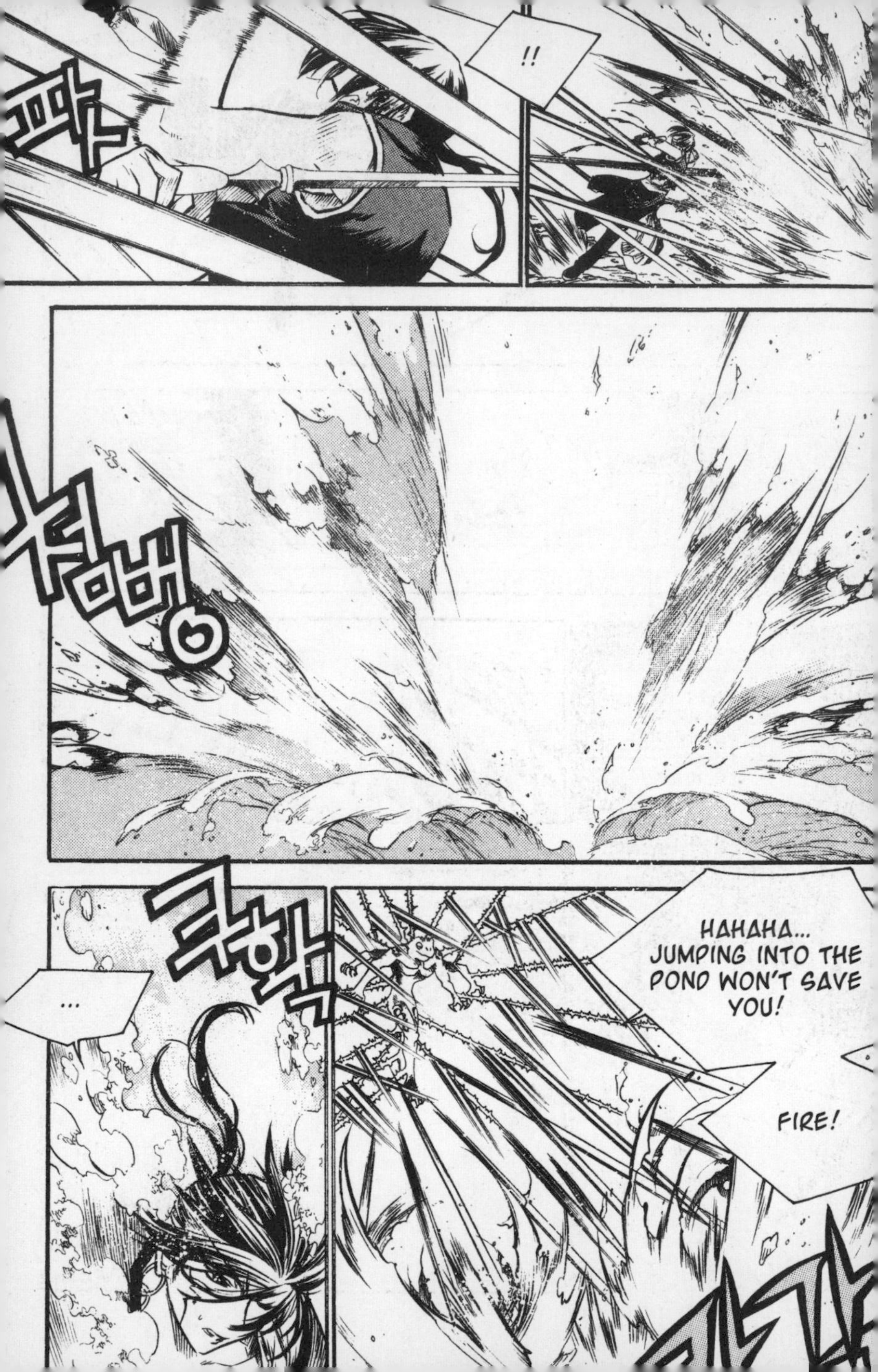
!!
...
HAHAHA... JUMPING INTO THE POND WON'T SAVE YOU!
FIRE!

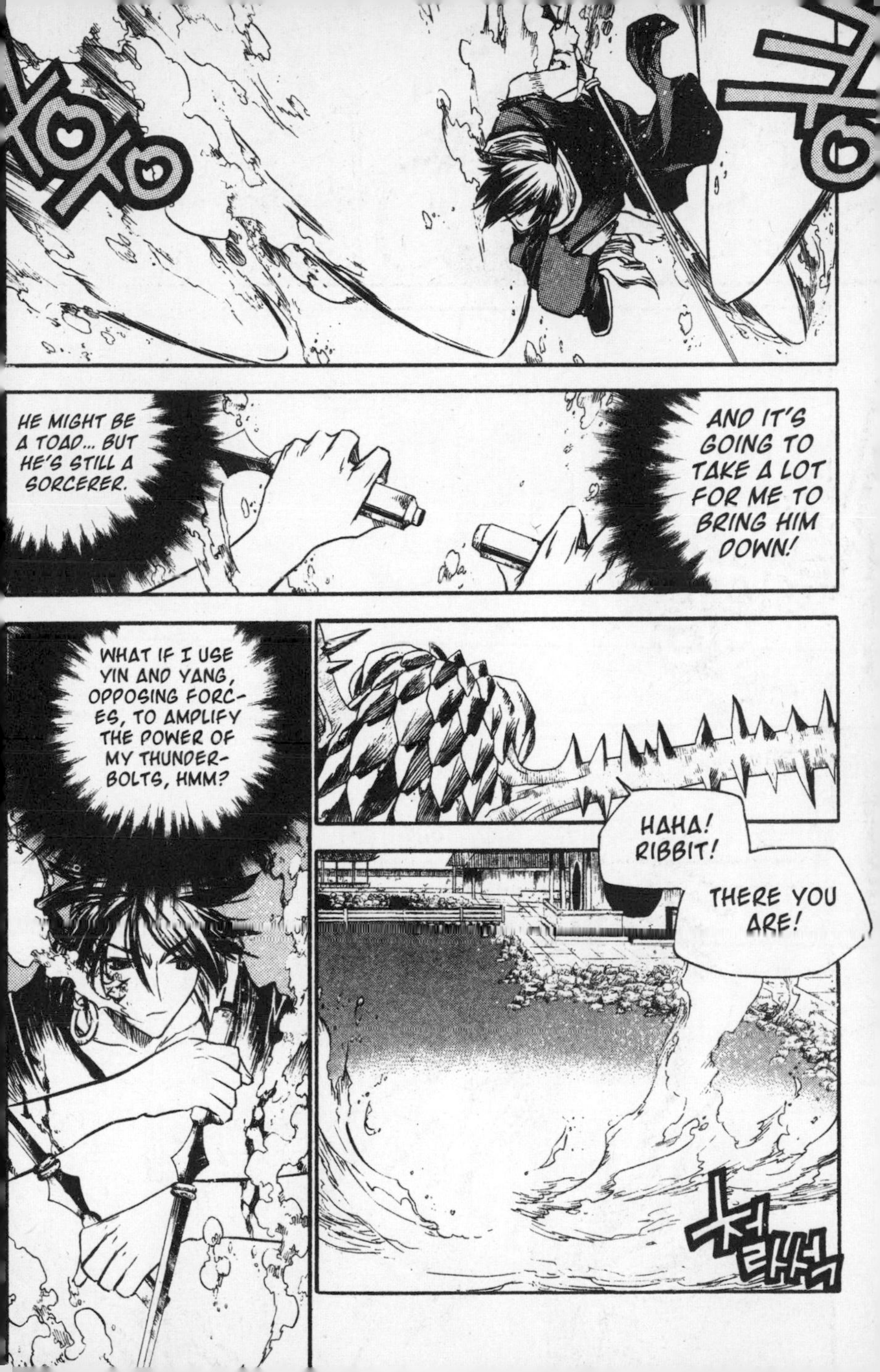
HE MIGHT BE A TOAD... BUT HE'S STILL A SORCERER.
AND IT'S GOING TO TAKE A LOT FOR ME TO BRING HIM DOWN!
WHAT IF I USE YIN AND YANG, OPPOSING FORCES, TO AMPLIFY THE POWER OF MY THUNDERBOLTS, HMM?
HAHA! RIBBIT!
THERE YOU ARE!

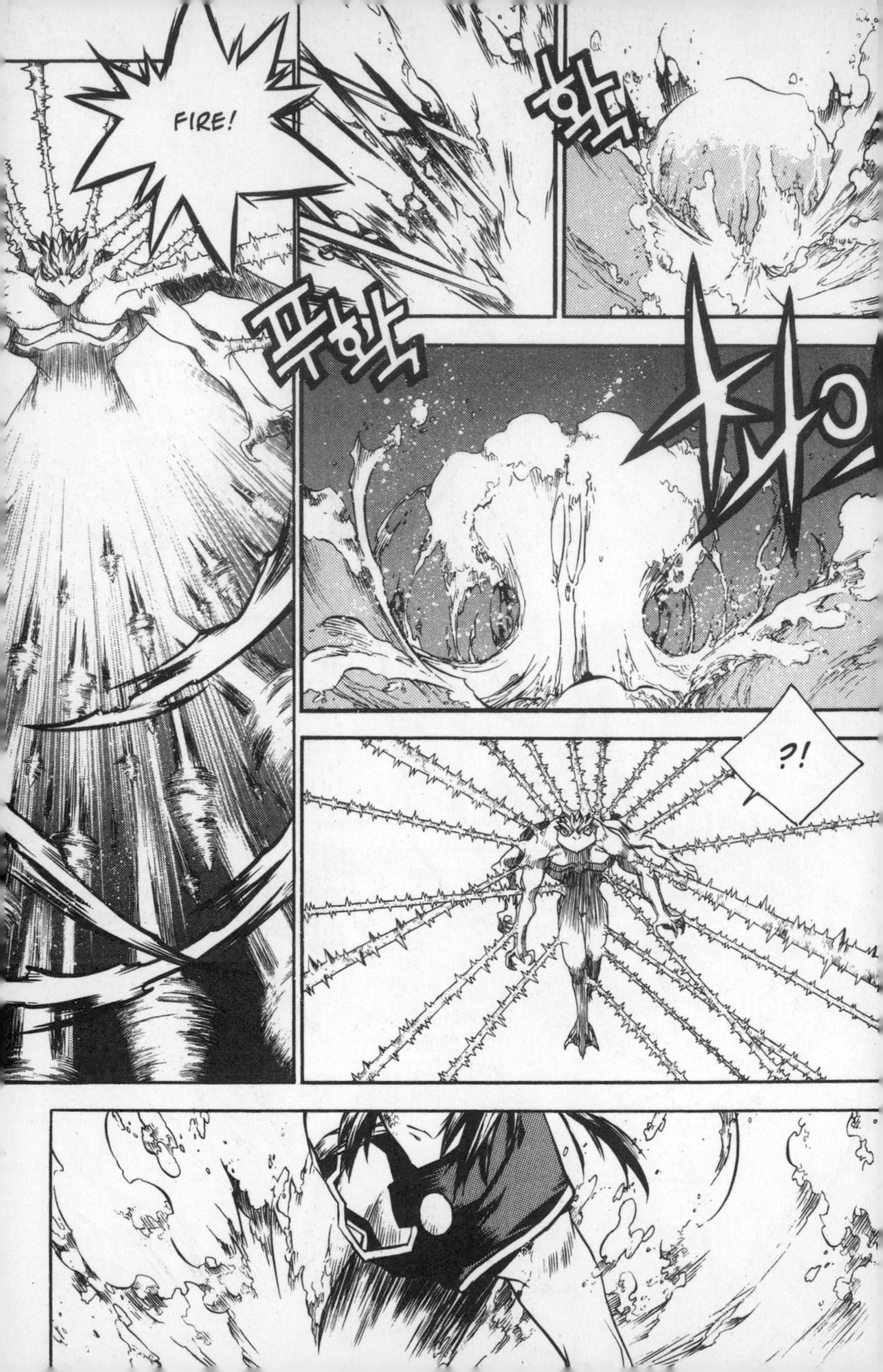
FIRE!
확
푸확
?!

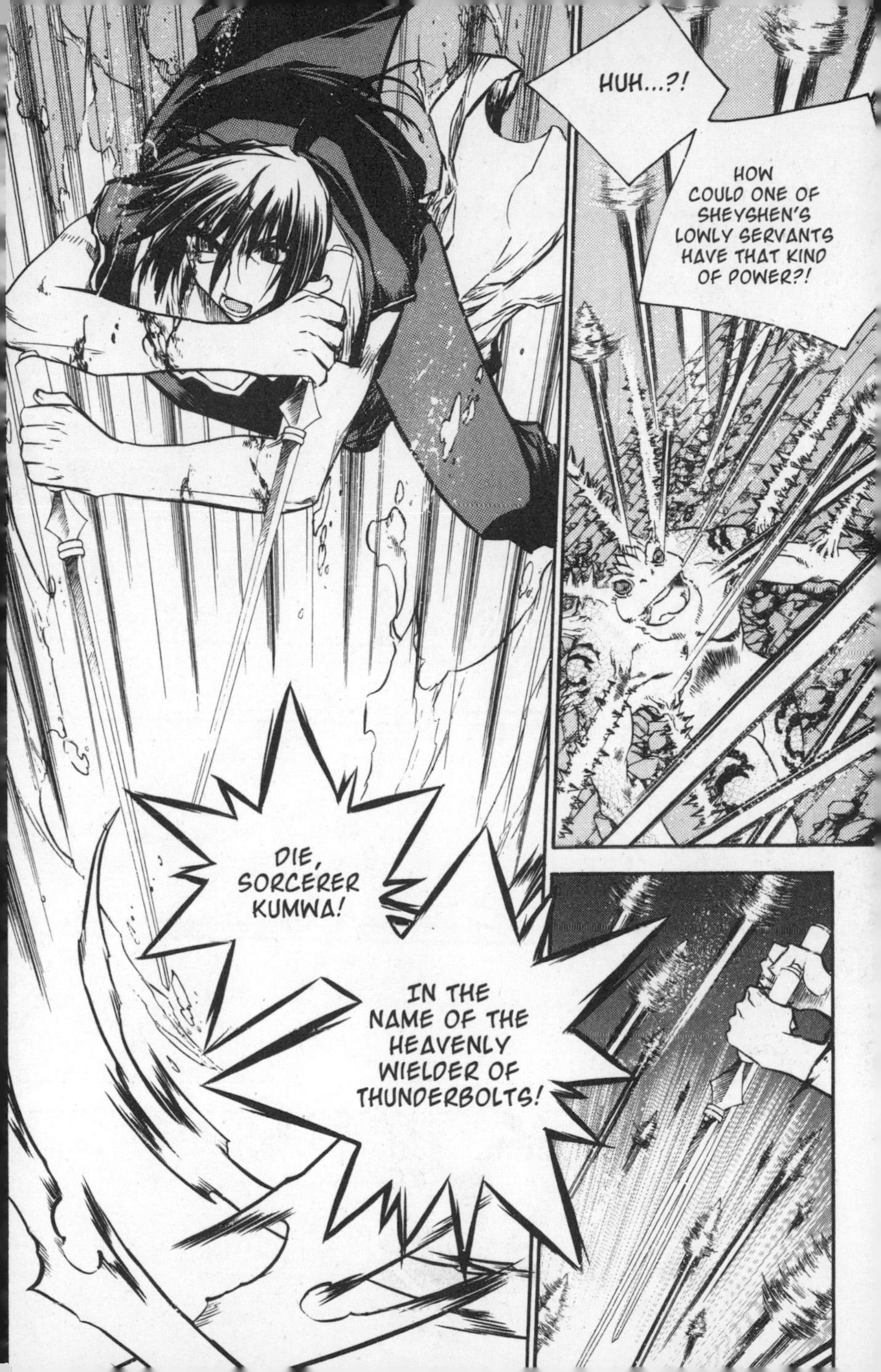
DIE, SORCERER KUMWA!
IN THE NAME OF THE HEAVENLY WIELDER OF THUNDERBOLTS!
HUH...?!
HOW COULD ONE OF SHEYSHEN'S LOWLY SERVANTS HAVE THAT KIND OF POWER?!

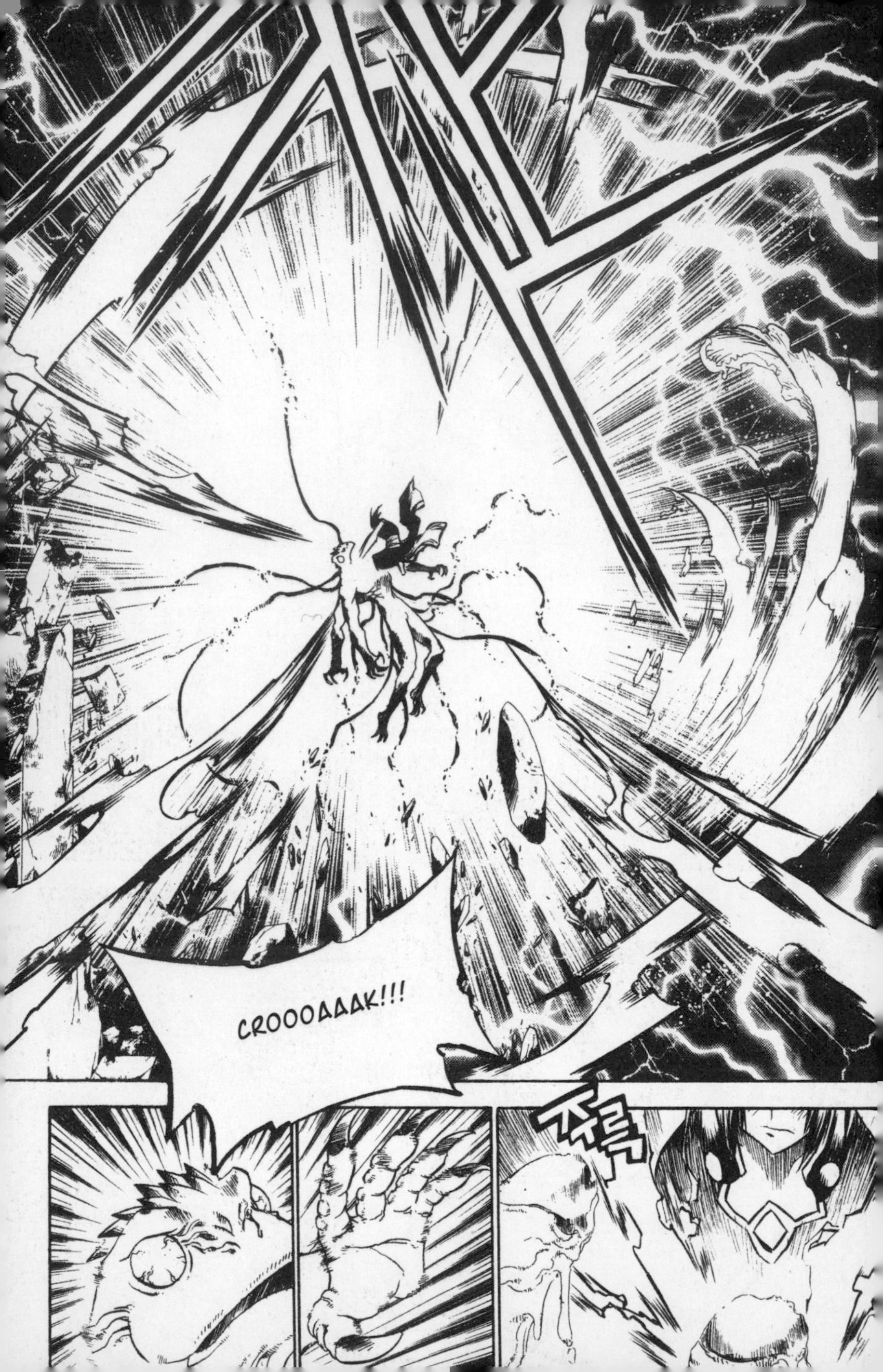
CROOOAAAK!!!

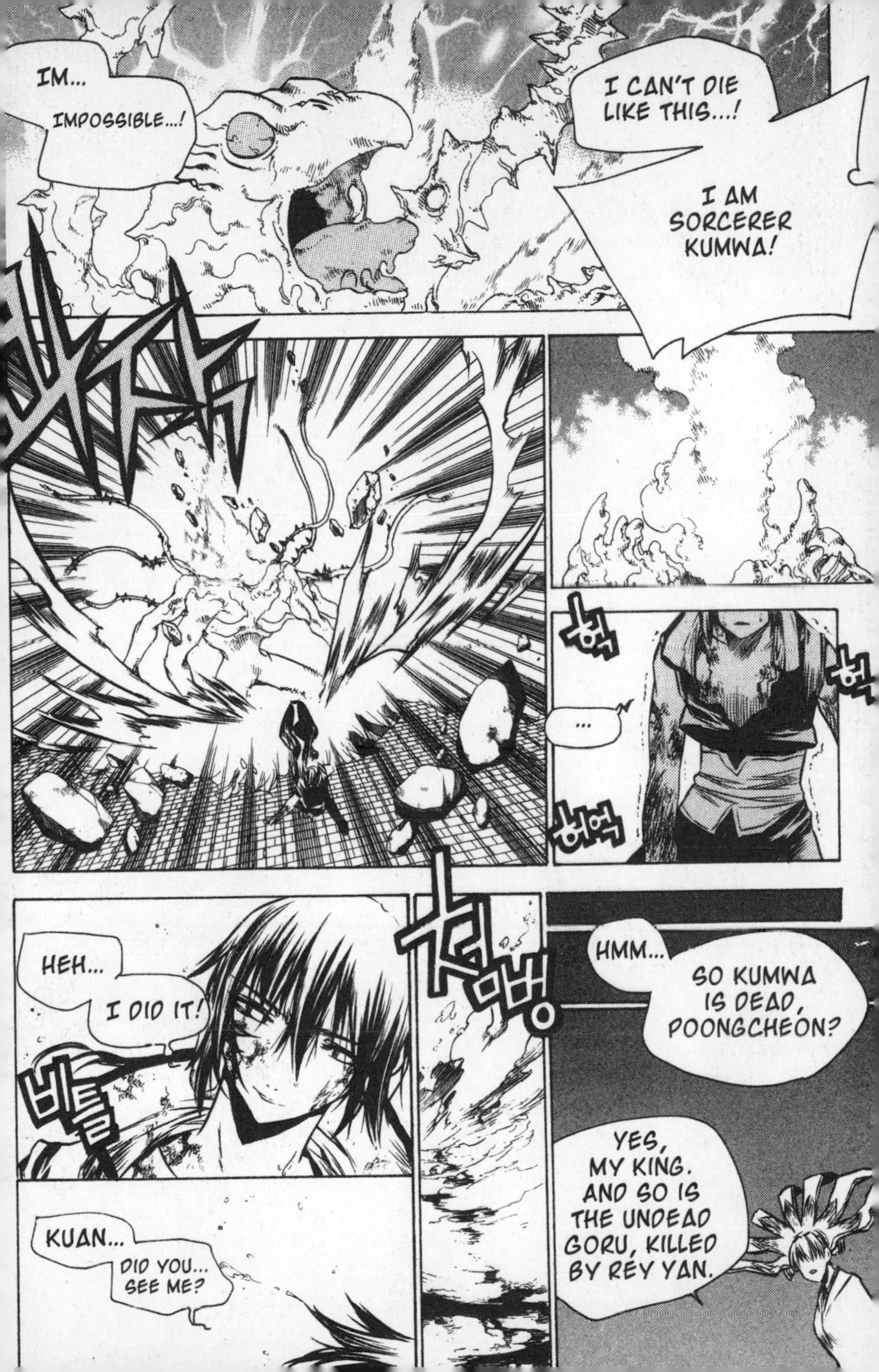

IM...
IMPOSSIBLE...!
I CAN'T DIE LIKE THIS...!
I AM SORCERER KUMWA!
...
HEH...
I DID IT!
KUAN...
DID YOU... SEE ME?
HMM...
SO KUMWA IS DEAD, POONGCHEON?
YES, MY KING. AND SO IS THE UNDEAD GORU, KILLED BY REY YAN.

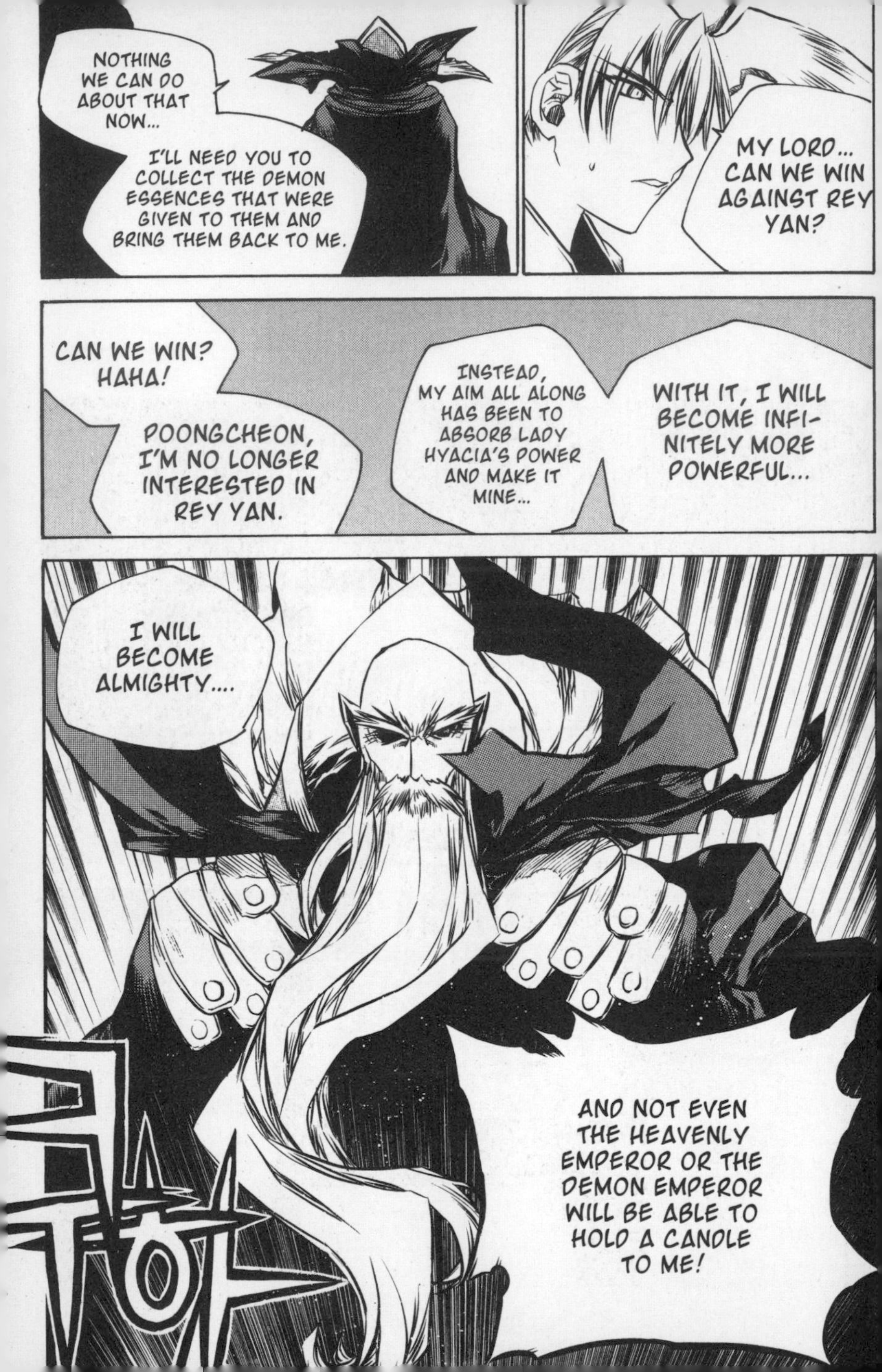
NOTHING WE CAN DO ABOUT THAT NOW...
I'LL NEED YOU TO COLLECT THE DEMON ESSENCES THAT WERE GIVEN TO THEM AND BRING THEM BACK TO ME.
MY LORD... CAN WE WIN AGAINST REY YAN?
CAN WE WIN? HAHA!
POONGCHEON, I'M NO LONGER INTERESTED IN REY YAN.
INSTEAD, MY AIM ALL ALONG HAS BEEN TO ABSORB LADY HYACIA'S POWER AND MAKE IT MINE...
WITH IT, I WILL BECOME INFI-NITELY MORE POWERFUL...
I WILL BECOME ALMIGHTY....
AND NOT EVEN THE HEAVENLY EMPEROR OR THE DEMON EMPEROR WILL BE ABLE TO HOLD A CANDLE TO ME!

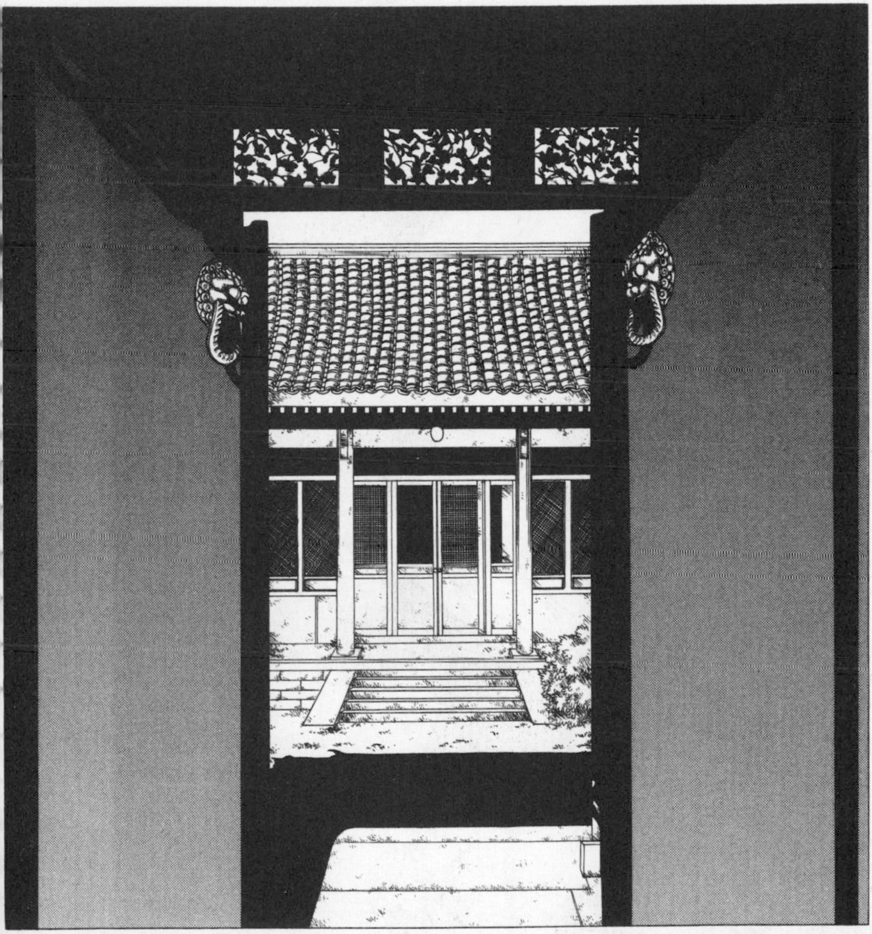

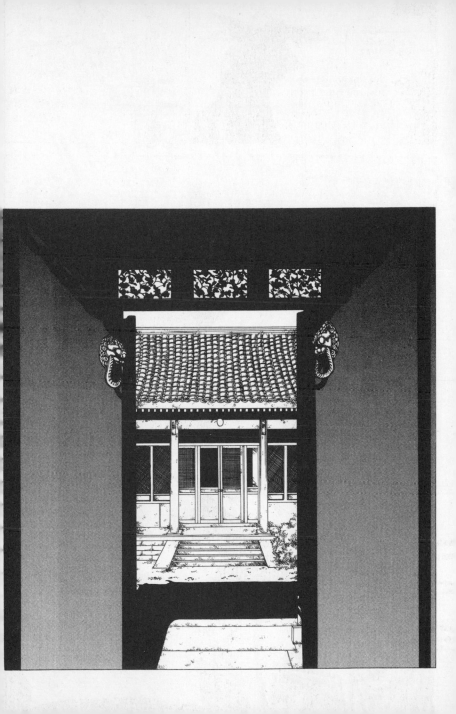

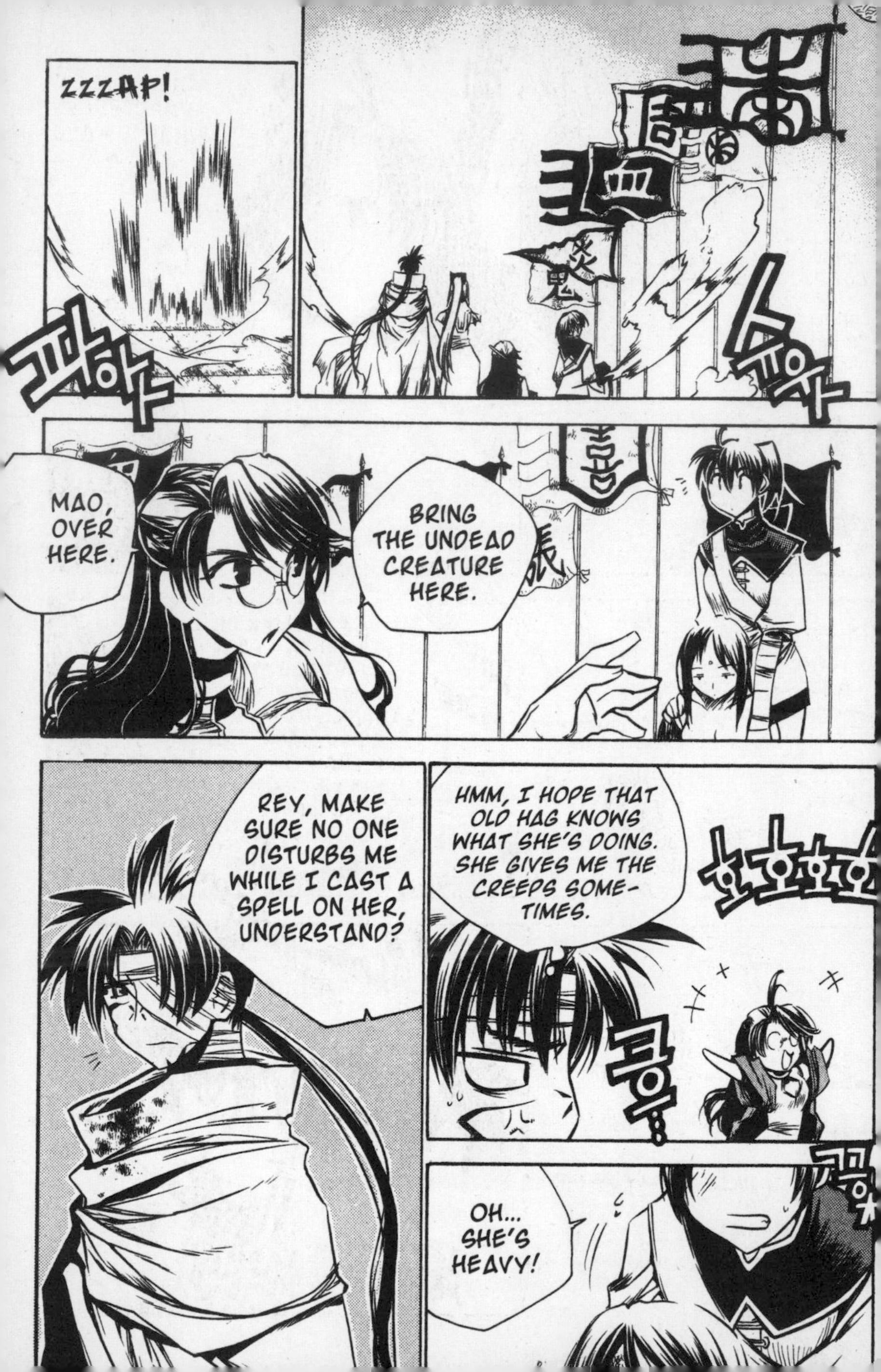
ZZZAP!
MAO, OVER HERE.
BRING THE UNDEAD CREATURE HERE.
REY, MAKE SURE NO ONE DISTURBS ME WHILE I CAST A SPELL ON HER, UNDERSTAND?
HMM, I HOPE THAT OLD HAG KNOWS WHAT SHE'S DOING. SHE GIVES ME THE CREEPS SOME-TIMES.
OH... SHE'S HEAVY!

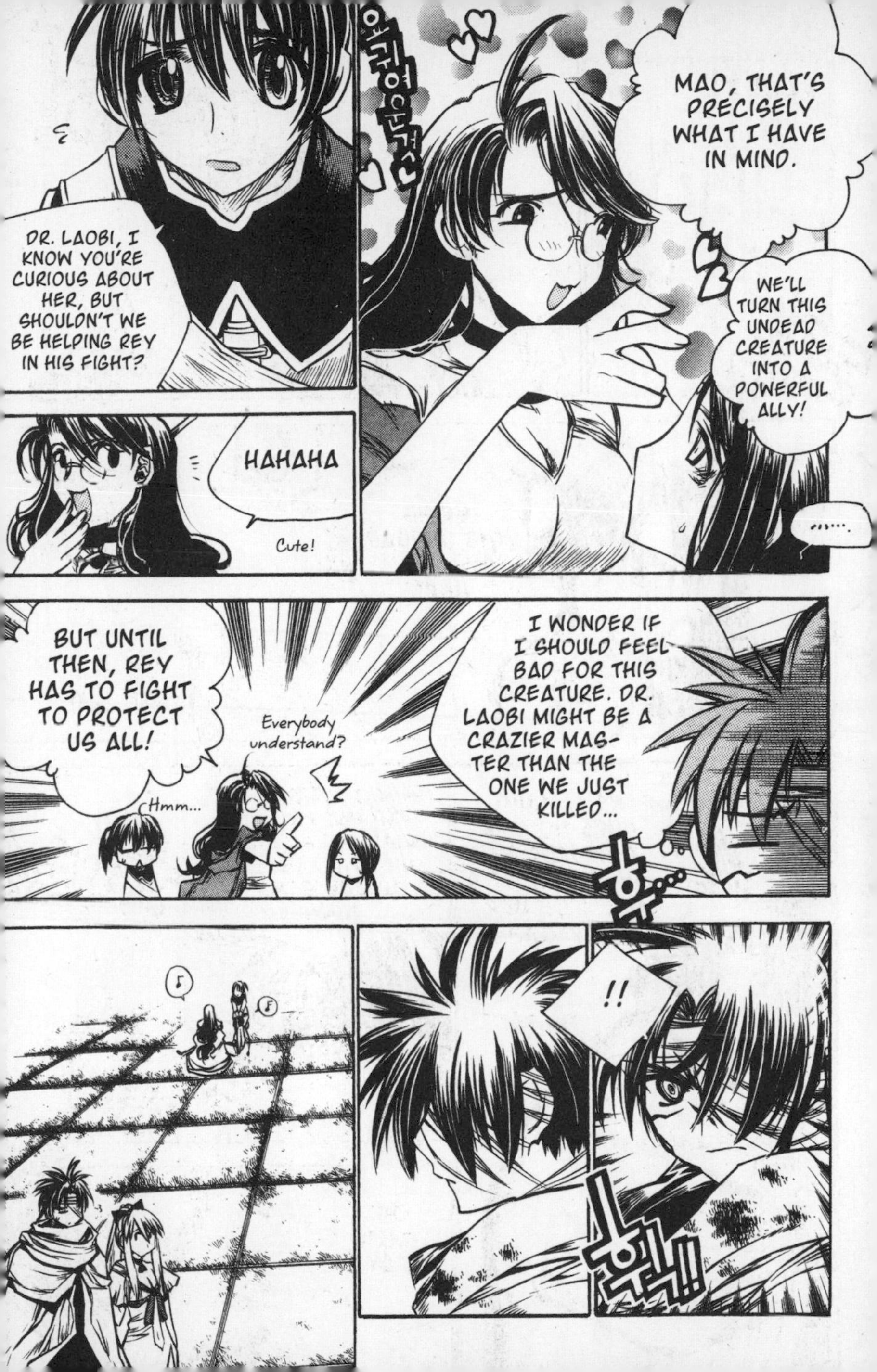
DR. LAOBI, I KNOW YOU'RE CURIOUS ABOUT HER, BUT SHOULDN'T WE BE HELPING REY IN HIS FIGHT?
HAHAHA
Cute!
MAO, THAT'S PRECISELY WHAT I HAVE IN MIND.
WE'LL TURN THIS UNDEAD CREATURE INTO A POWERFUL ALLY!
......
BUT UNTIL THEN, REY HAS TO FIGHT TO PROTECT US ALL!
Everybody understand?
Hmm...
I WONDER IF I SHOULD FEEL BAD FOR THIS CREATURE. DR. LAOBI MIGHT BE A CRAZIER MASTER THAN THE ONE WE JUST KILLED...
!!
헉!!

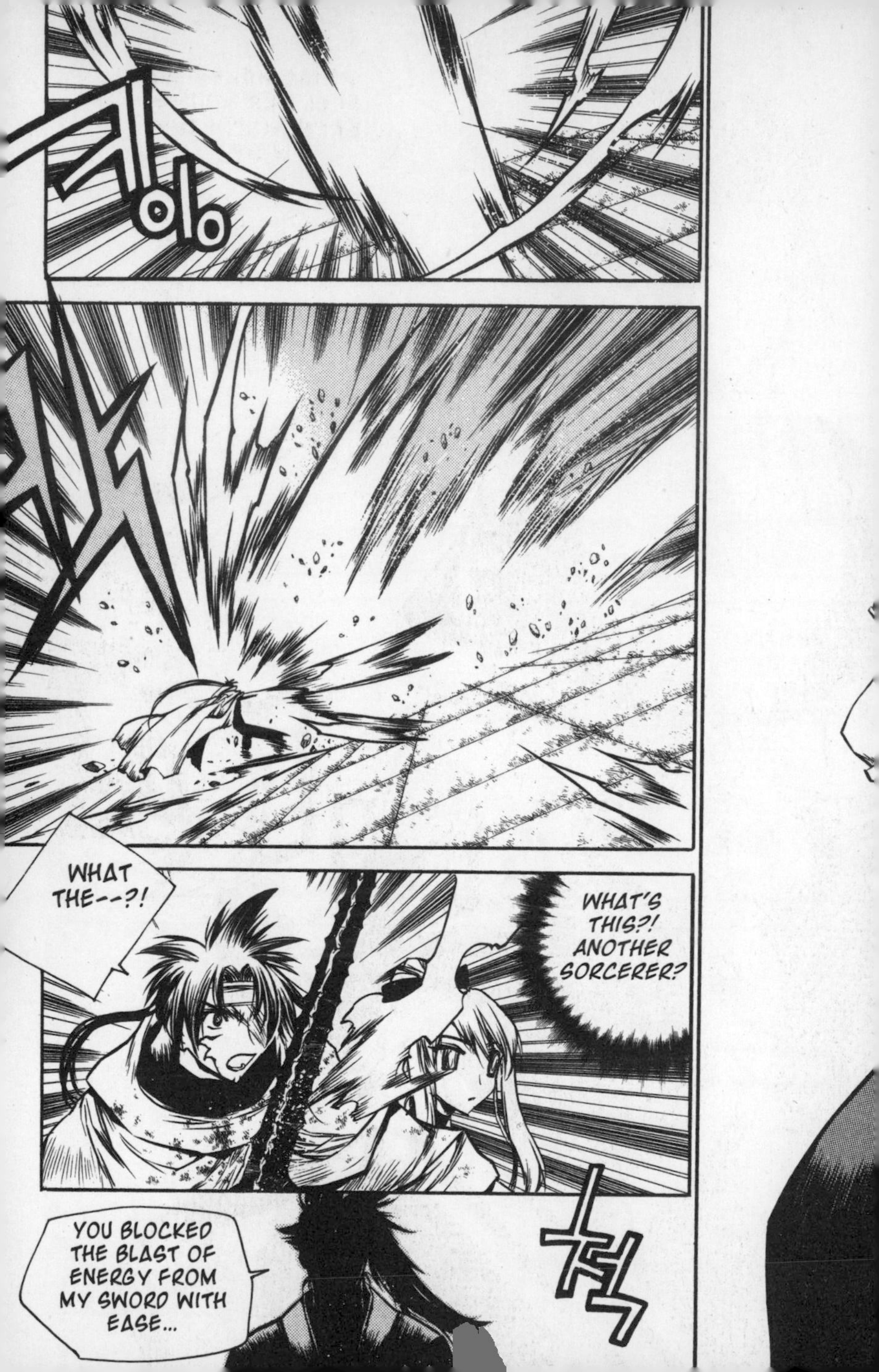
WHAT THE--?!
WHAT'S THIS?! ANOTHER SORCERER?
YOU BLOCKED THE BLAST OF ENERGY FROM MY SWORD WITH EASE...

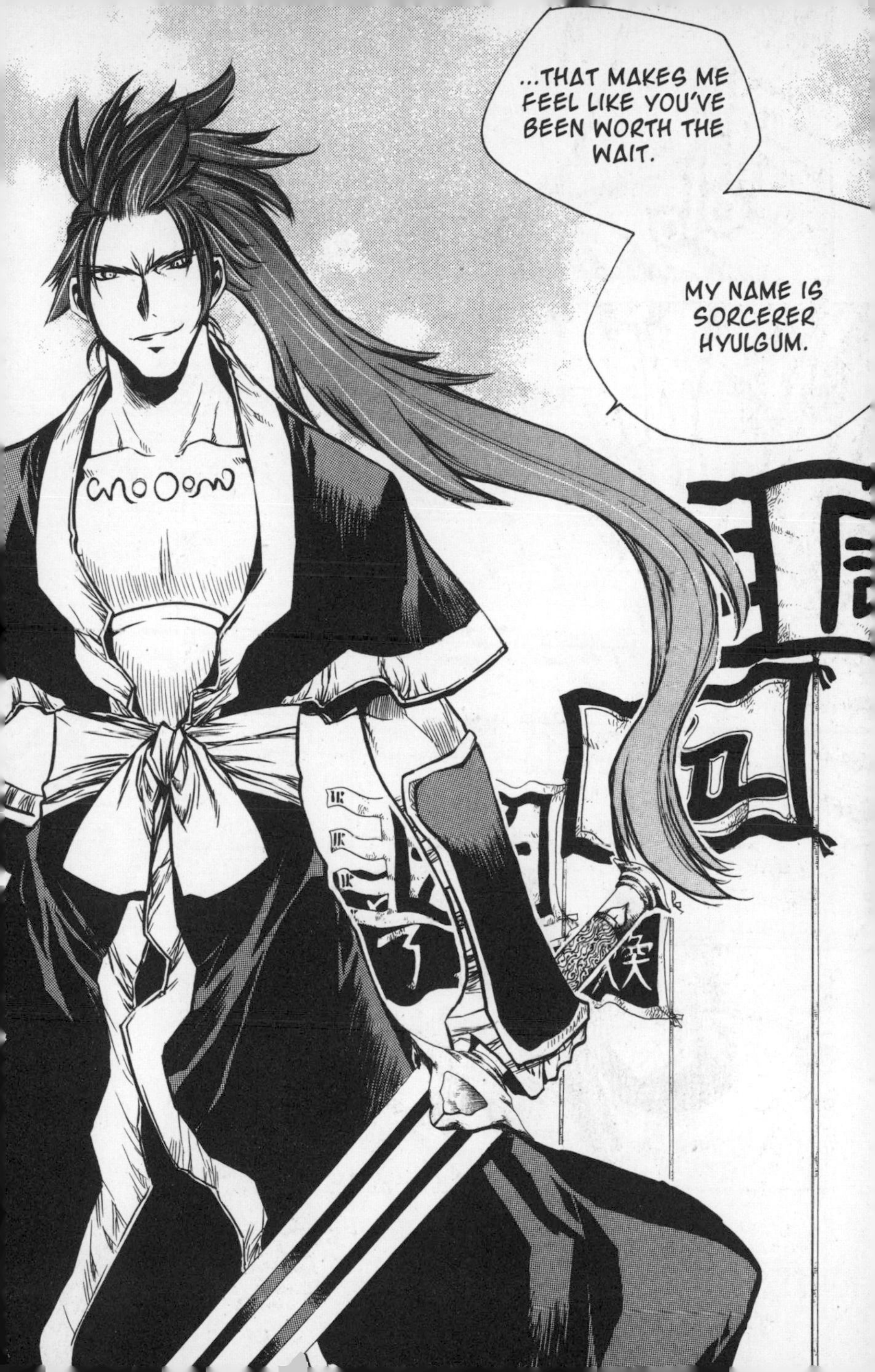
...THAT MAKES ME FEEL LIKE YOU'VE BEEN WORTH THE WAIT.
MY NAME IS SORCERER HYULGUM.

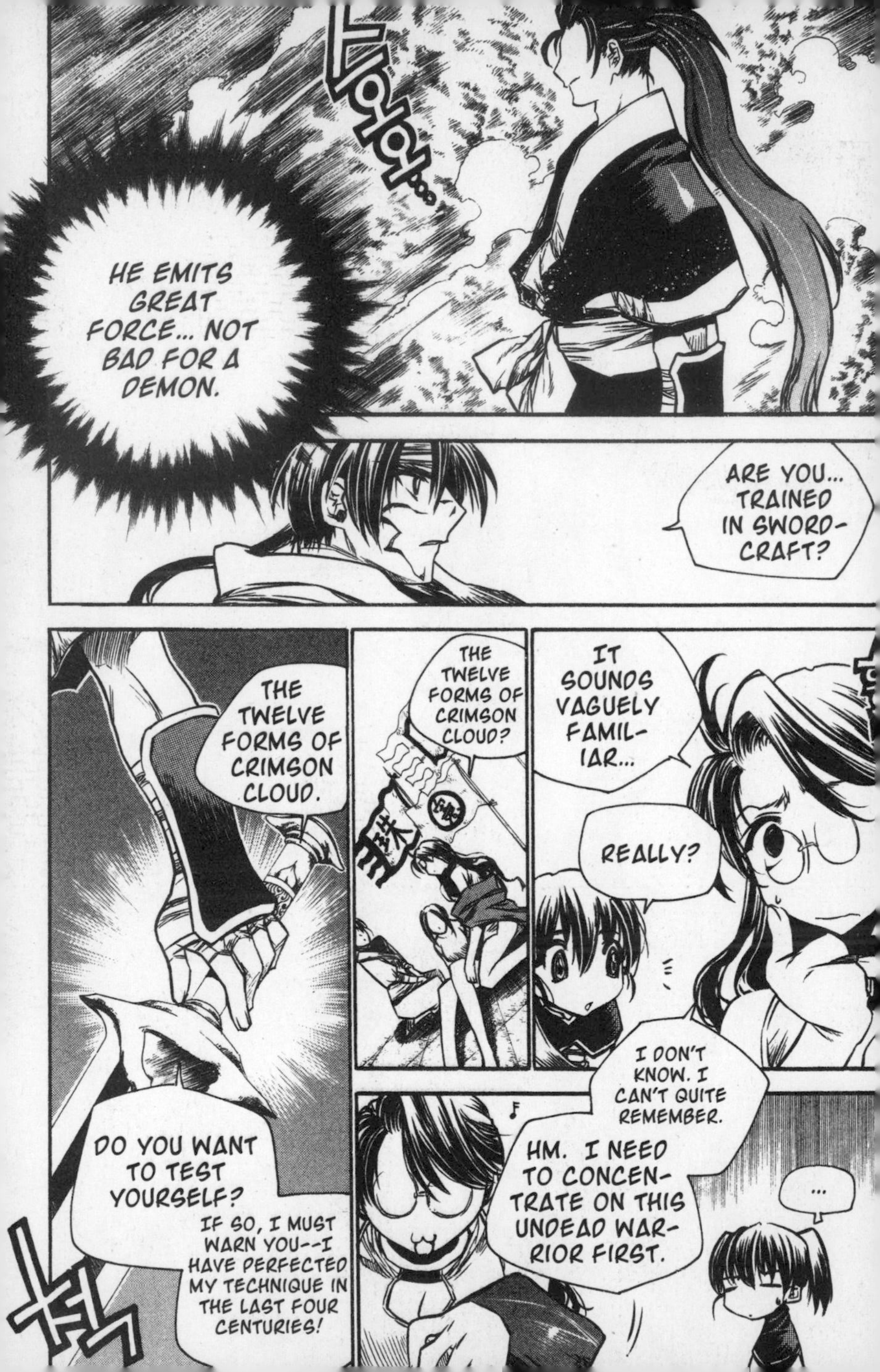
HE EMITS GREAT FORCE... NOT BAD FOR A DEMON.
ARE YOU... TRAINED IN SWORD-CRAFT?
THE TWELVE FORMS OF CRIMSON CLOUD.
DO YOU WANT TO TEST YOURSELF?
IF SO, I MUST WARN YOU--I HAVE PERFECTED MY TECHNIQUE IN THE LAST FOUR CENTURIES!
THE TWELVE FORMS OF CRIMSON CLOUD?
IT SOUNDS VAGUELY FAMILIAR...
REALLY?
I DON'T KNOW. I CAN'T QUITE REMEMBER.
HM. I NEED TO CONCENTRATE ON THIS UNDEAD WARRIOR FIRST.
...

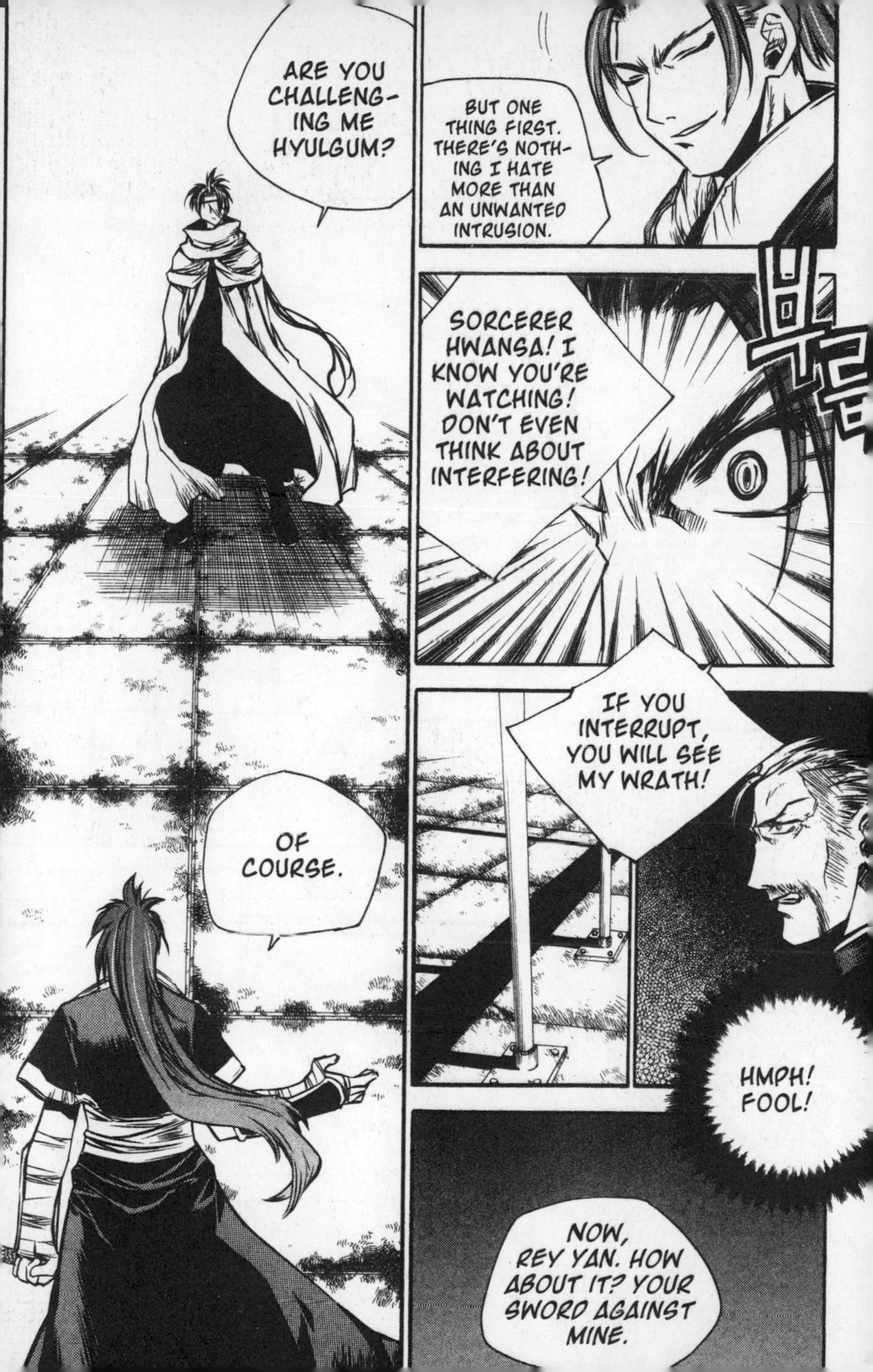
ARE YOU CHALLENG-ING ME HYULGUM?
OF COURSE.
BUT ONE THING FIRST. THERE'S NOTH-ING I HATE MORE THAN AN UNWANTED INTRUSION.
SORCERER HWANSA! I KNOW YOU'RE WATCHING! DON'T EVEN THINK ABOUT INTERFERING!
IF YOU INTERRUPT, YOU WILL SEE MY WRATH!
HMPH! FOOL!
NOW, REY YAN. HOW ABOUT IT? YOUR SWORD AGAINST MINE.

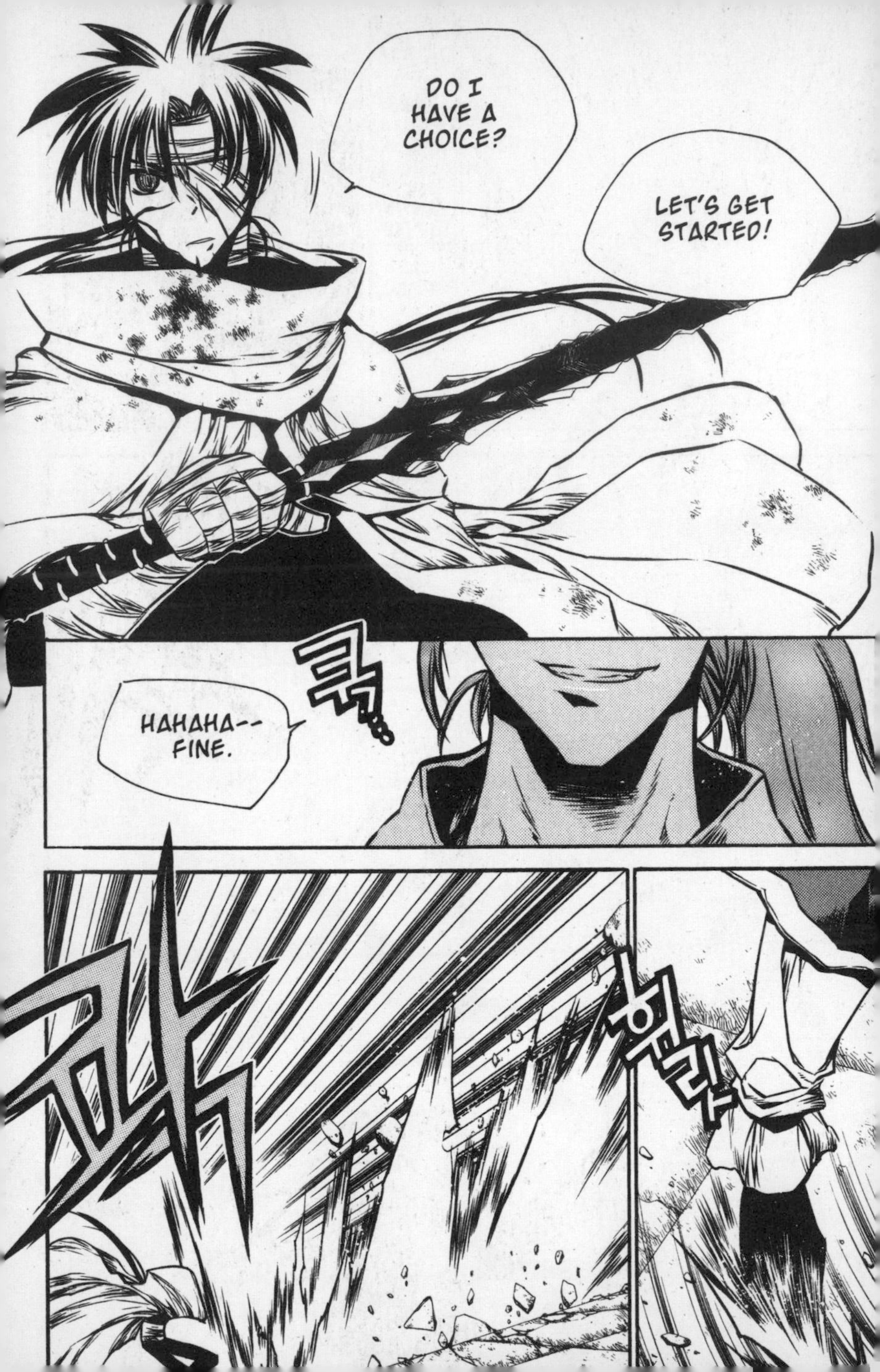
DO I HAVE A CHOICE?
LET'S GET STARTED!
HAHAHA--FINE.

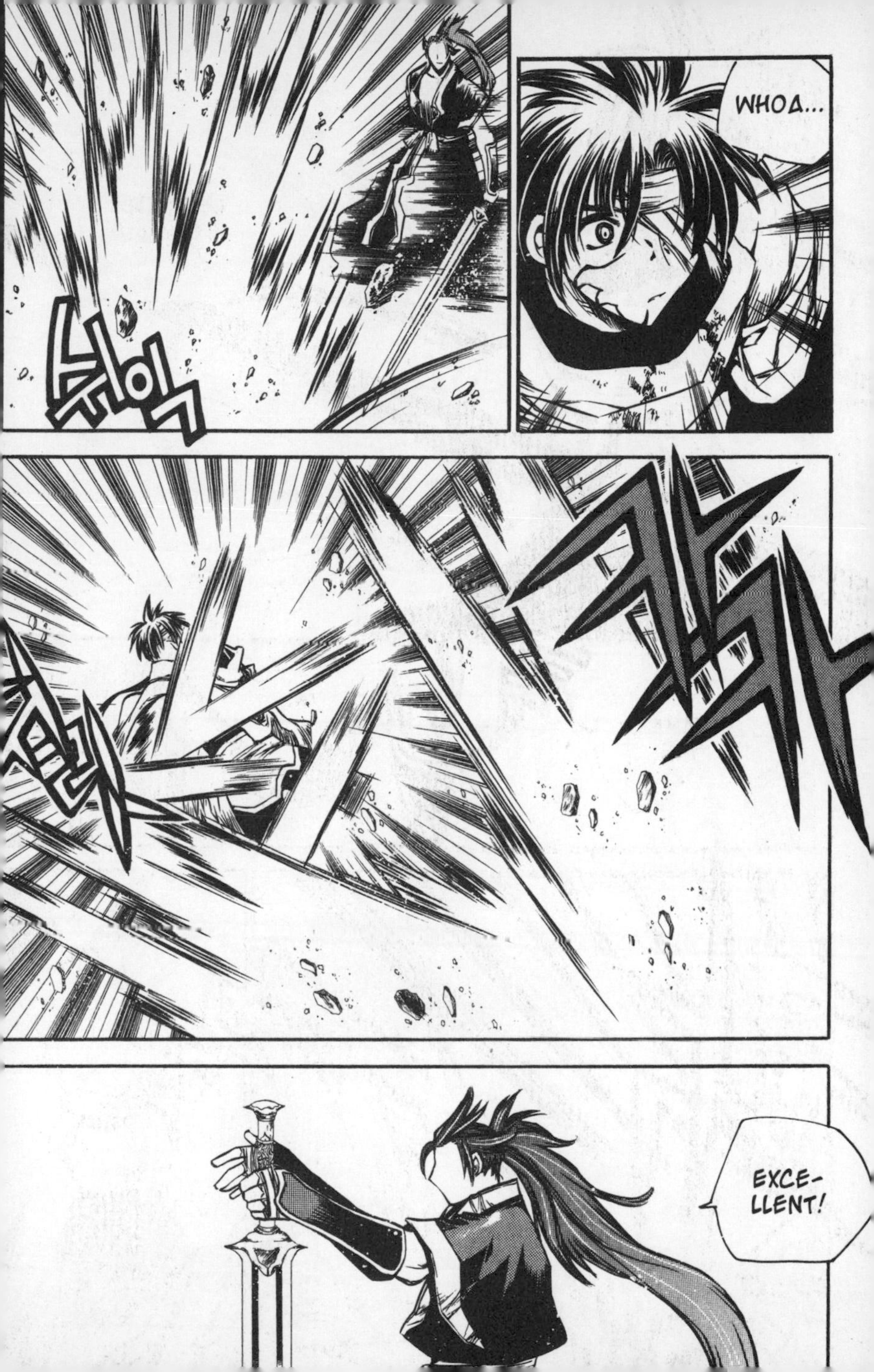
WHOA...
EXCE-
LLENT!

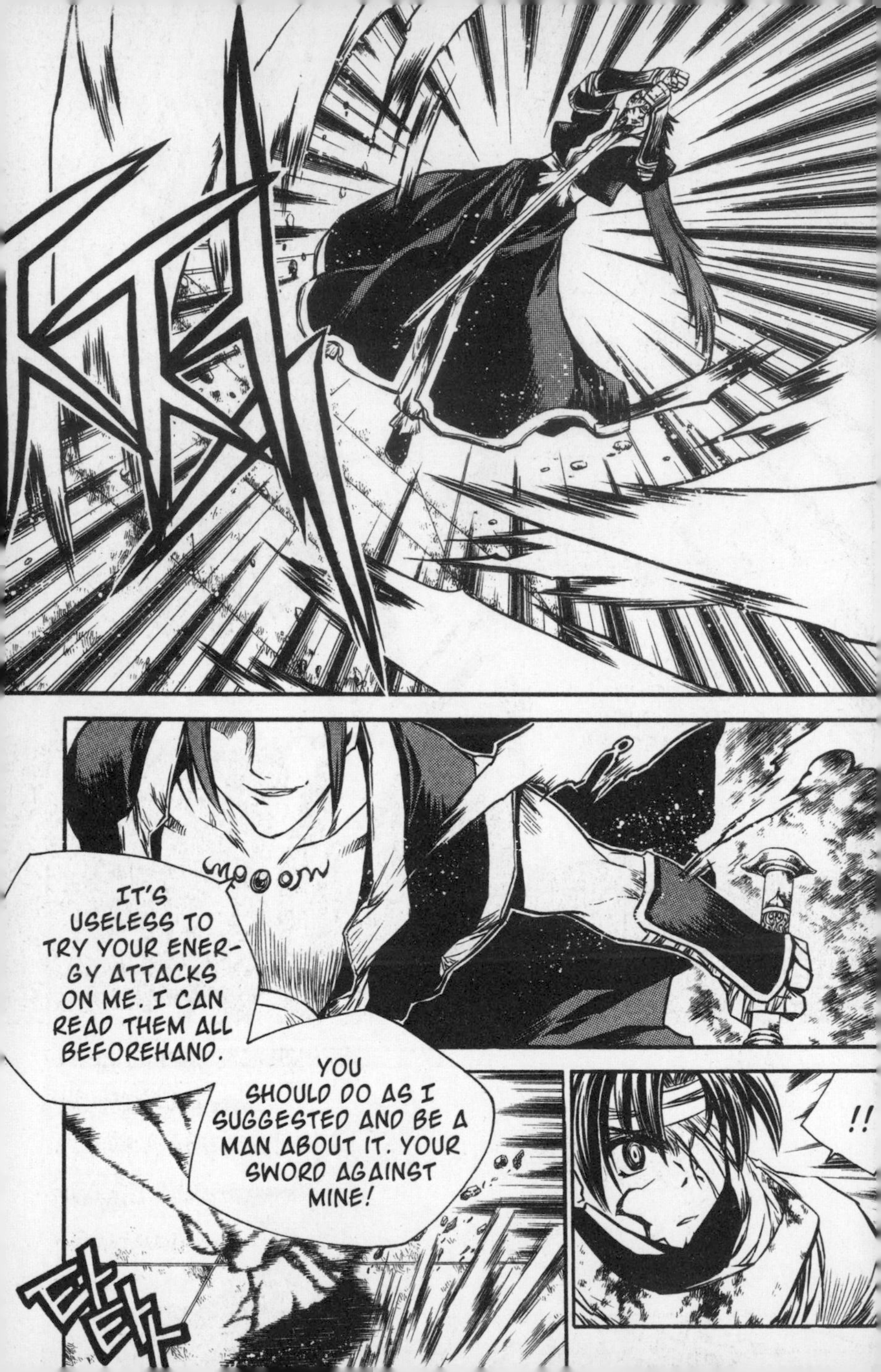
IT'S USELESS TO TRY YOUR ENERGY ATTACKS ON ME. I CAN READ THEM ALL BEFOREHAND.
YOU SHOULD DO AS I SUGGESTED AND BE A MAN ABOUT IT. YOUR SWORD AGAINST MINE!
!!

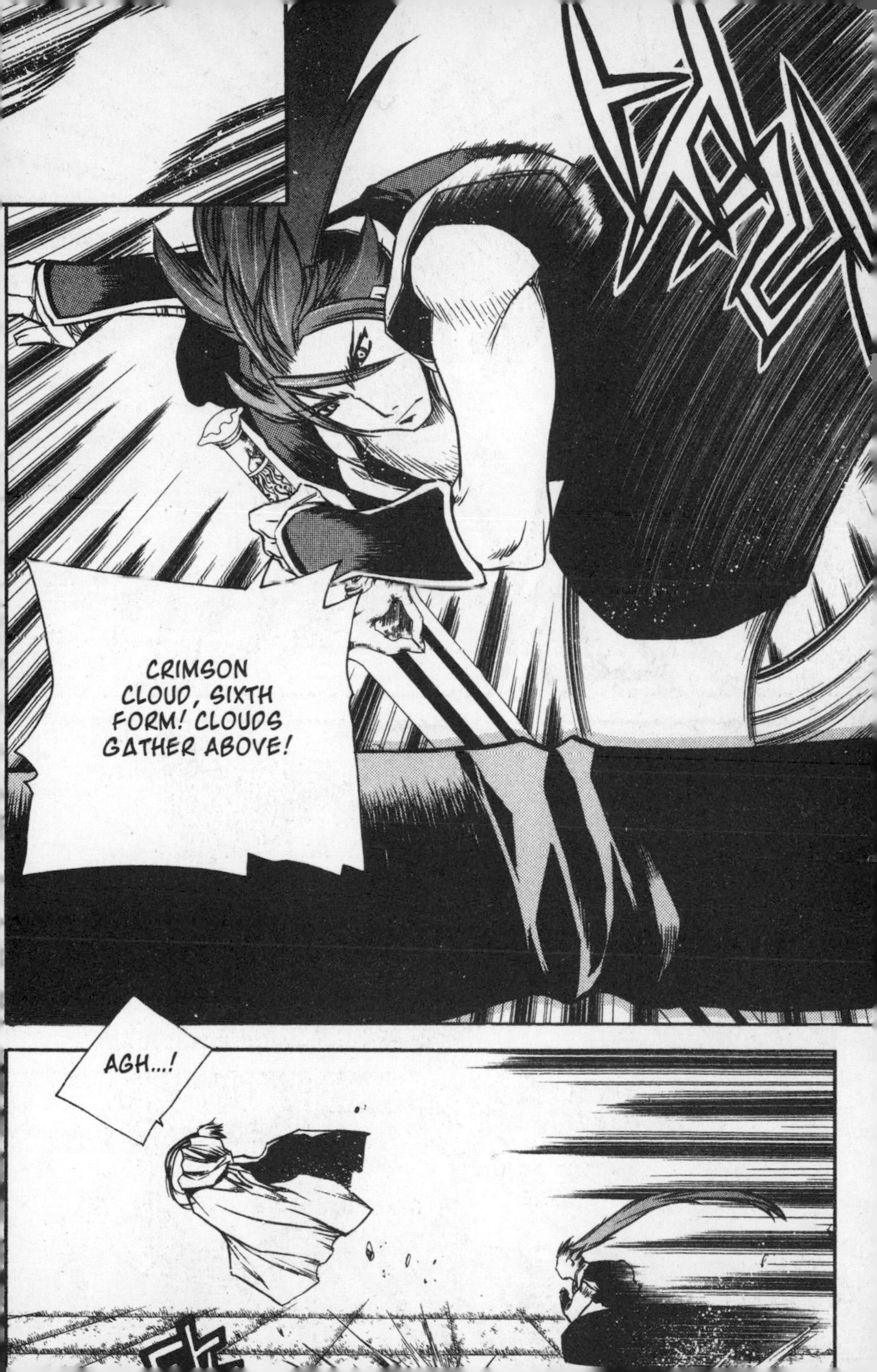
CRIMSON CLOUD, SIXTH FORM! CLOUDS GATHER ABOVE!
AGH...!

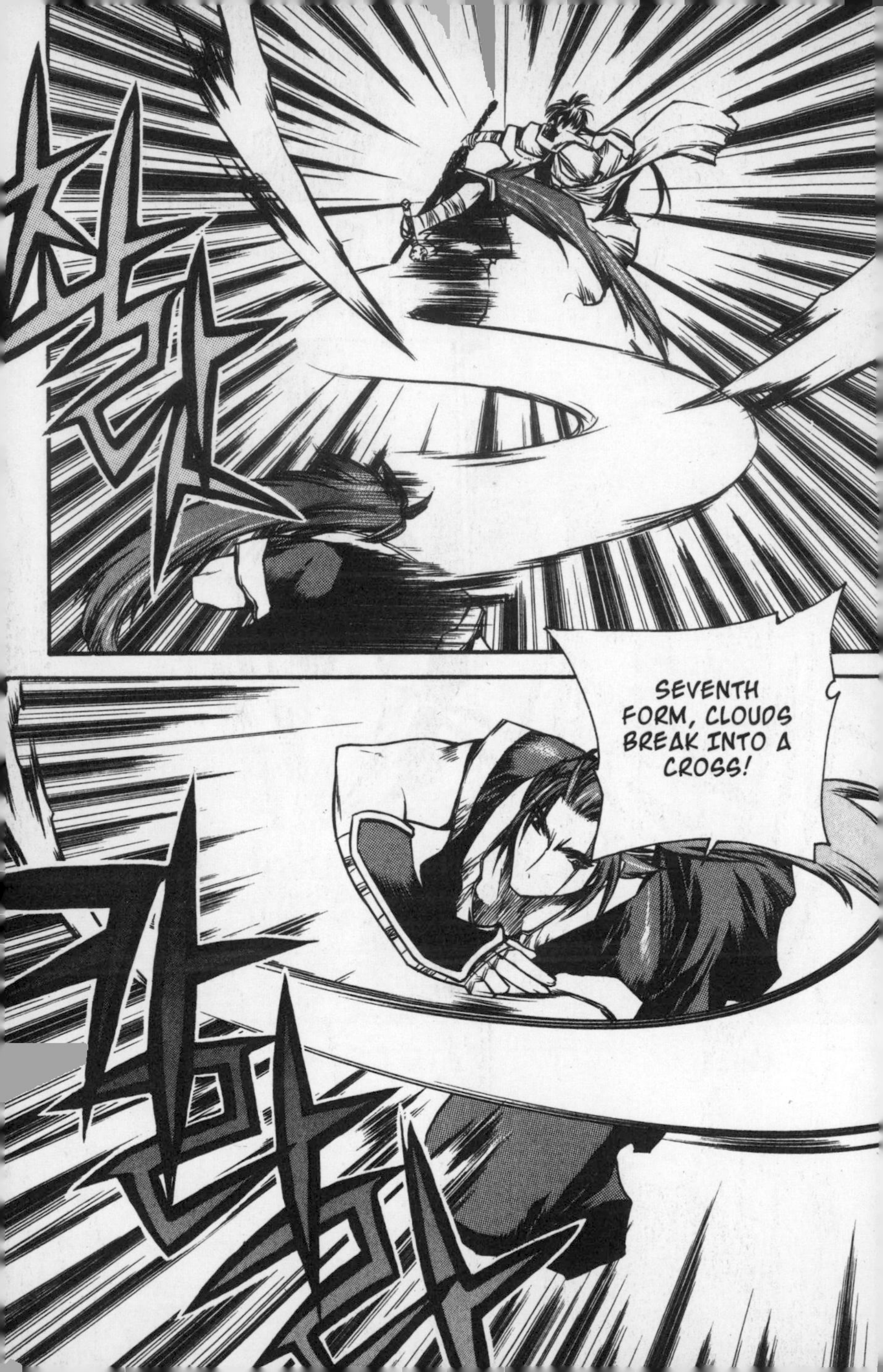
SEVENTH FORM, CLOUDS BREAK INTO A CROSS!

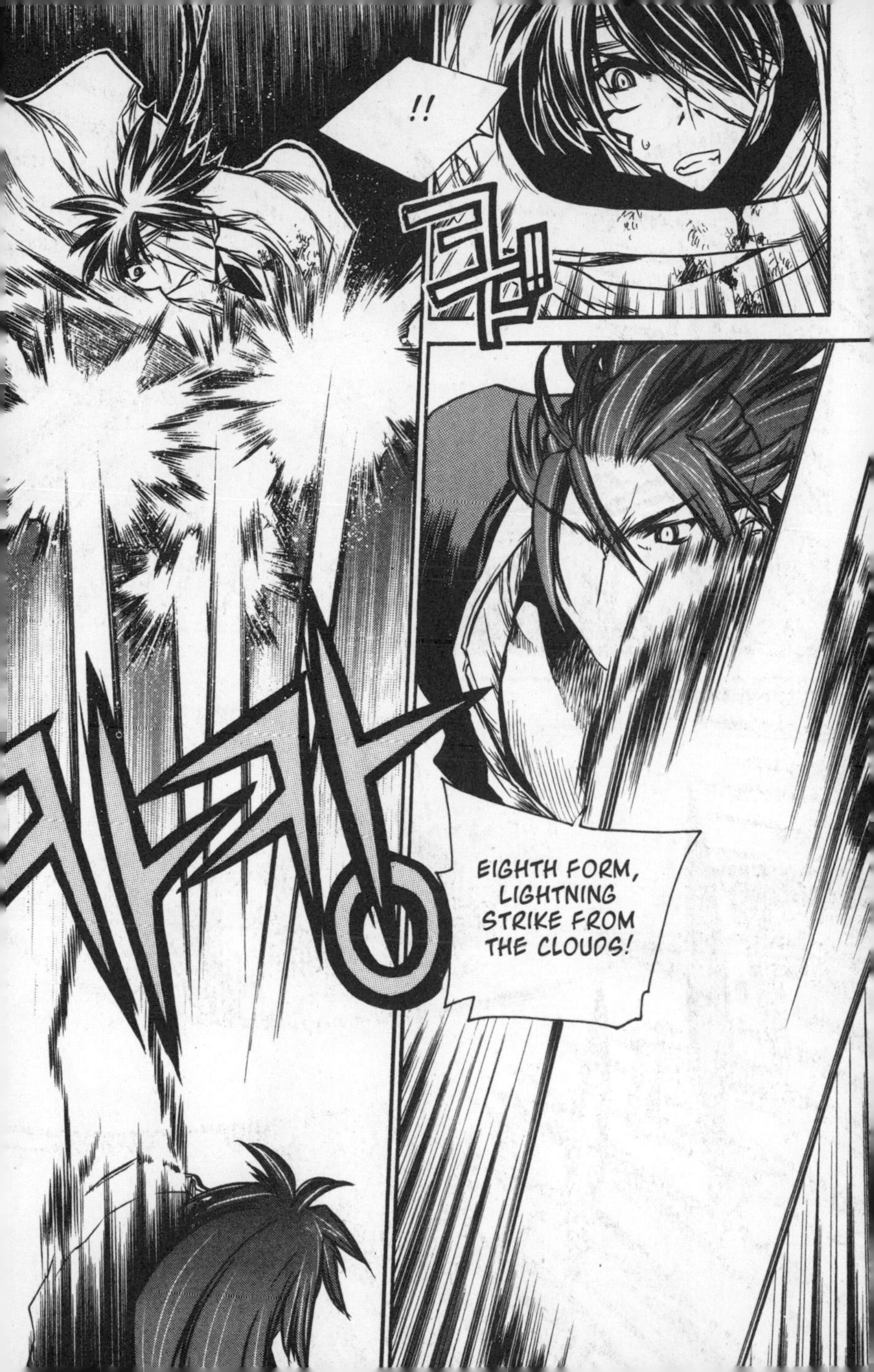
!!
EIGHTH FORM, LIGHTNING STRIKE FROM THE CLOUDS!

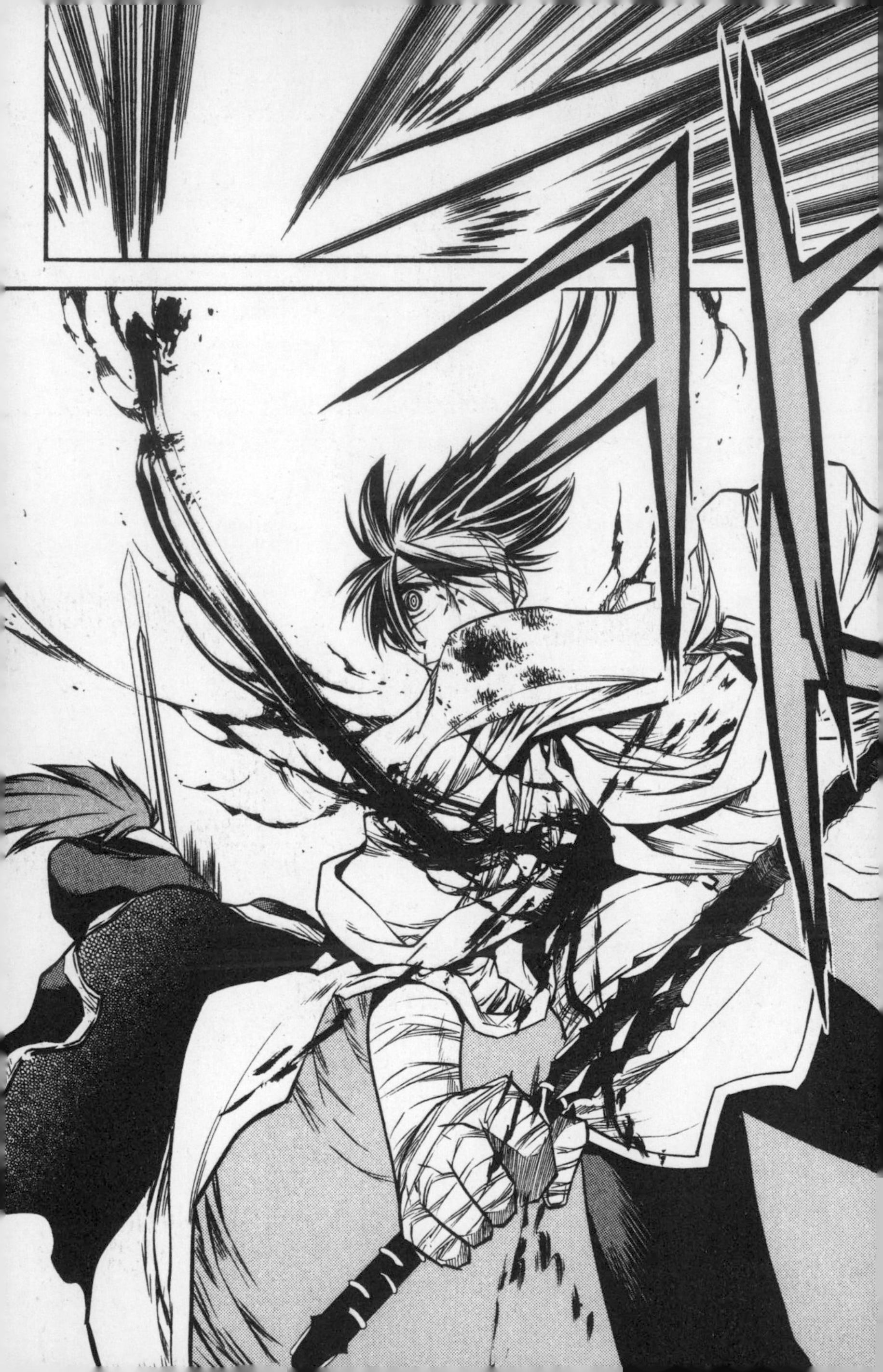

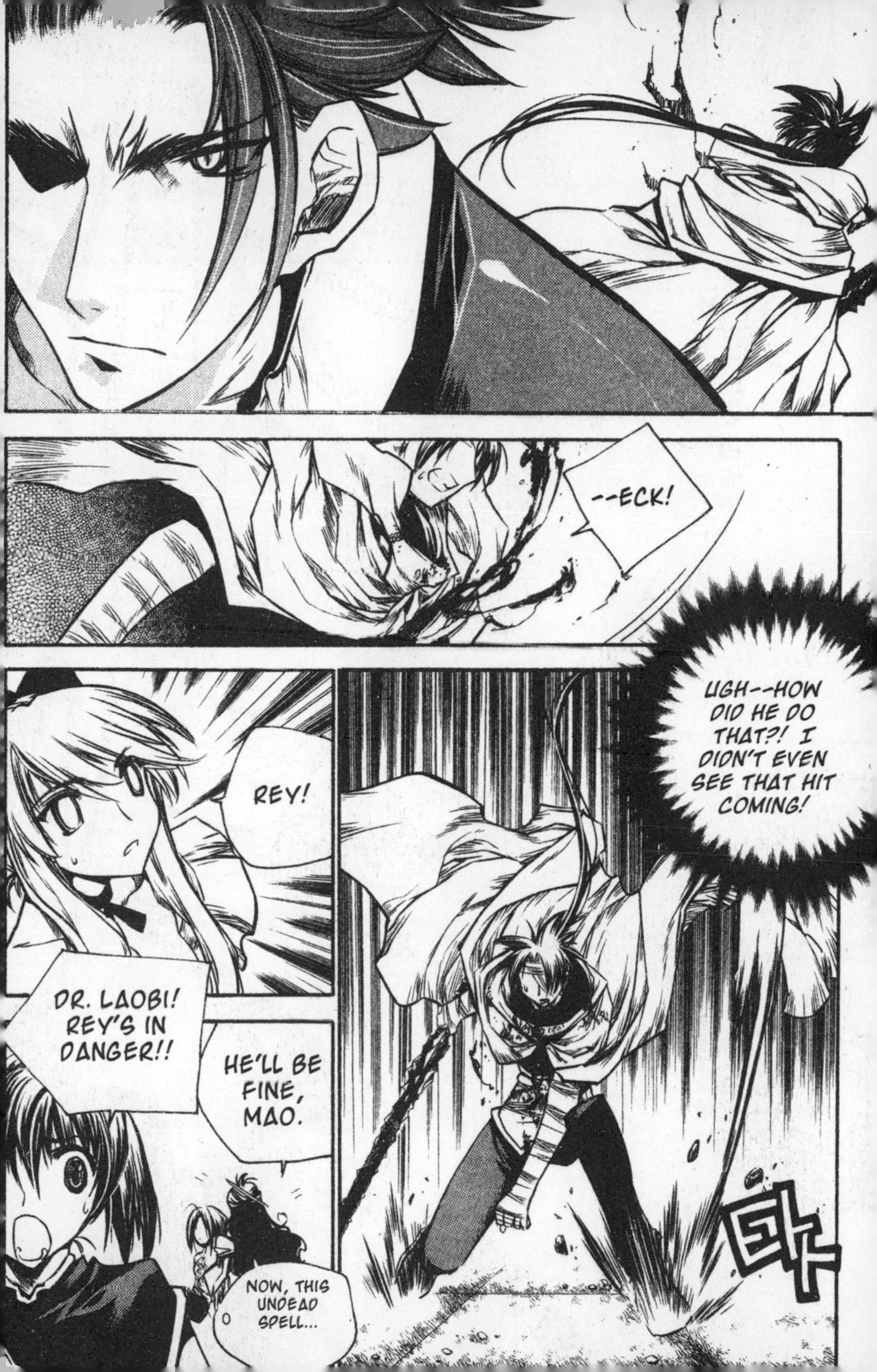
--ECK!
UGH--HOW DID HE DO THAT?! I DIDN'T EVEN SEE THAT HIT COMING!
REY!
DR. LAOBI! REY'S IN DANGER!!
HE'LL BE FINE, MAO.
NOW, THIS UNDEAD SPELL...

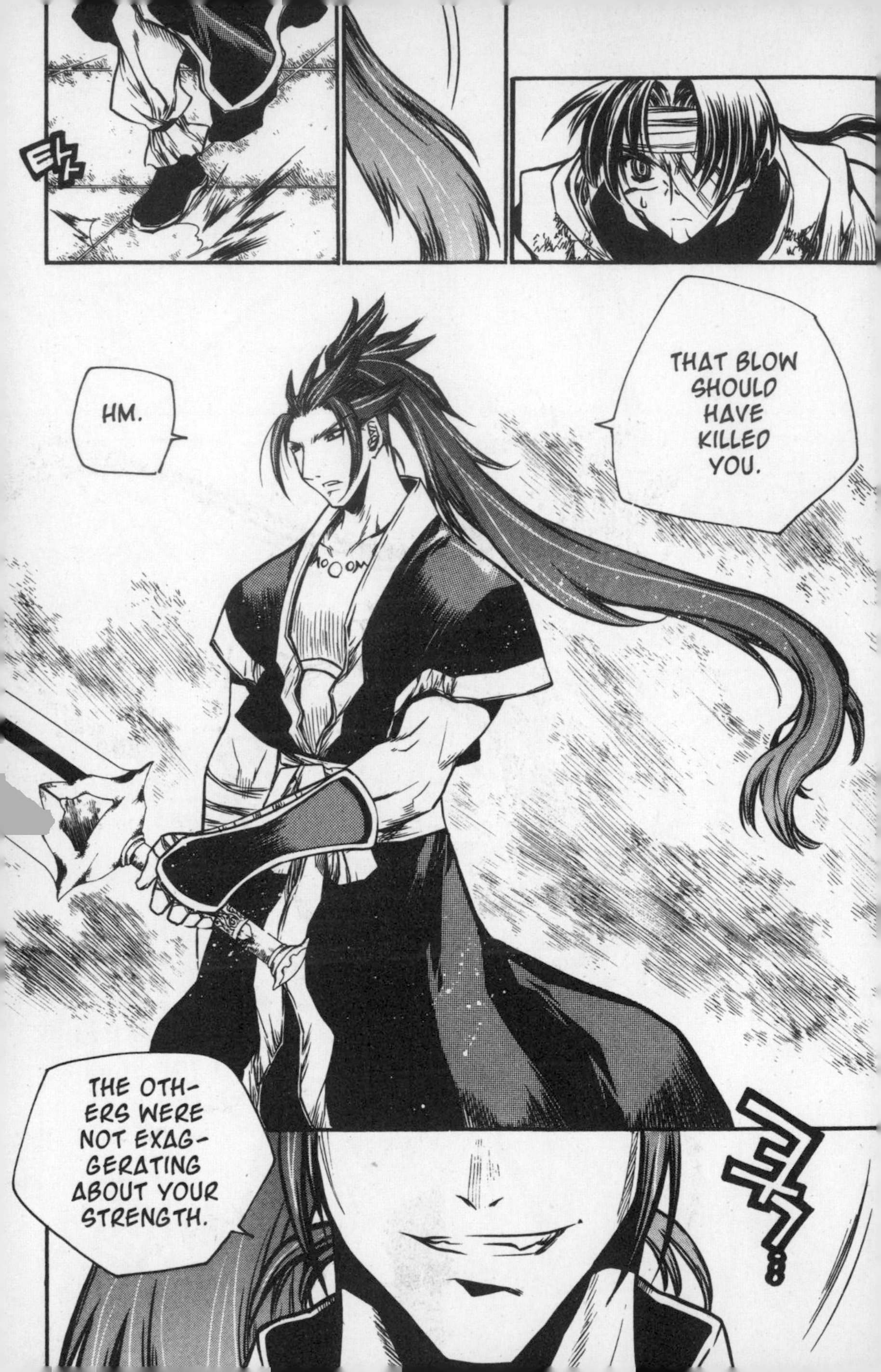
HM.
THAT BLOW SHOULD HAVE KILLED YOU.
THE OTH-ERS WERE NOT EXAG-GERATING ABOUT YOUR STRENGTH.

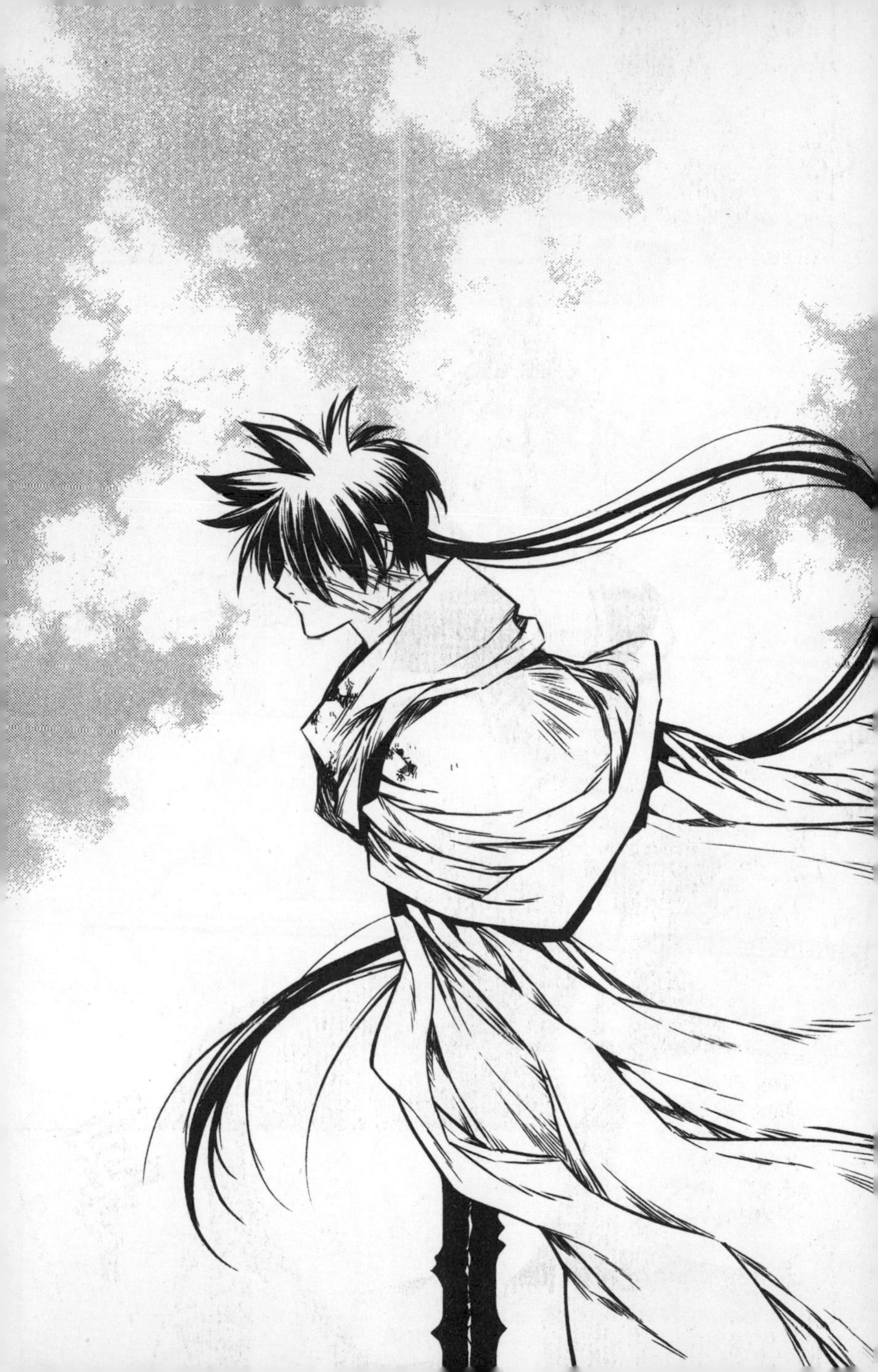

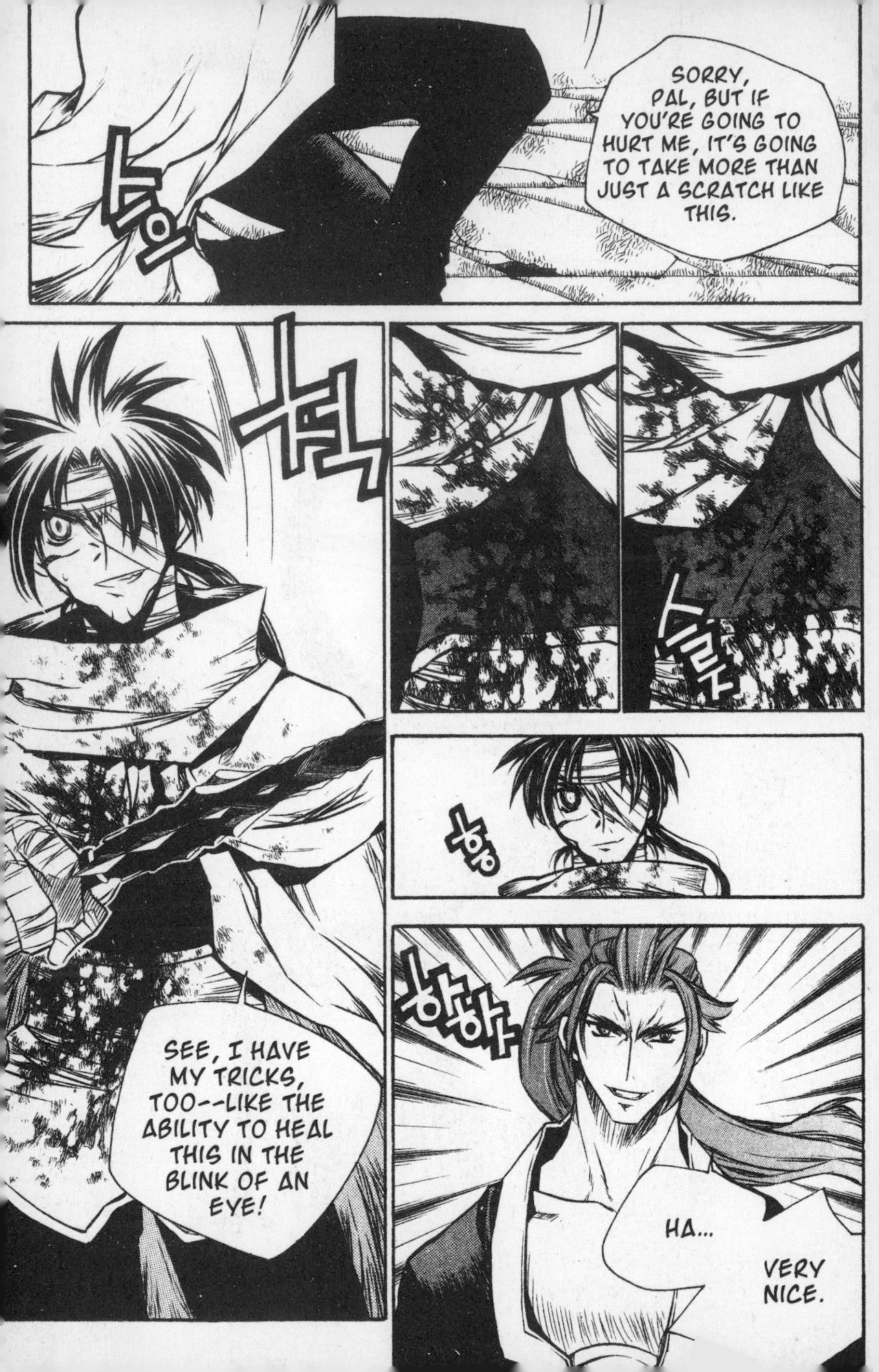
SORRY, PAL, BUT IF YOU'RE GOING TO HURT ME, IT'S GOING TO TAKE MORE THAN JUST A SCRATCH LIKE THIS.
SEE, I HAVE MY TRICKS, TOO--LIKE THE ABILITY TO HEAL THIS IN THE BLINK OF AN EYE!
HA...
VERY NICE.

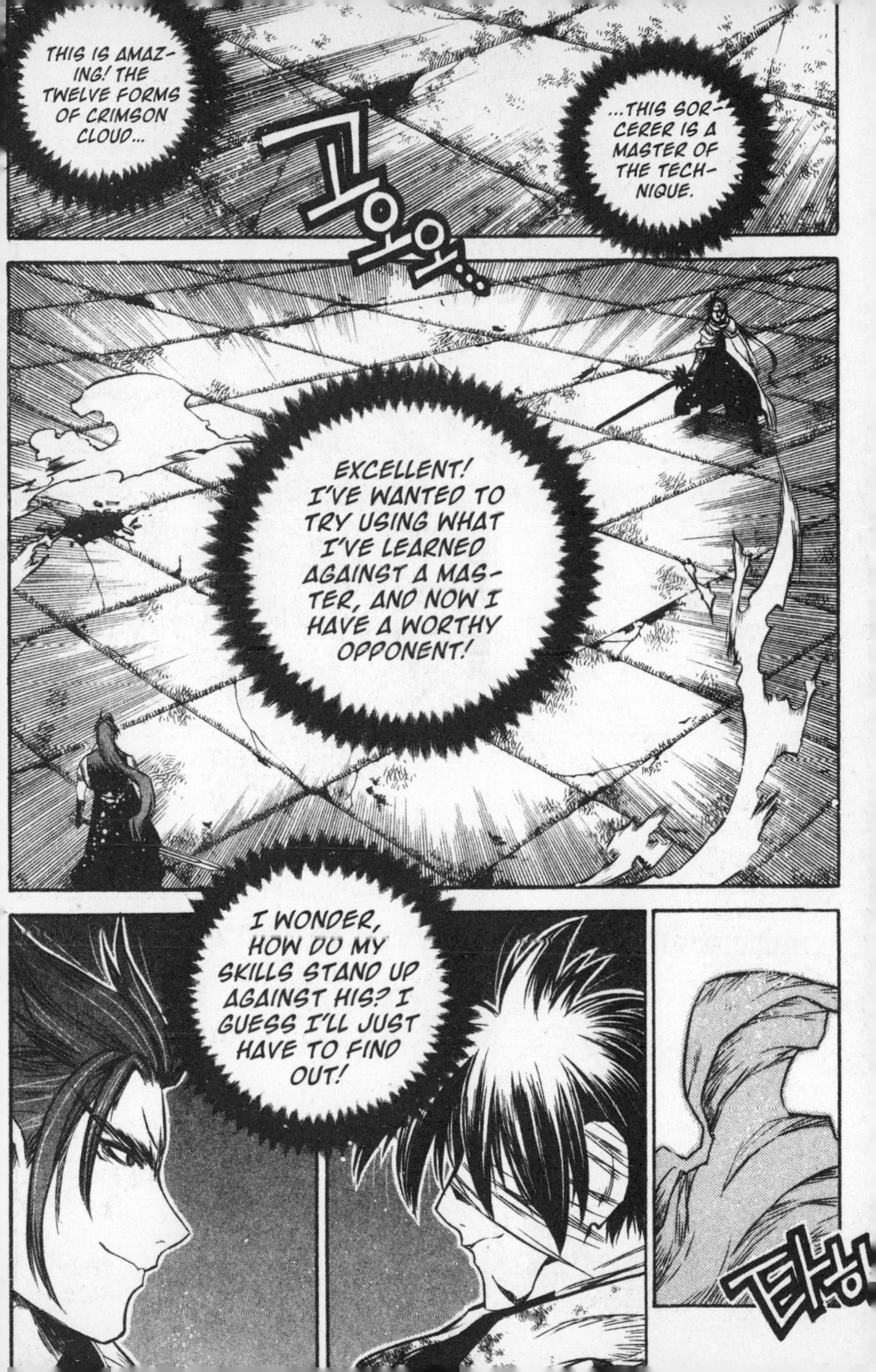
THIS IS AMAZING! THE TWELVE FORMS OF CRIMSON CLOUD...
...THIS SORCERER IS A MASTER OF THE TECHNIQUE.
EXCELLENT! I'VE WANTED TO TRY USING WHAT I'VE LEARNED AGAINST A MASTER, AND NOW I HAVE A WORTHY OPPONENT!
I WONDER, HOW DO MY SKILLS STAND UP AGAINST HIS? I GUESS I'LL JUST HAVE TO FIND OUT!

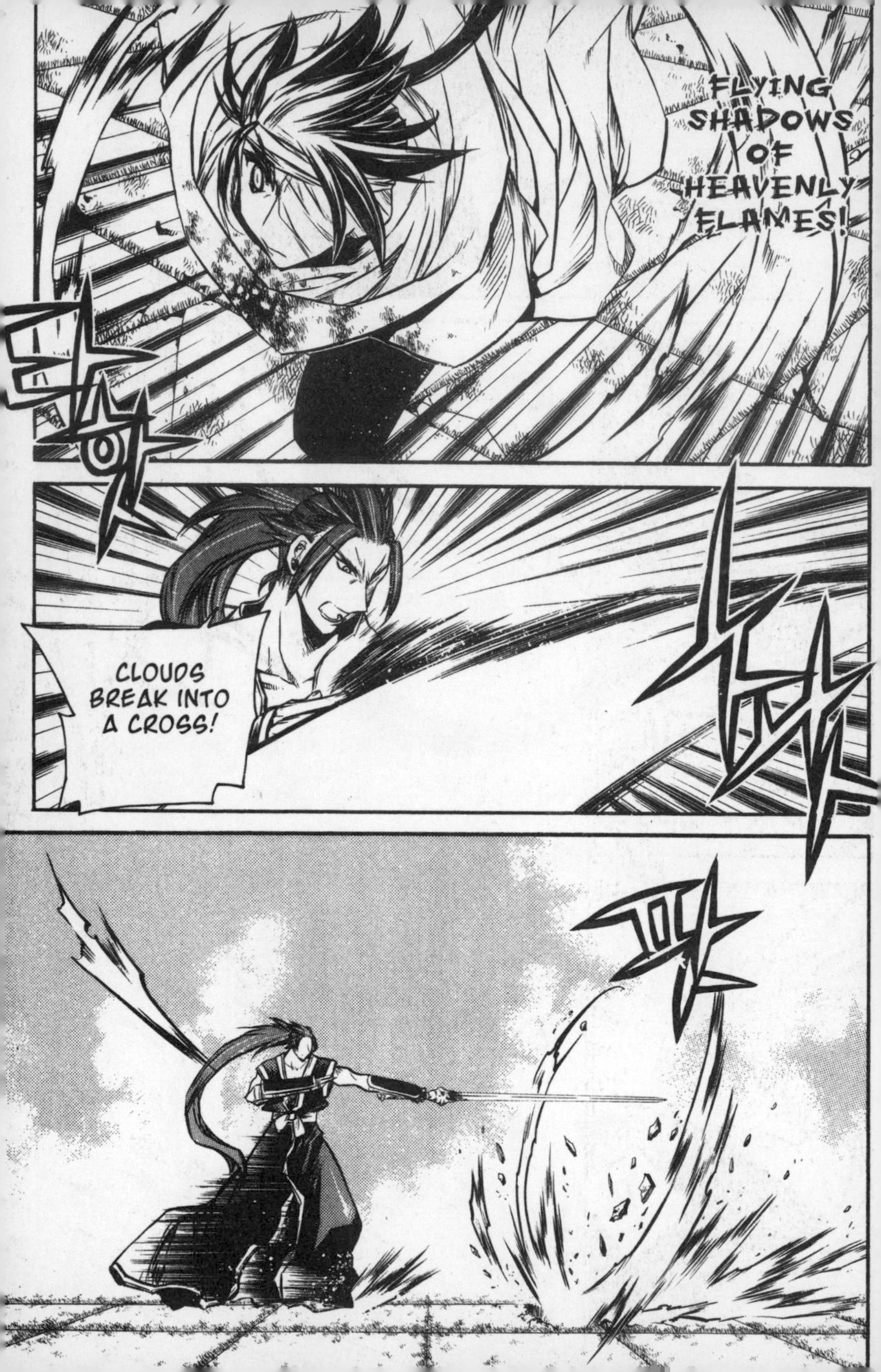
FLYING SHADOWS OF HEAVENLY FLAMES!
CLOUDS BREAK INTO A CROSS!

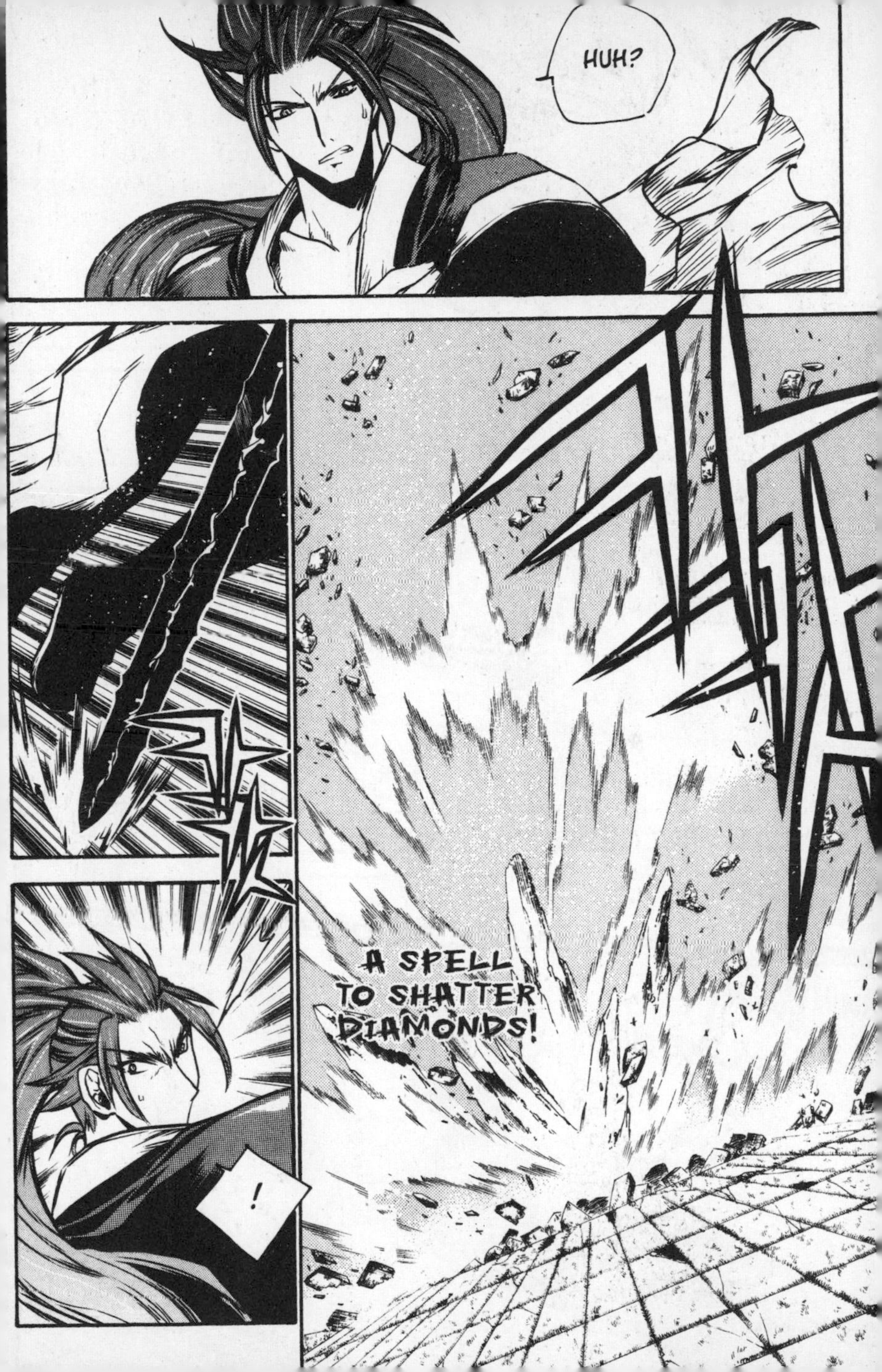
HUH?
A SPELL TO SHATTER DIAMONDS!
!

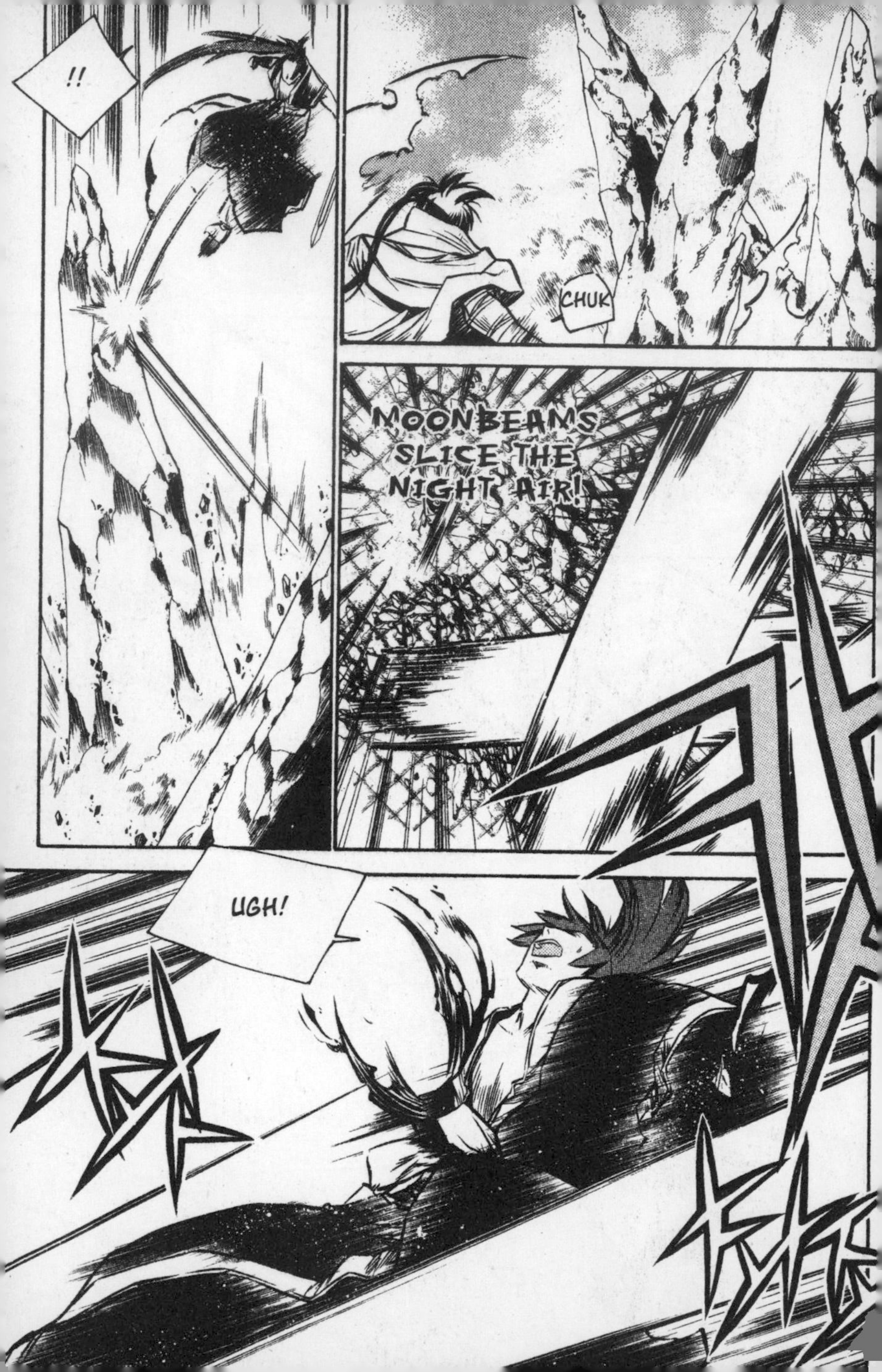
!!
CHUK
MOONBEAMS SLICE THE NIGHT AIR!
UGH!

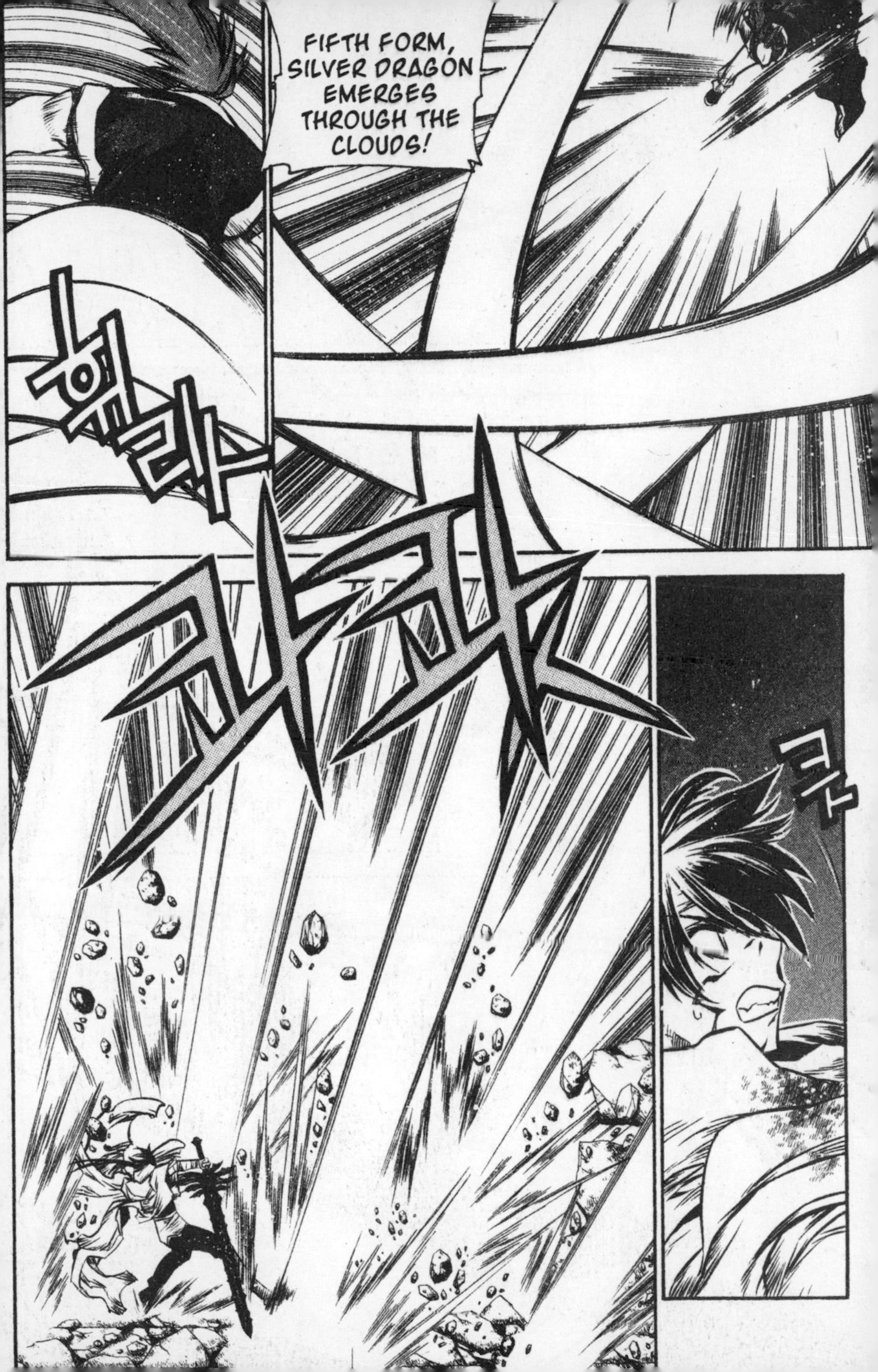
FIFTH FORM, SILVER DRAGON EMERGES THROUGH THE CLOUDS!

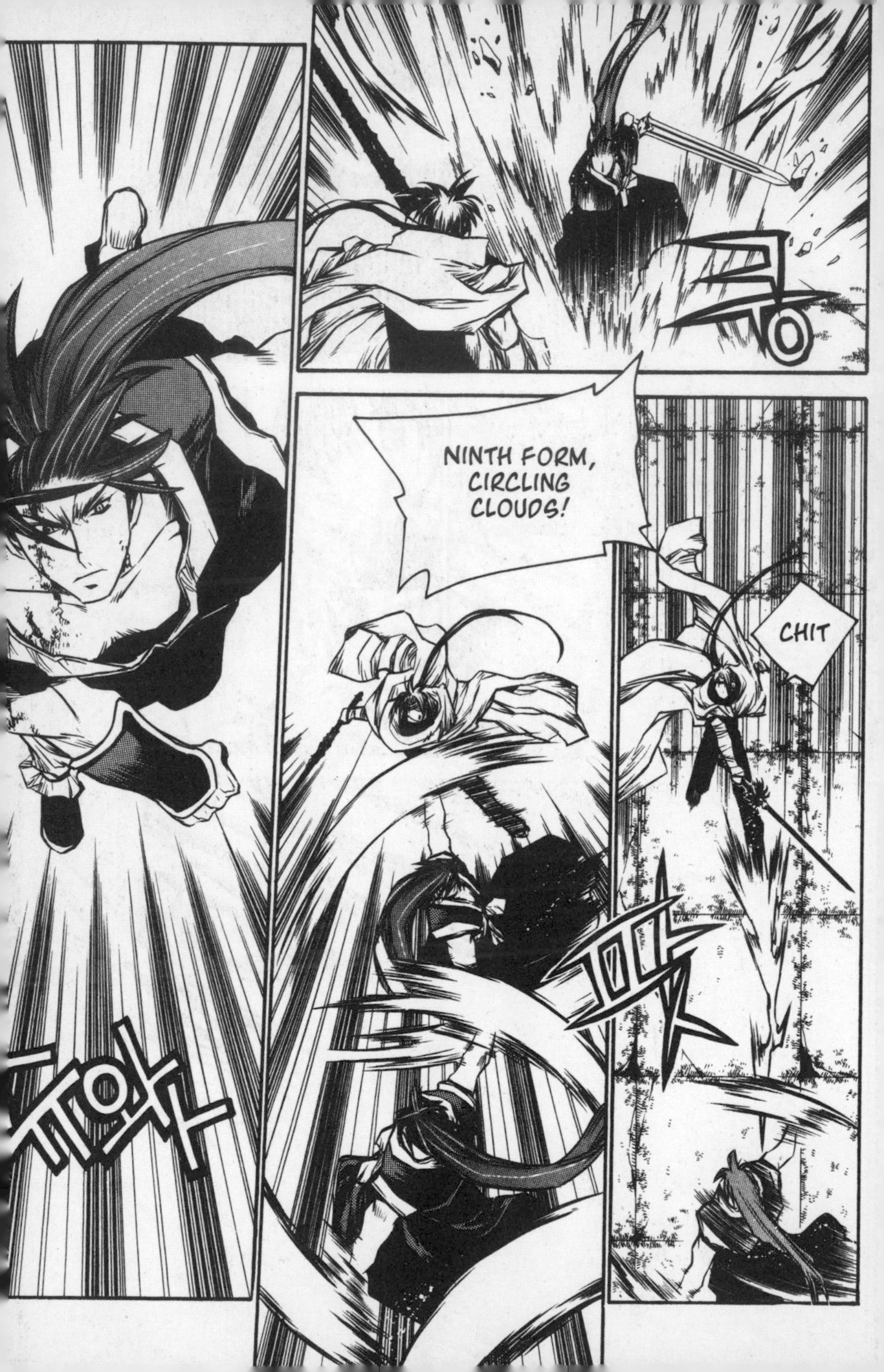
NINTH FORM, CIRCLING CLOUDS!
CHIT

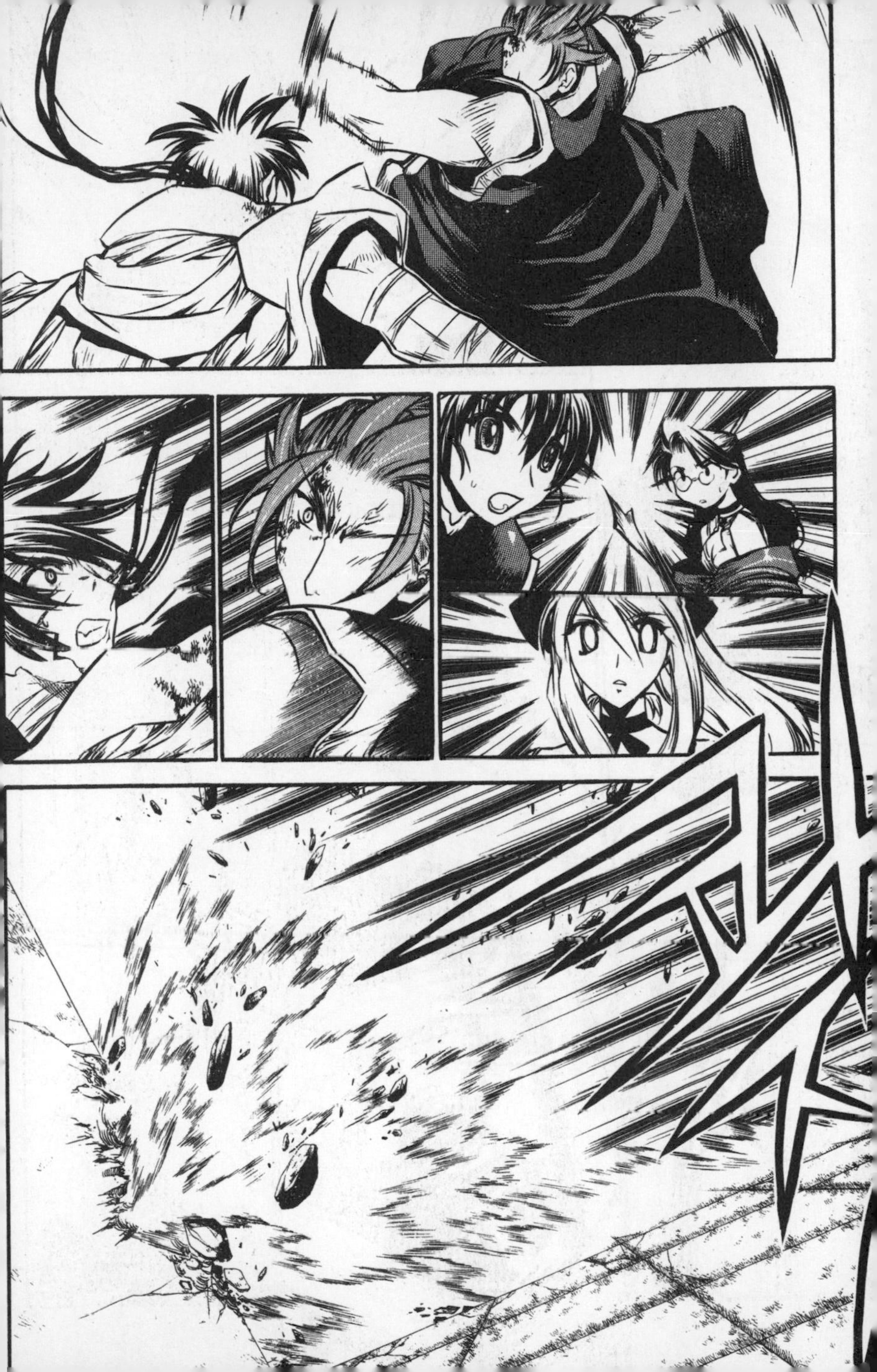

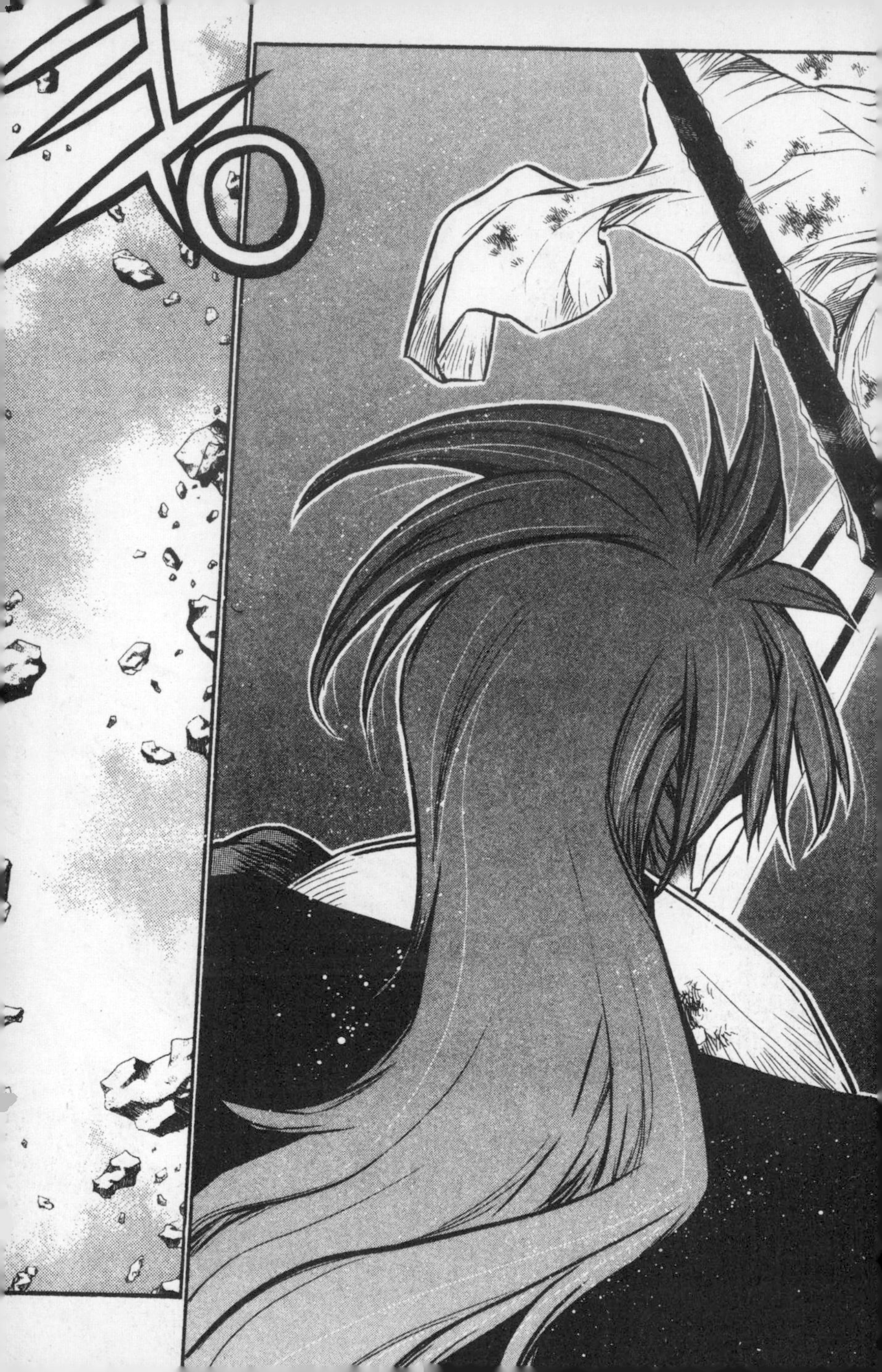

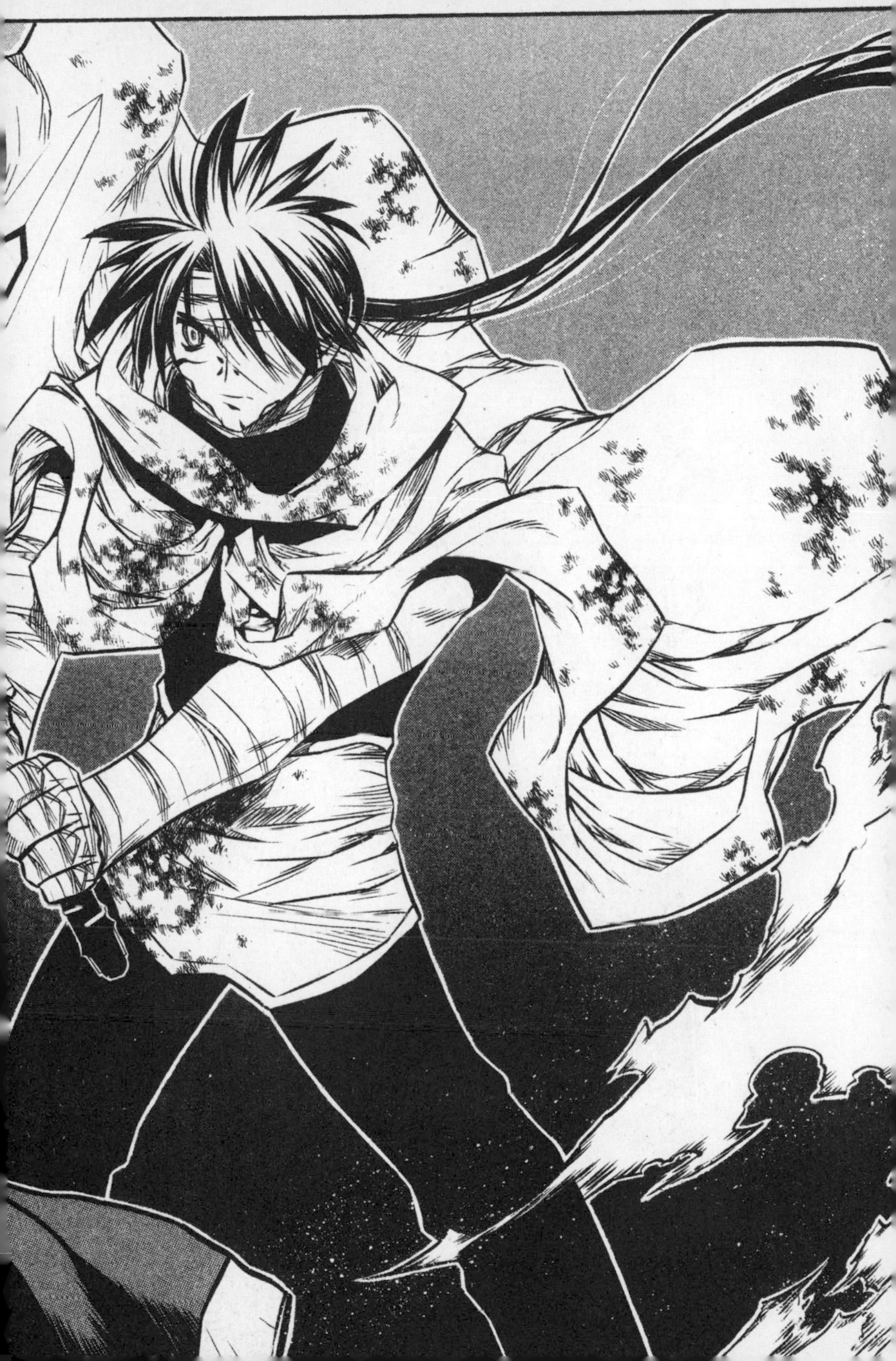

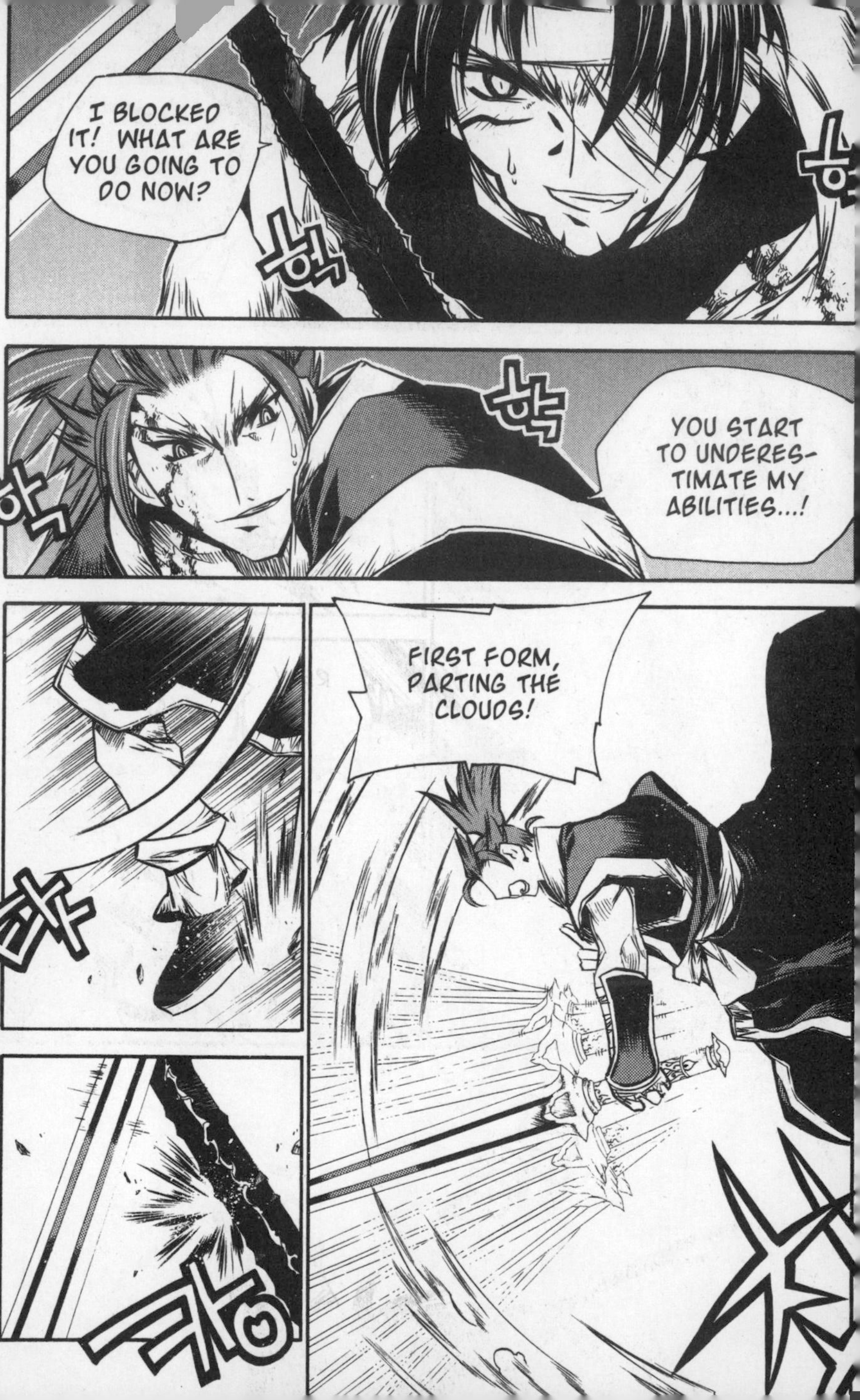
I BLOCKED IT! WHAT ARE YOU GOING TO DO NOW?
YOU START TO UNDERES-TIMATE MY ABILITIES...!
FIRST FORM, PARTING THE CLOUDS!

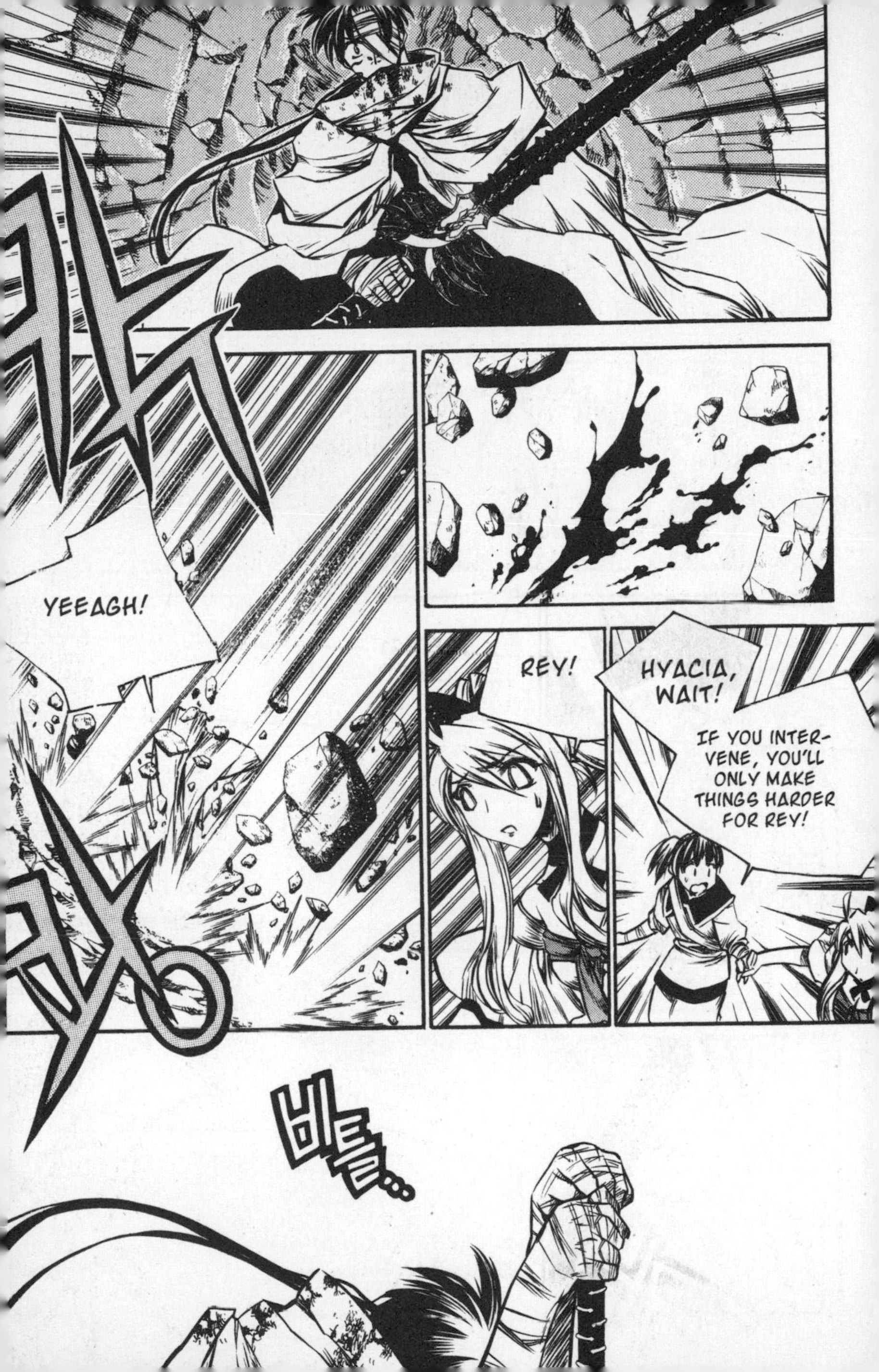
YEEAGH!
REY!
HYACIA, WAIT!
IF YOU INTER-VENE, YOU'LL ONLY MAKE THINGS HARDER FOR REY!

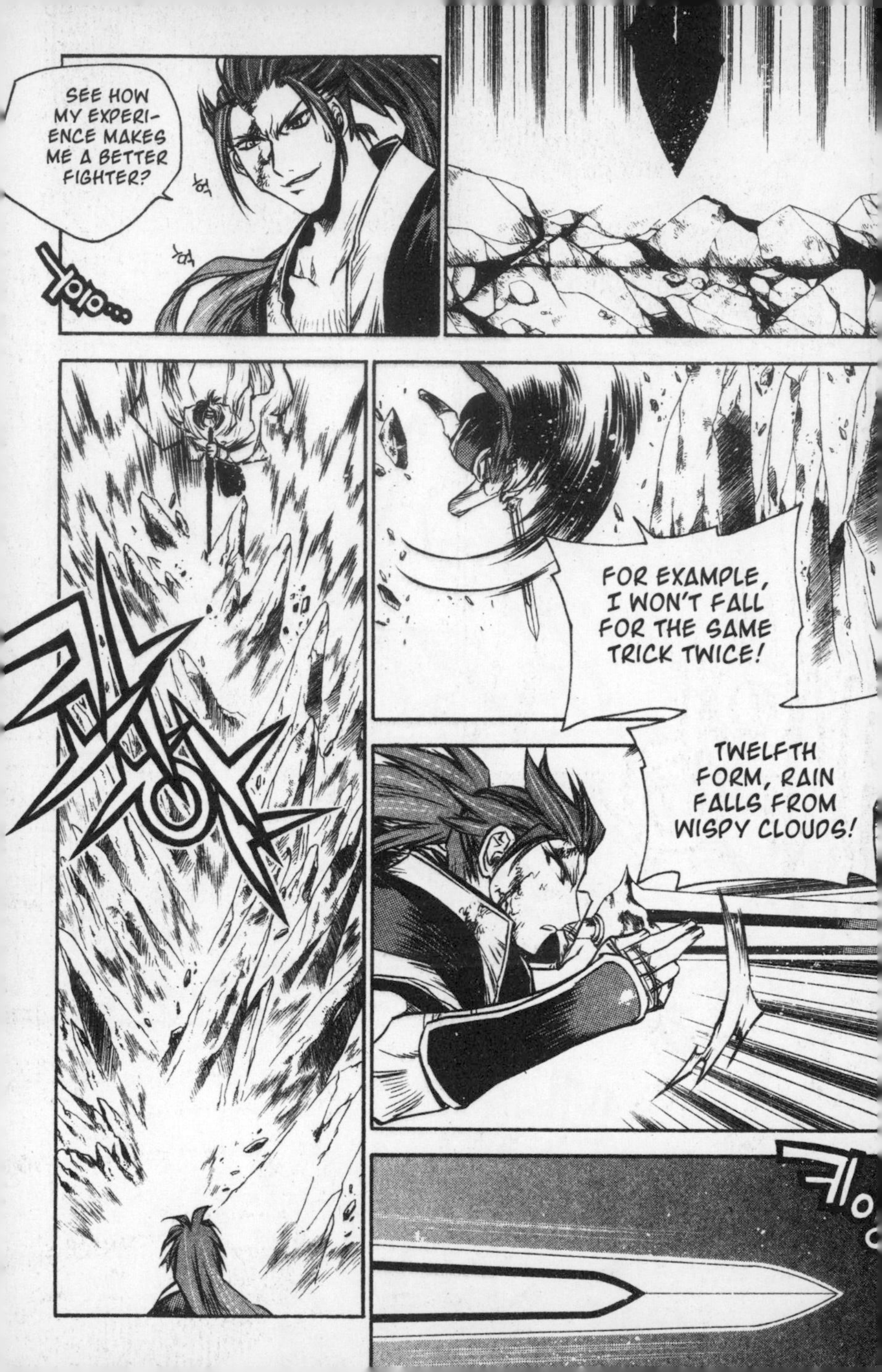
SEE HOW MY EXPERIENCE MAKES ME A BETTER FIGHTER?
FOR EXAMPLE, I WON'T FALL FOR THE SAME TRICK TWICE!
TWELFTH FORM, RAIN FALLS FROM WISPY CLOUDS!

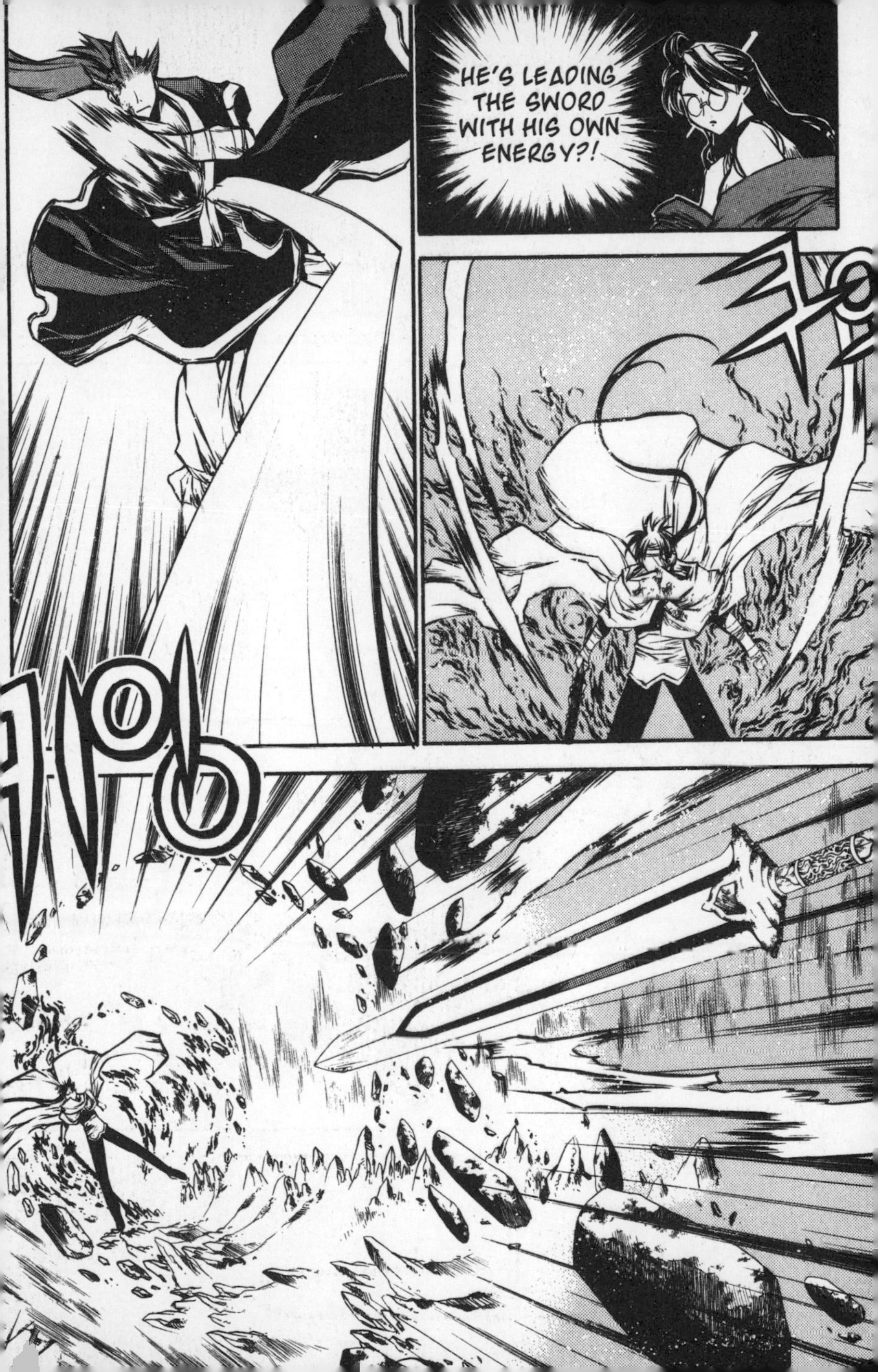
HE'S LEADING THE SWORD WITH HIS OWN ENERGY?!

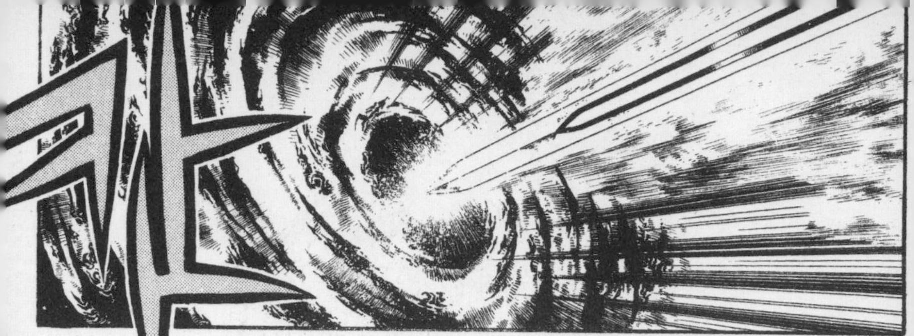
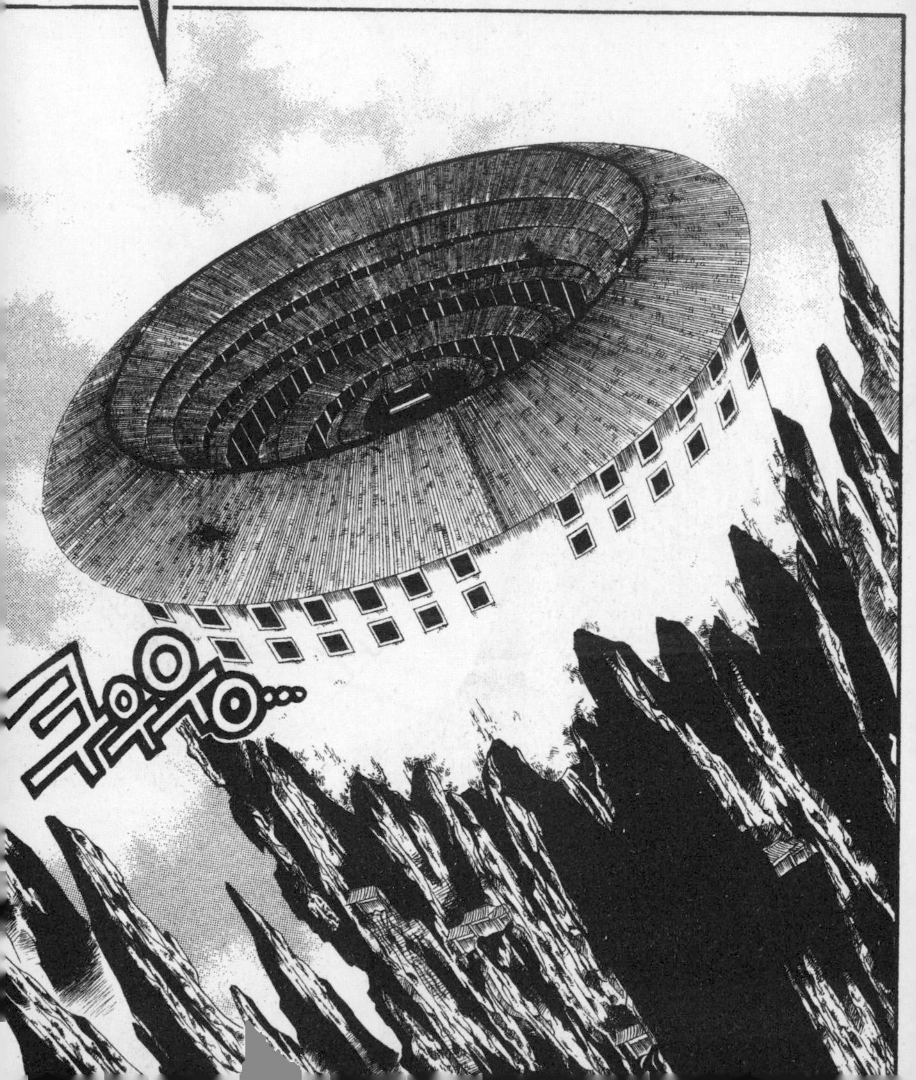

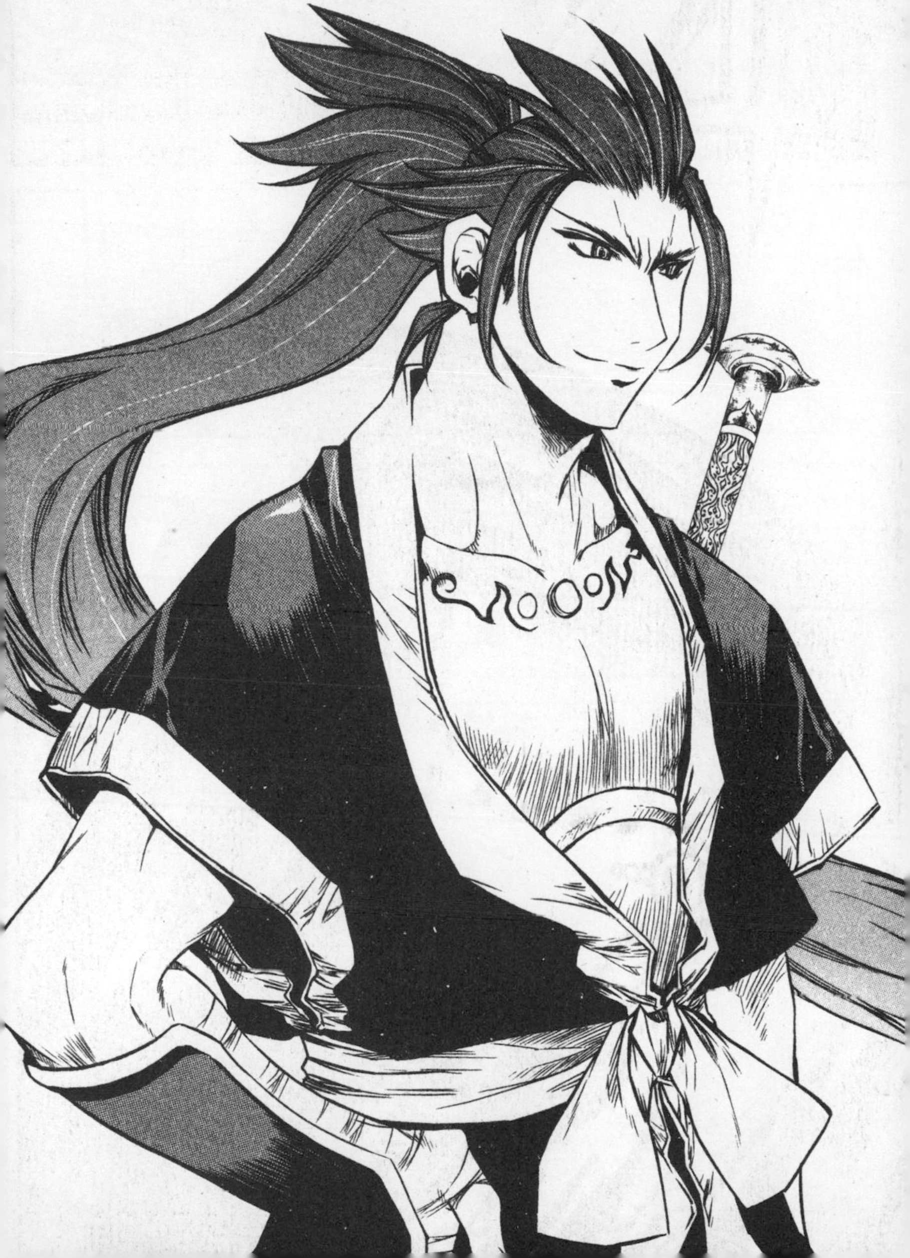

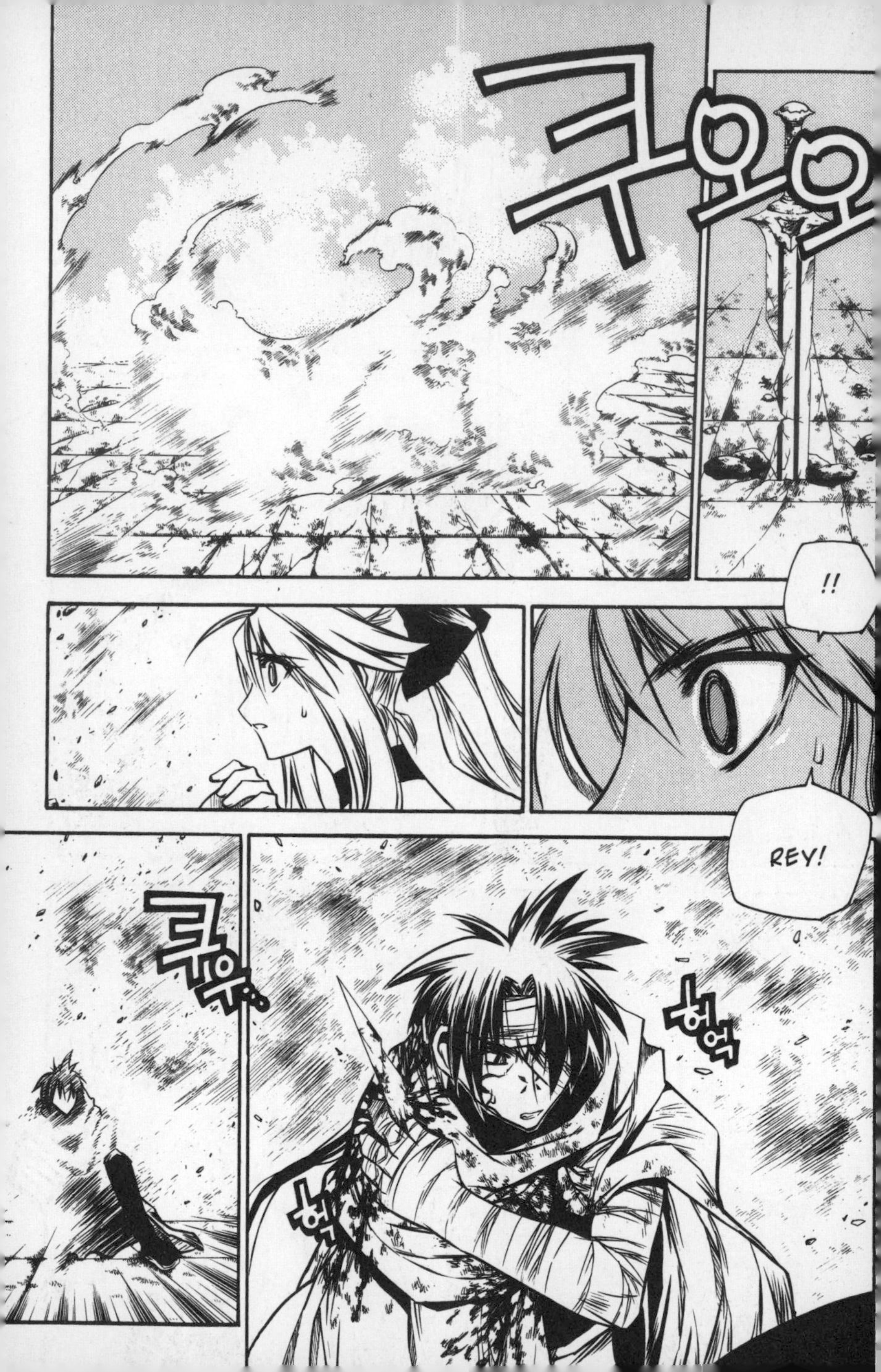

쿠오오
!!
REY!
쿠웅
허억
헉

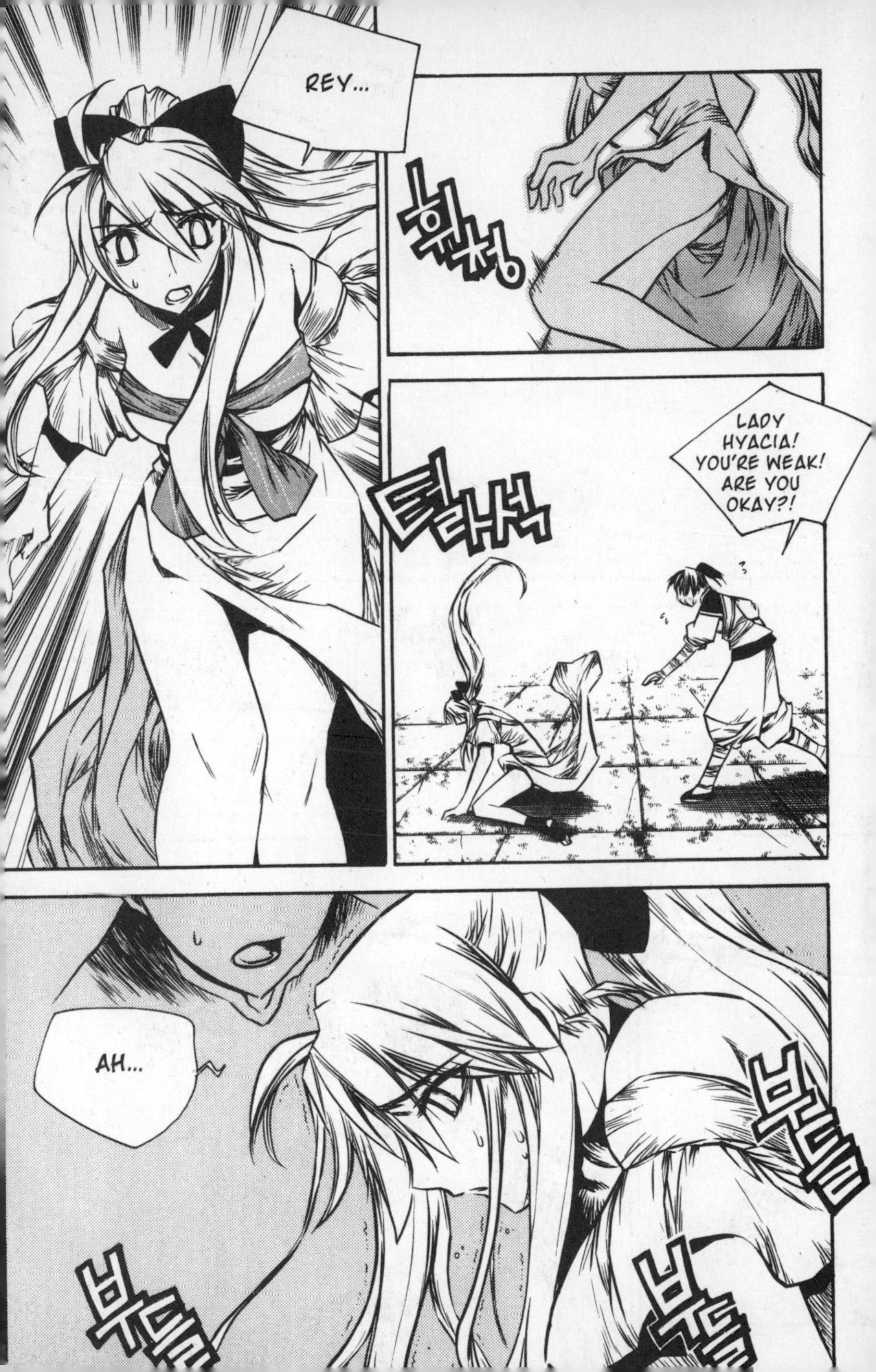

REY...
휘청
털썩
LADY HYACIA! YOU'RE WEAK! ARE YOU OKAY?!
AH...
부들
부들
부들

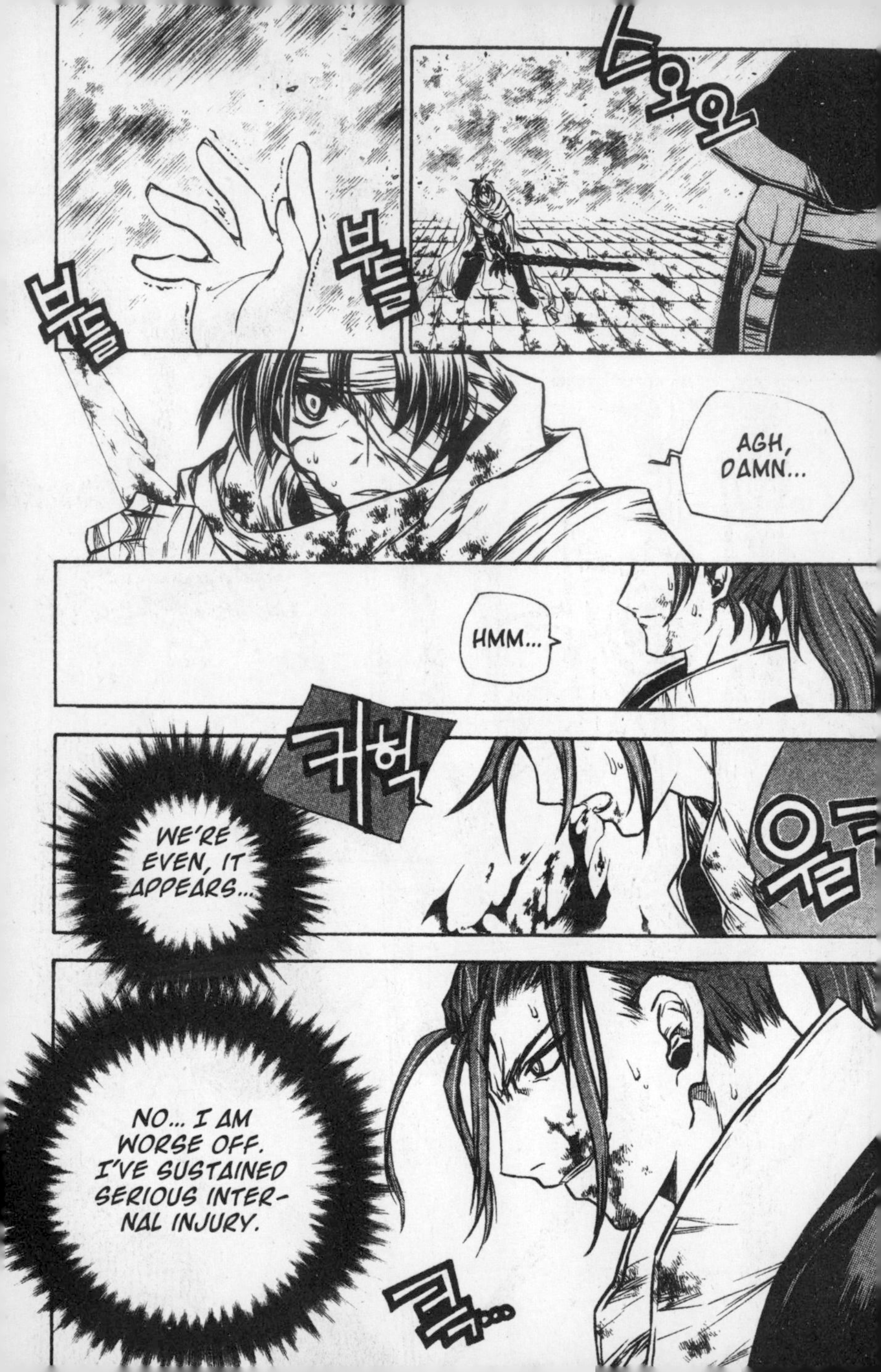

부들
부들
AGH, DAMN...
HMM...
커헉
WE'RE EVEN, IT APPEARS...
NO... I AM WORSE OFF. I'VE SUSTAINED SERIOUS INTER-NAL INJURY.
큭...

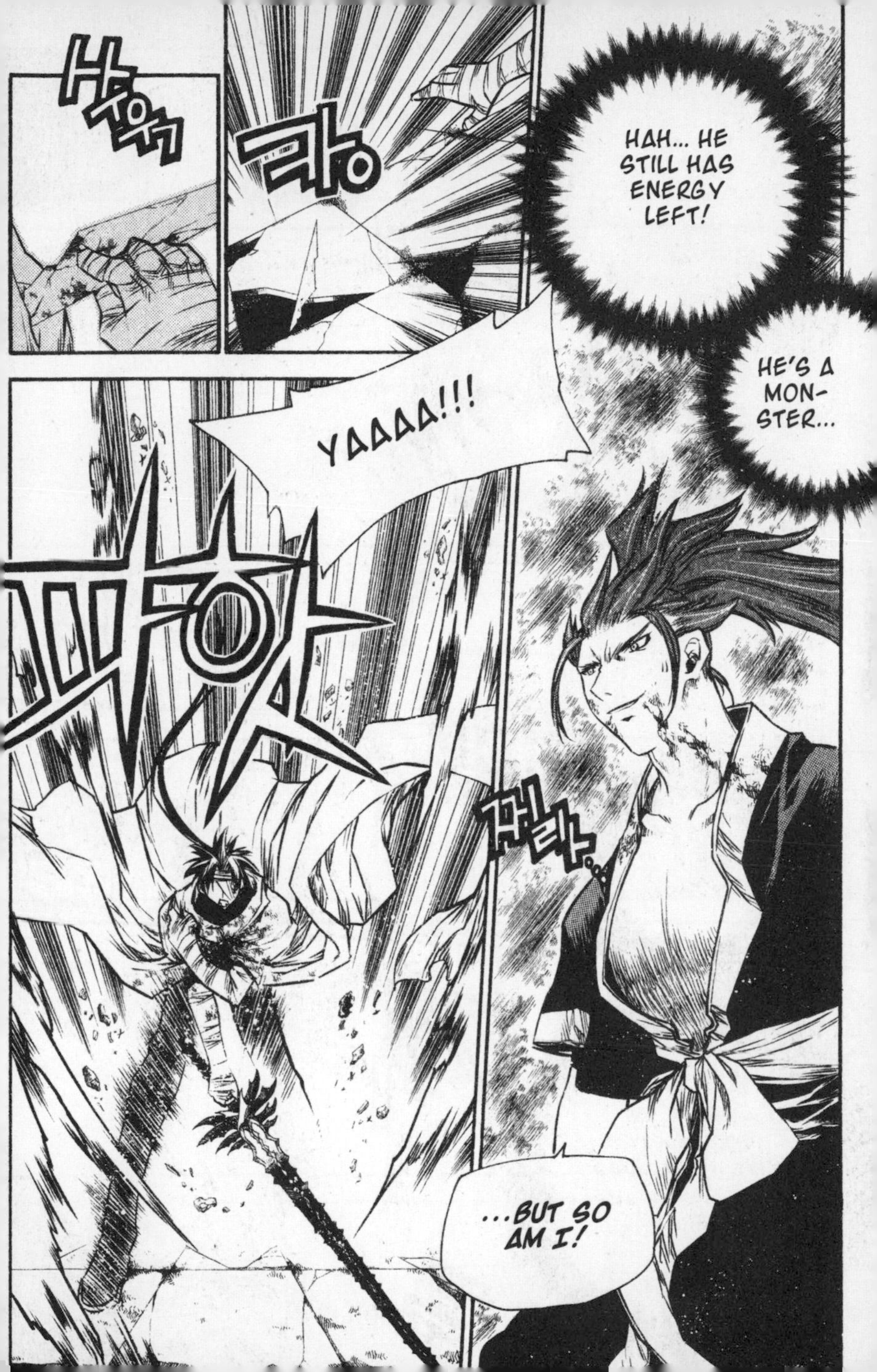
YAAAA!!!
HAH... HE STILL HAS ENERGY LEFT!
HE'S A MON-STER...
...BUT SO AM I!

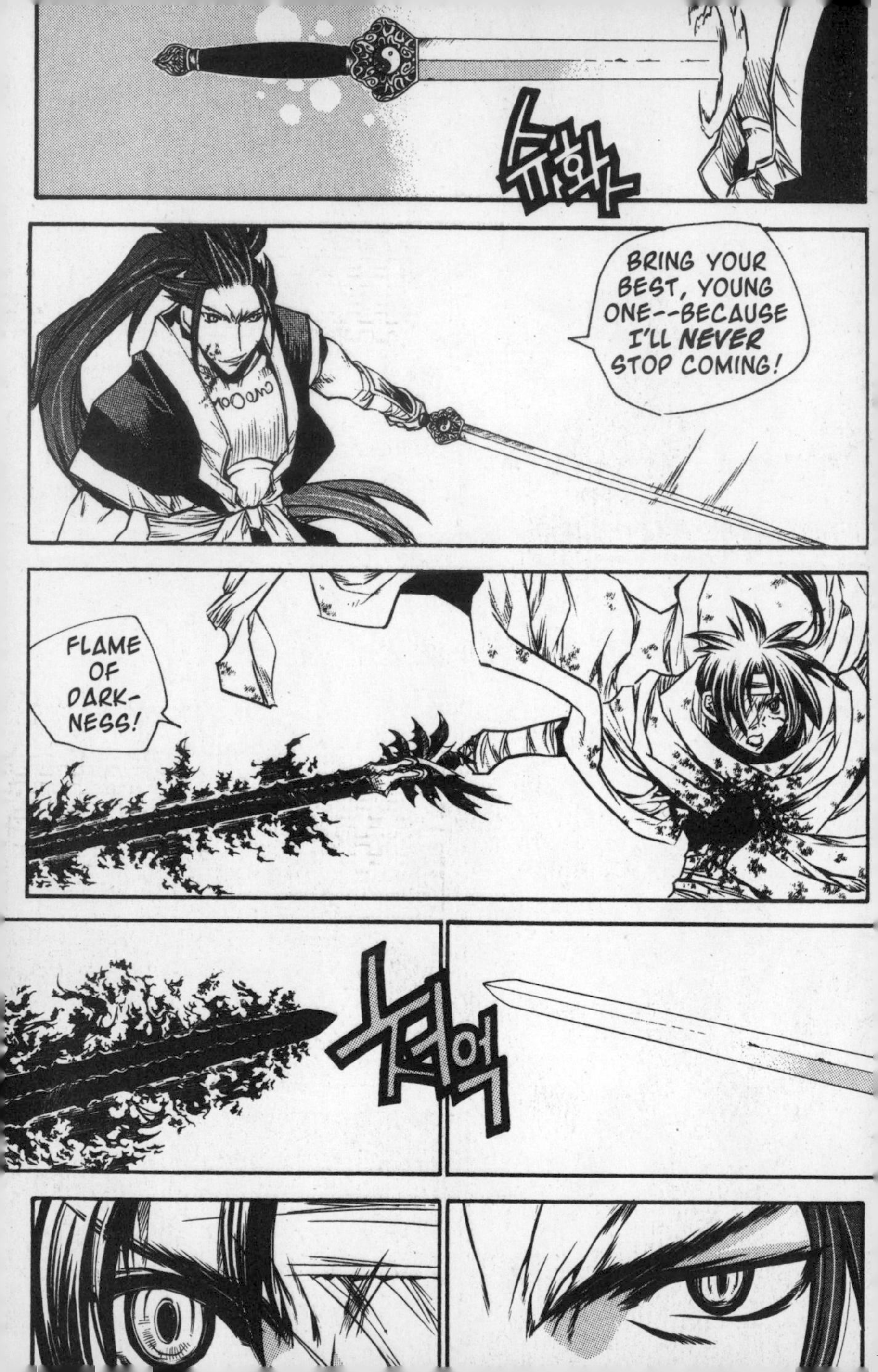
BRING YOUR BEST, YOUNG ONE--BECAUSE I'LL NEVER STOP COMING!
FLAME OF DARK-NESS!

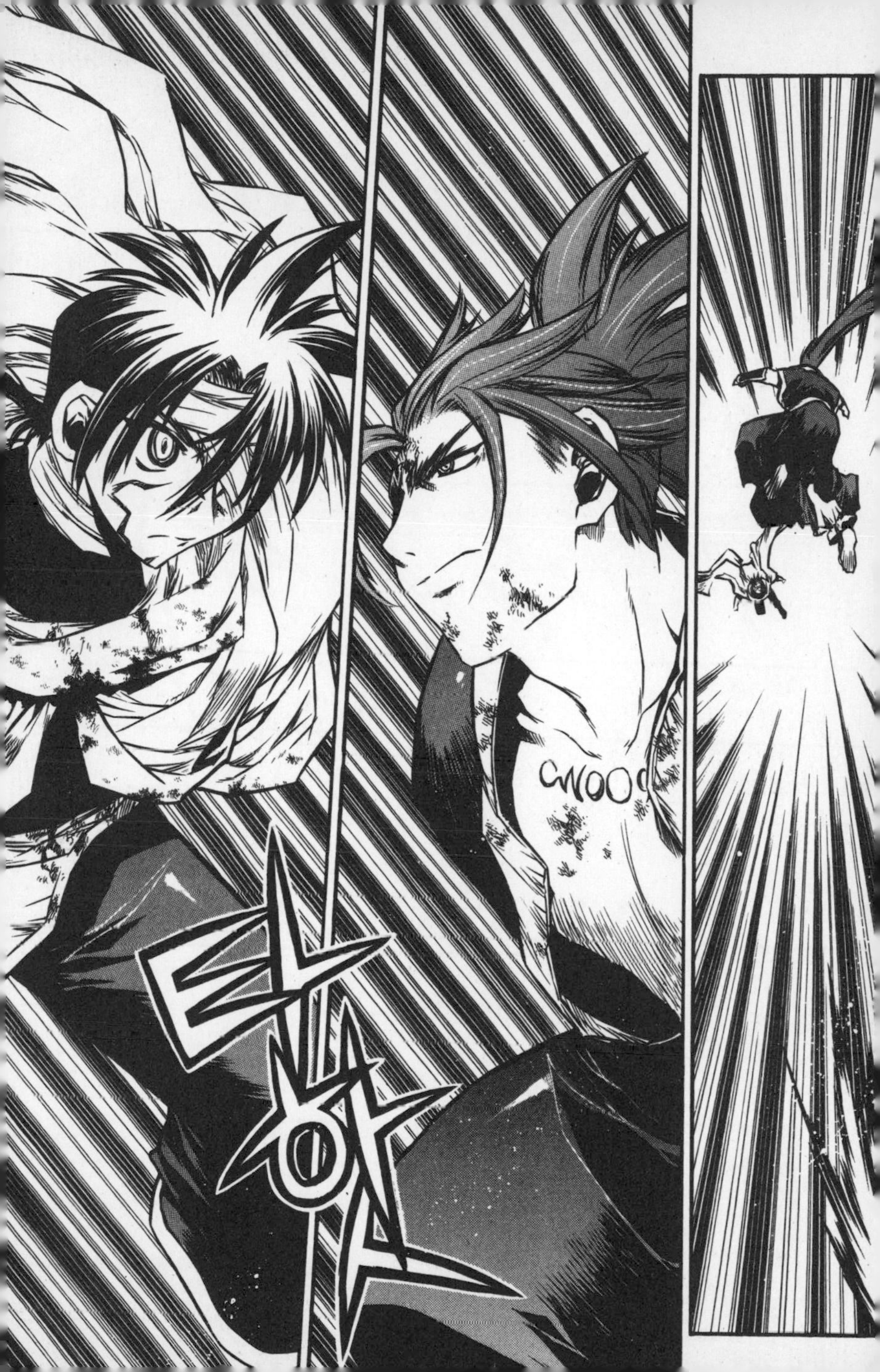
GWOOO

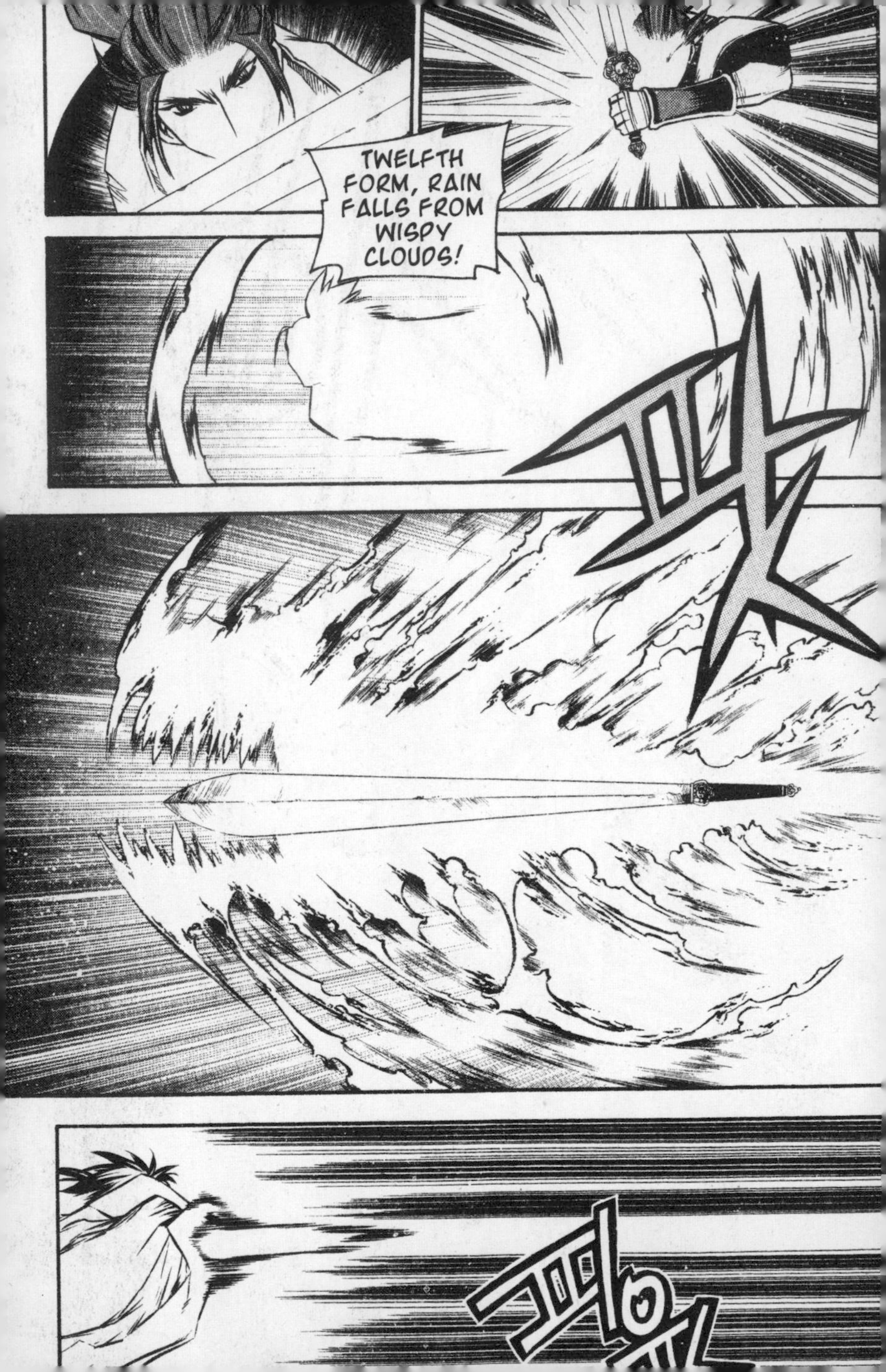
TWELFTH FORM, RAIN FALLS FROM WISPY CLOUDS!

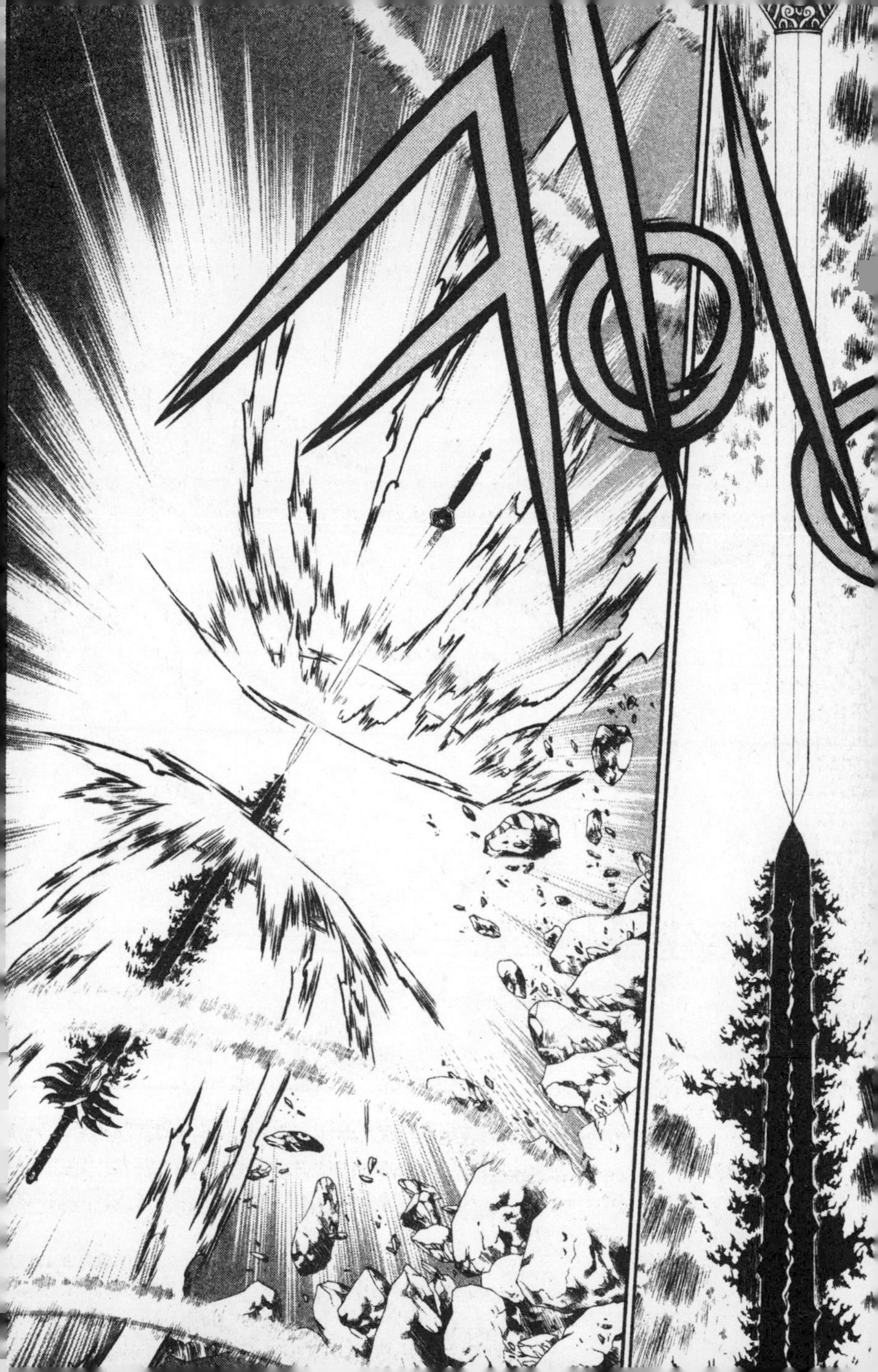

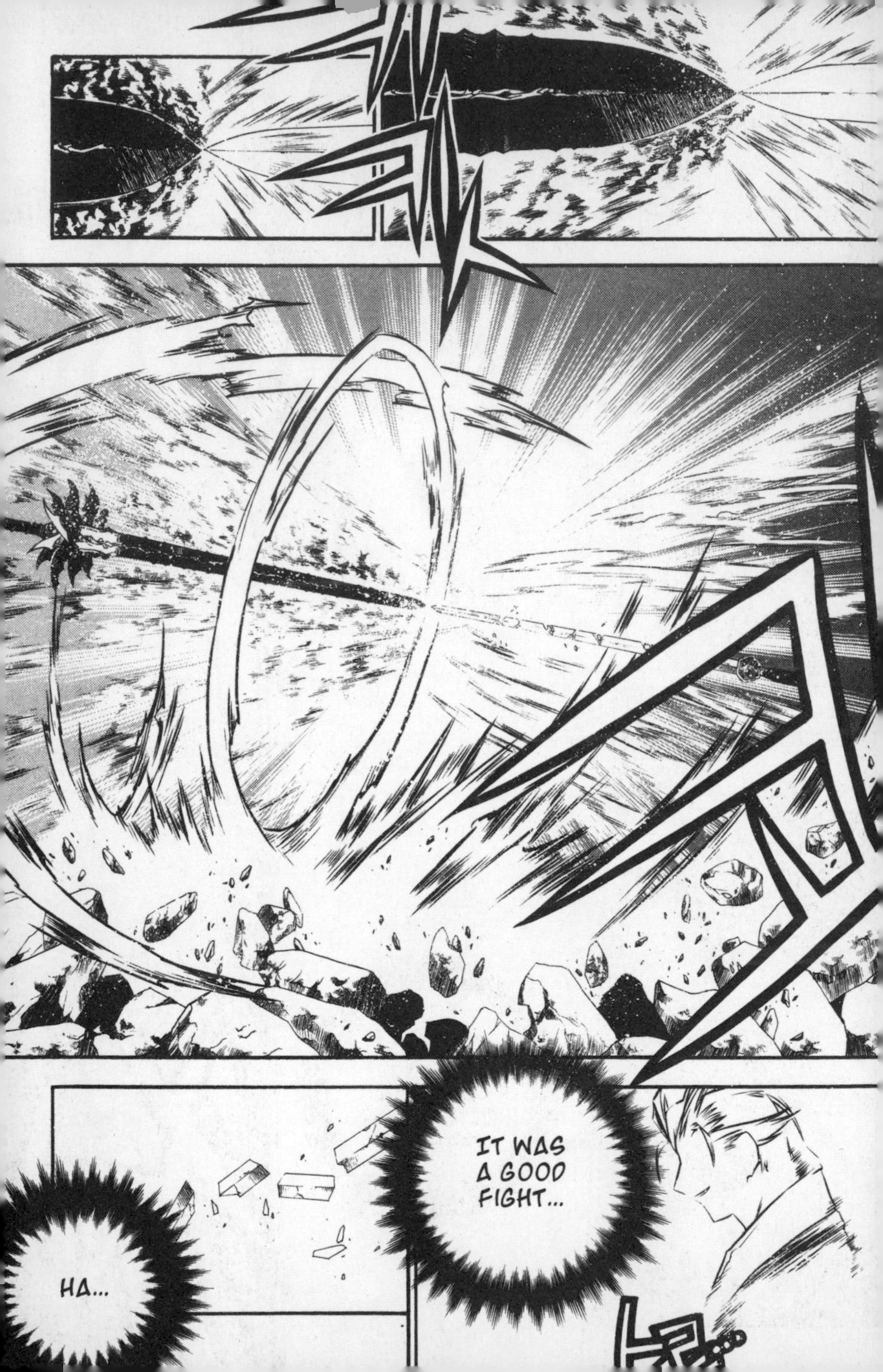
HA...
IT WAS A GOOD FIGHT...

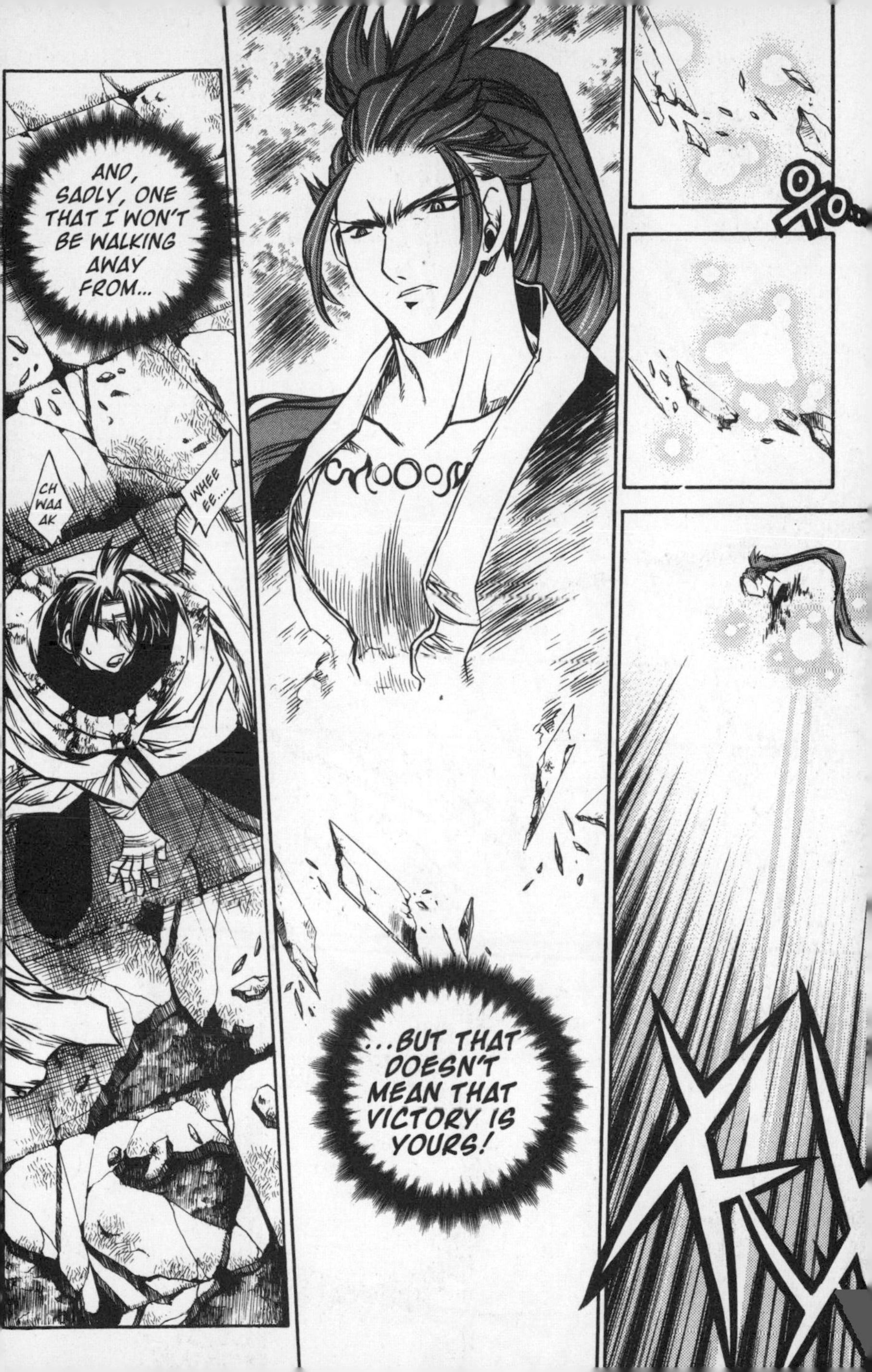
AND, SADLY, ONE THAT I WON'T BE WALKING AWAY FROM...
CH WAA AK
WHEE EE....
...BUT THAT DOESN'T MEAN THAT VICTORY IS YOURS!

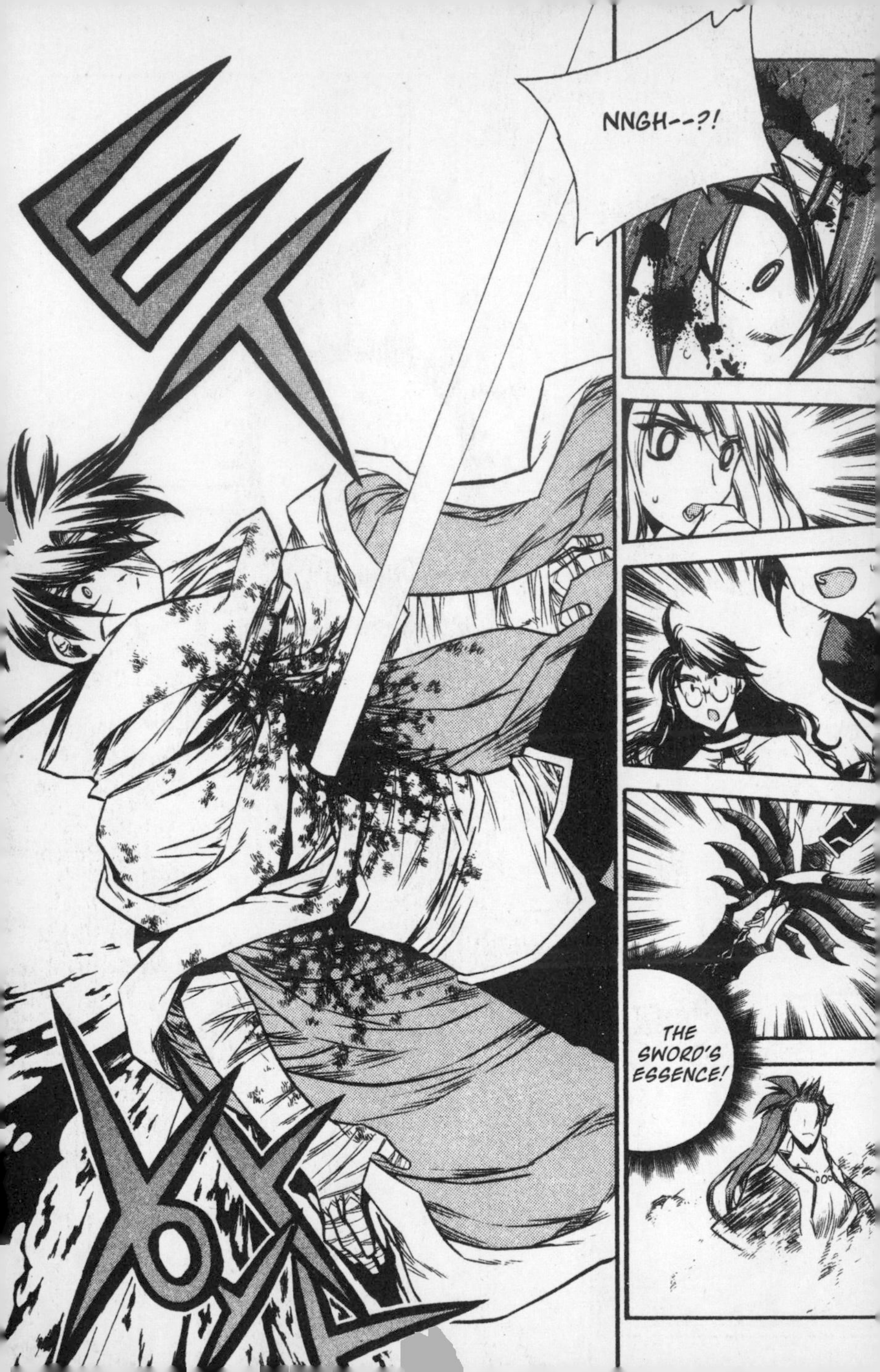
NNGH--?!
THE SWORD'S ESSENCE!

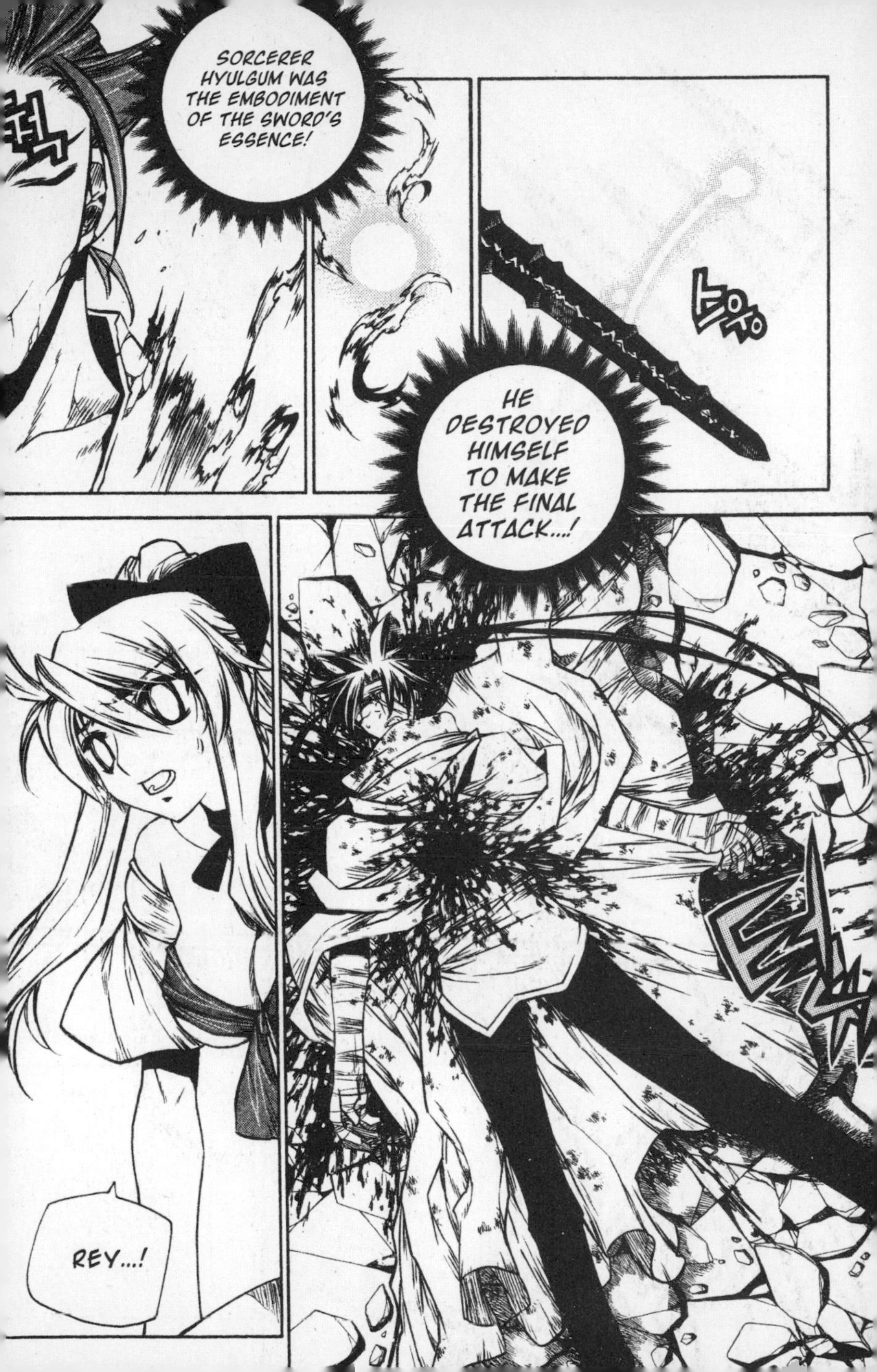
SORCERER HYULGUM WAS THE EMBODIMENT OF THE SWORD'S ESSENCE!
HE DESTROYED HIMSELF TO MAKE THE FINAL ATTACK...!
REY...!

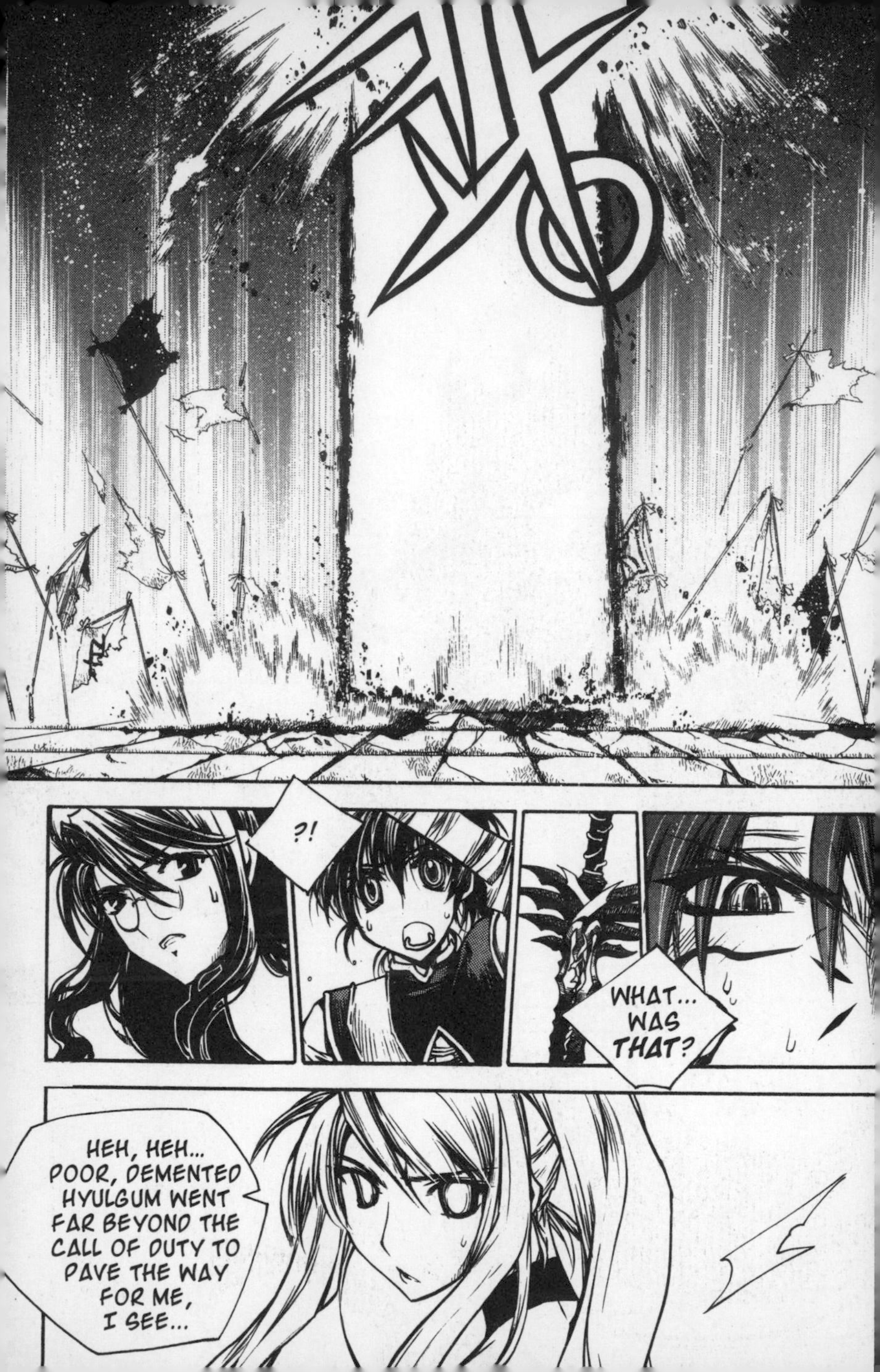
?!
WHAT... WAS THAT?
HEH, HEH... POOR, DEMENTED HYULGUM WENT FAR BEYOND THE CALL OF DUTY TO PAVE THE WAY FOR ME, I SEE...

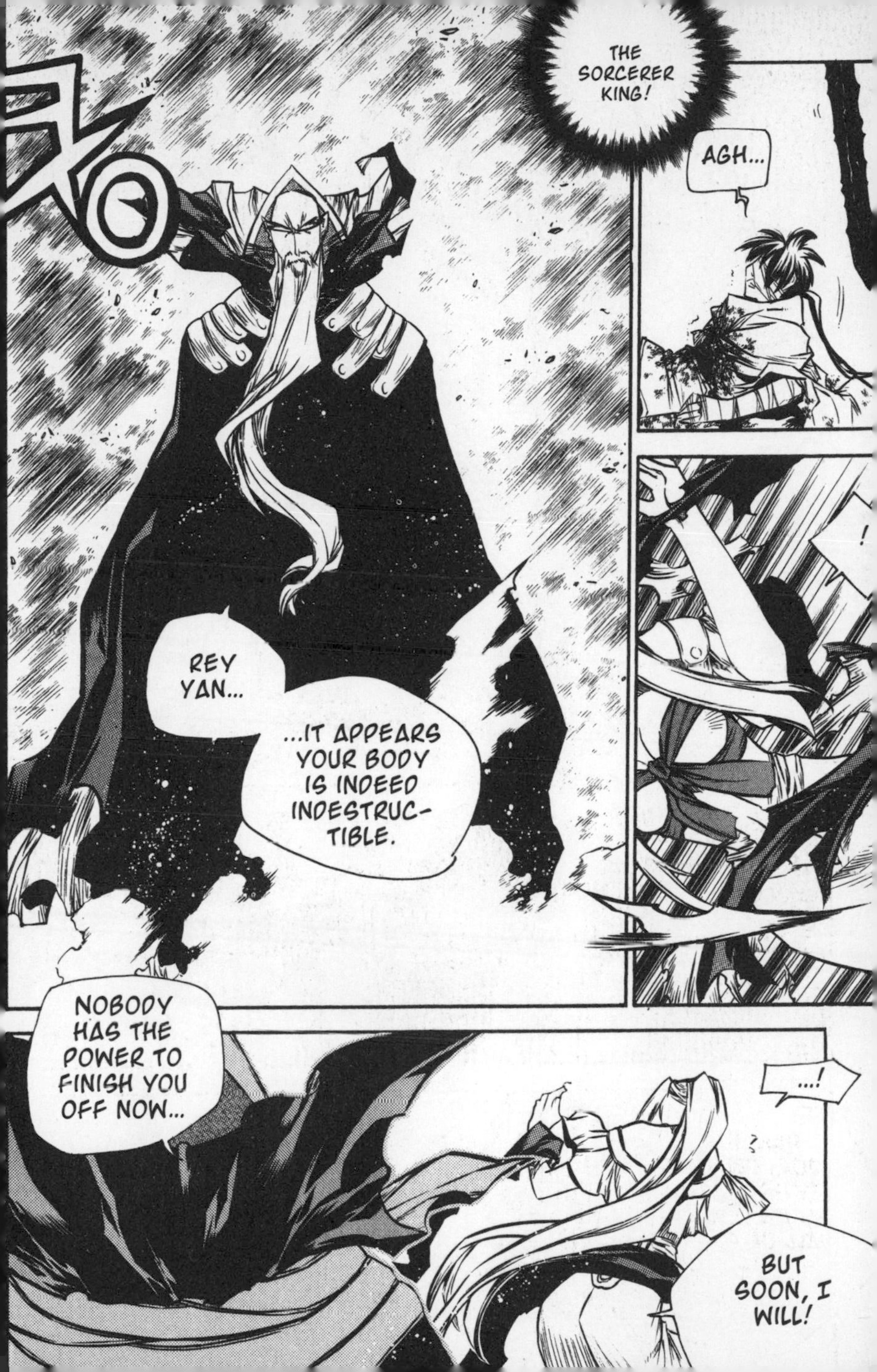
THE SORCERER KING!
REY YAN...
...IT APPEARS YOUR BODY IS INDEED INDESTRUC-TIBLE.
AGH...
NOBODY HAS THE POWER TO FINISH YOU OFF NOW...
...!
BUT SOON, I WILL!

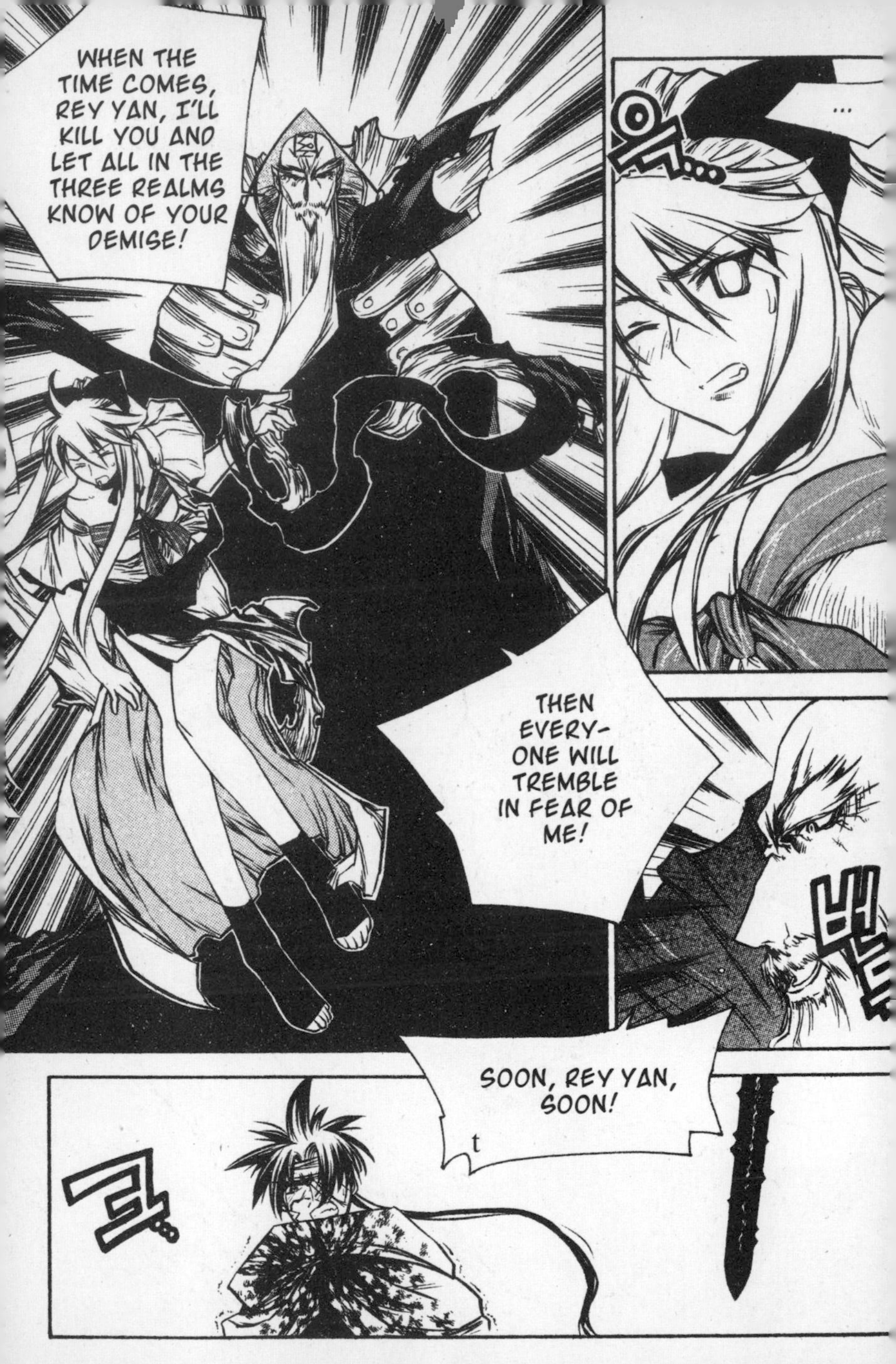
WHEN THE TIME COMES, REY YAN, I'LL KILL YOU AND LET ALL IN THE THREE REALMS KNOW OF YOUR DEMISE!
...
THEN EVERY-ONE WILL TREMBLE IN FEAR OF ME!
SOON, REY YAN, SOON!

Chapter 50
The Pillar of Enchanted Souls

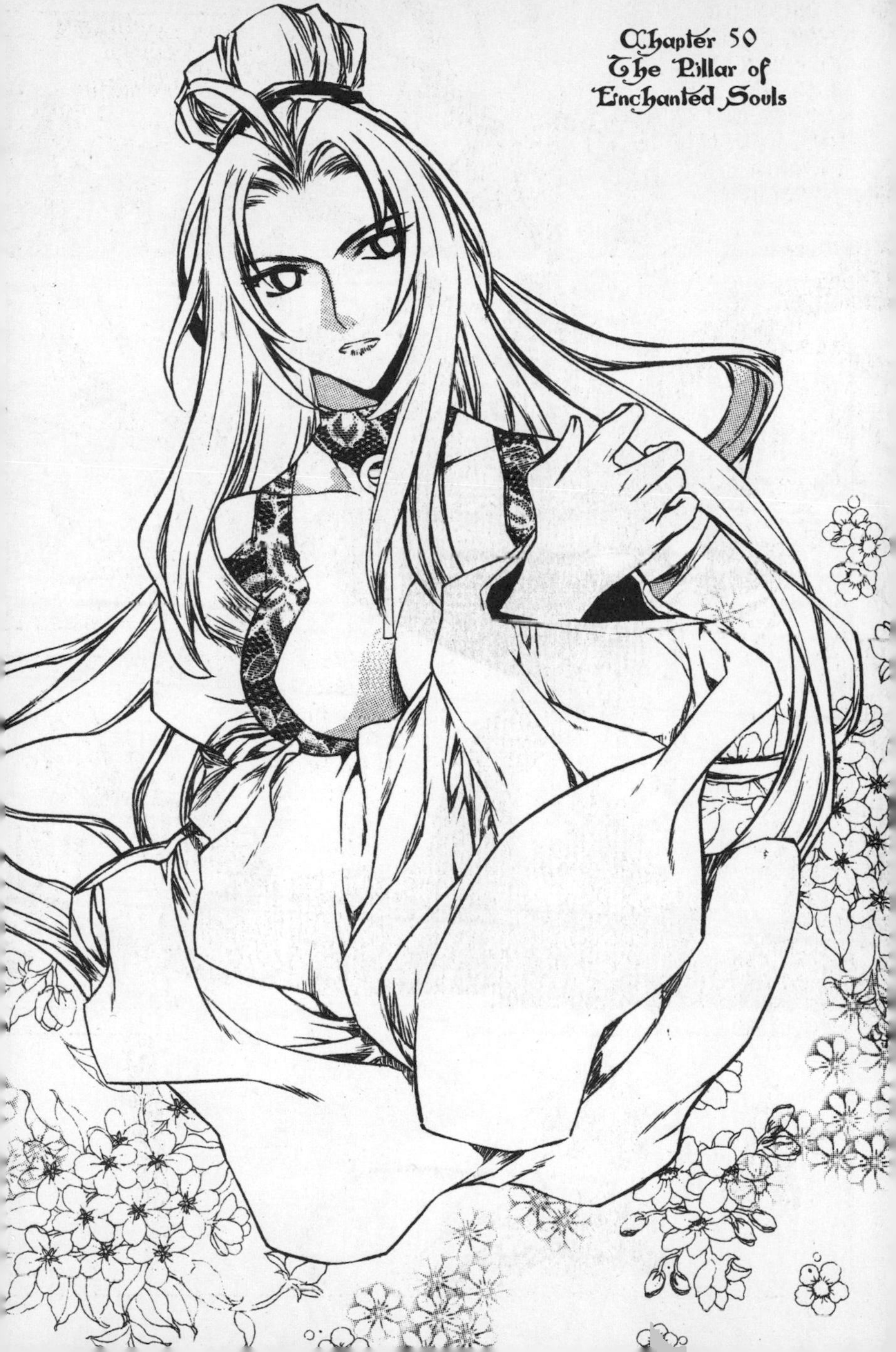

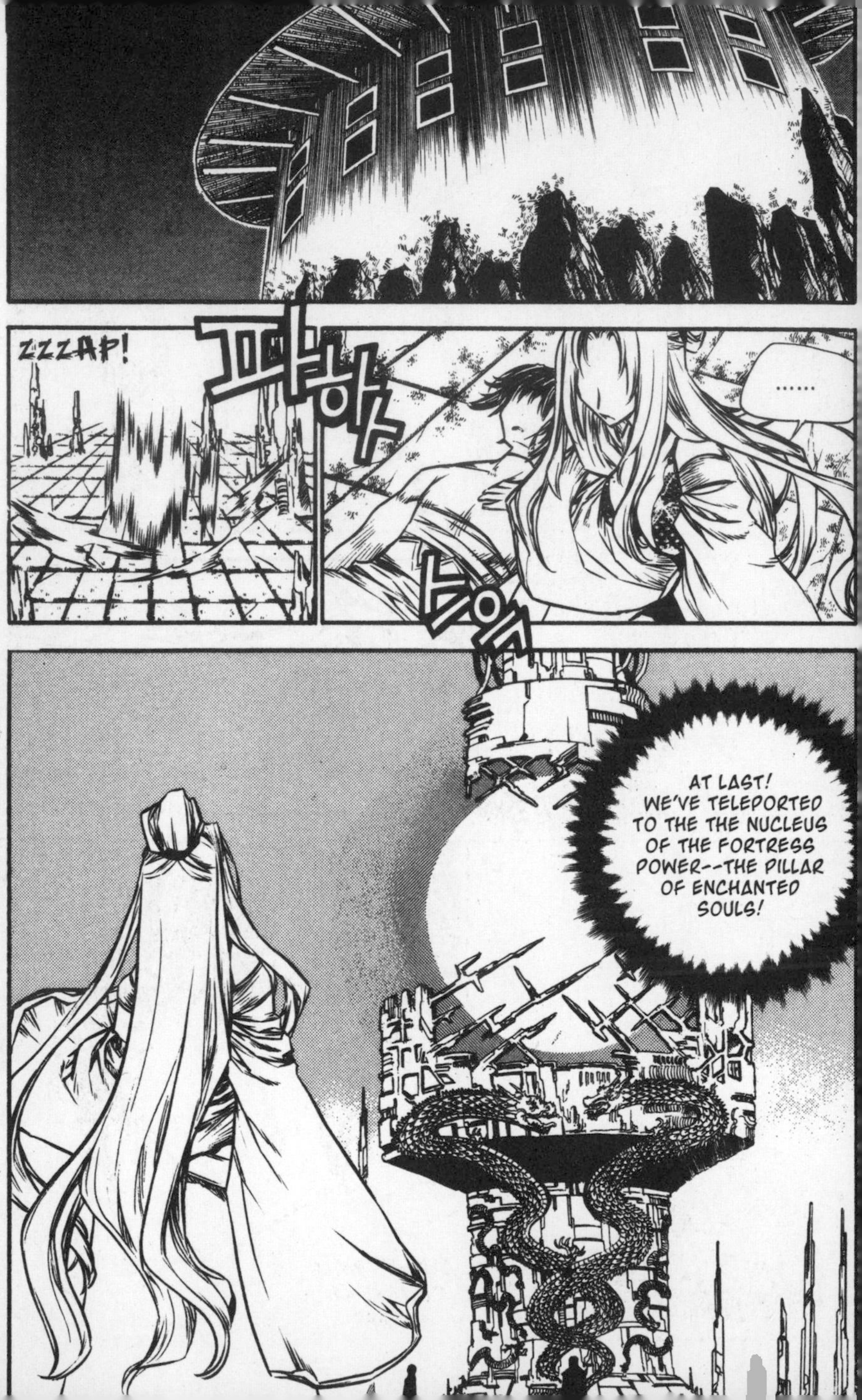
ZZZAP!
......
AT LAST! WE'VE TELEPORTED TO THE THE NUCLEUS OF THE FORTRESS POWER--THE PILLAR OF ENCHANTED SOULS!

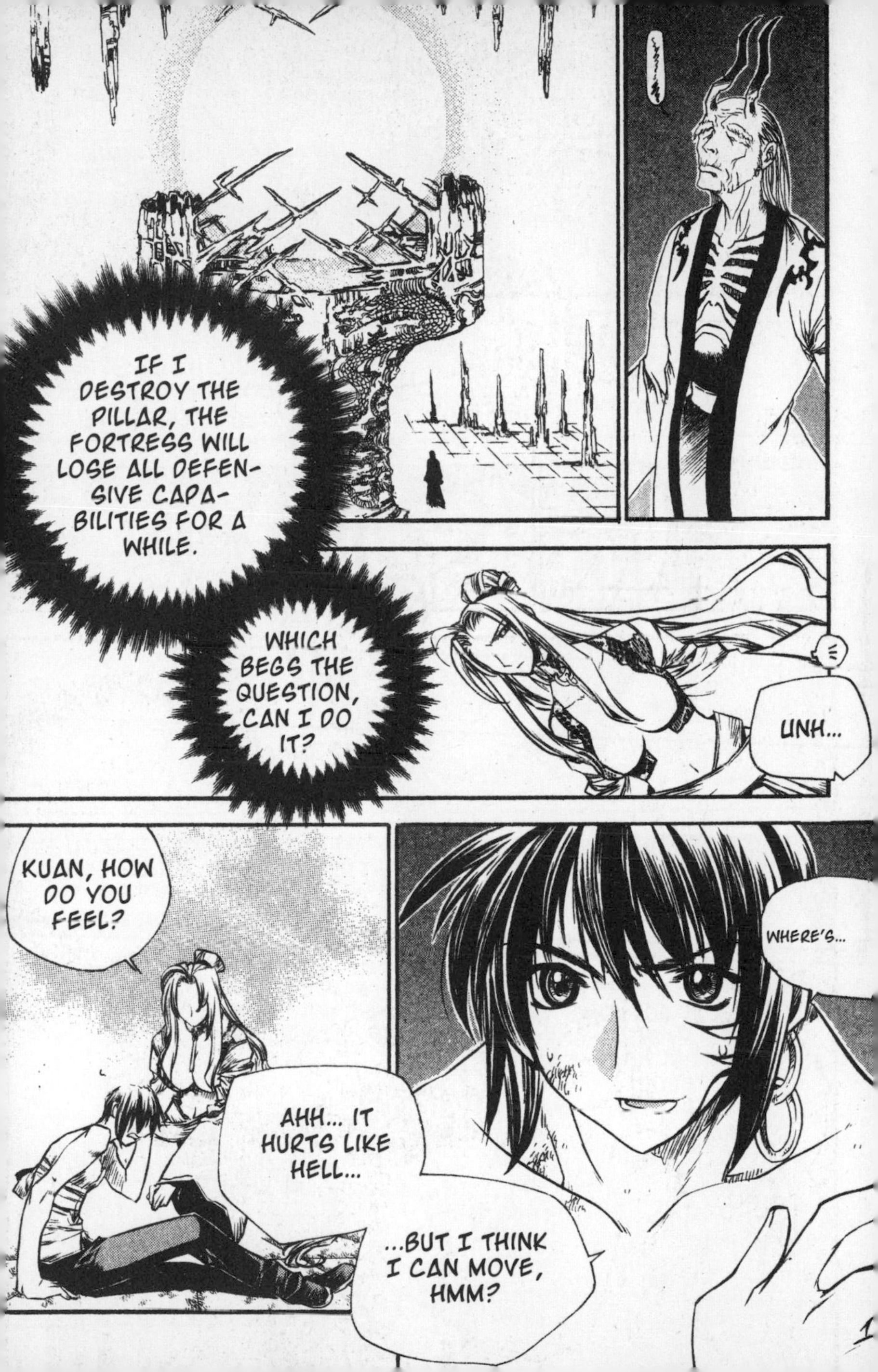
IF I DESTROY THE PILLAR, THE FORTRESS WILL LOSE ALL DEFENSIVE CAPABILITIES FOR A WHILE.
WHICH BEGS THE QUESTION, CAN I DO IT?
UNH...
KUAN, HOW DO YOU FEEL?
AHH... IT HURTS LIKE HELL...
...BUT I THINK I CAN MOVE, HMM?
WHERE'S...

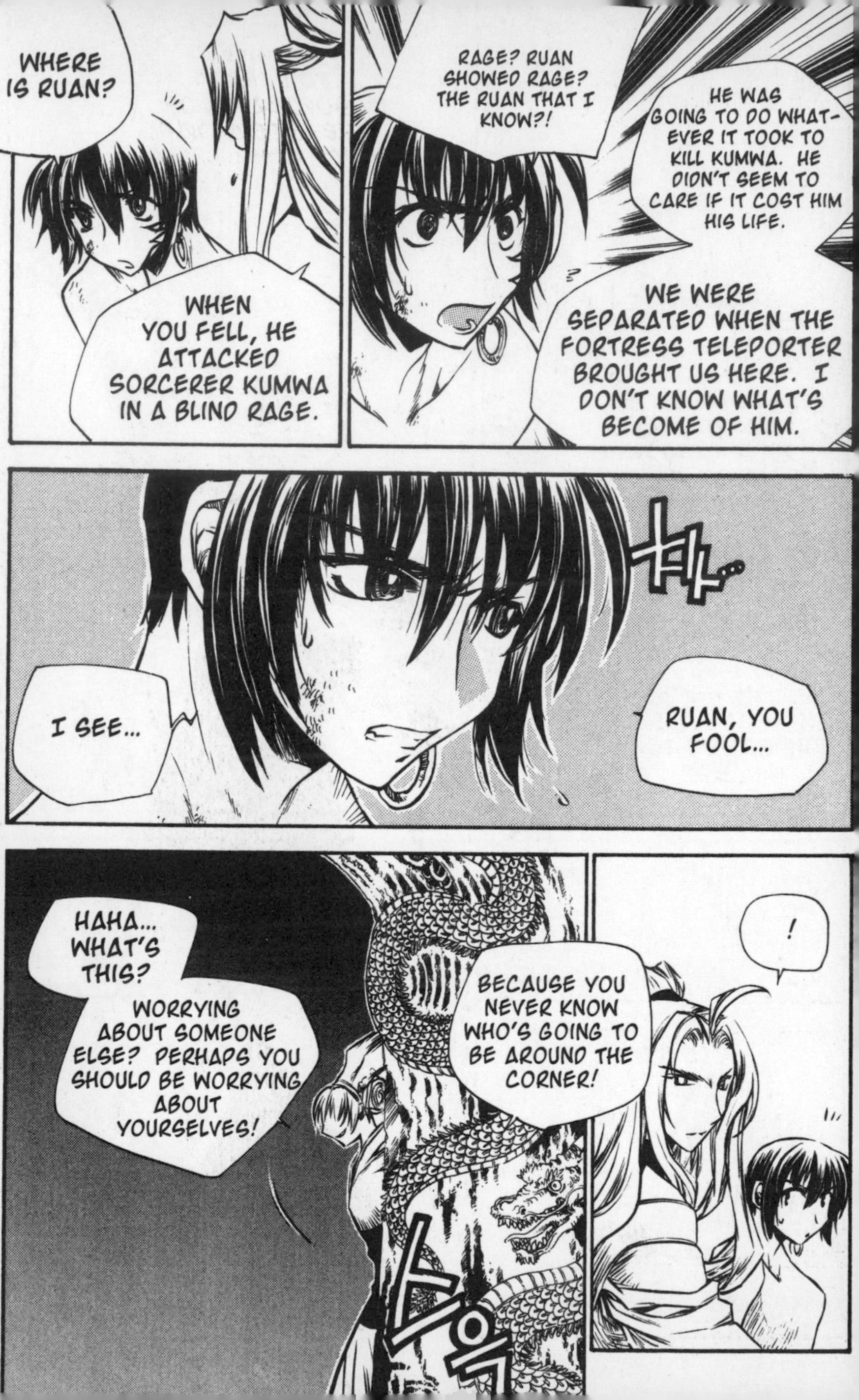
WHERE IS RUAN?
WHEN YOU FELL, HE ATTACKED SORCERER KUMWA IN A BLIND RAGE.
RAGE? RUAN SHOWED RAGE? THE RUAN THAT I KNOW?!
HE WAS GOING TO DO WHATEVER IT TOOK TO KILL KUMWA. HE DIDN'T SEEM TO CARE IF IT COST HIM HIS LIFE.
WE WERE SEPARATED WHEN THE FORTRESS TELEPORTER BROUGHT US HERE. I DON'T KNOW WHAT'S BECOME OF HIM.
I SEE...
RUAN, YOU FOOL...
HAHA... WHAT'S THIS?
WORRYING ABOUT SOMEONE ELSE? PERHAPS YOU SHOULD BE WORRYING ABOUT YOURSELVES!
BECAUSE YOU NEVER KNOW WHO'S GOING TO BE AROUND THE CORNER!
!

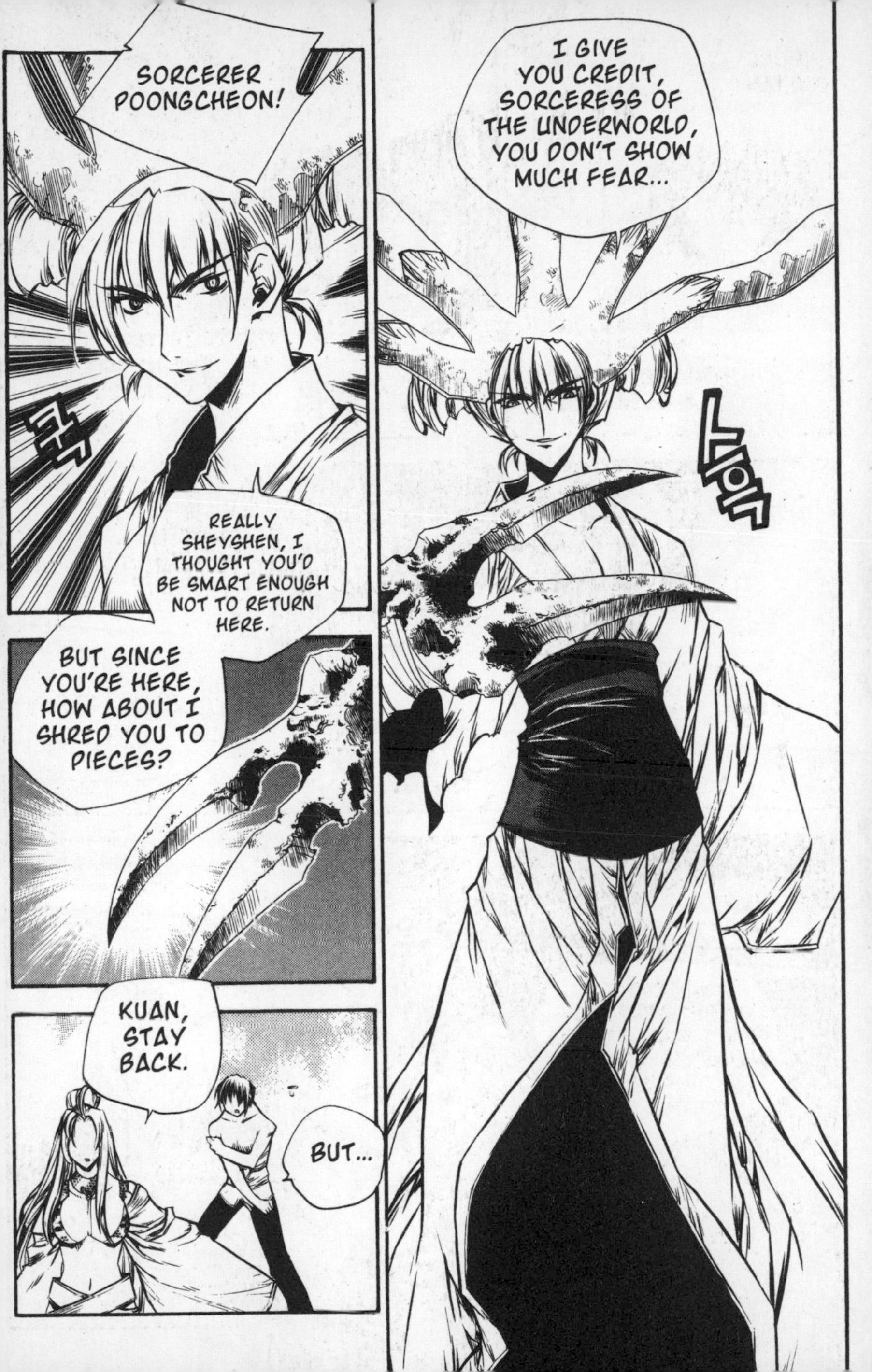
SORCERER POONGCHEON!
REALLY SHEYSHEN, I THOUGHT YOU'D BE SMART ENOUGH NOT TO RETURN HERE.
BUT SINCE YOU'RE HERE, HOW ABOUT I SHRED YOU TO PIECES?
KUAN, STAY BACK.
BUT...
I GIVE YOU CREDIT, SORCERESS OF THE UNDERWORLD, YOU DON'T SHOW MUCH FEAR...

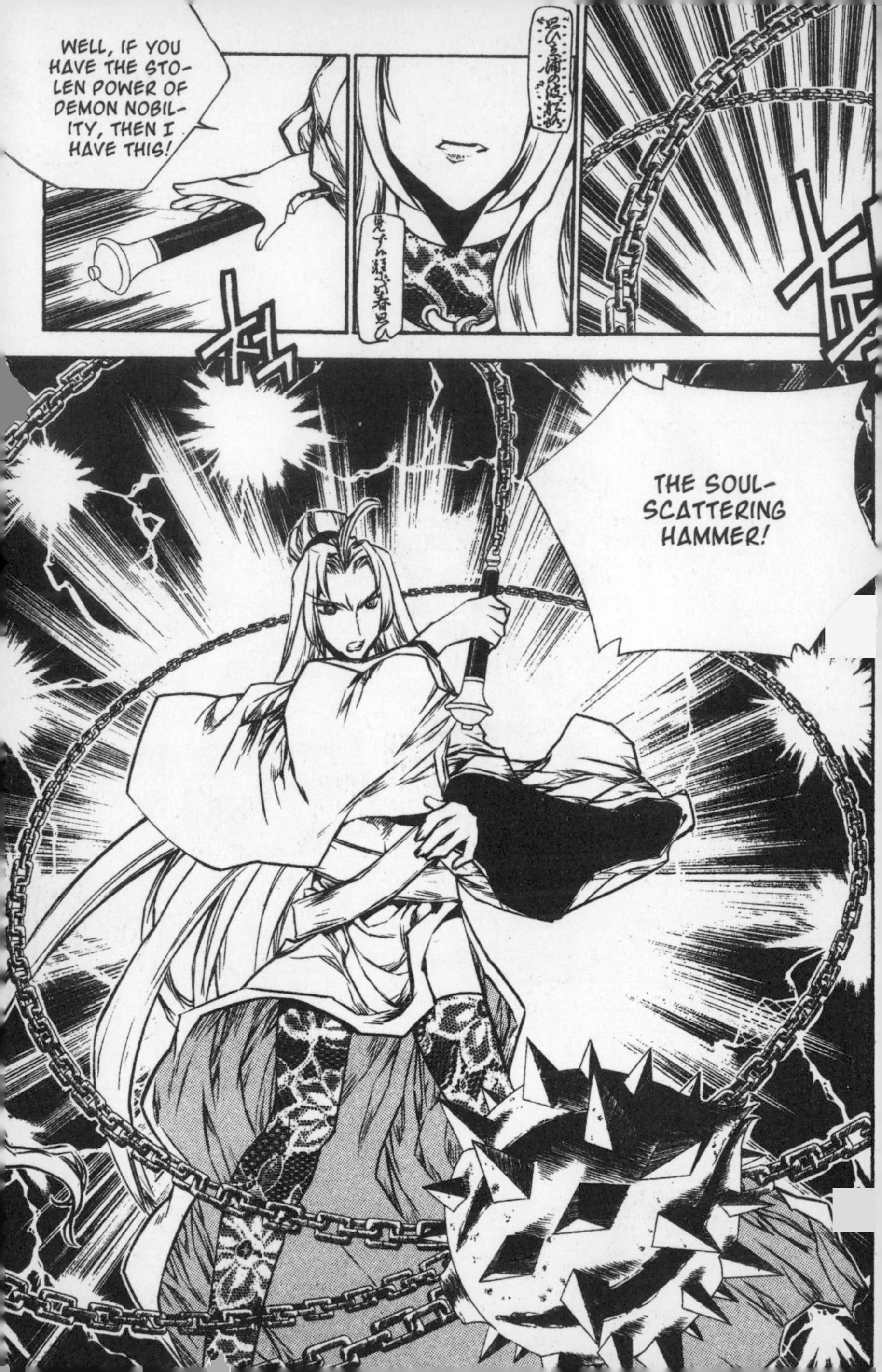
WELL, IF YOU HAVE THE STO-LEN POWER OF DEMON NOBIL-ITY, THEN I HAVE THIS!
THE SOUL-SCATTERING HAMMER!

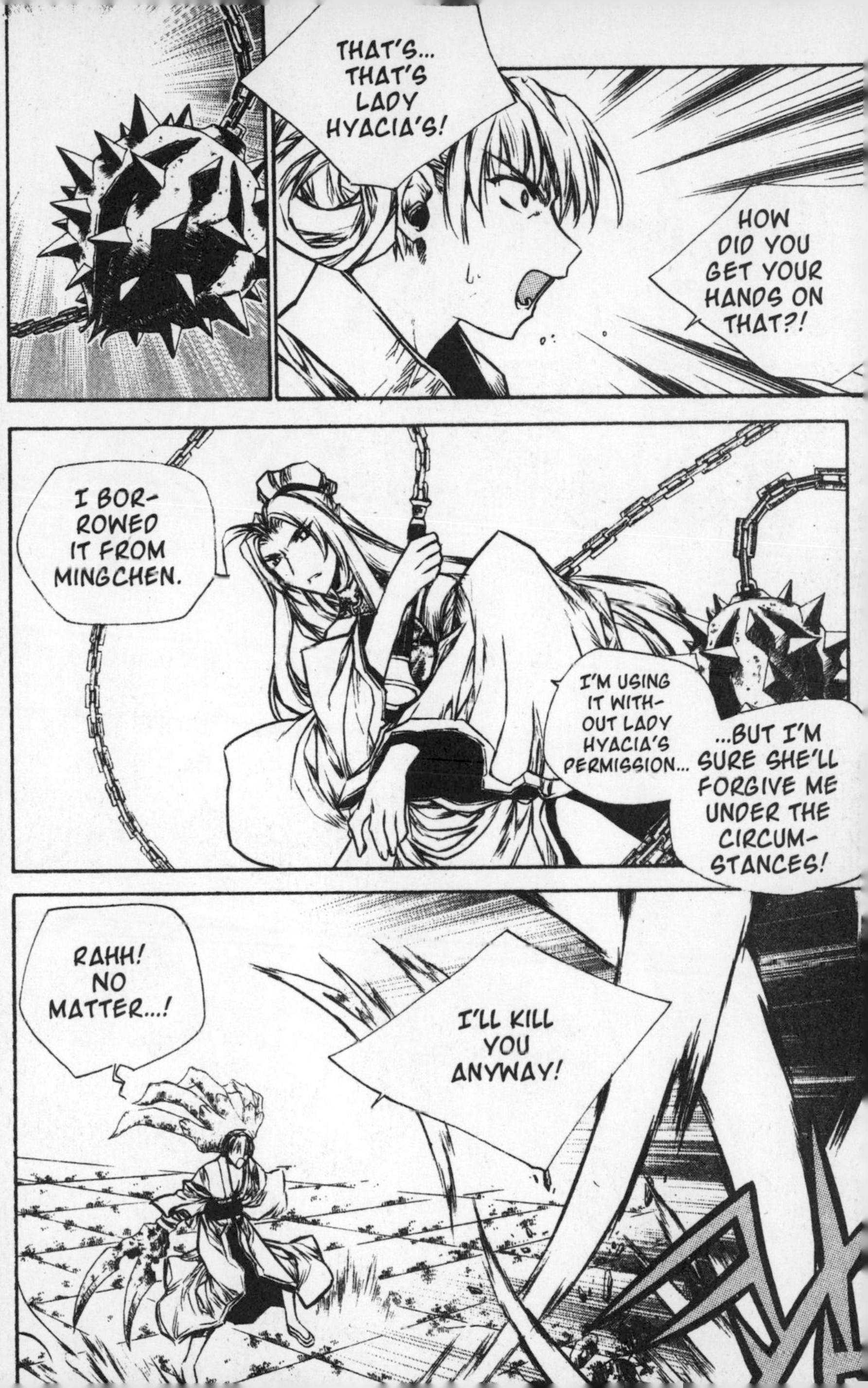

THAT'S... THAT'S LADY HYACIA'S!
HOW DID YOU GET YOUR HANDS ON THAT?!
I BOR-ROWED IT FROM MINGCHEN.
I'M USING IT WITH-OUT LADY HYACIA'S PERMISSION...
...BUT I'M SURE SHE'LL FORGIVE ME UNDER THE CIRCUM-STANCES!
RAHH! NO MATTER...!
I'LL KILL YOU ANYWAY!

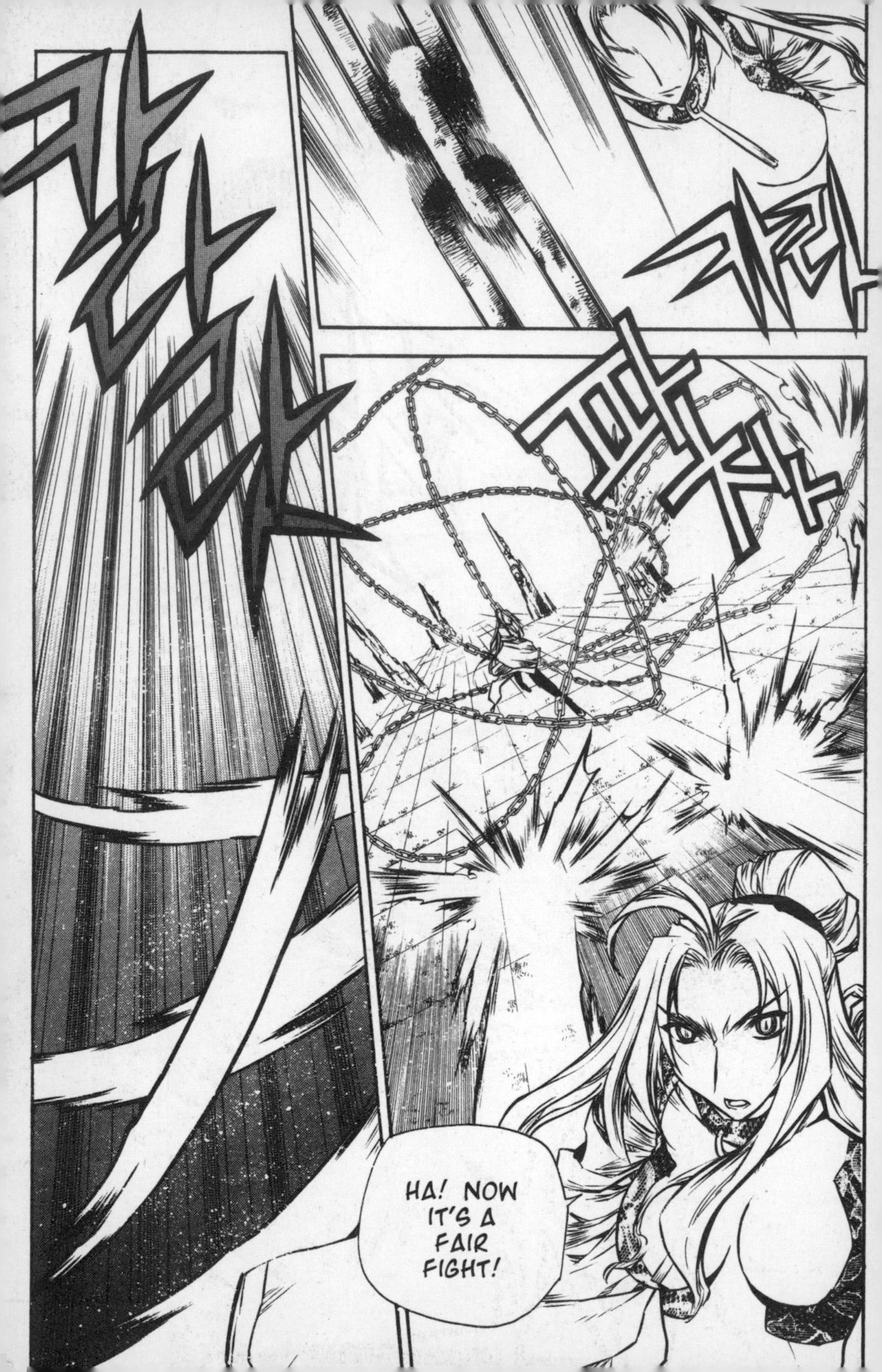
HA! NOW IT'S A FAIR FIGHT!

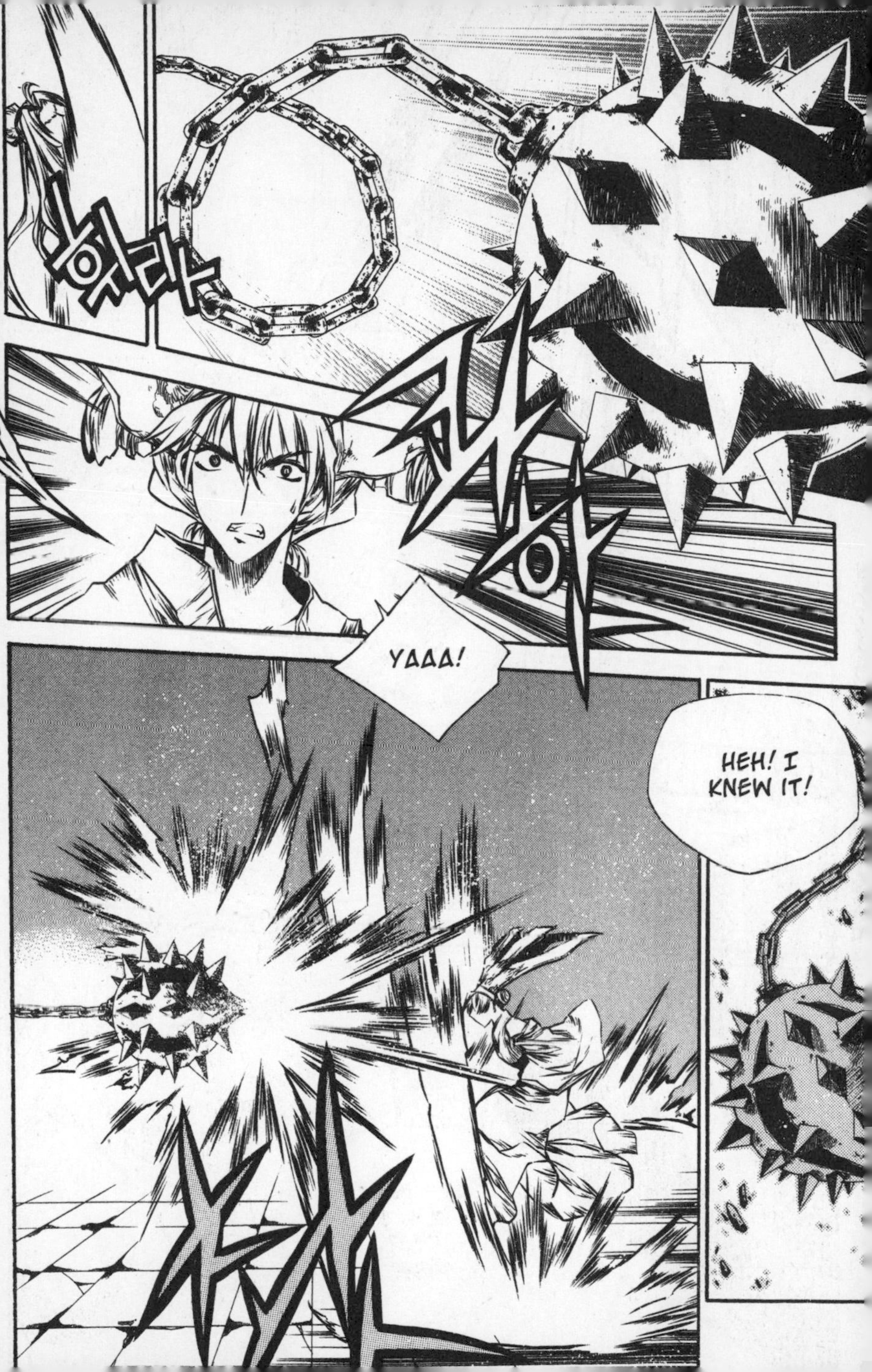
YAAA!
HEH! I KNEW IT!

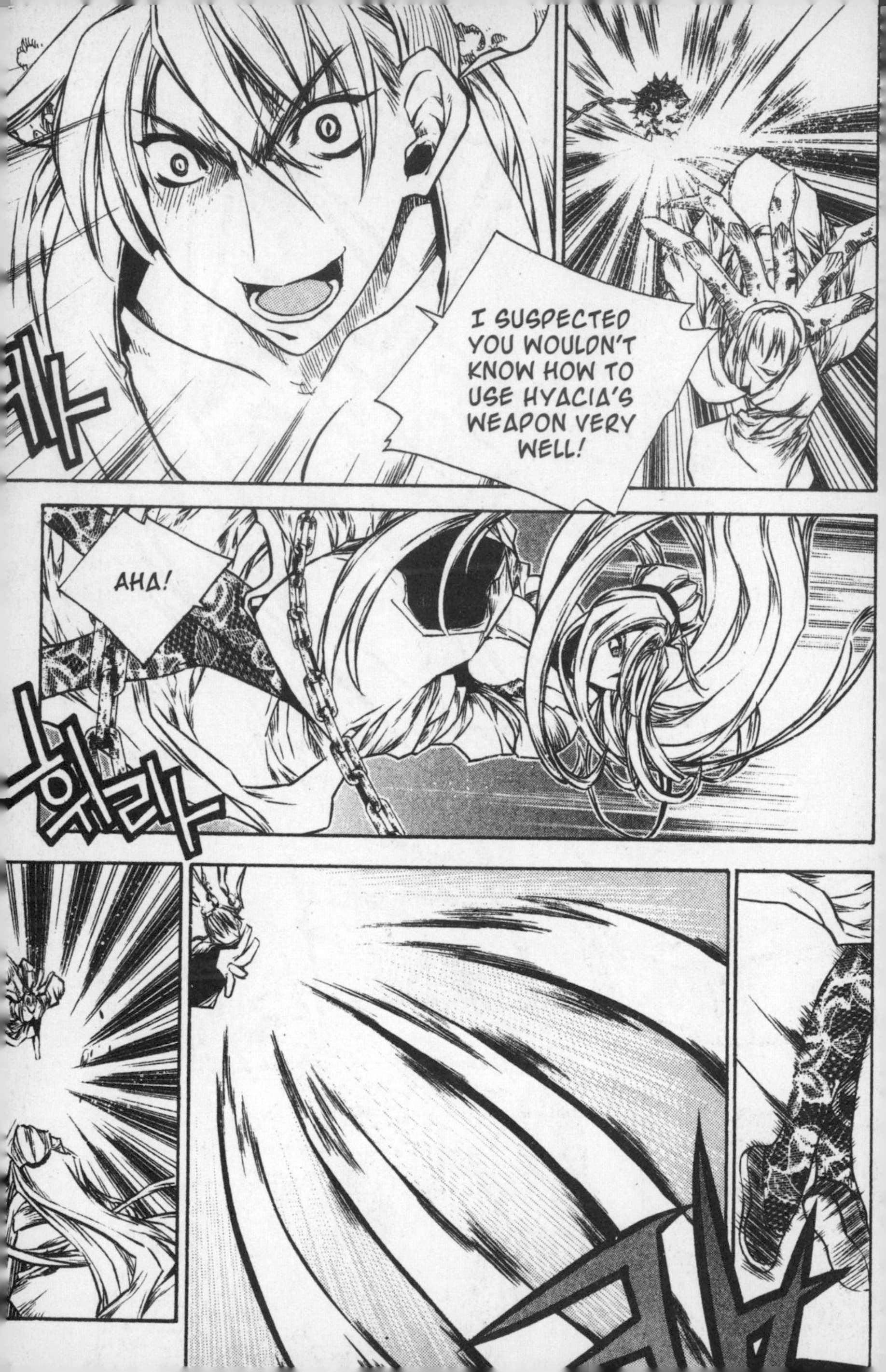
I SUSPECTED YOU WOULDN'T KNOW HOW TO USE HYACIA'S WEAPON VERY WELL!
AHA!

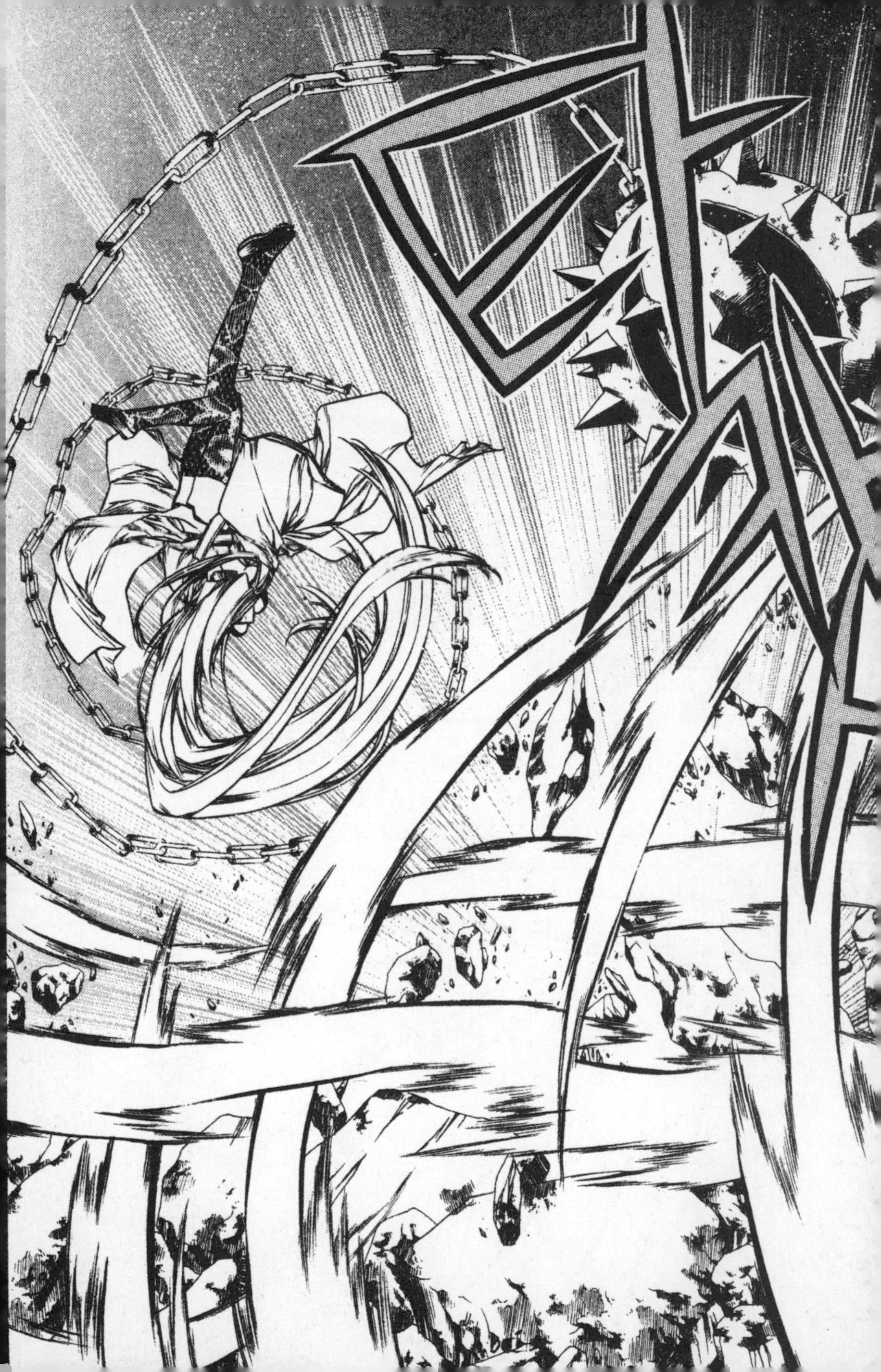

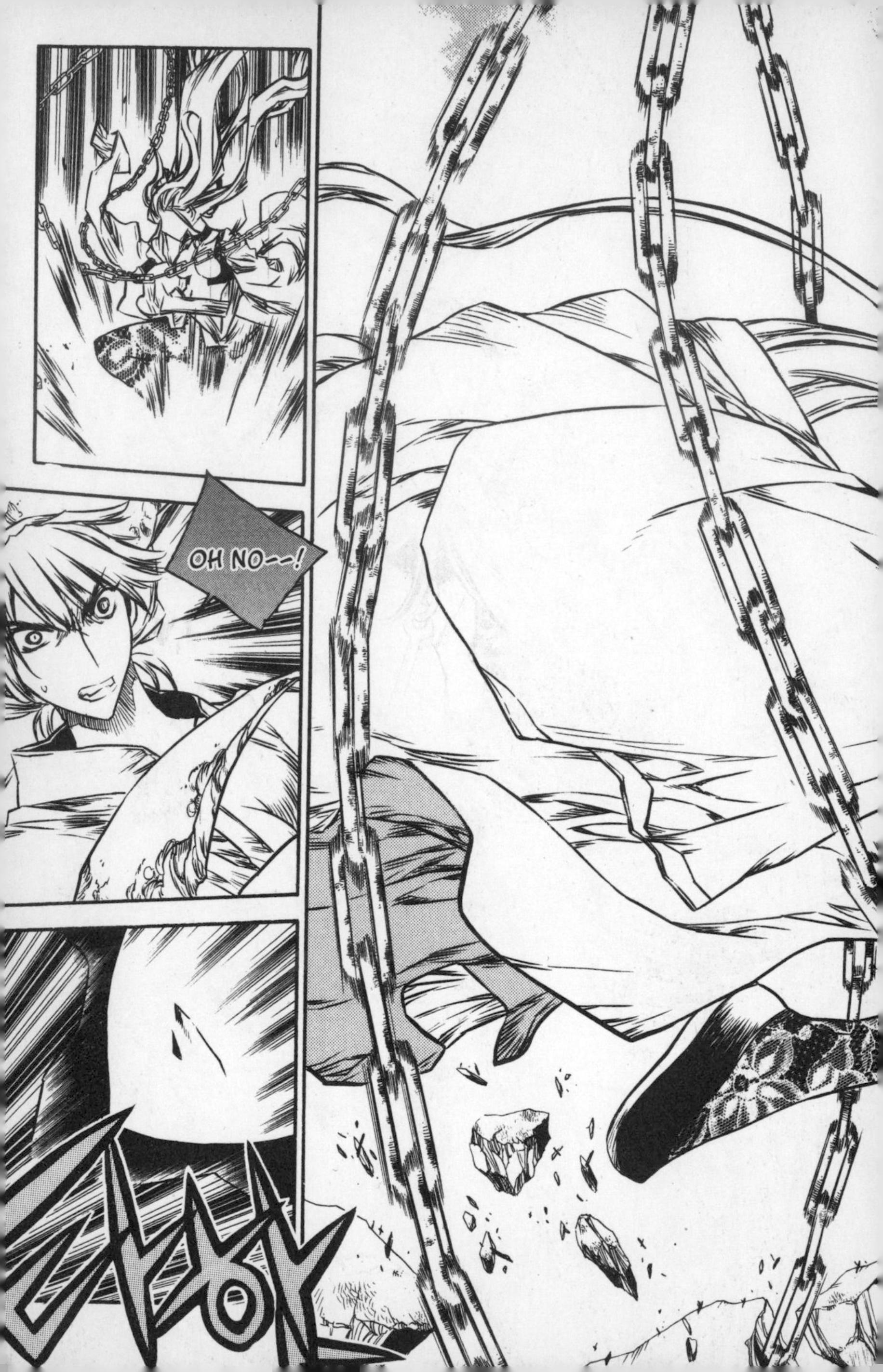
OH NO--!

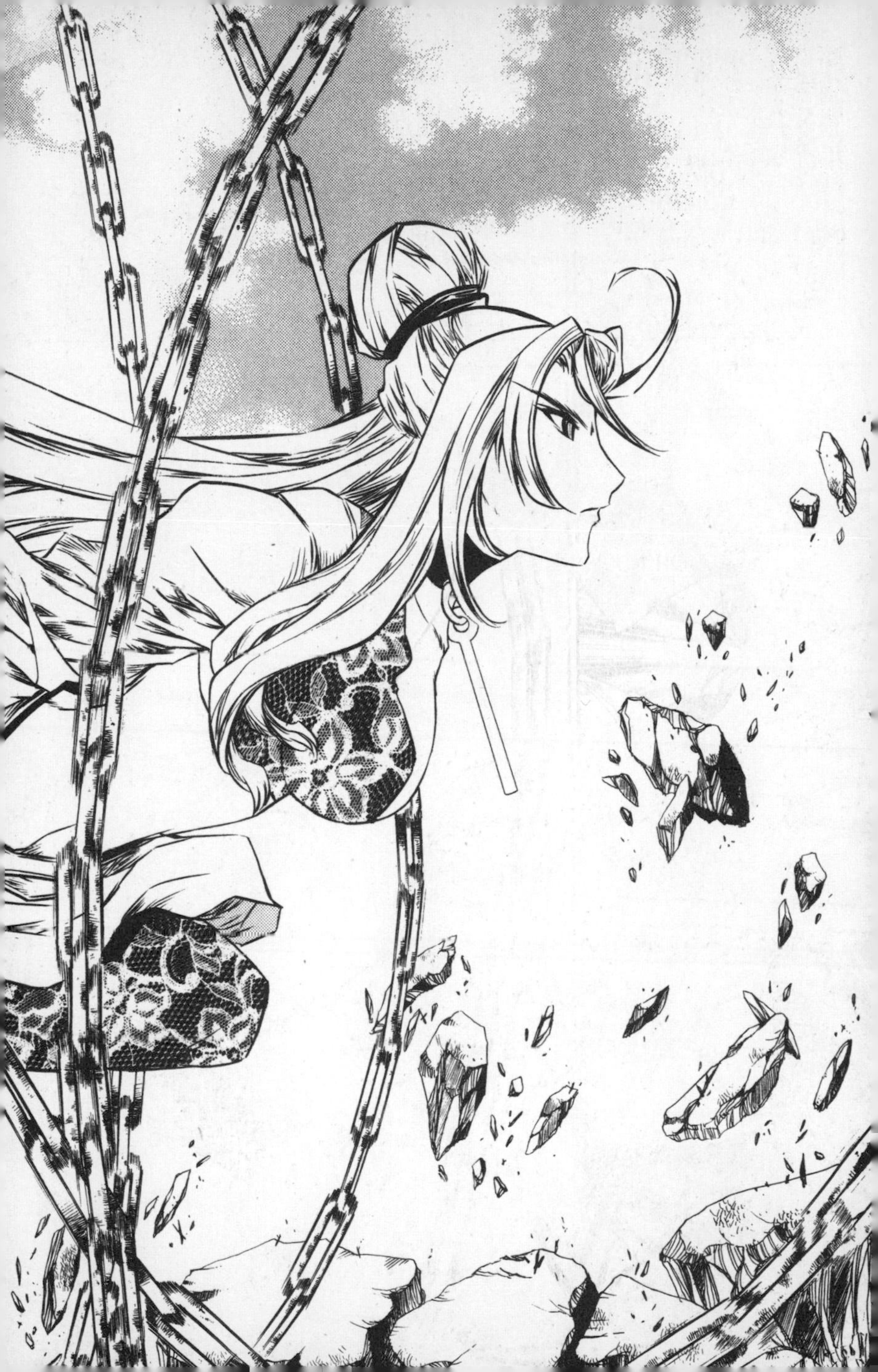

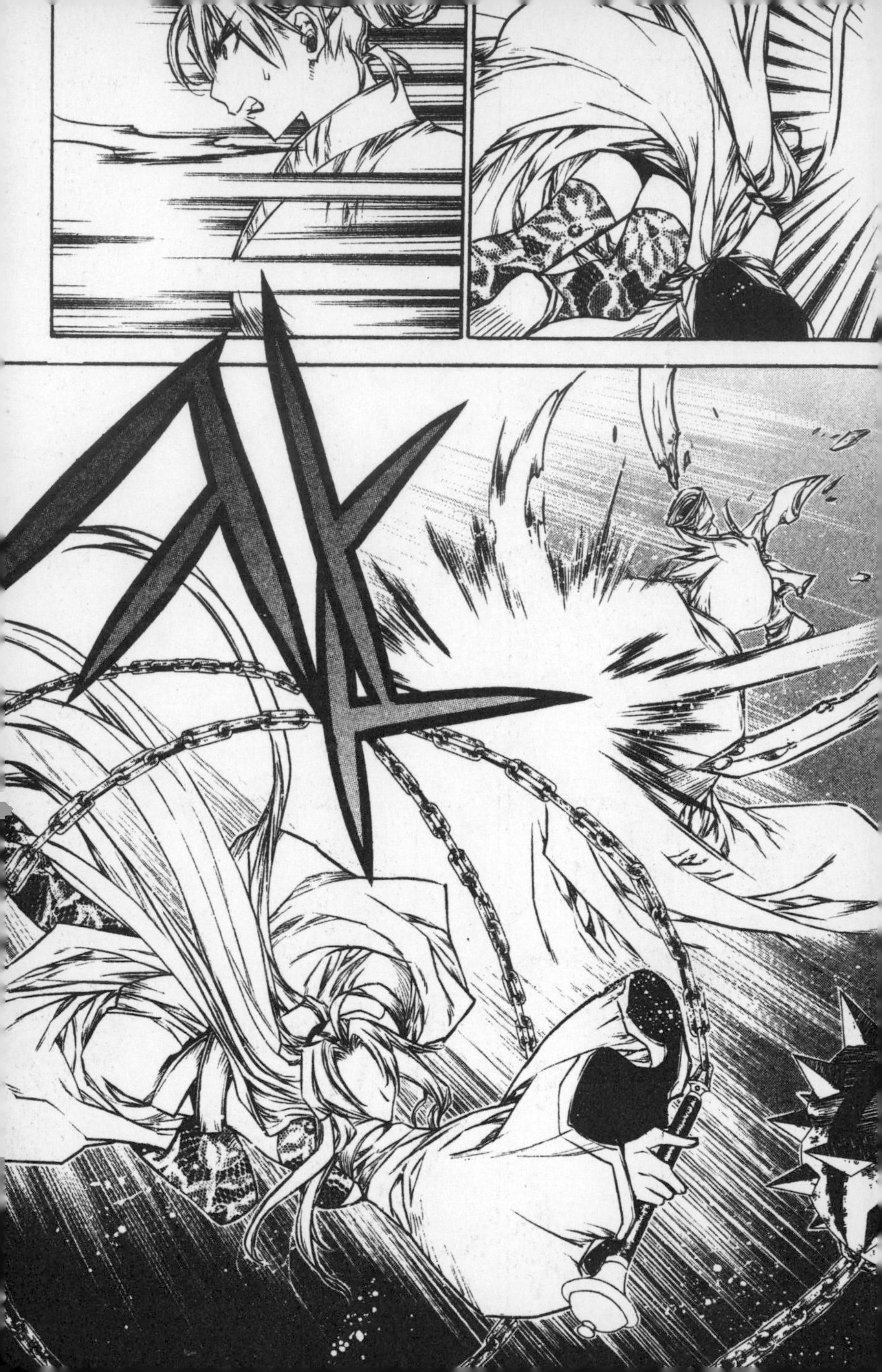

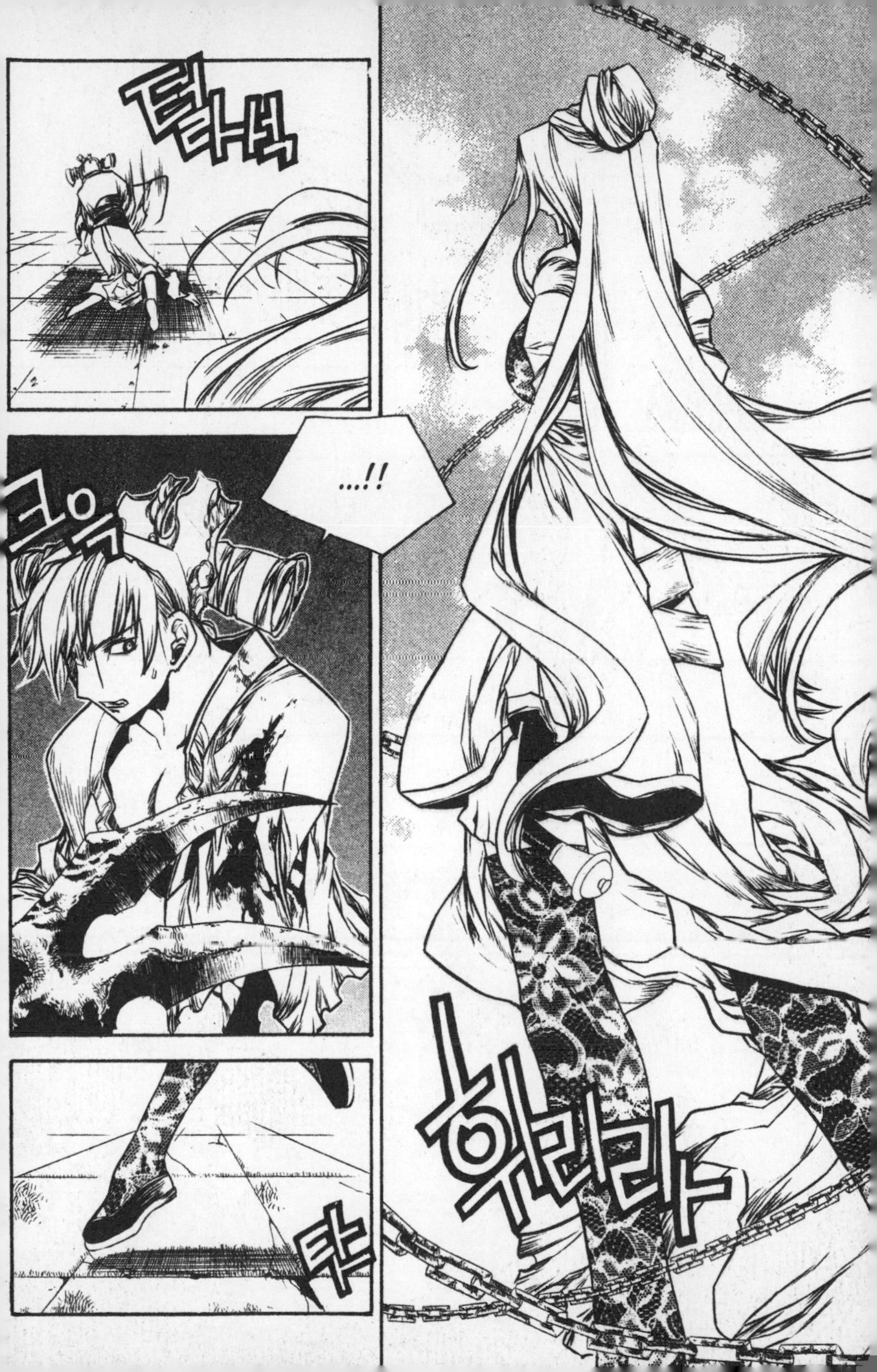
...!!
탁
휘리릭

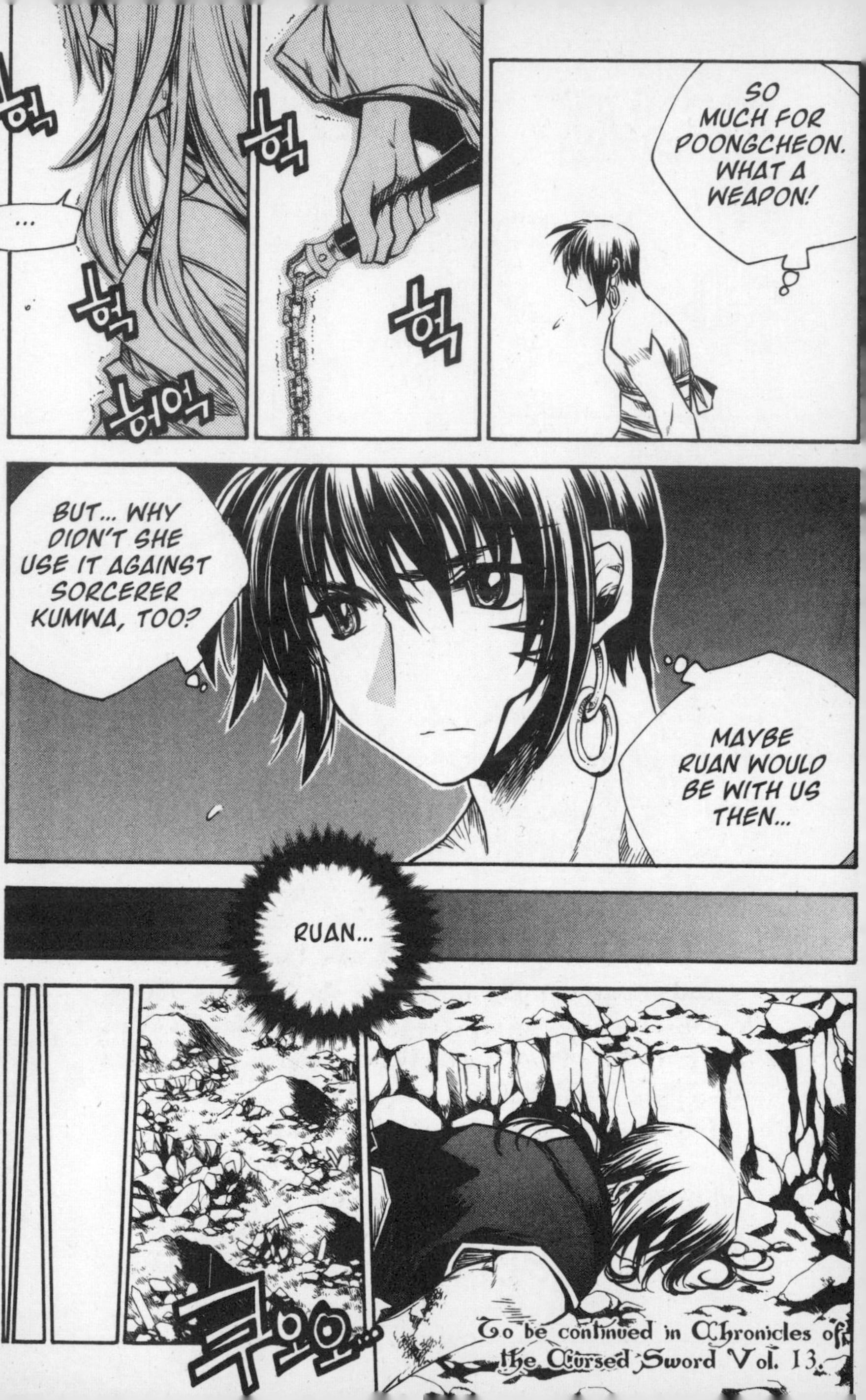
헉
...
헉
허억
헉
헉
SO MUCH FOR POONGCHEON. WHAT A WEAPON!
BUT... WHY DIDN'T SHE USE IT AGAINST SORCERER KUMWA, TOO?
MAYBE RUAN WOULD BE WITH US THEN...
RUAN...
쿠오오...
To be continued in Chronicles of the Cursed Sword Vol. 13.

NEXT VOLUME

In their struggle to save Lady Hyacia, Roy
and company finally succeed in shutting down the
treacherous defenses of the Sorcerer King's fortress...
only to be faced with new challenges from within. And
the final obstacle? A showdown with the Sorcerer
King himself! However, the Sorcerer King's new
powers are so great that he threatens all three
realms. Will Rey and the others be able to defeat
the corrupted King before it's too late?

PRINCESS AI

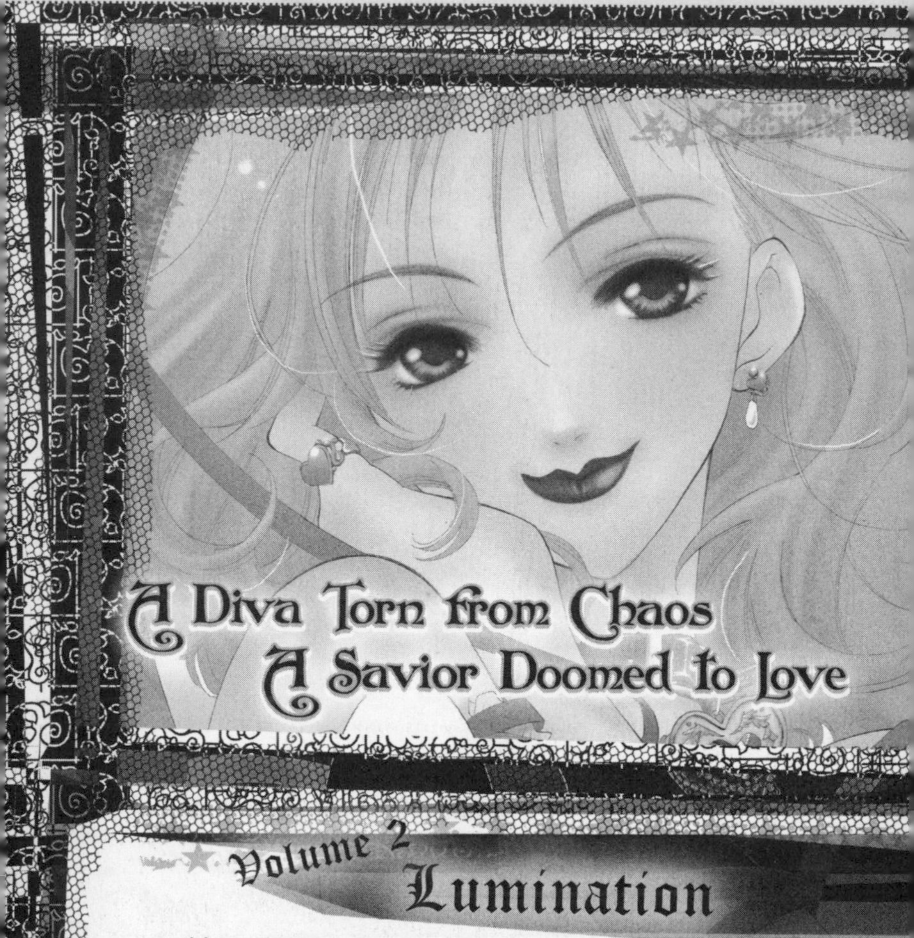
A Diva Torn from Chaos
A Savior Doomed to Love

Volume 2 Lumination

Ai continues to search for her place in our world on the streets of Tokyo. Using her talent to support herself, Ai signs a contract with a top record label and begins her rise to stardom. But fame is unpredictable—as her talent blooms, all eyes are on Ai. When scandal surfaces, will she burn out in the spotlight of celebrity?

T
TEEN
AGE 13+

Preview the manga at:

www.TOKYOPOP.com/princessai